PERSUASION:
GREEK RHETORIC
IN ACTION

Greek rhetoric and oratory are currently experiencing a renaissance of interest. Individual orators are receiving more attention in the form of editions and commentaries; Greek rhetoricians and rhetorical theories are undergoing new scrutinies and applications; and oratory and rhetoric are being linked together in studies of ancient Greece and its intellectual background, as well as providing a starting point for some modern discourse analysis. Other modern approaches draw out links with political science and dynamics, sociology and anthropology.

This book provides the most recent and wide-ranging treatment of Greek rhetoric and oratory at any level. The chapters are written by leading scholars in the field and deal with the influence of rhetoric on a particular historical aspect or literary genre of ancient Greece, taking advantage of the most recent trends and ideas. A chapter also discusses the influence of Greek rhetoric on modern theories of discourse. Law, politics, history, philosophy, rhetorical criticism and techniques, epic, tragedy, comedy and literacy are among the topics which are examined.

Persuasion: Greek Rhetoric in Action is an exciting and accessible introduction to rhetoric and oratory in ancient Greece. All Greek and Latin is translated. The book will be of interest to students and scholars of ancient history, communication, literature, philosophy and politics.

Ian Worthington is Lecturer in Classics at the University of Tasmania.

PERSUASION: GREEK RHETORIC IN ACTION

Edited by

Ian Worthington

London and New York

First published 1994
by Routledge
11 New Fetter Lane, London EC4P 4EE

Simultaneously published in the USA and Canada
by Routledge
29 West 35th Street, New York, NY 10001

Editorial material © 1994 Ian Worthington;
this collection © 1994 Routledge;
individual chapters © 1994 individual contributors

Typeset in Garamond by Megaron, Cardiff, Wales
Printed and bound in Great Britain by T. J. Press (Padstow) Ltd,
Padstow, Cornwall.

British Library Cataloguing in Publication Data
A catalogue record for this book is available from the British
Library

Library of Congress Cataloging in Publication Data
Persuasion: Greek Rhetoric in Action/edited by Ian
Worthington.
p.   cm.
Includes bibliographical references (p.) and index.
1. Greek literature–History and criticism–Theory, etc.
2. Greek language–Rhetoric.   3. Persuasion
(Rhetoric). 4. Rhetoric, Ancient.   5. Oratory, Ancient.
6. Literary form.   I. Worthington, Ian.
PA3074.P47   1993
808'.00938–dc20   93-2061

ISBN 0–415–08138–6 (hbk)
ISBN 0–415–08139–4 (pbk)

Contents

CONTENTS

Part III Contexts

Notes on contributors

Victor Bers Department of Classics, Yale University

Christopher Carey Department of Classics, Royal Holloway, University of London

David Cohen Department of Rhetoric, University of California, Berkeley

Michael Gagarin Department of Classics, University of Texas at Austin

Stephen Halliwell Department of Classics, University of Birmingham

Phillip Harding Department of Classics, University of British Columbia

Edward M. Harris Department of Classics, Brooklyn College and the Graduate Center/City University of New York

Josiah Ober Department of Classics, Princeton University

Carol G. Thomas Department of History, University of Washington

Peter Toohey Department of Classics and Ancient History, University of New England

Edward Kent Webb Department of History, University of Washington

Ian Worthington Department of Classics, University of Tasmania

Preface

Though distinct genres, Greek rhetoric and Greek oratory are intimately connected with each other: rhetoric is the intellectual art or study of persuasion; oratory is the actual verbal communication with the intent to persuade, the application of the art of rhetoric. One cannot live without the other, so to speak, and that is why this book is so titled since oratory *is* rhetoric in action. Rhetoric permeated and influenced (and, to an extent, was influenced by) other genres, concepts and features of ancient Greek life far more comprehensively than any other intellectual art or pursuit. This is reflected in Protarchus' words in Plato's *Philebus* (58a):

> I have often heard Gorgias constantly maintain that the art of persuasion surpasses all others; for this, he said, makes all things subject to itself, not by force, but by their free will, and is by far the best of all arts.
>
> (Trans. H. N. Fowler)

It is important, though, not to restrict the influence of Greek rhetoric just to the ancient world but to trace its continuity into our modern world, in the last instance perhaps most evident in the realm of communication.

Greek rhetoric and its effects on both its contemporary context and modern times are the scope of, and the justification for, the present book. In recent years there has been something of a renaissance of Greek rhetoric and oratory. Individual orators are receiving more attention in the form of editions and commentaries; Greek rhetoricians and rhetorical theories are undergoing new scrutinies and applications; critics of rhetoric, ancient and modern, are having their merits and views evaluated and re-evaluated; and oratory and rhetoric are rightly being linked together in studies of ancient Greece and its intellectual background. All of this is very welcoming, especially as many of what may be termed the 'standard' works on oratory and rhetoric have been around for a long time, and although many may still remain indispensable they naturally cannot reflect new trends, ideas and work in these two genres. Furthermore, it is still necessary to consult large numbers of modern works when interest centres on several aspects connected with rhetoric, such as its development; various rhetorical devices; the exploitation of rhetoric through the medium of oratory; or the relationship of rhetoric to other genres. I think it was while ploughing through a pile of books and articles on rhetoric and oratory that the idea for the present book hit me.

The aim of this book is to bring together within one set of covers discussions of the relationship of Greek oratory and rhetoric to a variety of important areas and genres, at the same time reflecting new trends and ideas now at work in the study of rhetoric. The book is divided into three parts to illustrate the influence and exploitation of rhetoric, and the reaction to it, at both the theoretical and practical levels. Although the focus is primarily the ancient Greek world, a chapter deals with the influence of Greek rhetoric on the sphere of modern communication. It is unavoidable in view of the wealth of source-material from Athens that attention will centre largely on Athenian sources and that city, yet it is as well to remember that although the Athenians transformed oratory into a fine art, the origins of oratory and rhetoric lay not in Athens but in Sicily. The history of those two genres, as Friedrich Blass would point out (*Die attische Beredsamkeit*, I, p. 4), began with Gorgias, and the directions which the Athenians took after Gorgias' visit illustrate the impact he had on them.

The book is aimed at student, scholarly and informed general audiences as is reflected in the varying pitches of the chapters. It serves as a starting point for those studying (or finding themselves interested in) ancient and modern rhetoric; politics and society; literature; philosophy; and the ancient world in general – as well as a stimulant to scholarly reaction and further work in rhetoric and its related areas.

There are several people I wish to thank, first and foremost being the other contributors for their enthusiasm and ready response to various comments and requests. I am also grateful to Dr Peter

Toohey, my colleague at my former institution the University of New England, for his constructive comments when the book was in its infancy and as it grew older. I thank Mr Richard Stoneman, Senior Editor at Routledge, for responding so positively to the proposal and for his advice when sought. My new colleagues at the University of Tasmania also deserve praise for putting up with a new member of staff trying to finish both his contributions to the book and the editing process at the same time as learning new ropes. Finally, I owe a special debt, as ever, to Tracy Furlonger, for her support throughout.

The following practices have been adopted throughout the book: Greek and Latin have been restricted to a minimum (where quotations in Greek and Latin occur they are translated); diacritical marks on transliterated terms (e.g. *diêgêsis*) have been omitted; in order to avoid an unduly large number of cross-references to other chapters (since the content of many chapters is often pertinent to others), I have added only a few such cross-references at some relevant points. Finally, all dates are BC except where indicated (in some instances BC has been retained for clarity).

I.W.
University of Tasmania

Abbreviations

Frequently cited ancient authors:

Aes.	Aeschines
Andoc.	Andocides
Antiph.	Antiphon
Arist.	Aristotle
[Arist.]	Pseudo-Aristotle
Aristoph.	Aristophanes
Dem.	Demosthenes
[Dem.]	Pseudo-Demosthenes
Diog. Laert.	Diogenes Laertius
Dion. Hal.	Dionysius of Halicarnassus
Isoc.	Isocrates
Lyc.	Lycurgus
Lys.	Lysias
Plut.	Plutarch
[Plut.]	Pseudo-Plutarch
Thuc.	Thucydides

The following modern works should also be noticed:

Cole, *Origins of Rhetoric*	T. Cole, *The Origins of Rhetoric in Ancient Greece* (Baltimore: 1991)
Kennedy, *Art of Persuasion*	G. Kennedy, *The Art of Persuasion in Greece* (Princeton: 1963)

Part I
COMMUNICATING

1

From orality to rhetoric: an intellectual transformation

Carol G. Thomas and Edward Kent Webb

Early in the *Phaedrus*, after Phaedrus has read Lysias' speech on love, Socrates opens his own speech on the subject with the invocation:

> Come then, ye clear voiced Muses, whether it be from the nature of your song, or from the musical people of Liguria that ye came to be so styled, 'assist the tale I tell' under compulsion by my good friend here, to the end that he may think yet more highly of one dear to him, whom he already accounts a man of wisdom.
>
> $(237a–b)^1$

Socrates begins the account only to interrupt himself, asking, 'Well, Phaedrus, my friend, do you think, as I do, that I am divinely inspired?' When Phaedrus replies 'Undoubtedly, Socrates, you have been vouchsafed a quite unusual eloquence', Socrates bids him 'listen to me in silence. For truly there seems to be a divine presence in this spot, so that you must not be surprised if, as my speech proceeds, I become as one possessed; already my style is not far from dithyrambic' (239c–d).

Socrates represented so many and differing images to his contemporaries that modern scholars must continue to seek the 'real' person. Even so, from the perspective of historical development, there is some agreement on at least one point: it is not uncommon to find Socrates described as a pivot between two phases of ancient Greek culture. Victor Ehrenberg ended his study of classical Greece with Socrates; F. M. Cornford saw the history of philosophy in terms of *Before and After Socrates*. We believe that Socrates' actions recorded in the *Phaedrus* are yet another illustration of his stance astride two ages with their quite different

3

intellectual attitudes. This position serves nicely, we think, to demonstrate the origins of the art of rhetoric. Socrates begins his discourse as one inspired by the Muses; he interrupts that discourse to question its effectiveness. These actions define two of the essential elements of formal rhetoric: oratory or actual speech, on the one hand, and the study of the theory and technique of speaking, on the other. The development that made oratory self-conscious by transforming the conception of speech was a new employment of writing. The transformation was sudden, occurring during Socrates' lifetime. His prayer for inspiration is a clue to the basic nature of the change.

This account will open with the role of oratory in ancient Greece, both in shaping the various aspects of Greek life and as indicative of a pre-rhetorical conception of the spoken word. Then, we will turn to the impact of increased reliance on written communication on the accumulated body of remembered tales, songs and accounts. Finally, the legacy of both parents – oratory and written analysis – will be viewed in the final product, the rhetorical theory of Plato and of Aristotle.

ORALITY AND POETICISED SPEECH

'Greek society relied on oral expression', George Kennedy states at the beginning of his survey of Greek rhetoric: 'Although literacy was clearly extensive in fifth- and fourth-century Athens, even then reading and writing, whether on stone, bronze, clay, wood, wax, or papyrus, was difficult and unnatural. Both the mechanics of ancient civilisation and its primary expression remained oral' (*Art of Persuasion*, p. 3). The recognition of the predominantly oral character of ancient Greek society, a prominent thread in the tapestry of Kennedy's account of Greek rhetoric, has quietly found its way into many descriptions of the origins of rhetoric, causing little debate. In the same year that Kennedy's study appeared, however, Eric Havelock's *Preface to Plato* (Oxford: 1963) broadcast a similar view of the mechanics of Greek civilisation. Havelock's account, by contrast, aroused passionate contention from its date of publication. The 'lively and iconoclastic mind' of this 'maverick' argued for the persistence of oral communication through virtually the whole of classical Greece.[2] Only towards the end of the fifth century, Havelock maintained, were the habits fostered by reliance on oral communication giving way to written communication. Plato's attack on Homer and poetry shows the conflict between the practices of literacy and orality. Until the end of the fifth century, oral, traditional modes of thought served as the foundation of Greek life and culture.

There is still no unanimity of opinion concerning the book's central thesis even as it was restated in Havelock's final book, *The Muse Learns to Write* (New Haven: 1986). For Murray, it 'begins to look as if Havelock was right after all in his basic contention', while in the eyes of T. J. Winifrith the book 'tries to provoke and merely succeeds in irritating'.[3] What can be agreed is that Havelock's advocacy of the fundamental role of oral communication in Greek culture has stimulated much interest in the issue. His views on the intellectual consequences of orality remain points of serious contention.[4] On the underlying question of the extent of literacy in the early Greek world, William Harris' recent *Ancient Literacy* (Cambridge, Mass.: 1989) inclines the balance in favour of Havelock's position. After a thorough survey of the evidence for literacy in ancient Greece, Harris concludes that even in Athens in the second half of the fifth century the rate of literacy did not exceed 10 per cent of the Attic population; for most states the percentage was even lower.[5]

The recognition of oral communication's central place in Greek society has significance for those who have searched for the origins of rhetoric. As natural speakers, *rhetors*, it comes as no surprise that the Greeks discovered the art of speaking, rhetoric. Its usual history is entwined with the newly established democracy in Syracuse during the second quarter of the fifth century which generated a need for training in the art of public speaking. Tisias and Corax, said to have produced the first handbooks on effective speaking in court, are credited with early responses to the need. In 427 the trail led to mainland Greece when Gorgias, a Sophist from Leontini, brought the art to Athens, where democratic processes caused it to flourish. From there, it passed on to the rest of antiquity. Such an interpretation assumes that the essential cultural and intellectual elements of rhetoric were present within the archaic and early classical periods – a 'protorhetoric', as it were – and needed only the right political circumstances to produce the formal and distinct practice of rhetoric. While recognising rhetorical theory as an important new development, this view sees the emergence of rhetoric as essentially an expression of cultural continuity.

This explanation has been rigorously challenged in a recent study by Thomas Cole, *Origins of Rhetoric*, who argues an alternative, 'revolutionary' interpretation of rhetoric's origins. Cole claims that the doxographical tradition attributing the creation of rhetoric to Tisias and Corax is erroneous. Because their handbooks were probably simple illustrations of contemporary oratory and not analyses of oratory in general, the two Sicilians' contribution to the art of rhetoric was minimal. Although the gradual spread of rhetorical texts is important in Cole's interpretation, it does not alone constitute the beginning of rhetoric. Instead, rhetoric was established as an art (*techne*) of speaking when Plato and Aristotle combined the study of manner with that of matter. In other words, an understanding of effective speech and knowledge of one's subject were equally essential to rhetoric. Since both Plato and Aristotle felt that truth derived from dialectical reasoning, Cole demonstrates how their arguments bound rhetoric and philosophy together inextricably. Throughout antiquity and even into the modern age, rhetoric was defined in Platonic and Aristotelian terms, determining the prerequisites for its very existence.

Cole's argument is rigorous, his analysis of the evidence is thorough and, according to the criteria of Plato and Aristotle, it correctly places the origins of rhetoric almost a century later than the usual date. If, however, one sees rhetoric not only as an achievement in theory and practice, but also as an intellectual development from which practice proceeded and theory arose, it is necessary to modify Cole's construction. By viewing rhetoric as an intellectual attitude, Cole's conception of the revolutionary change from pre-rhetorical to rhetorical Greece remains valid. However, the location of this shift from an unreflective conception of speech to one of self-conscious speech-making should be moved back to the traditional date of rhetoric's origins in the middle of the fifth century.

The Greeks' reliance on oral communication not only shaped the processes and institutions of their society, but also influenced their conception of speech itself. In the archaic and early classical world where the ability to read and write – even at Athens – was rare, and written texts even rarer, the spoken word assumed great burdens. One of the greatest was the preservation of important information. The need to be understood, even listened to, meant that expression was a vital skill. Words pleasing to the ear, woven together with eloquence, were more memorable than those without aesthetic merit. When Pindar sang, 'aboard the Muses' chariot I beg the eloquence that this occasion needs' (*Olympian* 9.79–81), he was voicing a general principle of ancient Greek life as well as honouring one man with a paean. A good measure of eloquence was needed so that 'winged words' would endure within another's memory. Even martial Tyrtaeus knew the value of 'a sweetly speaking tongue' (12.8).

The necessity for mellifluous verbal expression meant that speech was judged by the degree of charm it conveyed. The criteria by which we assess and classify oral communication – elements of speech, techniques of speaking and speakers' intentions – did not apply in this pre-rhetorical age. The first definition of poetry according to its metrical aspect, for example, did not appear until the second half of the fifth century when Gorgias stated that 'all poetry is simply speech with metre' (*Helen* 9).[6] Prior to this declaration, there is a telling absence of any analysis or criticism of poetic technique or form. Nor is there any suggestion that a clear distinction existed between poetic and prose speech. Not one of the early Greeks mentions the idea that there exists a type of speech that is not poetic; and before the fifth century no example of prose composition survives.

What does survive is comment on the quality of speech, a tendency suggesting that speech was conceived as a spectrum of progressive quality. Often such comments come in the form of a metaphor evoking sensory pleasure. Nestor's words flow sweeter than honey (*Iliad* 1.251) and Hesiod's good judges advise with soft words in order to bring harmony to the community (*Theogony* 89–90). Even the voices of the Sirens, which brought death to those who listened, are described in similar terms (*Odyssey* 12.187). The immediate pleasurable effect on the listeners determined a speech's effectiveness. The greater the effect of a speaker's words, the higher upon the spectrum of eloquence his speech fell. The words of men like Nestor, Odysseus and Hesiod's good judges, who could hold the attention and shape the attitudes of their auditors, occupied the higher end of the spectrum. The words of less noted, more laconic speakers like Menelaus fell somewhere below (*Iliad* 3.212–215).

Poetic speech, however, claimed the top of the spectrum. And poets were the most eloquent speakers. According to Greek legend, poetic skill was of divine origin: in order to assuage an angry Apollo, Hermes created the lyre and the speech appropriate to accompany its musical notes (*Homeric Hymn to Hermes* 4.420–435).[7] The Muses were the patrons of poetic speech and of those who practised it. The daughters of Mnemosyne and Zeus actively aided mortal singers and were not simply mythical personifications of a poet's abilities.[8] The Muses' contribution to the poet was often a grant of special knowledge. As Mnemosyne's children they could give a mortal access to vast, divine memory. On Hesiod, who calls himself a mere shepherd in the fields of Boeotia, they bestowed accounts of the gods and the past ages of the world. The poet of the *Iliad* and *Odyssey* begins with a general prayer for assistance to 'the Muse' (*Mousa*) in the *Odyssey*, to 'the goddess' (*thea*) in the *Iliad*. The singer of the *Iliad* requires fresh inspiration from the Muses to recount the Greek forces at Troy (2.484) and yet another nudge to recall the best and bravest (2.761).

The invocations and references to the Muses show that divinity was felt to be responsible for other aspects of the poetic performance.[9] Beyond stories, the Helicon Muses inspired (ἐνέπνευσαν) Hesiod to sing and taught (ἐδίδαξαν) him how to do so (*Theogony* 31, *Works and Days* 662).[10] Although Pindar repeatedly claimed that he possessed natural poetic ability, he required the Muses' inspiration to begin a song which his skills would then carry forward. Twice he uses the image of a gust of wind that fills a waiting sail in alluding to their gift to him (*Pythian* 11.39; *Nemean* 3.26).[11] In the *Homeric Hymns*, the Muses are regularly invoked to sing (*Hephaestus*), are thanked for inspiration (*The Muses, Apollo*) or are asked for information (*Pan, Aphrodite*). Phemius requires their inspiration but, at the same time, claims that he is self-taught (*autodidaktos*: *Odyssey* 22.346–347). The Phaeacian bard Demodocus, by contrast, is inspired and has been instructed in his art (*Odyssey* 8.480–481).

The marked presence of divinity in poetic speech was not limited to bards but was a far more general phenomenon. Skill in speaking was a gift of the gods granted to men other than specialists in the art of singing. As Odysseus reminds Eurylaus (*Odyssey* 8.166–173):

Friend, that was not well spoken, you seem like one who is reckless. So it is that the gods do not bestow graces in all ways on men, neither in stature nor yet in brains or eloquence; for there is a certain kind of man, less noted for beauty, but the god puts comeliness upon his words, and they who look towards him are filled with joy at the sight, and he speaks to them without faltering in winning modesty, and shines among those who are gathered, and people look on him as a god when he walks in the city.[12]

The gift was exceedingly valuable for it, along with skill as a fighter, defined a hero. Odysseus himself is compared to a singer by Eumaeus as that servant recounts his meeting with the hero to Penelope: 'But as when a man looks to a singer, who has been given from the gods the skill with which he sings for delight of mortals, and they are impassioned and strain to hear it when he sings to them, so he enchanted me in the halls as he sat beside me' (*Odyssey* 17.518–521). Odysseus has skills equal to a poet and his words have similar effects, but he is better known as king of Ithaca and renowned warrior at Troy.[13]

The brilliance of a speaker can be measured by the effect his words have on his audience. When Demodocus sings of the sack of Troy and the sufferings of the Achaeans, Odysseus is rendered helpless with grief (*Odyssey* 8.521–533). Nestor's speeches, among the most eloquent in the epics, are very like a bard's song. They consist of stories of the past which are as entertaining as they are persuasive or informative. As Cole has recognised (*Origins of Rhetoric*, p. 39), the tale Nestor relates often subsumes any message the Pylian king wished to convey (*Iliad* 1.254–284). Nestor's sheer volubility is also consistent with the picture of a bard who, once inspired, can sing for long stretches of time. Odysseus, too, holds forth before an assembly of men for a long time. The practical purpose of speaking is attested even more in the early archaic age as Hesiod reveals when he sings that the Muses 'bring honour upon a heaven-favoured lord and when they watch him being born, they pour sweet dew upon his tongue, and from his lips flow honeyed words'. Thus, 'speaking with assurance, he can stop great quarrels sensibly . . . such is the Muses' holy gift to men' (*Theogony* 80–94). Solon was certainly such a person.

The blurring of distinctions between poet and speechmaker calls into question the usual conception of speech in the pre-rhetorical age. A categorical division between poetry and oratory, rhetoric's precursor, is an anachronistic notion. Only when the elements of different types of speech could be set side by side and compared could poetic and prosaic expression become classifications. Such a comparison involves a critical reflection upon speech that did not occur in the archaic and early classical periods. As one scholar has observed, when early Greek poets do say something about their work it typically concerns its results and influence.[14] Their focus was on the effect their speech had on others, not on the techniques of fashioning that speech.

It was the Sophists who inaugurated the intensive study of language and its uses near the mid point of the fifth century. At that time a truly critical attitude towards oral communication took root. Aristophanes provides the first attested statement that poetic style should be consistent with subject-matter (*Frogs* 1057–1060). Distinction between non-poetic speakers and composers of poetry materialised in the fourth century, particularly in Plato's discussions. The word *rhetor* (ῥήτωρ) denoted the first, while *poietes* (ποιητής), derived from ποιέω, the second. Previously, a creator of poetry was designated by *aoidos*, singer, or by one of several words suggesting his submission to the divine force working through him (*therapon*: Hesiod, *Theogony* 100; Bacchylides 5.14; *opedos*: *Homeric Hymn* 4.450; *propolos*: Bacchylides 5.192). The poet's role in the poetic process is implicitly diminished; song, not the human singer, is the primary focus of attention.[15]

The further one moves from Gorgias' statement that poetry is simply words with metre, the clearer the lines of separation between poetry and prose become. With a developing consciousness of prose speech, the Greeks discovered how men create their own eloquence without the aid of the Muses. The origin of rhetoric lies here: with the awakening of a rhetorical conception of speech, the pre-rhetorical conception began to fade away. Rigid categories of distinct types of speech replaced the view of speech falling along a linear spectrum of eloquence according to its impact on an audience. Aristotle's *Rhetoric* and *Poetics*, meticulous definitions of their respective genres, are the culmination of this process. In order to understand how the Greeks moved to this new understanding of speech, we need to examine literacy's role in the creation of rhetoric.

LITERACY AND RHETORIC

The interplay between orality and writing in ancient Greece was complex. The common view is that the Dark Age was a time of total non-literacy.[16] Alphabetic writing made its earliest appearance during the eighth century but although the creation of the

Greek alphabet was a remarkable achievement,[17] it did not replace the spoken word and, in fact, grew slowly in quantity and kinds of use. Until at least the end of the sixth century, literacy's dissemination was slow and its application relatively limited. Powell's observations on the epigraphical evidence (see n. 5) are consistent with this view, but literacy's range of use for literary expression was equally narrow. Poetry was the only form of expression preserved in writing, and the works of Homer and Hesiod were the first subjected to the process of redaction. Thereafter, even as other poets employed the written word for compositions that went beyond epic and didactic genres, the forms themselves remained poetic.

Because of the scarcity and expense of writing materials in the Greek world, it is no surprise that this new technology was applied only to the most essential and the most eloquent examples of verbal communication. The result was the creation of performance texts of individual poets' works. Before the mid-eighth century, bards composed their songs unaided by writing through the patterning provided by oral formulas. Drawing on a reservoir of memorable tales, the bard recalled and retold his story with the help of metre, of set groupings of words that conveyed certain ideas and of framing sentences that offered a system of external structure. Composition was synonymous with performance and the immediate effect that words had on the audience was the measure of a bard's ability. Odysseus' remark to Alcinous that 'once properly told, a tale should not be repeated' (*Odyssey* 12.252–253), is thus not simply a matter of personal taste but a reflection of the conventions of a nonliterate environment. The poetry of a bard could not be replicated. A new song was expected every time a singer picked up his lyre.

When poetry began to be recorded in written form, however, this attitude was challenged. A text of a poet's work allowed for the recreation of the original occasion in which he had created his song. This additional dimension of Greek poetry stimulated composers to sing more than largely anonymous epic tales. Very soon, poetry that could be preserved in written form became a means of personal expression. Hesiod first broke out of the anonymity that epic tradition thrust on its bards. His version of Greek theology as well as his admonitions to his brother Perses are the earliest non-epic works to survive in written form. The lyric poetry that soon followed demonstrates even more vividly how

11

the introduction of literacy into the poetic process fostered a more intimate relationship between the composer and his composition. The personal emotions filling Sappho's poetry are but one illustration of the impact literacy made on poetic expression.

Yet the creation and use of texts did not bring the demise of the bardic tradition. Rather, it continued along several paths into the fifth century. Fragmentation of types of poetic expression accompanies the now-entwined course of written and sung poetry and indeed is reflected within the epic tradition itself. The existence of written versions of the Homeric epics to aid their memorisation created a class of professional reciters known as rhapsodes. Their title was derived from the verb *rhaptein*, 'to weave together', since rhapsodes wove together sections of the epics when reciting before an audience. Although the rhapsode eventually replaced the bard as the performer of the epic tradition, neither the application of writing to the epics nor the emergence of professional reciters vanquished oral formulaic poetry.[18] The singers of the 'Homeric Hymns' demonstrate the later history of this genre and we know of a Cynaithus of Chios who created new versions of the Homeric tales as late as 504 (Schol. 1 Pindar, *Nemean* 2).

Thus, in the words of Bruno Gentili, 'repetition and creation continued to coexist . . . even in the sixth century' (*Poetry and Its Public*, p. 7). The application of the written word to the poetic process created new forms of poetic expression without destroying the old. Nor did it affect the nature of the poetic experience itself. As we have said, the Muses played an important role in Pindar's poetry. A condition akin to religious ecstasy invaded the poet's being, while he sang a 'superior language, the expression of a single divine entity'.[19] In turn, spectators found themselves in a position of dependency upon the rhapsode who bewildered and numbed them. It was this condition, according to Havelock's argument, that troubled Plato, for poetry remained 'a possession, not an autonomous exercise of the mental faculties' (*Preface to Plato*, p. 156). In other words, writing did not immediately alter the nature of either poetic creation or performance. The change required a new application of writing. To anticipate: only when it was trained on the low end of the spectrum of poetised speech could a new conception of speech emerge. A newly emergent art of written prose is both the culmination and the major tool of the process.

12

Consequently, Tisias and Corax are restored as the agents of momentous change. In the special circumstances that unfolded in Sicily in the mid-fifth century, they produced the first texts of non-poetic speech in creating speeches for those in need of improving their ability to speak in court. The speeches offered examples of effective verbal argument. No longer inelegant speech at the low end of the spectrum, non-poetic speech had a true, empirical value. These collections of examples would be useful in constructing speeches for the assembly, the courts or other polis occasions, and had the practical value of providing aid in planning a speech. As Kennedy concluded, 'it is clear that these commonplaces or specimens of oratory were like building blocks from which a speech could be constructed. The actual composition was often largely extempore, the orator drawing on the material in his memory' (*Art of Persuasion*, p. 53). In style, too, they were pragmatic in that they taught straight-speaking or *orthoepeia*.

Such collections were largely illustrative, *not* analyses of method. They may have been similar to the performance texts used for memorisation of poetry and for the presentation of dramatic performances. Handbooks of these sample speeches soon circulated widely in the Greek world. Kennedy believes that written handbooks became fairly numerous although there were not likely to be many copies of each one. Nevertheless, the existence of illustrations of effective prose speech allowed a critical attitude towards verbal communication to develop for the first time. Even speech that was not a gift of the Muses was preserved alongside highly esteemed poetry. It could be analysed by any wanting to discover its components. Different examples of prose speech could be compared to learn why one was more effective in its purpose than another. There arose an interest in the nature of discourse, the stirrings of a *logon techne* that sought 'to discover, identify and illustrate the minimal components of discourse'.[20] This new technical interest in the nature of prose discourse is the birth of rhetorical analysis.

Particularly important at this stage were the Sophists. From Tisias' and Corax' creation of written texts, they went on to study the mechanics of speech and to make a profession of teaching the practical application of their research. Protagoras studied argumentation, debate, grammar and diction. In his efforts to understand not only speech's mechanics but also its purposes, he drew together *Refutory Arguments* and two books of Antilogies.

Thrasymachus is said to have paid especial attention to rhythm, perhaps also to sentence structure and avoidance of hiatus. His writing of an *ars* points to a concern with style or *lexis*. He is credited with a treatise on rhetoric. A study of style – *peri lexeos* – is ascribed to Polus in the *Suda* while Aristotle (*Rhetoric* 1414b13 ff.) describes a handbook of Theodorus of Byzantium in which subdivisions of a speech form at least part of the account. Hippias wrote works on grammar and prosody; Prodicus was best known for his study of language and he may have prepared a work known as *On the Correctness of Names*.

But it is Gorgias of Leontini who seems to have been most prominent in the study and practice of prose speech employing, according to Diodorus Siculus (12.53.4), such new devices as antithesis, isocolon, parison and homoeoteleuton. Consideration of the opportune, *to kairon*, also marked Gorgias' style. The occasion of a speech dictates its organisation, its style and its contents. In the words of M. Untersteiner, *to kairon* is 'the adaptation of the speech to the manifold variety of life, to the psychology of speaker and hearer'.[21] For J. Swearingen, the products of Gorgias 'were among the earliest rhetorical "works"' providing 'the raw material for technical rhetoric and ultimately for what we now know as rules of composition'. Their traits include more diverse lexical repertoire and discourse structures; philosophical abstraction; an argumentative structure; a move away from narrative; and a self-referential habit, all of which are absent in the traditional Homeric canon.[22]

Rightly, then, did the chorus in *The Clouds* yearn to hear the newly trained Pheidippides argue (1397–1398; trans. M. Hadas):

> Thou mover and shaker of novel words, now 'tis time to seek
> Persuasiveness, to make it seem you naught but justice speak.

His trainer, in Aristophanes' eyes, had been Wrong Logic, who could ask (1038–1042; trans. M. Hadas):

> The Lesser Logic am I? Your sages call me so
> Because the pioneer was I in devising refutations
> Of laws that on conventions rest and codified traditions.
> To win a case for the weaker side at higher value I rate
> Than a hundred moneybags bulging with pieces of eight.

Both chorus and Wrong Logic emphasise novelty ('novel words', 'the pioneer was I') as part of the means to persuade an audience.

14

Composed for performance in 423, the description appears to reflect recent developments. Right Logic, modelling itself on traditional education and values, is only now being worsted by voices modulated to entice a lecherous ear.

Out of this interest in the mechanics of speech rules eventually emerged. In the career of one of Gorgias' students rhetorical theory expanded significantly. Isocrates claimed and seems to have genuinely believed that 'speech is the marshall of all actions and of thoughts and those most use it who have the greatest wisdom' (2.5 ff.). His philosophy aims at 'a wisdom in practical affairs resulting in high moral consciousness and is equated with a mastery of rhetorical technique'.[23] His view found concrete expression in his two schools, the first in Chios at the very end of the fifth century and the second in Athens. Students improved a natural ability by practice and study of theory (*Against the Sophists* 14 ff.).

In spite of his belief that 'men may become better and worthier if they are anxious about speaking well' (15.274 ff.), Isocrates was akin to the fifth-century Sophists in feeling that abstract truth is not possible or, even if possible, useless.[24] The final component in the true art of rhetoric was supplied by Plato and Aristotle who, correcting the amoral stance of the Sophists and Isocrates, sought 'to show how poetry and oratory can make truth sound like truth'. For them rhetoric was the 'art of harnessing and focussing poetical and oratorical energy with such ends in mind'.[25]

Example and analysis interweave in Plato's discussions of rhetoric. Perhaps the best examples are the funeral oration of the *Menexenus*, the speeches of Phaedrus and Socrates in the *Phaedrus* and Socrates' defence in the *Apology*. But speeches abound in all the dialogues, many of which could serve as examples for imitation. Plato also contemplates and analyses the nature of discourse generally, particularly in the *Phaedrus* and the *Republic*. Writing and discourse complement one another: living speech is 'the original of which the written discourse may fairly be called a kind of image' (*Phaedrus* 276a).

In the work of Aristotle, on the other hand, illustration yields to analysis, 'analysis based on an abstract conception of speeches of different kinds, not actual speeches' (Kennedy, *Art of Persuasion*, p. 123). We should not attribute the difference to changed political conditions since debate continued to be the vehicle of polis activity. After all, Aristotle was defining rhetoric during the lifetime of Demosthenes, Aeschines, Apollodorus, Lycurgus,

Hyperides and Dinarchus – all, apart from Apollodorus, members of the Canon of Ten Attic Orators. The role of public speaking had not diminished. Instead, the alliance between speech and writing resulted in a new manner of composition and a body of lasting examples that could be studied apart from the occasion of actual delivery. Comparison between examples could show that which was common to every instance, just as the search for beauty could move beyond specific instances of beauty in order to discern beauty itself. Analysis could occur at a higher level through a language of analysis, a metalanguage.[26] The development of this metalanguage required that writing be involved in the whole process of oratory from composition to delivery to analysis.

The one hundred years that separate Tisias and Corax from Plato and Aristotle saw rhetoric's birth, childhood and adolescence. Tisias and Corax sparked the development of a rhetorical conception of speech; possessing this conception, the Sophists studied speech and applied their knowledge to practical situations; Isocrates made the first attempt at formulating a theory of effective speaking. Only with the work of Plato and Aristotle did rhetoric take the form by which it would be recognised for the rest of antiquity. Even so, the intellectual reaction set in motion by Tisias' and Corax's handbooks of speeches transformed the traditional Greek conception of speech from a spectrum of relative eloquence into categories of poetic and prosaic expression. Eloquence became a quality that any person could attain in either category. The symbol of this transformation is the figurative death of the Muses. Soon after the dawn of the rhetorical era, invocations to the Muses become merely a literary motif. In the rhetorical age, humans had learned to acquire what previously the Muses had bestowed.

LEGACY

We have argued that orality was the first component of rhetoric. Not only did ancient Greeks rely on speech to direct their communal life, but also they took delight in their exact, subtle and clear language. Muteness was a powerfully negative sign. Demeter's refusal to speak until the fate of her daughter is decided is a clear token of her overwhelming grief (*Homeric Hymn* 2.24–33). Its consequences are fearful: the withdrawal of fruitfulness from the earth.

The reflection enabled by writing was the second necessary component. Both were present in Greek culture from the eighth century but reliance on writing was limited until the late fifth century when it became a valuable tool rather than a suspicious ability. The changed regard for written documents is apparent in the few years that separate the generations of Herodotus and Thucydides. Herodotus believes that written records indicate the exercise of absolute, and often arbitrary, power. They can lie and they often involve trickery. The safest communication is by word of mouth: Themistocles relayed his secret information to the Persians through the words of his messenger Sicinnus (8.75). In contrast, Thucydides' regard for writing is surely echoed by the thoughts attributed to Nicias (7.8):

> He was afraid, however, that the messengers might not report the facts as they really were, either through lack of ability in speaking, or bad memory or a desire to say something which would please the general mass of opinion. He therefore wrote a letter, thinking that in this way the Athenians would know what his views were without having them distorted in the course of transmission, and would so have the truth of the matter in front of them to discuss.

The rising regard for writing brought it into equal partnership with discourse, giving rise to the origin of a number of new applications. These applications, in turn, yielded new products, one of which was rhetoric, which shows the legacy of both components. We will consider the twin legacy in four of its features: its uses, persuasive intent, magical aura and the esteem accorded to speakers.

Consider, first, its goals. According to Aristotle, rhetoric is the faculty of discovering the means of persuasion in each of three kinds of oratory: judicial, deliberative and epideictic. In sketching the role of speech in the polis, we must acknowledge how crucial it was in the administration of public and private affairs. As J. de Romilly sums up the situation for the fifth century: 'All major decisions were the outcome of public debates. Speech was thus an important mode of action'.[27] The assembly and council relied on debate to reach decisions in deliberating on all state affairs; the law courts entrusted judicial decision-making to debate between involved parties; and the community celebrated its human and divine constituents through speeches of praise. In other words, the

17

three categories of oratory recognised by Aristotle are the three public functions of public speech cementing the bonds of the polis. Aristotelian theory is a statement of earlier practice.

The rising importance of writing in Hellenic culture contributed equally to rhetoric's uses. The Sophists are remembered for the compilations of examples they supplied to aid their students. Collections are attributed to Thrasymachus in his *Subjects for Oratory* as well as compilations of deliberative speeches; Gorgias' *Helen* and *Palamedes* are regarded as two examples of legal speeches; Protagoras drew together three collections; and Antiphon's *Tetralogies* is a series of examples. And the Sophists went beyond compilation of samples; they sought to understand the very nature of language. To this end, they treated linguistic theory – *orthoepeia* – through study of grammar, prosody, arrangement of elements, and style. We have surveyed the titles of works associated with Corax and Tisias, Thrasymachus, Protagoras, Hippias and Prodicus. Gorgias is identified as even 'more of a theorist and abstract thinker than the other Sophists'.[28]

Such interests manifest more than expansion of interest in speech-making; they show a new kind of regard for words. When content and method separated, a realisation arose that the study and use of words might be ends in themselves, with no regard to the purpose to which they were put. Rhetoric, in other words, might have no relation to truth. As we have seen, Isocrates undertook to heal the breach between words and truth, demonstrating that a need to persuade will guide a speech to accepted opinion which, while not absolute truth, is the received truth for most people.[29] While Plato mistrusted most rhetorical displays because they were just that, not searches for truth, he believed that there could be another rhetoric that expressed the truth. That rhetoric appears when, as Socrates relates in the *Gorgias* (504d–e), 'the good and true artist [has] his mind always occupied with one thought, how justice may be implanted in the souls of the citizens and injustice banished, and how temperance may be implanted and indiscipline banished, and how goodness in general may be engendered and wickedness depart' (trans. Woodhead). Aristotle forged a tighter bond between rhetoric and philosophy. In doing so, the abstract analysis fostered by writing was embedded deeper in the now many-faceted discipline of rhetoric. As Kennedy noted, Aristotle is 'not intoxicated with speaking . . . his analysis is based on an abstract conception of speeches of different kinds, not actual speeches' (*Art of Persuasion*, p. 123).

The dual legacy from discourse and writing to rhetoric is also apparent in the tendency to regard words as magical and a speaker as a magician.[30] An orator, like a poet, is one who is capable of leading souls of his hearers through the hypnotic charm of words; a *psychagogas*, he weaves his web of *psychagogia*, or the enchanting of souls. The magical character of speech is inherent in the earliest nature of composition and we have mentioned the persistence of this conception (see p. 12). To be successful, oral discourse must enchant the soul; without the power to draw listeners into the spell of words, a speaker will lose his audience. The composer himself was inspired; the bards are taught their songs by the Muse who loves the tribe of *aoidoi* (*Odyssey* 8.480–481).

The means of enchantment is provided by the nature of oral composition. Lacking writing from the late Bronze Age until the end of the Dark Age, the Greeks preserved information through an increasingly elaborate means of composition, patterning human speech and thereby memory.[31] The form was poetic, easier to recall though more difficult to produce initially as it required conformity to the specific requirements of metre. Language was structured in another way: blocks of words, sometimes many lines in length, took shape as formulas; that is, expressions that revealed certain ideas in fixed metrical fashion. The composer worked with formulas that had been tested by time and found satisfactory in terms of the two essential criteria, comprehension and aesthetic pleasure. Once a singer began his song or tale, the well-learned formulas welled up spontaneously within him, for, as we have seen, the Muses bestowed both skill in speaking and the substance for song. The formulas, carried along by narrative, attached themselves in their right places to the thread of narrative as it passed through his mind. If he was making a new song they must rise naturally as the rhythm flowed into new patterns. The patterns carried the utterance forward almost like a boat upon a stream. An old song stayed the same because the bard knew the patterns; even the audience would recall long stretches as the bard sang and would catch him if he slipped. New song melded organically out of old, reborn phrases.

A song would bring praise if it were not problematic, either in content or in form. It must be immediately persuasive. As Powell reminds us: 'Silence and incomprehensibility destroy the rhetor's control. The rhetor gains his power by thinking aloud for the audience, replacing their thoughts with his own. Silence returns thought to the audience: they may question his point' (*Homer and the Origin of the Greek Alphabet*, p. 223). Powell is describing the Homeric bard. His choice of titles is instructive in that the art of the later orators, or *rhetors*, apparently differed little from that of the oral composer of the eighth and seventh centuries. In fact, Powell continues the parallel: 'Redundancy is for the rhetor what the formulaic style is for the singer of tales . . . It is an irony in the history of literary theory that the original functions of repetition – to facilitate oral composition and to reduce the discrepancy between rates of thought and speech – gave rise to theories of poetic and prosaic diction' (p. 223).

The magic of words is well attested in the fourth century by Plato, who had a gift for creating his own spells of enchantment. In listening to the public orations, Socrates tells Menexenus that 'The speakers steal away our souls with their embellished words . . . I feel quite elevated by their laudations, and I stand listening to their words and become enchanted by them' (*Menexenus* 235a). And when Protagoras ends 'his long and magnificent display of eloquence', reported by Plato in the dialogue named for the Sophist, Socrates admits, 'For a long time I gazed at him spellbound, eager to catch any further word that he might utter. When I saw that he had really finished, I collected myself with an effort' (*Protagoras* 328d).

The psychological element of oratory was very similar for the audiences of a bard and of a later public orator. And the ingredients were much the same: powerful images, mellifluous language, careful patterning, even rhyme and metre, remained vital to effective discourse.[32] Caught up in a stream of words, the listeners must be swept along by the unfolding narrative or argument. Formulas impel the stream for a singer of tales; topoi are similar aids for the *rhetor*. The dactylic hexameter coupled with familiar narrative provides firm structure for the oral bard; extremely elaborate ring composition is the counterpart for at least some fourth-century orators.[33] In both instances, the audience is aided by the condition of awareness of the direction the account will take. In bardic performances, use of traditional tales – slices from the banquet of Homer – provides this direction. For later orators, the careful structuring described by Socrates performs the same function.

However, the orators of Socrates' day cast their spell by other means than the formulaic narrative of the bards. The *Phaedrus* describes the more recent means. In the first place, discourse is carefully constructed 'like a living creature, with its own body, as it were; it must not lack either head or feet; it must have a middle and extremities so composed as to suit each other and the whole work' (264c); 'a speech must begin with a preamble . . . And next comes exposition accompanied by direct evidence; thirdly, indirect evidence; fourthly, probabilities; besides which there are the proof and supplementary proof mentioned by the Byzantine master of rhetorical artifice' (266d–e). It is essential that the student of the art of rhetoric make a systematic division of words (263b). Along with that knowledge, he must know how to apply them by understanding 'what types of soul there are . . . To the types of soul thus discriminated there corresponds a determinate number of types of discourse. And when he is competent to say what type of man is susceptible to what kind of discourse; when further, he can, on catching sight of so-and-so, tell himself, "That is the man, that character now actually before me is the one I heard about in school, and in order to persuade him of so-and-so I have to apply *these* arguments in *this* fashion" ' (271d, 272a).

In sum, the would-be speaker learned how to steal away the souls of his audience; he need not wait for a gift from the Muses. Moreover, the vehicle was prose not poetry, even though it was often 'poetical prose'. Yet while the elements of effective speech are so similar, the nature of composition is fundamentally different: as Socrates' words show at every turn, by the late fifth century the art of speech can and must be calculated to be effective. Calculation meant study. Innate ability was important, certainly, but only when leagued with knowledge and practice. 'If you lack any of these three', Socrates told Phaedrus, 'you will be correspondingly unfinished' (269d). One had to build a store of elements of speeches or even entire speeches in order to be prepared to address an audience at a moment's notice (*Menexenus* 235c–d). The availability of written treatises offered a ready supply of examples for, as Phaedrus acknowledged, 'there is plenty of matter in the rhetorical manuals' (266d). This is the gift of literacy to rhetoric.

A final mark of the dual inheritance appears in the *rhetor*'s status. As we have stressed, bards were honoured as those whom the Muse cherished. Phemius, the Ithacan bard, rued the honour the suitors had paid him as Odysseus was taking his vengeance. With

21

Telemachus' aid, however, he was spared along with the herald (*Odyssey* 22.330–360). Prized for their ability to charm with song, bards also served very important practical roles: it was an *aoidos* who was entrusted with the care of Clytemnestra when Agamemnon left for Troy (*Odyssey* 3.267–268). The status of orators is never in doubt during the classical age. Plato vents his anger on orators and oratory precisely because they are so important in Hellenic society. The specific object of his attack (*Phaedrus* 272d) was not speech-making but the view that:

> There is . . . absolutely no need for the budding orator to concern himself with the truth about what is just or good conduct, nor indeed about who are just and good men whether by nature or education. In the law courts nobody cares a rap for the truth about these matters, but only about what is plausible. And that is the same as what is probable, and is what must occupy the attention of the would-be master of the art of speech.

Plato did care a rap about the truth. His attempt – in defining rhetoric or education or love or friendship – was to uncover the true, unchanging meanings. In defining proper rhetoric he allied speaking with the truth: 'If we are to address people scientifically, we shall show them precisely what is the real and true nature of that object on which our discourse is brought to bear' (*Phaedrus* 270e). In fact, Plato's definition of proper rhetoric may be closer to its oral antecedents than the view of most fifth-century instructors had been. Acknowledging that written words can be aids to memory, Plato is firm in believing that spoken discourse, brother to the written speech, is of unquestioned legitimacy. It 'goes together with knowledge, and is written in the soul of the learner, [that] can defend itself and knows to whom it should speak and to whom it should say nothing' (276a). Plato would strip away some of the current features of public speaking leaving out of the picture Evenus of Paros, 'the inventor of covert allusion and indirect compliment and, according to some accounts, of the indirect censure in mnemonic verse' (267a). Nor would he 'disturb the rest of Tisias and Gorgias, who realised that probability deserves more respect than truth, who could make trifles seem important and important points trifles by the force of their language, who dressed up novelties as antiques and vice versa' (267a). He had little to say of Polus and 'his *Muses' Treasury of Phrases* with its reduplications and maxims and similes' (267b). Such elements were part of the instruction using written manuals; Plato's programme would purge many of these practices.

Thus, Plato himself strengthened the twofold contribution to the formal art of rhetoric: while seeking to define its function through the critical faculties sharpened by written discourse, he pressed the priority of oral discourse in discovering the truth. The two gifts have truly become entwined. Only the Muses have withdrawn to Olympus.

NOTES

1 Translated by R. Hackforth; other translations from the *Phaedrus* are also by him.

2 The description is that of Oswyn Murray in his careful review of several accounts of oral tradition in *The Times Literary Supplement*, 16–22 June 1989, pp. 655 ff.

3 Murray, op. cit., pp. 655–6; T. J. Winifrith, *CR*[2] 38 (1988), p. 158. *The New York Review of Books* offers a more recent illustration of the debate. In a review of several books, Hugh Lloyd-Jones (5 March 1992) challenged the importance of oral composition even for the Homeric poems, a challenge that brought quick response in later issues (14 May 1992).

4 For example, the devastating critique of J. Halverson, 'Havelock on Greek Orality and Literacy', *Journal of the History of Ideas* 53 (1992), pp. 148–63.

5 Harris argues that literacy will spread only when certain preconditions are fulfilled: there must exist widespread formal education, a mechanism for diffusion of texts and the ideological notion that citizens should be literate. Harris' findings have not been accepted by all. In his review of the book, G. Bowersock, (*The New Republic*, 2 April 1990, pp. 37–9), said: 'It will remain for at least a generation as the most authoritative and accessible general survey of literacy in classical antiquity.' At the same time, Bowersock questioned the validity of the central thesis, that literacy was extremely limited in ancient Greece and Rome.

In another recent study, B. Powell, (*Homer and the Origin of the Greek Alphabet*, Cambridge: 1991), examines epigraphic remains of the archaic period, roughly fifty-five short inscriptions, along with a handful of longer ones. These surviving inscriptions for the first 150 years or more of Greek literacy, five generations of men as Powell has put the situation, were employed in a limited number of ways. Powell writes: 'The inscriptions are wholly private, but they do not include private topics frequently attested later in Greece: no legal documents, manumissions of slaves, contracts, mortgages, transfer of land; nothing to do with real property; no *tabella defixionum*. There is nothing in these alphabetic inscriptions, either to suggest mercantile interests, public or private: no financial accounts, not even any numbers of evidence that a numerical system existed, until *c.* 600 BC. . . . Nothing public and nothing economic'

(p. 182). This conclusion does not tell us that early Greek society had no political, economic or legal dimensions. Rather, the lack of written documentation indicates that public and private matters were conducted by other means, namely direct, oral communication.

6 Cole, *Origins of Rhetoric*, p. 35, makes the same observation.

7 A. Sperduti, 'The Divine Nature of Poetry in Antiquity', *TAPhA* 81 (1950), pp. 209–40, is a thorough treatment of this subject.

8 Contra Havelock, *Preface to Pluto*, pp. 154 ff.

9 E. R. Dodds, *The Greeks and the Irrational* (Berkeley and Los Angeles: 1981), pp. 80–2, did not recognise this fact.

10 For an interesting interpretation of Hesiod's encounter with the Muses see K. Latte, 'Hesiods Dichterweihe', *Antike und Abendland* 2 (1946), pp. 152–63.

11 C. M. Bowra, *Pindar* (Oxford: 1964), p. 11.

12 Translated by R. Lattimore; other translations from the *Odyssey* are also by him.

13 Even the word in the epics normally translated as orator, *agoretes*, has an etymological meaning of 'one whose speech is god-given'.

14 Bowra, *Pindar*, p. 1.

15 Democritus was the first to express the idea of the ecstatic poet, possessed by a god, as a person separate and distinct from others types of speakers (frgs 18, 21). Plato developed the notion of divinely inspired poetry further (*Ion* 533d–534e): see Dodds, *The Greeks*, p. 82.

16 J. A. Davison, *Companion to Homer* (London: 1962), p. 217. A. Heubeck, 'L'origine della lineare B', *SMEA* 23 (1982), p. 197: 'Contemporaneamente alla distruzione violenta della cultura micenea è andata dunque perduta anche l'arte della scrittura.' On the return of literacy: L. Jeffery, *Archaic Greece: the City States c. 700–500 B.C.* (London: 1976), pp. 25 ff.

17 See Havelock, 'The Greek Alphabet', in *The Literate Revolution and Its Cultural Consequences* (Princeton: 1982), pp. 77–88.

18 B. Gentili, *Poetry and Its Public in Ancient Greece*, trans. T. Cole (Baltimore: 1988). Gentili has shown how oral formulaic poetry of early modern Italy flourished in spite of the fact that literacy had been part of Italian culture since antiquity: see especially pp. 3–23. R. Sealey, 'From Phemios to Ion', *REG* 57 (1970), pp. 312–55, presents a strong case for the use of writing for new literary efforts during the sixth century.

19 M. Massenzio, 'Il Poeta che Vola', in B. Gentili and G. Paioni (eds), *Oralita: Cultura, Letteratura, Discorso*, Atti del Convegno Internazionale, Urbino, 1980 (Rome: 1985), pp. 161–77, at p. 163.

20 Cole, *Origins of Rhetoric*, p. 85.

21 M. Untersteiner, *The Sophists*, trans. K. Freeman (Oxford: 1954), p. 197.

22 C. Jan Swearingen, 'Literate Rhetors and their Illiterate Audiences; the Orality of Early Literacy', *Pre/Text* 7 (1986), pp. 145–62. These developments are also apparent in the thought of Parmenides.

23 Kennedy, *Art of Persuasion*, p. 178.

24 ibid.

25 Cole, *Origins of Rhetoric*, p. 140.

26 ibid., p. 92.

27 J. de Romilly, *The Great Sophists in Periclean Athens* (Oxford: 1992), p. 57.

28 ibid., p. 63.

29 ibid., pp. 71 ff.

30 J. de Romilly, *Magic and Rhetoric in Ancient Greece* (Cambridge, Mass.: 1975).

31 The description of oral composition in the Homeric poems was developed by Milman Parry and continued by his associate Albert B. Lord in numerous articles and books. For a recent account of oral composition with full bibliography, see J. M. Foley, *The Theory of Oral Composition: History and Methodology* (Bloomington: 1988).

32 Alcidamus (fr. B XXII 15.13) urges that a speech must at least appear improvised.

33 Ian Worthington, 'Greek Oratory, Revision of Speeches and the Problem of Historical Reliability', *C&M* 42 (1991), pp. 55–74. In an analysis of ring composition in Dinarchus 1 *Against Demosthenes*, Worthington finds that the major framework, or primary level of the speech, is divided into eleven parts. Each part divides into a secondary level and some split again at a tertiary stage and even beyond. Worthington concludes, quite legitimately we believe, that 'ring composition provides evidence for the amount of effort expended in producing a circulated version of a speech, and thus may be taken as further evidence that speeches were indeed revised before publication' (p. 69). See also his *A Historical Commentary on Dinarchus: Rhetoric and Conspiracy in Later Fourth-Century Athens* (Ann Arbor: 1992), pp. 27 ff., and below, chapter 6. The role of writing seems essential.

2

Rhetorical means of persuasion

Christopher Carey

In the *Rhetoric* (1356a) Aristotle distinguishes three means of persuasion (*pisteis*) which can be produced by the rhetorician's art. The term used, *pistis*, though frequently translated 'proof', is broader in its semantic range than the English word would suggest. Its use encompasses the related qualities of trust, trustworthiness, credence and credibility, and extends to objects and means used to secure trust or belief. This breadth of usage explains the disparate contents of Aristotle's list, and his inclusion of items which have no bearing on factual proof; he lists argument (as Aristotle puts it, 'to demonstrate something or appear to demonstrate'), the character of the speaker, and the disposition created in the hearer. Aristotle considers the first of these to be the the proper task of rhetoric, the other two being additional effects necessitated by the nature of the audience. Certainly this item is different in kind from the others in that demonstration by argument addresses itself more or less directly to the issue to be decided, while the other two *pisteis* listed have only an indirect bearing at most on the issue. These indirect 'proofs' do however play a major role in Attic oratory, and accordingly Aristotle feels compelled to accept and advise on their use. In this chapter I shall examine the range of effects sought by their deployment in the Attic orators, and the means used.

1

Pathos is defined broadly by Aristotle (*Rhetoric* 1356a, 1377b) as 'creating a certain disposition in the audience'. Aristotle was not the first rhetorician to stress the importance of *pathos*. Emotional appeal formed a major component of the rhetorical handbooks circulating in his day (*Rhetoric* 1354a). Gorgias in his *Helen* (9–10) lays great emphasis on the emotive power of the spoken word. Quintilian attests Prodicus' interest in emotional effect (*Institutio Oratoria* 3.1.12). Thrasymachus dealt with pity in a work called *Eleoi*, literally *Pities* (Plato, *Phaedrus* 267c; Arist. *Rhetoric* 1404a). The treatment went beyond the contents of emotional appeal to embrace the acting skills necessary for effective delivery. The generation and removal of anger were also dealt with. In this as in many respects classical rhetoric is merely systematising existing practice, for emotional appeal is the product neither of Athenian democracy nor sophistic teaching. Emotional appeal figures in the arsenal of the Homeric speaker, and is a pronounced feature in the political oratory of Solon and Alcaeus.[1] The speech of Sthenelaidas urging the Spartans to vote for war against Athens in the first book of Thucydides (1.86) is not noticeably lacking in emotional appeal; nor is his Spartan audience any less moved by this appeal than the democratic Athenian assembly which voted with Alcibiades for war on Syracuse in 415 (Thuc. 6.8–24). In the forensic process too, emotional appeal predates sophistic rhetoric. Hesiod's warnings to the nobles who will judge his suit with his brother Perses (*Works and Days* 202 ff., 248 ff.) are designed to intimidate as well as reform. Aeschylus' *Eumenides* (633 ff., 711 ff.) demonstrates that emotional appeal was well established in Athenian trials by the early 450s.

Common to all speakers is the basic need to secure the goodwill of the hearer.[2] The speaker will often use the *prooemium* to lay claim to qualities which the audience will respect,[3] or stress the disadvantages of his situation as a claim to sympathy. Thus the speaker of Demosthenes 54 says (1):

> Since all my friends and relatives, whose advice I sought, though they stated that his actions rendered him liable to the procedure of summary arrest for muggers and the indictments for malicious assault (*hubris*), none the less advised and urged me not to take on a task beyond my abilities, nor to be seen bringing a complaint beyond my years for the injuries I suffered, I did just this and because of them I brought a private action, though I should have preferred most of all to put him on trial for his life.

The projection here of the modesty which the Athenians expected of the young makes a powerful initial demand for a sympathetic hearing. Likewise we find speakers stressing the magnitude of the danger facing them (Lys. 19.1), the extent of the wrong done to them (Dem. 45.1), their inexperience in speaking or their complete inexperience of the legal system (Antiph. 1.1; Isaeus 10.1; Dem. 41.2) as a claim for sympathy. An important component in the establishment of goodwill is the neutralisation of any hostility against the speaker, a topic to which the theorists devoted a great deal of attention.[4] This hostility can arise from a number of sources. It may be generated by previous speakers. This is especially so in the case of a defendant in court, since the prosecutor as first speaker was in a position to create a prejudice against the defendant before the latter uttered a word (see especially Dem. 45.6). The hostility could also arise from the matter itself or the political climate. Demosthenes 57 was delivered during a court hearing by a man ejected from his deme under the general scrutiny of deme members authorised by the Demophilus decree of 346/5. It is clear from the proem that there was a general prejudice against the individuals ejected by the demes. The speaker is therefore obliged to plead at length for a fair hearing (1–6). The nature of the brief could also adversely affect audience reception. In forensic cases where the law allowed rewards for successful prosecutors it was necessary to establish at the outset that profit was not the motive (as [Dem.] 53.1 ff., 59.1 ff.), since this suspicion would inevitably arise in the jurors' minds. Equally, when bringing a serious charge in matters which did not affect the prosecutor directly, it was useful, given the instinctive public hostility towards meddlesomeness (*polypragmosyne*), to stress the public spirit (Lyc. 1.3–6) or paradoxically the private hostility which motivated the action (Lys. 14.1 ff.; Dem. 22.1 ff.; [Dem.] 58.1 ff.; Aes. 1.1–2). Prosecution of relatives inevitably excited hostility in a society which placed enormous weight on the solidarity of the family. In such cases it was important to quell the prejudice by stressing the importance of the issue or to transfer the hostility by presenting the resort to legal action as a course forced on oneself by the intransigence of the opponent (cf. Antiph. 1.1–4; Lys. 32.1; Isaeus 1.6; Dem. 39.1, 41.1–2; [Dem.] 48.1). Prejudice could also arise from the identity or circumstances of the speaker. One important factor singled out by Anaximenes is age (*Rhetorica ad Alexandrum* 1437a). Given the diffidence expected of youth, the jurors might feel that a youthful prosecutor was displaying precocious legal expertise or excessive ambition. This had to be countered by presenting recourse to law as forced upon one by the opponents or stressing the lack of supporters to undertake the burden of prosecution (Isaeus, fr. 6; [Dem.] 58.2–4).

The discussion of *eunoia* so far has concentrated on the opening, in accordance with the narrow approach of the classical handbooks (*Rhetoric* 1415a; *Rhetorica ad Alexandrum* 1436b, 1441b) and the inescapable fact that the introduction of any speech must establish a bond between speaker and audience if the rest of the speech is to do its work. However, the bid for *eunoia* is not confined to the proem. We find attempts to counter prejudice directly in the proof section, as at Demosthenes 37.52–3:

> Well now, when anyone asks him: 'And what case do you have in response to Nicobulus?' he says: 'The Athenians hate money lenders. Nicobulus is unpopular; he walks fast and has a loud voice and carries a stick. All this', he says, 'is in my favour.' And he is not ashamed to say this, nor does he think that his hearers understand that this is the reasoning of a sycophant, not a victim.

We may also compare Demosthenes 45.77 and Lysias 16.20. The positive bid for *eunoia* is equally at home in proof and in the narrative section. In both it may be achieved subtly through the personality projected by the speaker, which can be used to create or sustain the required bond of sympathy. This is dealt with in section 2 below.

Beyond the basic need for a hearing, the precise effects sought depend on the situation of the speaker. In forensic oratory this amounts in part to the role in court, prosecution or defence. Common to both is the need to arouse hostility against the opponent. However, this inevitably figures more prominently in the speech of the plaintiff, who must move the jurors first to convict and then (where appropriate) to impose the desired penalty. The appeal for anger is often (at least to the reader accustomed to modern legal hearings) surprisingly explicit, with the use of key words such as *orge* ('anger'), *misein* ('hate'), *aganaktein* ('resent'). So for instance Lycurgus 1.134: 'Yet when a man is hated and ejected even by those who have suffered no wrong, what should he suffer from you who have been treated in the most monstrous manner?' Commonly the audience is made to feel that they have been wronged personally. In the case of political trials this is easy enough, for by definition the defendant is accused of an offence against the city. But even in trials with no political dimension there is a consistent tendency to present the offence as an attack on values important to the city as a whole, and to induce the jurors to register the feelings they would have if they themselves were the victims, as at Demosthenes 54.42: 'I urge you then, jurymen . . . just as each of you would hate the perpetrator if he himself were the victim, to register anger in the same way against Conon here, and not to regard as private any such offence of this sort which might perhaps happen to another too.'

The above examples of appeal to anger come from the proof section. But the narrative may contain such appeals in the form of explicit value judgements intermingled with the statement of the 'facts' of the case in order to give the narrative a pronounced bias, as in the following extract from Aeschines (1.40):

> For this man, first of all, as soon as he was past boyhood, used to sit in the Piraeus at the medical establishment of Euthydicus, on the pretext of learning the trade but in reality because he had made a firm decision to sell himself, as the sequel showed. The names of all the merchants or other foreigners or citizens who had the use of Timarchus' body during that period I shall pass over, so that no one can accuse me of going into excessive detail about everything. But I shall confine my account to the people whose house he has lived in, disgracing his body and the city and earning money by the very means for which the law forbids a man from political action or speech.

Anger may however be aroused less overtly by the manner of the presentation of the offence. The following account of the funeral of Lysias' brother Polemarchus is a particularly fine example (12.18–19):

> And when after his death he was taken forth from the prison for burial, though we owned three houses they would not even let him be carried out from one of them, but they hired a tent and laid him out. And though we had many robes they gave none for the burial in answer to our request, but one friend gave a robe, another a pillow, others various items for his funeral. And though they had six hundred shields belonging to us, though they had so much silver and gold, and bronze and jewellery and furniture and women's clothing, more than they ever expected to acquire, and a hundred and twenty slaves, of whom they took the best and

30

gave the rest to the public exchequer, this is the extent their insatiable and petty greed reached and the demonstration they gave of their character: the gold ear-rings of Polemarchus' wife, which happened to be the ones she possessed when she first came to his house, Melobius took from her ears.

The brutality of the murderers is compounded by their pettiness in refusing even the resources for a basic funeral. Pity for the victims, hence anger against the prepetrators, is aroused by the humiliating need for a rich man's family to beg such trifling items from friends and by the contrast between the generosity of private citizens and the meanness of those in power. The climax is the petty greed of the perpetrators, effectively presented by the long list of confiscated goods, leading to the act of wrenching a pair of ear-rings from the widow's ears. Authorial judgement is explicitly present, but far more telling is the skilful use of detail. Examples from Lysias might be multiplied. But this effect is not confined to him. The following passage is taken from the prosecution of the ex-prostitute Neaira ([Dem.] 59.38):

Stephanus spoke encouragement to her in Megara and inflated her confidence, saying that Phrynion would regret it if he laid hands on her; he would keep her as his wife and introduce the children she had at that time into his phratry as his own and give them citizenship; nobody in the world would harm her.

This account is designed to raise anger at the casual abuse of the solemn right of Athenian citizenship. It achieves its effect by the vivid presentation of male bravado designed to impress a mistress.

Another common approach is to generate prejudice against the opponent by means of matters tangential or irrelevant to the issue. This practice falls under the general heading of *diabole*. This word is derived from the verb *diaballein*, which means 'to cause hostility between/against'. Aristotle (*Rhetoric* 1415a) and Anaximenes (*Rhetorica ad Alexandrum* 1436b–1437b, 1441b–1442b, 1445a) associate the creation or removal of *diabole* with conclusion and introduction, respectively. But this element is at home in any part of the speech. In narrative one can deploy tangential material to create hostility. Thus the narrative in Pseudo-Demosthenes 53.4–18, which bases the decision to prosecute in a public action on grounds of personal enmity, in passing destroys the good character of the opponent by accusing him of a range of actions of which base ingratitude to a loyal friend is the least. Such allegations are particularly effective if repeated, for the effect, even without independent support, is to create the plausibility which comes from internal consistency, as in the repeated presentation of Stephanus as a sycophant in Pseudo-Demosthenes 59 or the repeated references to drunkenness in Lysias 3.5–9 and Demosthenes 54.3–6. The range of prejudices manipulated by speakers, in both narrative and proof, is very wide. We find allegations of luxury (Dem. 21.158, 36.45; Aes. 1.42, 53, 95–100); sexual incontinence or deviation (Andoc. 1.100, 124–127; Lys. 14.25, 26; Isaeus 8.44; Dem. 36.45; Aes. 2.99); theft or violence (Isaeus 4.28, 8.41–42; Lys. 14.27; Dem. 57.65); political misconduct or (after 403) unsoundness (Lys. 18.19, 30.9–14; Isoc. 16.42–44; Dem. 21.202–204; Aes. 1.106–115); lack of patriotism, evidenced in evasion of public taxes and duties (Isaeus 5.45; Dem. 21.154 ff., 54.44; [Dem.] 42.22; Aes. 1.101); spurious citizenship or base or servile extraction (Lys. 30.2; Dem. 18.129–130, 21.149–150; [Dem.] 59.44); and of course sycophancy ([Dem.] 40.32, 58.6, 10, 11, 12, 59.41, 43, 68; Aes. 1.1). Given the general hostility to professionalism in legal contexts, expertise in the law and oratorical skill are also charges to be hurled at adversaries (Isaeus 10.1; Dem. 21.189, 57.5; Lyc. 1.31). Allegations of misconduct may concern associates and relatives (Lys. 13.67–68, 14.30, 35–40; [Dem.] 25.77). Moreover, since the litigant sought to benefit from the status of his witnesses and supporting speakers, his opponent's *diabole* might be extended to them (Lys. 30.34; Dem. 54.34 ff.; Aes. 1.131, 181).

A related emotion triggered in particular by prosecutors is fear. Litigants insist that a judgement for the opponent will open the door to unbridled wrongdoing (Dem. 19.342 ff.; [Dem.] 59.112–113; Aes. 1.192). We also find attempts to intimidate the jurors either by suggesting that the gods will take note of and action for a misjudgement, or that the jurors will disgrace or compromise themselves in the eyes of their loved ones, the city or the rest of Greece. Lycurgus (1.146) warns the jury: 'Rest assured, gentlemen, that each of you now while voting in secret will make his attitude clear to the gods';[5] the speaker of Pseudo-Demosthenes 25.98 says: 'Suppose then you leave the court, and the bystanders, both foreigners and citizens, watch you and look at each man as he passes and gauge the acquitters from their faces. What will you say, men of Athens, if you abandon the laws before you leave?'

The counterpart to the prosecutor's demand for anger is the plea for pity from the defence. Appeals for pity are not confined to the defendant. However, for the prosecutor they are largely a means to an end. Pity for the victims of the opponent's wrongdoing is stimulated in order to excite anger against the perpetrator. But it is the defendant who needs to move the jurors to gentler emotions. The crudest method, much criticised and satirised (cf. Aristoph. *Wasps* 568 ff., 976 ff.; Plato, *Apology* 34c–d), but still effective (or considered effective) enough to remain a standard procedure, was to have one's family mount the stand, weeping and wailing, in order to bring home to the jurors the damage which conviction would inflict. The same effect might be sought with words, either with reference to the speaker himself (Lys. 4.20, 24.22 ff.; Isaeus 2.44; Dem. 57.70), or with reference to defenceless or infirm relatives entirely dependent on him (Lys. 7.41; [Dem.] 40.56).

An overlapping appeal is that for gratitude. The importance of gratitude was universally acknowledged, and it is common for litigants to remind the jury of benefactions bestowed on the city by self or family, including ancestors, in order to stake a claim, often explicit, to their gratitude (Lys. 3.47, 18.27, 20.30; Isaeus 4.27, 7.37–41; [Dem.] 50.64). And just as the litigant hopes to gain from the stature of his supporting speakers, so he hopes that some measure of the gratitude due for their benefactions will accrue to himself.

The discussion so far has largely concentrated on the lawcourts. But *pathos* as a means of persuasion is not confined to forensic oratory. It is also at home in deliberative oratory. It is important for the modern reader to bear in mind that the neat divisions in classical rhetoric are the product of schematisation by theorists rather than oratorical practice. In addition to the inevitable overlaps between political and forensic oratory in a political system which relied on the lawcourts, there were in classical Athens significant similarities between the political and forensic processes. From the speeches in Thucydides it is clear that already in the fifth century political oratory concerned itself with many of the topics found in judicial oratory, expediency, justice, honour.[6] The mode of argument is the same. And the need to direct the emotional response of the jurors is the same. For the politician proposing alliance or intervention, attack or retaliation, is in part an advocate for or against friend or foe. He is moreover in direct competition for the hearers' favour no less than the litigant. The political process was highly competitive, and the speaker supporting any policy is almost by definition impinging on the interests of a political faction.

The similarity between forensic and political oratory becomes explicit on occasion, most notably in the speech which Thucydides attributes to Cleon in the debate on the fate of Mytilene in 427. Cleon seeks to excite hostility against the opposing speakers by alleging that they have been bribed, an example of *diabole*, as his opponent Diodotus notes (Thuc. 3.42; cf. 3.38, 3.40.1). Diodotus also complains that Cleon treats the debate as a trial of the Mytilenaeans, and Cleon makes explicit his desire to stimulate the Athenians to anger (Thuc. 3.44, 3.38.1, 3.40.7). This procedure is not peculiar to Cleon or the Athenians. The Corinthians at Sparta before the Peloponnesian War, when arguing for war against Athens, in effect appear as speakers for the prosecution, as the Athenian ambassadors note (Thuc. 1.68–71, 1.73). They accuse the Athenians of wrongdoing and explicitly appeal for Spartan anger. Demosthenes' anti-Macedonian policy inevitably involves an attempt to stimulate hostility against Philip (Dem. 2.6-10, 4.9–11, 37, 42, 6.6–20). Nor is Cleon unusual in attacking his political opponents as part of the deliberative process. Demosthenes' assault on the dominant faction in the *Third Olynthiac* is even more virulent (21–32).[7]

Another emotion equally at home in political contexts is fear. The Corinthian criticism of Athens at Sparta is designed to appeal to existing Spartan fear of Athenian expansion, just as Demosthenes seeks to arouse Athenian fear of Macedonian expansion. The reverse of this effect is confidence, noted by Aristotle (*Rhetoric* 1378a) as an important factor in deliberations about the future. The clearest examples are the speech of the Corinthians before the outbreak of the Peloponnesian War in the first book of Thucydides, which is full of quite wild speculation about the prospects for success (1.121–122), and the speech of Alcibiades in support of the Sicilian expedition in the sixth book, which is equally unrealistic (17.2–18.2).[8]

2

For Aristotle the use of *ethos*, moral character, as a means of persuasion consists in creating through the speech a character

(*Rhetoric* 1377b) which will induce the required degree of trust on the part of the hearer. As with *pathos*, practical usage predates theory. Nestor's appeals to his age and experience in the *Iliad* (as at 1.260 ff.) constitute a claim to personal authority in military debate, just as Pindar's references to his poetic authority or relation to his patron (*Olympian* 1.111 ff., *Nemean* 7.61 ff.) constitute a claim to authority for his praise. In practice, *ethos* and *pathos* are closely connected, for one effect of *ethos*, as well as inducing a degree of trust, is also to produce a feeling of goodwill in the audience towards the speaker, so that the projection of the appropriate character achieves more subtly the effect sought by explicit appeals for a favourable hearing.[9] Reference to civic virtue, which establishes overall good character, also involves an implicit appeal for gratitude. Moreover, one effect of *diabole* is to undermine the credibility of the opponent as well as inducing hostility, by suggesting that his way of life is such as to render statements from him unreliable.

Aristotle regards *ethos* as more at home in deliberative oratory and *pathos* in forensic (*Rhetoric* 1377b), according to a tendency towards schematisation typical of the treatise and the writer. This view is reflected in the list of desired characteristics singled out by Aristotle as the province of *ethos*: wisdom, virtue and goodwill towards the audience. Certainly Aristotle is right to stress the significance of *ethos* in deliberative oratory. The need to project a trustworthy character was especially important in the Athenian context of individual competition for influence. And the characteristics singled out can certainly be exemplified in surviving speeches. Virtue, for instance, is exemplified in the claim to honesty of Pericles in Thucydides 2.60 and Demosthenes at 5.12, goodwill towards the audience in the readiness to take the risk of telling the unpalatable truth at Demosthenes 3.21, 32 (cf. 4.51), or the high-minded devotion to the city's good at 8.1, 21–23, 24 (cf. 16.1). Wisdom appears in various guises, as the bluff, straight-talking simplicity of Cleon in the Mytilenaean debate or of Demosthenes at 5.11, for instance, or the cool-headed calculation of Cleon's opponent Diodotus. Aristotle's list is incomplete however even for deliberative oratory, since other effects may be sought, as when the young Demosthenes diffidently apologises for speaking first in a debate at 4.1, or when the same author modestly attributes part of his success in public deliberation to good fortune at 5.11.

Furthermore, *ethos* was equally important in the lawcourts. In addition to the basic need to project a personality which invited belief, the Athenian tendency to view the trial as a detail in a broader canvas rather than an occurrence isolated from the rest of the life of litigants and city made appeal to activity beyond the courts inevitable. In such a context, the general conduct of an individual offers a useful means of determining the balance of probability in the individual instance. This implicit view was reinforced during the classical period by the increased reliance on argument from probability. *Ethos* may thus overlap implicitly with explicit argument. The simplest way to project the appropriate persona was to list explicitly the services one had bestowed on the city. The kind of services mentioned naturally depend on the status of the speaker. Unfailing performance of military service, scrupulous, generous or enthusiastic payment of property taxes (*eisphorai*) or performance of public duties (*leitourgiai*), loyalty to the democracy during the period of the Thirty, tend to figure (cf. Lys. 13.77, 24.25; Isaeus 7.38–42; [Dem.] 34.38–39; Dem. 54.44).

Less blatant is the use of value judgements and general observations. By laying claim to certain beliefs which agree with accepted social values a speaker can with contrived inadvertence reveal something of his character. A wide range of effects may be sought. Patriotism and public-spiritedness are evident in the following remark from the first defence speech of Antiphon's *Second Tetralogy*: 'I thought in training my son in skills which especially benefit society that some good would emerge for both of us; the result has been the reverse of my expectations' (3). The javelin throw which killed a fellow athlete is placed in the context of training for war, and both the boy who threw the javelin and his father are presented as contributing to the well-being of the state. Respect for the laws is exemplified in the opening words of Demosthenes 47: 'I think the laws are quite right, jurymen' (cf. Antiph. 1.1, 5.75). The point the speaker goes on to make is quite specific to prosecutions for false witness. But the opening strikes exactly the right general note. Nobody ever alienated a Greek jury by praising the laws. Respect for parents is evidenced in the following passage ([Dem.] 40.12):

> [My father] urged me as soon as I reached eighteen to marry the daughter of Euphemus, because he wished to live to see children born from me. I for my part obeyed, jurymen, because I thought it my duty, both beforehand and when

these men were causing him pain by suing him and making trouble, to do the opposite and give pleasure by doing everything which might gratify him.

Openness, manifested explicitly in a readiness to reveal things which one might be expected to conceal, or a promise to tell the whole story from the beginning, helps to establish trust (Lys. 1.5, 3.10; Dem. 39.1, 45.2). Simplicity, manifested in inexperience of public speaking and ignorance of the lawcourts (Antiph. 1.1, 5.1; Lys. 1.5, 12.4; Isaeus 8.5; Dem. 27.2), offers the promise of unadorned fact. A display of piety, expressed either (where the magnitude of the issue and the stature of the participants warrant, as at Dem. 18.1; Lyc. 1.1) in prayers or in judgements on the alleged piety or impiety of others (Dem. 54.39–40; [Dem.] 59.72–78, 109, 116–117, 126), appeals to a very basic value. Particularly important in lawsuits is the quality of restraint. The speaker should in general avoid appearing weak. But in the context of a society which believed that the courts should be a last rather than a first resort, a readiness to tolerate a degree of discomfort or disadvantage rather than sue both establishes a commendable disposition and emphasises the magnitude of the injuries suffered, so that again *ethos* overlaps with argument. An explicit example is Pseudo-Demosthenes 56.14: 'We agreed to this proposal, not because we were ignorant, jurymen, of our rights under the contract, but because we thought we should tolerate some degree of disadvantage and reach agreement and not give the appearance of fondness for litigation.' Such restraint is especially commendable in the context of a family quarrel, as at Demosthenes 39.36: 'Why are you so quarrelsome? Don't be. And don't be so hostile towards us. I'm not hostile towards you; for even now, just to make this clear to you, I'm speaking more for your good in insisting that we should not have the same name.' Wisdom (or at least a capacity for reflection), given prominence by Aristotle, can be conveyed by the use of generalisation (as at Dem. 57.27), though in general sententiousness is more at home in trials with a pronounced political flavour, or involving public figures. In such cases the scope for self-importance allows for appeal to the model of the jurors' ancestors or other political systems and for quotations from the poets,[10] all of which, apart from any overt message or emotional appeal, help to convey an impression of sagacity and moral weight. The elevated moral sentiments also help to create a bond of sympathy between the speaker and his audience.

For the projection of *ethos* what is unsaid may be as important as what is said. The 'rules' (in the limited sense of tacitly accepted norms) of decorum in an Athenian court were essentially the same as for everyday life. Though potentially a limiting factor where unsavoury matters must be discussed, in practice this etiquette allowed a speaker credit for good moral character by refusing, implicitly or explicitly, to call a spade a spade. The most sustained example is the prosecution of Timarchus by Aeschines, the basis of which is an allegation that Timarchus has forfeited the right to participate in politics by prostituting himself. At no point does Aeschines make explicit what exactly Timarchus has done. He makes clear that Timarchus has allowed himself to be used sexually for money, but he is content to refer in roundabout ways to the activity involved. The result is a sustained presentation of the speaker as a man who will not stoop to describe vile behaviour, and the effect is to create a rapport between speaker and audience and commensurate gulf between audience and opponent, an individual who stoops to do what decent men will not even say. The same sustained effect is created throughout Pseudo-Demosthenes 59. Much of the character assassination of the defendant Neaera relies on the undisputed fact that she was in her earlier days a prostitute. The speaker Apollodorus refers repeatedly to her sexual career, but always by means of periphrases. The silence may become explicit, as at Demosthenes 21.79 (cf. 54.9, 17; Aes. 1.55): 'And then in front of my sister, who was in the house then and still a girl, they said disgraceful things, the sort of things their sort would say (I could not be induced to repeat to you any of the things said then), and to my mother and me and all of us they uttered insults speakable and unspeakable.'

In the passages considered so far the presentation of *ethos* is explicit or nearly so. However, all the effects listed above can be achieved more subtly, as in the case of *pathos*, by the adroit presentation of the 'facts' of the case. Here at least Aristotle shows an awareness, largely missing in his own treatise and (to judge by the bland generalisations about narrative quality which he attributes to his predecessor at *Rhetoric* 1416b) largely lacking from contemporary and earlier rhetorical theory in general, of the potential of narrative as proof. He notes (*Rhetoric* 1416a) in his brief discussion of narrative: 'You may slip into your narrative such things as relate to your virtue, such as: "I was constantly advising him, telling him what was right, not to abandon his children", or your opponent's villainy: "He answered me that wherever he himself was he would get other children".' The advantages of this technique are that the exposition of character appears uncontrived and that the hearer draws the character by inference for himself. The resultant persona is therefore more plausible. The account of the dealings of Apollodorus with Nicostratus ([Dem.] 53.5 ff.), as well as revealing the latter's ingratitude, also testifies to the generosity of Apollodorus and his adherence to the time-honoured ethic of supporting friends in need. The following passage ([Dem.] 47.38) for all its brevity is no less revealing: 'I went into the house to make seizure of furniture; the door happened to be open when Theophemus came and he had still not gone in; and I had ascertained that he was not married.' The last clause hints delicately at the complex of ideas regarding women in Greek society. It presents the speaker as a man who avoids any risk of disturbing the seclusion of decent women unrelated to him. He thus reveals himself as a man of decency and restraint even in the heat of a dispute.

There is another aspect to the use of character as a means of persuasion; that is dramatic characterisation. In any legal hearing the listener will be on the alert for signs of dissimulation. In the Athenian context the tradition that the litigant represent himself, together with the scope for the use of bought material or expertise (from commonplaces to whole speeches), made the 'fit' between speech and speaker a factor of some importance, at least to the extent that any obvious dissonance would jar. Here again, as so often, there is an overlap between *ethos* and *pathos*, since the general disapproval of professionalism in the lawcourts would render the jurors sympathetic to a speaker who could present himself convincingly as an untutored novice attempting to present the unadorned truth in his own words.

It would appear that the potential of character in this theatrical sense was grasped only imperfectly by theoreticians. Aristotle touches briefly on this aspect of character in his discussion of 'appropriateness'/ 'propriety' of style (*to prepon*)[11] at *Rhetoric* 1408a, where he says that the use of language appropriate to such external characteristics as age, sex, nationality, and to the way of life of the individual imparts *ethos*. Here and at *Rhetoric* 1417a, where he advocates the inclusion in the narrative of details appropriate to 'each *ethos*' in order to make the narrative *ethikos*, he has in mind not just moral character but also plausibility. What Aristotle has in mind is expressed more lucidly in chapter 15 of *Poetics*: 'Secondly, characters must be fitting; for it is possible for a woman to be manly in character, but it is not fitting for her to be so manly or clever [sc. as a man].' The same section of *Poetics* includes another specification which is relevant to the courts, the requirement that character should be consistent (*homalos*). The absence of any hint of this quality in *Rhetoric* suggests that Aristotle has not thought through the implications for rhetorical theory of the notion of character as dramatic construct. And even in the discussion of propriety he does not go beyond the inclusion of detail.

Practitioners too were slow to grasp the potential of dramatic characterisation. The verbal pyrotechnics of Gorgias and the ornate manner of Protagoras and Prodicus as presented by Plato and Xenophon (Plato, *Protagoras* 320d–322d; Xenophon, *Memorabilia* 2.2.34) would lend themselves badly to dramatic characterisation since the style, while suitable perhaps to a political figure who has less need to conceal his training, could not plausibly be used by an ordinary man. The earliest of the logographers, Antiphon, though aware of the importance of moral character, appears to have had no conception of the potential of *ethos* in the dramatic sense. The speakers in his *Tetralogies* all have a uniformity of manner which betrays the author's hand no less than that of the speakers in Thucydides. The same is true of the speeches written for real court cases. The speaker of Antiphon 5, Euxitheus, as a young man complains of the inadequacy of his speaking skills to present his case convincingly, but does so in a style heavily influenced by the Gorgianic love of balance and assonance (5.1). His successors however show an awareness that the manner of utterance should reflect the status and circumstances of the speaker. When writing for private individuals they generally avoid a style whose sophistication would jar with the client's claim to be an ordinary man. Speakers other than major political figures also avoid grandiose effects such as appeal to poets. And as a rule they do not lay claim to a greater degree of knowledge than that of the audience.

Only one writer, however, fully appreciated the potential of dramatic characterisation, the speechwriter Lysias, who in several surviving speeches creates a vivid and consistent portrayal of the speaker. This does not amount to a detailed character portrayal.

Too much detail would obtrude, and might actually impede the purpose of the speech by diverting attention from the 'facts' and the speaker's arguments. Lysias simply selects one or two distinctive characteristics and by presenting these consistently creates the illusion of depth of characterisation.

The first speech in the corpus, *On the Killing of Eratosthenes*, composed for a man accused of homicide, whose defence is that the killing was lawful since he caught Eratosthenes in adultery with his wife, presents us with a simple individual. The circumstantial narrative shows us a man who foolishly trusted his adulterous wife until his eyes were opened. It also tells of the hasty attempt on the night of the killing to put together a posse since the speaker was unprepared for what happened. One effect is to induce a feeling of sympathy for the speaker as a decent man whose trust has been abused. Another is to strengthen his 'factual' case. Since, as we subsequently learn, the relatives of the dead man are alleging that he was the victim of a plot, the characterisation is central to the defence case, for the personality which emerges from the narrative is too simple to be capable of the cunning attributed to him.

In the third speech, *Against Simon*, a defence against a charge of intentional wounding, we are presented at the outset with a retiring figure, a man of mature years acutely embarrassed to find himself in court because the case arose from a dispute between two rivals for the sexual favours of a young man. The detailed narrative then presents us with two contrasting portraits, the shameless and violent Simon who does not scruple to harass and assault the speaker and the boy, and the speaker, who repeatedly strives to avoid any trouble. The speaker's retiring disposition is germane to the charge against him, since the effect of the characterisation is to suggest an individual who is incapable of behaving in the ostentatiously aggressive manner alleged.

Speech 16, written for a man who has been opposed at his scrutiny as member of the Boule on the grounds that he served in the cavalry under the Thirty, opens with an expression of confidence in his ability to satisfy even his enemies of his worth. After briefly answering the charge against him he proceeds to give an account of his way of life, which in both public and private spheres shows the same generosity towards others and attests his readiness to face danger on behalf of the city. Implicit in the claims of energy, courage and generosity is a suggestion that the city will be deprived of important qualities if he is not allowed to serve it.

Implicit in the frank self-praise is a suggestion of candour, which further implies an inability to deceive by concealing the past.

Lysias 7 presents us with an individual whose explicit claim to cleverness is supported by the thorough and astute array of arguments to demonstrate his innocence. He is charged with the removal of a sacred olive stump from his property, an act which he presents as reckless folly. The calculating personality projected by the speech appears incapable of such recklessness. Finally, in Lysias 24, composed for a cripple faced with the termination of his disability pension, we are presented with a cheeky, irreverent character who alternates between humour and pathos. The effect aimed for is in part the impression of a 'rough diamond' speaking in his own words, in part an obfuscation of the factual case by emotional appeal and humour.[12]

As this survey indicates, Lysias uses dramatic characterisation to secure two effects. The first, tactical, effect is a plausible 'fit' between the alleged or discernible circumstances of the speaker and what he says so that the intervention of the professional speechwriter is concealed. The second effect is strategic. The characterisation in all but one of the above cases is intended to confirm the speaker's version of his case by presenting an implied argument from probability; the implication, sometimes reinforced elsewhere in the speech by explicit argument, is that the character before the jury is incapable of behaving in the manner alleged. In the case of Lysias 24, the character still contributes to the refutation of the opponent's case, but only in a more general way by allowing the speaker to present his evasion of the allegations against him as the normal behaviour of a naturally humorous disposition. Thus again the classical distinction between the different sections of the speech, while it is of value as a formal description, is inadequate as a description of purpose, for the narrative is capable of sustaining the burden of proof, and the method used, argument from the general (the evidence of character implicitly presented to the court) to the particular (the specific allegations) on the basis of probability, is the staple of argumentation from the birth of Greek rhetoric.

The only other Greek writer of the period to achieve comparable vividness of characterisation is Demosthenes in the speech *Against Conon* (54), a speech which bears so strong a resemblance to Lysias 3 that one is inclined to suspect direct influence. In both speeches we have the same structural feature of the preliminary narrative (Lys. 3.5–10; Dem. 54.3–6), and in both one effect of the narrative is to present the speaker as a model of restraint. Since the opponent Conon intends to argue that what Ariston presents as a gratuitous assault was no more than a battle between rival gangs, and since he may well be arguing that Ariston was the instigator, it is as useful for Demosthenes as it is for Lysias to present his client as a model of *apragmosyne*.

There is a complementary aspect to dramatic characterisation: that is, the presentation of the opponent. In the passage from *Rhetoric* 1416a cited above, Aristotle shows an awareness that use of narrative details to suggest the character of the opponent can be rhetorically effective, though it is not clear whether he would class this with *ethos* or *pathos*. Something has already been said on this subject under the heading of *diabole* (see Section 1). In its more developed forms however this technique belongs as much with *ethos*, in that the presentation of character is being used not merely to secure an emotional effect but to create a consistent picture of the opponent which increases the plausibility of the allegations against him. The shameless and relentless Simon of Lysias 3, the greedy and petty Diogeiton of Lysas 32, Stephanus in Pseudo-Demosthenes 59, who sells his services for unscrupulous gain and engages in blackmail and false accusations, the arch-betrayer Alcibiades in Lysias 14, the violent and drunken Conon and his family in Demosthenes 54,[13] are all presented with a consistency and vividness which through intrinsic plausibility invite belief, irrespective of the degree of supporting evidence.

3

A persistent theme in this discussion has been the flexibility of oratorical practice of the classical period in comparison with rhetorical theory. Like other fourth-century writers Aristotle subdivides the speech and recognises appropriate points in the speech for specific effects. Actual orators and logographers are less tidy; they tend to blur distinctions between these subdivisions, as far as deployment of *ethos* and *pathos* are concerned. In particular, the narrative, especially but by no means exclusively in Lysias, proves to be far more flexible than classical rhetoricians supposed. From what we can gather, instructions for narrative tended to be simplistic and uniform; Aristotle at least shows an awareness that narrative can be varied, and that it can achieve more than one effect.

Aristotle's threefold division of *pisteis* proved very influential with his successors, and deservedly so. There are however pronounced overlaps in effect between *ethos* and *pathos*, just as there are overlaps in effect between different parts of the speech. And in the hands of a master, *ethos*, in the sense of dramatic characterisation, may fulfil the role of argument. Like all schemata, it is useful as a rough guide only.

NOTES

1 Cf. Solon, fr. 4W (fear), Alcaeus, fr. 129V (anger), 130 (pity), 74 (fear).
2 Writers of the Roman period tend to confine *pathos* and equivalent terms to more powerful emotional effects. The goodwill of the audience on the other hand is treated under *ethos* ('character'). Cf. for example Cicero, *De Oratore* 2.27.225, and see in general R. Volkmann, *Die Rhetorik der Griechen und Römer in systematischer Übersicht*[2] (repr. Hildesheim: 1963), pp. 272 ff. However Aristotle in his definition of *pathos* in oratory speaks in very general terms of creating a 'disposition' (the verbs *diatithenai*, *diakeisthai*) and of emotions as 'all those factors through which people undergo a change of attitude towards their decisions' (*Rhetoric* 1378a), and he locates *eunoia* with *philia* among the emotions (*Rhetoric* 1378a). This broader approach corresponds better with observable practice in the orators; since *eunoia* can be invited with reference to the situation as well as the personality projected by the speaker, it does not belong exclusively in the sphere of *ethos*.
3 For the overlap between *pathos* and *ethos* see below, section 2.
4 Cf. Thrasymachus, *apud* Plato, *Phaedrus* 267d, Arist. *Rhetoric* 1354a on his predecessors, and his own precepts *Rhetoric* 1415a, 1416a–b, Anaximenes, *Rhetorica ad Alexandrum* 1436b–1437b and 1442a–b.
5 Cf. Lys. 12.100 (the dead), [Dem.] 59.109 and 126.
6 Cf. Kennedy, *Art of Persuasion*, p. 204.
7 Cf. also Thuc. 2.63.2–3, 6.12.2 and Lys. 34.1–2.
8 Cf. Pericles at Thuc. 1.141.2–143.5, 2.62.1–2. Thucydides praises Pericles' ability to stimulate fear and confidence in the Assembly as necessary: 2.65.9.
9 For *ethos* as a means of creating *eunoia* see, n. 2. For the overlap between *ethos* and *pathos* cf. D. A. Russell, 'Ethos in Oratory and Rhetoric', in C. Pelling (ed.), *Characterization and Individuality in Greek Literature* (Oxford: 1990), p. 212.
10 Dem. 18.289, 19.247, 255, 21.143–150; Aes. 1.128–129, 143–152, 180–181, 182; Lyc. 1.98–100, 102–110, 111–123 and 128–129.
11 Dion. Hal. *Lysias* 9 likewise sees *to prepon* solely in terms of style.
12 For detailed discussion of the presentation of character in these speeches see S. Usher, 'Individual Characterization in Lysias', *Eranos* 63 (1965), pp. 99–119; C. Carey, 'Structure and Strategy in Lysias XXIV', *G&R*[2] 37 (1990), pp. 44–51, and *Lysias: Selected Speeches* (Cambridge: 1989), pp. 10, 61–2, 89–90 and 116–17.

13 See Carey, *Lysias*, pp. 207 and 210 ff., C. Carey and R. A. Reid, *Demosthenes: Selected Private Speeches* (Cambridge: 1985), pp. 78 and 82; and C. Carey, *Apollodoros Against Neaira: [Demosthenes] 59* (Warminster: 1992), p. 90.

3

Probability and persuasion: Plato and early Greek rhetoric

Michael Gagarin

It is no secret that our view of early (that is, before the influence of Plato, during the period *c.* 450–390) Greek rhetoric has been strongly influenced by the hostile attacks levelled at it and at the sophists in general by the philosopher Plato, but recognition of this fact has not eliminated the influence and Plato's criticisms continue to shape our understanding of the formative period of Greek rhetoric in ways that are not fully appreciated. My intention in this chapter is to consider the force of Plato's criticisms, to examine closely one issue on which modern scholars still follow Plato's lead, even though he is demonstrably wrong, and then to suggest some features found in the rhetorical and sophistic works themselves that should form the starting point for a more accurate picture.

According to the current view,[1] rhetoric originated in Sicily with the handbooks of Corax and Tisias as a response to the large number of legal suits which arose after the overthrow of the Syracusan tyrants in 467. The study of rhetoric then became a primary interest of the sophists, who advertised their skills to young men desirous of getting ahead in the world of the democratic polis, especially at Athens. Success in these circumstances depended on one's ability to persuade large audiences in the Assembly or the courts, the latter of which became more important after the judicial reforms of Ephialtes in 462. The main vehicle for persuasion was rhetoric, a *techne* whose subject-matter covered the wide range of activity of the Greek word *logos*, which could mean 'word', 'speech', 'argument', 'reasoning', and more, and which included everything from small grammatical details, such as Protagoras' criticism of Homer for phrasing the first verse of the *Iliad* as a command rather than a request (Arist. *Poetics*

1456b15), to large matters of composition, structure and argumentation. For the sophists and their pupils, rhetoric was a means to worldly success in the contests (*agones*) of life, and any interest a sophist might show in such matters as truth, justice, or virtue was motivated by the primary goal of his rhetoric, namely persuasion.

Fifth-century evidence confirming this picture of rhetoric can, it seems, be found in Aristophanes. In the *Clouds* Strepsiades is driven by mounting debt to study with Socrates, who is pictured as a representative sophist, so that he can learn how to escape from his creditors, whose cases against him are otherwise valid. Strepsiades' only reason for wanting to learn the tricks of the sophists is to cheat others. In the *Wasps* Aristophanes reinforces this view of sophistic rhetoric by painting a picture of the typical Athenian juror as blinded by prejudice and utterly unconcerned with the truth of a litigant's case. This ignorant juror is the perfect foil for the sophists' tricks of persuasion. Despite the obvious danger of reading comic parody as social history, because Aristophanes' evidence seems to confirm the picture of early Greek rhetoric at which Plato directs his criticism, many scholars have accepted it more or less uncritically. We should note, however, that some of the humour of the *Clouds* comes from Socrates' continual insistence that Strepsiades study subjects he does not want to learn, such as geometry, and that the ambivalence of the long *agon* between the stronger and weaker *logoi* leaves one in doubt about the rhetorical or 'moral' winner. Moreover, although the striking caricature of Philocleon remains in our imagination as typifying the Athenian juror, the accuracy of the portrayal can surely be doubted. There probably were jurors like Philocleon voting on actual cases, but that these constituted the majority or even a large minority of jurors is doubtful. If they had, the Athenian legal system could hardly have survived long.

Aristophanes' comic caricature of rhetoric as a vehicle for persuasive falsehood that will sway a largely ignorant audience is the product of a fundamentally conservative critical position.[2] The same basic attitude underlies the sustained philosophical attack on rhetoric in the *Gorgias*. Here Plato's opposition to rhetoric is set forth with such clarity and force that this remains the best place to begin for anyone seeking to understand the issues.[3] Socrates' discussion with Gorgias and Polus proceeds step by step: rhetoric is a *techne* (449a), whose special quality is the ability to persuade others (452e) about matters of justice and injustice

(454b). It brings conviction, however, without knowledge (455a), since it addresses an audience that has no knowledge and is only effective on such an audience (459a–b). The *rhetor* thus has the ability to persuade but has no knowledge of justice and injustice (459d–e).[4] Socrates then defines rhetoric not as a *techne* but as a 'knack' (*empeiria*), which together with cooking, sophistry and cosmetics make up the category of flattery (463a–b). As such, rhetoric is concerned with appearances, not knowledge, and can give no rational account (*logos*); it is as far from real justice as cooking is from medicine (465a–b). True justice would require that someone who has done wrong confess and demand the proper punishment (even death!) rather than seek to persuade jurors of his innocence (480b–d).

At the heart of this account is the distinction between the form of a *logos* and its content: a *rhetor* takes a certain content (usually a case that is not true) and applies his empirical 'knack' to giving this content a form that will make this false case persuasive for jurors who are necessarily ignorant of the truth. The truth or falsity of the content is not the *rhetor*'s concern, only the persuasiveness of the form his *logos* takes. Neither rhetoric nor the *rhetor* places any value on the truth *per se* and Gorgias cannot be concerned with justice or (by extension) *arete*.

Plato's hostility towards rhetoric, which is also evident in the *Phaedrus*, is clearly part of the general hostility towards sophists and poets expressed throughout his works. Thomas Cole has recently argued that there was an even wider gap than is usually thought between Plato's view of 'rhetoric' and the actual achievement of the fifth-century thinkers he attacks.[5] Cole notes that the earliest occurrence of the word *rhetorike* (sc. *techne*) is probably in Plato's *Gorgias*,[6] and concludes that Plato may have invented the term himself, perhaps for the precise purpose of stigmatising the work of his sophistic predecessors and contemporaries. According to Cole's view, fifth-century sophists and other intellectuals[7] (such as Thucydides) composed *logoi* for the purpose of practice and demonstration; these *logoi*, which were often presented in opposed pairs, illustrated arguments on issues of contemporary concern, but these thinkers did not engage in the intellectual analysis of oratory implied by the term 'rhetoric'. They were doing something quite different.

There is much in Cole's challenge to the traditional view with which I would agree, but I will suggest that with or without the term *rhetorike techne*, intellectuals before Plato were probably writing about oratory in ways that resembled later rhetoric, and they were undoubtedly talking about theories and techniques of oratory among themselves and with their pupils. Plato's misunderstanding (or worse, conscious distortion) lies not so much in the fact of fifth-century rhetoric but in its purpose and accomplishment. Perhaps the best illustration of the gap between the fifth-century evidence for rhetoric and its later critics is furnished by what was called the argument from *eikos*, 'probability' or 'likelihood'. Since we are frequently told that the first Greek rhetorical theorists, Corax and Tisias, made important advances with regard to probability arguments, and this type of argument was clearly an important concern of many early orators, it is worth examining it at some length.[8]

Modern scholars are essentially in agreement about the status of probability arguments in early Greek rhetoric. W. K. C. Guthrie in *The Sophists* (Cambridge: 1971), considers the theoretical perspective: 'The essential theoretical basis of rhetoric was that which distinguished it from the beginning . . . namely that "they held the probable (or likely-seeming, plausible, *eikota*) in more honour than the true" ' (p. 180). Kennedy's assessment in *Art of Persuasion* focuses on more practical concerns: 'In practice probability appeared safer than witnesses who were only too easily corrupted, for probabilities could not be bought' (p. 32). Even Brian Vickers accepts this conclusion, although a major purpose of his *In Defence of Rhetoric* (Oxford: 1988) is to attack Plato's view of rhetoric. As he puts it, 'probability . . . in Graeco-Roman law – strange though it may seem to modern ears – . . . was deemed more credible than the "truth" of witnesses or evidence' (pp. 69–70). One might think the very strangeness of these views, which Vickers notes, would lead these scholars to question them, but apparently the grip of tradition has too powerful a hold, even on critics hostile to Plato.

All these assessments ultimately go back to Plato. Guthrie, who is largely echoed by Vickers, is quoting from *Phaedrus* 267a, where Plato ridicules the work of earlier and contemporary rhetoricians: 'We will let Tisias and Gorgias rest in peace, who saw that probabilities should be more honoured than truths, and who make small things appear great and great things small by the power of speech.' Plato provides no evidence to support his statement about the value of probability; none the less, critics ever since have largely accepted his views. Kennedy is paraphrasing Aristotle,

Rhetoric 1376a17–23: 'As for witnesses, someone who has no witnesses can affirm that one must decide from probabilities . . . and that probabilities cannot be bribed or convicted of bearing false witness; but someone who has witnesses when his opponent does not can say that probability arguments have no liability[9] and there would be no need for evidence if a case could be settled by arguments alone.' Aristotle's advice is twofold: when the direct evidence of witnesses is against your case, you should promote probability ahead of witnesses; but when you have witnesses on your side, then you should promote direct evidence. Kennedy takes only the first part of this advice and promotes it to a single unconditional view; by such a method he could just as easily have concluded that the Greeks thought witnesses safer than probabilities because witnesses were answerable for their testimony. That he chooses to cite only the part of Aristotle's advice that casts rhetoric in a negative light is the result of Plato's influence: scholars are so conditioned by Plato's basic assumptions that they only respond to the negative side of what is in fact a more balanced view of rhetoric. Apparently none of these scholars has sought to test Plato's claim against the actual probability arguments in early rhetoric. Such a test will show that – strange as it may seem to some – the Greeks were not so strange after all: they did not, in fact, deem probability more credible than truth; Plato's claim is simply wrong.

The earliest discussion of the use of probability arguments in rhetoric was apparently that of Corax and Tisias, around the middle of the fifth century. Although nothing survives of their writing, both Plato and Aristotle cite them on the subject of probability. In *Phaedrus* 272d–273c Plato elaborates the difference between rhetoric and dialectic in much the same terms he used in the *Gorgias* and criticises the orators for not caring at all about truth. He supports this assessment by citing Tisias' example of a fight between a strong coward and a weak brave man. According to Plato, Tisias maintained that both men should conceal the truth about their behaviour, replacing it with assertions that seem plausible (*pithanon*) but are in fact false: the strong man should argue that the weak man attacked him with the help of others (since he would not likely do so alone) and the weak man in turn should argue that it is highly unlikely that he would attack such a strong man. Each man, on this account, is concealing a crucial fact: the strong man conceals his cowardice, the weak man his bravery.

If this is all that Tisias' teaching about probability amounted to, it would not have won recognition for originality, since probability arguments had long been known and used. The earliest explicit example[10] is in the Homeric *Hymn to Hermes*,[11] where in a quasi-legal setting[12] Hermes argues that he, a mere babe, is not like a cattle thief (265: οὐδέ . . . ἔοικα) and thus did not steal Apollo's cattle. The earliest explicit probability argument in tragedy is probably Pasiphaë's speech in Euripides' lost play, the *Cretans*, usually dated to the 430s;[13] and Herodotus too is fond of *eikos*-arguments (for example, 3.38.2).

A close study of these and other early uses of probability argument would show that the cases they support range from clearly false (that the day-old Hermes could not have stolen Apollo's cattle) to probably true (that Cambyses was mad) to cases which are not questions of fact but of interpretation (that Pasiphaë is not to blame for her lust). For us the important point is that Tisias and Corax did not invent the form of argument from probability. They did, however, develop a new form of this argument – what I shall call the 'reverse probability' argument. The classic example of this is attributed by Aristotle to Corax (*Rhetoric* 1402a17–28): in a fight between a weak man and a strong man, the weak man gives the traditional probability argument: it is not likely that he, a weak man, assaulted a strong man. The other counters with a reverse probability: he is not likely to have assaulted a weak man, since he, a strong man, would immediately be suspected of the crime. It should be noted that neither of the parties in this case conceals a truth about himself, as in Plato's example. This may be why Plato does not cite the same details as Aristotle; it is quite possible that he is referring to the same written example of Corax or Tisias but is adjusting the details to better support his point.

The reverse probability argument is a typical product of the intellectual experimentation characteristic of the sophistic 'enlightenment' in the second half of the fifth century.[14] It was a clever, turning-the-tables type of argument that would certainly make an impact on an audience gathered for a debate. This sort of argument also fostered the sense that if one was clever enough, one could find arguments to support any position. The sophists did indeed practise such cleverness, and not always with any serious purpose. But many of their 'experiments', even those that may seem at first glance to be nothing but clever showmanship, have, or may have had, a serious intellectual purpose. For example, Protagoras' clever analysis of the apparent contradiction in Simonides' poem (Plato, *Protagoras* 339a–d) is dazzling and effective in the contest with Socrates, but also raises serious questions about the nature of virtue. Similarly, the reverse probability argument can form an important part of an examination of the validity of probability arguments relative to arguments based on direct evidence, since a demonstration that probability can be used on either side of a case can form the basis for a rejection of probability in favour of direct evidence. This may be the conclusion we are meant to draw from Antiphon's *First Tetralogy* (2.2.6), where we find the only other fifth-century example of the reverse probability argument. This work shows quite clearly, in my view, that the fifth-century intellectuals recognised the limited value of probability arguments and did not ascribe to them the power Plato alleges.

The *Tetralogies* present fictitious cases, constructed by Antiphon in such a way as to demonstrate or rehearse arguments he was interested in exploring.[15] The *First Tetralogy* concerns a straightforward factual dispute: did the accused kill the victim or did someone else? Antiphon constructs the case in such a way that the direct evidence, which consists only of the reported testimony of a slave who later died, supports a guilty verdict but is far from conclusive. This allows him to explore various arguments regarding other likely suspects. The plaintiff argues that there is no other likely suspect and that the defendant is the most likely because of his previous relationship with the victim. The defendant must be guilty, he argues, since both the direct evidence and the likelihood point to him. The defendant responds that the direct evidence is doubtful, since the victim's slave had good reason to make a false accusation, and that many others are more likely than he to have killed the man. In addition, he is very unlikely to have killed the man, since he knew he would immediately be suspected; indeed, if he had known that another person was intending to kill the victim, he would have tried to prevent it, knowing that he himself would be the prime suspect.

In his second (and last) speech the defendant also adds an alibi to show 'not in likelihood but in fact' (οὐκ ἐκ τῶν εἰκότων ἀλλ' ἔργῳ, 2.4.8) that he could not have been the killer: he was at home all that night and has slaves to prove it. This last claim directly raises the question of the relative value of probability arguments and the evidence of facts (*erga*); and the conclusion we are apparently meant to draw from this late introduction of the alibi is that in the end a direct knowledge of the facts will overcome arguments from likelihood, which only have force when the facts are not known. The same impression is conveyed by the rest of the work, if we look carefully at what both litigants say about probability and 'truth', by which they clearly mean the actual facts as supported by direct evidence, if possible.

The plaintiff begins by apologising for his use of probability arguments, which are made necessary by the difficulty of knowing what happened in cases like this (2.1.1–2). Later the defendant argues that if the plaintiff is going to consider likelihoods (*ta eikota*) equal to the truth, then he too should be allowed to do the same, and since the likelihood in fact supports his side, he should be acquitted (2.2.8). This claim does not imply the primacy of likelihood, but indeed just the opposite: it implies that factual truth is normally primary but that the plaintiff in this case has wrongly implied that likelihood should be equated with truth. The defendant later begins his second speech by asserting that he is trusting in 'the truth of the things that were done by me' (τῇ ἀληθείᾳ τῶν ἐξ ἐμοῦ πραχθέντων, 2.4.1). This and similar expressions imply that there exists a 'factual truth' which, if known by all, would settle the matter. The difficulty is that up to this point there is no good direct evidence for this factual truth, and thus the indirect evidence of probability naturally enters in.

The arguments conclude with the defendant's alibi. The conclusiveness of the alibi, which can be supported by the testimony of household slaves, demonstrates (as I have said) that probability arguments are of less value than direct evidence; but since direct evidence will often be lacking, one needs to learn how to use probability arguments when necessary. The purpose of the *First Tetralogy*, then, is to explore ways of learning the 'truth' and to rehearse the use of probability arguments at the same time. Far from establishing probability as 'more honoured than truth', it establishes just the opposite: that probability arguments only have value in the absence of direct evidence; direct evidence, when available, is better.

Examination of other surviving speeches of the period leads to the same conclusion, that the orators resort to probability only when the truth is unknown, or unclear, or subject to differing interpretations. In some of these cases, moreover, probability supports a case that we know is true. In other cases, probability does not enter into the argument.

Gorgias' most notorious surviving rhetorical work is his *Encomium of Helen*, in which he argues that Helen should not be blamed, as she traditionally is, for running off with Paris. The case seems well suited for giving probability a higher value than truth, since many different versions of Helen's actions existed, including several (Stesichorus, Euripides' *Helen*, Herodotus) in which she did not go to Troy. Herodotus, in fact, uses an indirect probability argument (2.120) that Helen did not go to Troy: he argues that Priam and the Trojans were suffering such losses during the war that they would have given her up (that is, it is likely that they would have given her up), if she had been in Troy. Here a probability argument supports a rejection of the traditional version of the facts. Gorgias' approach is different. He adheres to the traditional version of the facts about Helen, namely that she went to Troy with Paris, but he suggests a different understanding of her involvement in or responsibility for this action.[16] Thus Gorgias does not dispute a matter of factual truth or falsehood – did Helen go to Troy? – but rather accepts the factual truth of the tradition and challenges only the traditional interpretation or evaluation of these facts. Gorgias only uses likelihood once in his argument, when he lists all the likely causes of Helen's behaviour: force, the gods, verbal persuasion and love.[17] The arguments that follow have nothing to do with likelihood; Gorgias has no reason to resort to probability arguments, since the basic facts are known and accepted.

In his *Defence of Palamedes*, on the other hand, Gorgias *is* concerned with the facts. In this speech he argues for the side that, according to the traditional version of the story, was right. The vast majority of ancient sources agree that Palamedes was falsely accused and convicted, and Gorgias follows this tradition closely.[18] Since the facts in this case are not clearly known to the jurors, however, Gorgias uses several probability arguments[19] on Palamedes' behalf to support a case his (Gorgias') audience knew to be true: I would not have betrayed the Greeks for money, since I have as much as I need; I would not have wanted to rule over either Greeks or Barbarians; etc. Virtually the entire case is an attempt to refute the direct, but false, evidence of Odysseus by means of probability arguments in support of the truth. By arguing in this fashion Gorgias does not imply that probability arguments are a better guide to the truth than direct evidence; rather, he shows that probability arguments, though not always effective, are sometimes the only means available for supporting a true case. Thus, when there is a clear-cut opposition between truth and falsehood, Gorgias uses probability in the service of truth. In *Helen*, on the other hand, where the issue is not factual truth but the complex question of causation and responsibility, probability plays no significant role in the argument.

Probability arguments play almost no role in three other mythological speeches surviving from this period. First, a speech attributed to Gorgias' pupil Alcidamas[20] presents the prosecution's case against Palamedes. Alcidamas' *Odysseus* is a pastiche of different arguments, including some that are quite irrelevant but characteristic of Attic oratory, such as a long *ad hominem* attack on Palamedes' claims to have made many inventions. The facts Odysseus introduces, albeit circumstantial and quite possibly falsified, are supported at one point (7) by witnesses, and one inference is drawn by likelihood (10).[21] This is the only mention of likelihood in the speech. Nor does likelihood play any significant role in a pair of speeches composed by Socrates' pupil Antisthenes. These present the two sides of the dispute between Ajax and Odysseus about who should be awarded the arms of Achilles. The arguments are mostly *ad hominem*; each speaker accepts the traditional dichotomy of powerful, honest, simple-minded Ajax and versatile, clever, deceitful Odysseus, and each cites specific deeds to support his contention that the other is unworthy. The only occurrence of the word *eikos* is of no relevance to the argument.[22]

The primary use of probability arguments in early rhetorical exercises is thus in factual disputes where direct evidence is inconclusive. Several actual courtroom speeches confirm that the orators understood this function of probability arguments and differentiated clearly between them and the direct evidence. I cite just two examples. In his fifth speech, *The Murder of Herodes*, Antiphon makes a clear distinction (5.26) between facts (τὰ γενόμενα) and probabilities (τὰ εἰκότα). If the speaker spends more time arguing the latter, this does not mean he considers probabilities more valid but only that they require more argument in this particular case. Most scholars consider the speaker's alibi (supported by witnesses) the strongest part of his case,[23] but whether or not his claim of innocence is true, he presents facts and probabilities as two complementary means of supporting a true case. If his case is false, then both kinds of evidence are falsely used. Second, in Lysias' first speech, Euphiletus argues that he lawfully and properly killed Eratosthenes when he caught him in adultery. The speech is famous for its long and convincing narrative account of the events, which is supported by the direct testimony of witnesses. Towards the end, however, Euphiletus introduces probability arguments to refute the charge that he entrapped his victim with a premeditated plot. He argues that it is unlikely that he would have behaved as he did if this had been his intent. Probability arguments form only a small part of Euphiletus' case, but here too they clearly are used in support of a position established primarily by direct evidence.

All this evidence indicates that the early orators – Corax and Tisias, Gorgias, Antiphon and Lysias – were interested in the use of probability arguments but did not advocate giving these arguments more credence than directly established truth, as Plato charges. Probability arguments could supplement the direct evidence of witnesses, or could be used when direct evidence was absent or inconclusive. If the theorists paid more attention to the rhetorical use of probability than direct evidence, then this was because probability arguments have more varied uses and require, or allow for, more rhetorical skill. Probability arguments also serve pedagogical needs because they can be applied *mutatis mutandis* to many different cases, whereas direct evidence is more case-specific. A *Tetralogy* where all the facts were clearly established by witnesses would be of little pedagogical or theoretical interest. The earliest theorists, Corax, Tisias and Antiphon, were the most interested in probability; they seem to have exhausted theoretical speculation on the subject, and later thinkers turned to other types of argument.

In sum, there is no evidence to support Plato's claim, echoed nearly unanimously by modern scholars, that Greek orators and rhetoricians valued probability more highly than the truth. Undoubtedly probability was sometimes used to support a false case, but so too was direct evidence; and the surviving speeches, at least, indicate that orators at this time had a clear and reasonable understanding of the value of probability arguments and considered them valid only to the extent that direct evidence for the truth was absent or inconclusive. Plato's criticisms on this point reflect his own concern with the overriding primacy of an absolute standard of truth, which is tied to and validated by his Forms; for him anything less than absolute truth was no truth at all.[24]

The fifth-century sophists and orators, however, did value truth and did appreciate the distinction between truth and opinion, even if they did not share Plato's view of the nature of truth. At the same time, they understood the fundamental importance of rhetoric, oral and written, in situations where truth is not clear. Perhaps the most obvious of such situations were legal cases, since very few of these involve a clear set of agreed-upon facts. The cases that end up in court are those where the facts or their interpretation are in dispute, and in these cases litigants need to look for means of discovering truth other than direct evidence, even if the truth that is discovered by these means is less certain. Thus, the earliest rhetorical theorists devoted considerable attention to understanding the various ways probability arguments could be used to sway opinion precisely because they recognised the practical need for such arguments.

The theorists' attitude towards truth and opinion is best revealed in a passage in Gorgias' *Helen* (11), where he is describing the power of *logos*:

> For if all men on all subjects had memory of the past, (understanding) of the present, and foresight into the future, *logos* would not be the same in the same way;[25] but as it is, to remember the past, to examine the present, or to prophesy the future is not easy; and so most men on most subjects make opinion (*doxa*) an adviser to their minds. But opinion is perilous and uncertain, and brings those who use it to perilous and uncertain good fortune.

Gorgias implies that since knowledge of the truth is in most cases unattainable, rhetoric must concern itself with people's opinions, but this is a far cry from saying that opinion is held in more honour than truth. Indeed, Gorgias implies a clear preference for the truth, when it is knowable. But he recognises that often it is not knowable, and so he and others concern themselves with and train their pupils in the use of probability arguments and other devices for swaying human opinion.

Gorgias gives three examples of the importance of opinion (13):

> One must first study the arguments of astronomers, who replace opinion with opinion: displacing one but implanting another, they make incredible, invisible matters apparent to

the eyes of opinion. Second, compulsory debates with words,[26] where a single speech to a large crowd pleases and persuades because it is written with skill, not spoken with truth. Third, contests of philosophical arguments, where it is shown that speed of thought also makes it easy to change a conviction based on opinion.

Most relevant for us is the second example, 'compulsory debates with words', where Gorgias praises a speech 'written with skill, not spoken with truth' (τέχνῃ γραφείς, οὐκ ἀληθείᾳ λεχθείς). Gorgias may be more concerned with the rhetorical assonance than the epistemological implication of this pair of oppositions (skill/truth, written/spoken),[27] but he seems to say that truth is, at least in some cases, of secondary importance compared to the orator's (or speechwriter's) skill in composing the speech. This can be taken to mean that with rhetorical skill one can win any case, no matter how strongly the facts favour the other side, but the parallel with Gorgias' other examples – astronomical and philosophical debates, in which the facts are evidently unclear – suggests rather that Gorgias has in mind cases like Palamedes' defence, in which the skill with which one presents probability arguments or uses other rhetorical techniques may be the key to reaching a just verdict in cases where a simple assertion of the truth would fail. Gorgias' remarks recognise the need for rhetorical skill in many areas of life and imply that the sophists' contributions to the study of rhetoric have played an important role in the intellectual progress of his day.

The contributions of the sophists did not, of course, come in a vacuum: oratory played an important part in Greek life from the beginning. Oratorical skill is recognised in Homer;[28] Hesiod stresses the oratorical ability of the good king in settling disputes (*Theogony* 80–92);[29] historians speak of the oratorical ability of Athenian statesmen such as Themistocles; and oratory in the form of a long, set speech was probably an important feature of tragedy from the beginning (for example, Aeschylus, *Persians* 353–432). The development of democratic institutions in Athens during the fifth century provided more opportunities for addressing a large audience, just as the replacement of tyranny with democracy in Syracuse reportedly stimulated the interest of Corax and Tisias in rhetorical theory.

Also fundamental to Greek culture from the beginning was the institution of the contest or *agon*. The contest may first have evolved out of military combat, which in Homer, at least, is primarily a matter of one-on-one combat between heroes, but even by the time of Homer and Hesiod the Greeks were engaging in contests in non-military settings.[30] Our earliest references are to athletic contests, such as those in *Iliad* 23, and poetic contests, such as Hesiod's victory at Amphidamas' funeral games (*Works and Days* 551–557). But by the fifth century the basic pattern of the *agon* could be found in many other areas. As noted above, Gorgias (*Helen* 13) refers to debates between astronomers or philosophers in addition to legal disputes, and the *agon* was a well established feature of fifth-century tragedy and comedy.[31]

Particularly important for the history of rhetorical theory in Athens was the great increase in the use of the popular courts in the second half of the fifth century. As more and more citizens found themselves in court before large bodies of jurors, intellectuals also turned their attention to forensic rhetoric. The ancient testimony is divided on the question whether the primary impetus for the earliest rhetorical theory in Syracuse was the need for good speakers in the newly democratic Assembly or the need for forensic skill for the legal suits resulting from the overthrow of the tyrants;[32] but whether Corax and Tisias were more concerned with legal disputes or political debates is less important for us than the fact that their best known contribution (discussed above) pertains to a legal dispute stemming from an assault. Most of the other fifth- and early fourth-century speeches that survive, moreover, were written for real or hypothetical court cases or are modelled on legal disputes. I include here not just Antiphon's *Tetralogies*, Gorgias' *Palamedes* and *Helen*, Antisthenes' *Ajax* and *Odysseus*, and Alcidamas' *Odysseus*, but also Prodicus' speeches by Vice and Virtue in *The Choice of Heracles*, and the *agones* of tragedy and comedy (Jason and Medea, Clytemnestra and Electra, the stronger and weaker *logos*, etc.), which take the form of a quasi-legal debate between two opposed positions. Even the deliberative speeches in Thucydides are often structured in pairs in the manner of a legal dispute.[33]

A related development was the transition to written composition. The first speeches to be written down were evidently forensic, and this was no accident. Debates in the Assembly would not always fall into two clearly opposed positions, as they did in legal cases, and it would not be as easy to predict the arguments of one's opponents or the precise terms in which an issue would be debated. Thus speakers in the political debates in the Assembly would normally have been unable to write their speeches before a debate, and would have had to speak extemporaneously. In the lawcourts, however, each litigant could predict with reasonable certainty the arguments his opponent would use,[34] and so a speech could be composed beforehand. Traditionally, litigants composed their own speeches and spoke without a written text. We can imagine, however, that they often consulted with family or friends, and in the second half of the fifth century some speakers began seeking the advice of 'professionals'. The first of these (to our knowledge) was Antiphon, who, we are told, was the earliest Athenian to leave behind written speeches.[35] His three surviving courtroom speeches and the datable fragments of his other speeches all were written during the last two decades of his life (430–411), and it is thus reasonable to date the beginning of written oratory in Athens to about 430. But Antiphon apparently took an interest in legal affairs before this time,[36] since most of his other works (the *Tetralogies* and *On Truth*) also involve legal issues. The *Tetralogies* are frequently dated to the 430s or even earlier,[37] and Antiphon's reputation for giving good advice to those in legal difficulty (Thuc. 8.68) is likely to have preceded his being asked to write down speeches. Thucydides also reports that Antiphon shunned the courts himself, preferring to remain in the background and advise others; and as an adviser, Antiphon would quite naturally be asked for more than general advice. At some point a litigant asked for the actual text of a speech, and Antiphon would then need to write down the text for his client to read and memorise. Antiphon never appeared in court himself, and thus never wrote a speech for a case of his own, until his famous speech in his own defence when he was brought to trial after the revolt of 411. Although Antiphon lost the case (and his life), his speech was much admired by Thucydides and others. This was the first time, to our knowledge, that someone wrote down a speech for himself to deliver at a trial, but this practice was followed by Antiphon's younger contemporaries: Andocides, who himself delivered all three of his genuine speeches in the period 408–392, and Lysias, who probably delivered, or intended to deliver, his earliest speech (12) himself.

The full impact of writing on the study of rhetoric is difficult to assess,[38] but writing was almost certainly an important factor for Antiphon as he developed the practice of logography into a *techne*, or 'profession'.[39] The writing down of speeches must have influenced their composition and contributed to the professionalisation of the study of rhetoric. Writing allowed those interested in rhetoric to focus on fine details of style both in composing a speech and in studying the effect of the speeches of others. We can scarcely imagine a speech like the *Encomium on Helen* being composed without the aid of writing. The importance of writing in the development of early rhetoric is confirmed by contemporary critics. Alcidamas describes the process of writing in the course of his protest against it in *On Those Who Write Speeches or On Sophists*, which may have been written around 390 as a response to Isocrates' *Against the Sophists*.[40] Alcidamas' first objection is that writing is too easy (4), and although few might agree with this conclusion, his description provides a good illustration of the process of writing a speech at this time:

> To write something over a long period of time, to revise it at one's leisure, to consult the works of earlier sophists gathering together their arguments on the same topic and imitating passages that happen to be expressed well, and then in some places to make further revisions on the advice of laymen and in others, after investigating the matter thoroughly by oneself, to delete everything and write it over again – this is naturally easy even for those with no education.

Alcidamas admits that written composition can achieve greater precision and artistry but this very fact, he maintains, causes distrust in the audience (12). Written composition also slows down a person's mental processes (17) and does not allow for the insertion of last-minute or chance arguments (24–25). Thus, extemporaneous oral composition is both more difficult and more effective.

Alcidamas' criticisms of the art of written composition give us a good picture of the rhetorical training being given at the start of the fourth century by those who held themselves skilled in this *techne*. Another source of information is Isocrates, whose criticisms, though quite different from those of Alcidamas, also contain clues about the nature of rhetorical training. Most interesting is his description of the process of composition (13.16): 'To select the points that are necessary for each case, to combine and arrange them properly, to meet the needs of the occasion, to adorn the whole speech with appropriate arguments, and to deliver it with rhythmical and poetical expressions.'[41] This list suggests an important thesis of classical rhetoric, explicitly attested only later, that its five parts are invention, arrangement, style, memory and delivery. All these save memory are included, in order, in Isocrates' description.

These passages in Alcidamas and Isocrates present obstacles to Cole's thesis that the successors of Tisias and Corax 'continued to deal in illustration rather than analysis, merely replacing sample instances of a single type of speech with a more diversified collection of reusable "speech components" ' (*Origins of Rhetoric*, p. 83). By the early fourth century, at least, the sophists and teachers of rhetoric were discussing, teaching, and very likely writing about 'rhetoric' as a *techne*, in much the same sense as Plato uses the term in the *Gorgias*, even if they did not use the expression *rhetorike techne*. Thus, Plato distorts the nature of early Greek rhetoric, but not the fact of its existence.

Other features of early rhetoric also suggest an awareness of and interest in rhetorical theory. For instance, the speeches of Gorgias and Antiphon indicate an implicit understanding of basic differences between kinds of legal cases that formed the basis of later *stasis* theory (Latin *status*). The theory as developed by Hermagoras[42] set forth four basic *staseis* or kinds of cases, but the most important division was between the *stasis stochasmos* (or *status coniectura*), where the dispute concerns a question of fact ('did the defendant do the deed or not?'), and the other three (in some versions four) *staseis*, all of which involve not denying the deed but denying one's guilt or some other aspect of the case (such as the jurisdiction of the court). Both Gorgias and Antiphon appear to recognise this basic division, which corresponds roughly to our distinction between questions of fact and questions of law.[43] Gorgias' *Palamedes* involves a factual dispute, whereas in *Helen* the facts are admitted but Helen's guilt is denied; similarly, Antiphon's *First Tetralogy* disputes the facts, whereas in the *Second* (and less explicitly the *Third*) the litigants debate the legal consequences of an admitted action. These pairings are unlikely to be mere coincidence; more likely both Antiphon and Gorgias were aware of the basic division between these two kinds of cases and consciously devoted a work to each kind.

The sophists also took an interest in new forms of argument. In addition to the method of arguing on both sides of an issue, the invention of which is usually attributed to Protagoras,[44] Gorgias developed a method sometimes called 'apagogic',[45] in which the speaker sets out all the possibilities and then argues against each in turn. Gorgias makes use of this method in *Helen* and *Palamedes*, as well as in *On Non-Being*, and the plaintiff in Antiphon's *First Tetralogy* catalogues the other likely suspects, arguing against each in turn. The method became popular in actual court speeches, especially among defendants who argue that they have no motive for the alleged crime (for example, Antiph. 5.57–61): they list all the motives commonly alleged for the sort of crime they are charged with and then deny each in turn. The apagogic method can be seen as a forerunner of Plato's method of diaeresis, whereby a subject is broken down by repeated division into parts. Plato's method seeks to eliminate the 'loophole' in the apagogic method, namely that the list of possibilities may not be exhaustive, and thus provides a stronger philosophical proof, but the apagogic method is often more useful in the kinds of cases for which rhetoric is actually used.

In assessing the positive contributions of early Greek rhetoric, we should not forget that the influence of rhetoric was felt not just in speeches, real and imaginary, but also in many of the written treatises of the time, works like Gorgias' *On Non-Being*, the *Dissoi Logoi*, and (probably) Protagoras' *Antilogiae*, Antiphon's *Truth*, and others. As far as we can tell (or in some cases speculate), these works shared an interest in juxtaposing contrasting arguments, following Protagoras' dictum that 'there are two opposed sides to every issue' (δύο λόγους εἶναι περὶ παντὸς ἀντικειμένους ἀλλήλοις: Diog. Laert. 9.51). Some of these works (notably the *Dissoi Logoi*) seem primarily aimed at a display of virtuosity (or would-be virtuosity), and with their clever turns of phrase and ingenious, table-turning arguments they may appear fully deserving of Plato's criticisms. And we can hardly imagine that Gorgias was not aware of the shock value of both the form and content of works like *Helen* and *On Non-Being*. But in this respect the sophists resembled many of the Presocratic 'philosophers' (notably Heraclitus, Parmenides and Zeno), and like them the sophists could use their shocking new arguments and stylistic effects to explore issues that we can properly call philosophical,[46] such as cause and effect, the responsibility for action, the relation between truth and reality, and aspects of language and human psychology. Gorgias' *Helen* contains some striking observations on language, truth, sense perception, psychology and responsibility; and Antiphon's *Tetralogies* address several serious philosophical issues.

The *Second Tetralogy* in particular provides the most sophisticated examination of cause and responsibility before Aristotle. Although he lacks the technical language of the later philosopher, Antiphon's defendant takes an apparently straightforward example of causation – the thrower of a javelin causes the death of the boy who was hit – and by a subtle, 'sophistic' argument[47] shows that the boy in fact caused his own death by running out on to the throwing field at the wrong time, whereas the thrower acted properly in throwing when he ought to and when the others were throwing, and thus should incur no responsibility. The philosophical argument is that when (as often) there are several causes of an event, the cause that involves the greatest error should incur the primary responsibility (see especially 3.2.3–8). The question of causation was of great interest during the second half of the fifth century,[48] and Antiphon's treatment of the issue is the most advanced before Aristotle.

Less obvious, perhaps, are the positive implications of the *First Tetralogy*: by combining probability and reverse probability arguments with the manipulation of direct evidence, first of the slave's reported testimony and then of the available alibi, Antiphon explores the relative value of probability and direct evidence. The *First Tetralogy* can be understood as suggesting a conclusion much like that reached by Aristotle in *Rhetoric* 1402a12–13, quoting the late fifth-century tragedian Agathon's couplet: 'One might say that this too is likely (*eikos*), that many unlikely things happen to mortals' (τάχ' ἄν τις εἰκὸς αὐτὸ τοῦτ' εἶναι λέγοι | βροτοῖσι πολλὰ τυγχάνειν οὐκ εἰκότα). In other words, probability has its use but also its limitations.

I have tried in this chapter to show that early Greek rhetoric did not suffer from the faults attributed to it by its most vehement critic Plato, but on the contrary contributed in positive ways to the intellectual ferment of the period – even in ways that later influenced Plato. Let me conclude by noting the one critic of early rhetoric we have left out of this discussion, Thucydides. Thucydides was fully aware of the potential danger of rhetorical manipulation, as his brilliant analysis of the misuse of language at Corcyra shows (3.83), and his work as a whole could be taken as a conservative warning against this danger. But Thucydides was also so thoroughly influenced by the sophists that it would only be a slight exaggeration to call him a sophist himself. Moreover, much of his analysis of the fundamental issues of war, peace and the human condition is conveyed through the stunning rhetoric of his speeches.[49] Thucydides' intellectual accomplishment is inconceivable without the advances made by the sophists and orators, and it is clear from the debate about rhetoric contained in the Mytilenean debate (3.37–48) that he was aware of, and acknowledged, this debt. That is more than one can say for Plato.

NOTES

1 The most convenient summary with references to earlier scholarship is in Kennedy, *Art of Persuasion*, pp. 26–70; see also M. Lavency, *Aspects de la logographie juridique attique* (Louvain: 1964). The relevant texts are collected in L. Radermacher, *Artium Scriptores* (Vienna: 1951).

2 This is not to say that Aristophanes is simply a conservative critic. As noted above, this position is only one part of his comic creation; other positions are also present in his work and the author's views are not reducible to one or the other of these.

3 It is legitimate to speak of Plato's views in the *Gorgias* since 'Socrates' does not just elicit answers about rhetoric from others but presents substantial positive arguments of his own. As G. Vlastos has argued (*Socrates*, Ithaca: 1990), the presentation of positive views is characteristic of the Platonic Socrates, in contrast to the earlier, aporetic Socrates, who is closer to the 'historical' figure. There is, to be sure, some irony in Plato's treatment, as when Polus asserts that Socrates' view is fantastic, though irrefutable, and Callicles then asks whether Socrates is really serious or just joking (480e–481b), but the irony does not mean that Plato is distancing himself from the views of 'Socrates', but rather that he is aware that these views are in some ways extreme.

4 Note that Gorgias objects at this point (460a) that his students do learn about justice, but he then yields his role as interlocutor to Polus.

5 Cole, *Origins of Rhetoric*; some of the same points are made by E. Schiappa, 'Did Plato Coin *Rhetorike*?', *AJPh* 111 (1990), pp. 457–70; *Protagoras and Logos: A Study in Greek Philosophy and Rhetoric* (Columbia, SC: 1991); and '*Rhetorike*: What's in a Name? Toward a Revised History of Early Greek Rhetorical Theory', *QJS* 78 (1992), pp. 1–15.

6 ῥητορική *(rhetorike)* also occurs in Alcidamas' *On the Sophists* (1, 2). This work cannot be dated with certainty; most scholars would put it around the same time as Plato's *Gorgias* (c. 386), but Cole argues (*Origins of Rhetoric*, p. 173 n. 4) that parallels with the *Phaedrus* suggest a date for Alcidamas' work in the 360s. Even if the word *rhetorike* first occurs in the *Gorgias*, this does not prove that Plato invented it, since it could have been used for many years in oral discussions among orators and philosophers, and the expression ἡ καλουμένη ῥητορική *(Gorgias* 448d9) suggests that this was not its first use. The word may have been invented or made

prominent in oral discussion in Plato's circle. See also S. Halliwell, chapter 11 below.

7 I use the term 'intellectual' for sophists, orators, rhetoricians, and others influenced by the new ideas of the last half of the fifth century. The categories designated by these names were not differentiated in the fifth century, and even in the fourth century 'sophist' can designate an orator like Lysias as well as a thinker like Socrates: see M. Gagarin, 'The Ancient Tradition on the Identity of Antiphon', *GRBS* 31 (1990), pp. 27–44, especially p. 31, and also Lavency, *Logographie*, p. 55: 'Rhétorique et sophistique, *ces deux genres d'une même espèce*, poursuivent les mêmes intérêts' (his emphasis).

8 Cole includes a brief discussion of the views of both Plato and Aristotle of *eikos* (*Origins of Rhetoric*, pp. 96–7); he rightly concludes that an *eikos*-argument was often necessary in the absence of other adequate evidence and that it would have served a legitimate legal, not rhetorical, purpose.

9 False witnesses were liable for prosecution in Attic law.

10 For convenience I shall distinguish between explicit probability arguments, in which the word *eikos* itself appears, and implicit probability arguments, which take forms like 'Why would I do this?' or 'I would not do that.'

11 The date of the *Hymn* is uncertain, but virtually all scholars date it before 450 and most date it around 500 or earlier: see R. Janko, *Homer, Hesiod and the Hymns* (Cambridge: 1982), pp. 140–3.

12 Apollo is searching Hermes' home for stolen cattle; eventually the two of them take their dispute to Zeus, acting as judge: see M. Gagarin, *Early Greek Law* (Berkeley and Los Angeles: 1986), pp. 40–1.

13 See G. Goebel, *Early Greek Rhetorical Theory and Practice: Proof and Arrangement in the Speeches of Antiphon and Euripides* (Ph.D. dissertation, Madison: 1983), pp. 290–301. There are, of course, many probability arguments in tragedy where the word *eikos* is not used, such as Creon's famous defence in *Oedipus the King* 583 ff.

14 See F. Solmsen, *Intellectual Experiments of the Greek Enlightenment* (Princeton: 1975).

15 I accept the *Tetralogies* as fifth-century works, probably by Antiphon; *contra* R. Sealey, 'The *Tetralogies* Ascribed to Antiphon', *TAPhA* 114 (1984), pp. 71–85. I shall argue this point at greater length elsewhere.

16 Gorgias may have been influenced by the arguments of Helen in Euripides' *Trojan Women* (produced in 415) but we cannot be certain, since we cannot date Gorgias' speech.

17 Section 5: τὰς αἰτίας, δι' ἃς εἰκὸς ἦν γενέσθαι τὸν τῆς Ἑλένης εἰς τὴν Τροίαν στόλον (literally, 'the causes on account of which it is likely that Helen's journey to Troy took place'). The only other use of the word in the *Helen* is when Gorgias asks rhetorically: 'Why is it not reasonable to pity Helen?' (7: πῶς οὐκ ἂν εἰκότως ἐλεηθείη).

18 The only argument to the contrary is Alcidamas' *Odysseus* (see p. 55), in which Odysseus' case is transparently weak on the facts: for a full discussion of the evidence for the myth see R. Scodel, *The Trojan Trilogy of Euripides, Hypomnemata* 60 (Göttingen: 1980), pp. 43–63.

19 Only one of the probability arguments is explicit (section 9).

20 The current consensus (for example, Kennedy, *Art of Persuasion*, pp. 172–3) is that *Odysseus* is probably not the work of Alcidamas, first because it is of poor quality, and second because in his other surviving work, *On the Sophists*, Alcidamas criticises those who write speeches. Neither reason carries much weight; the second is especially questionable in view of the fact that the other notable fourth-century attack on writing comes in a work (*Phaedrus*) by Plato, a master of the written word.

21 'We should also infer from this evidence a likely explanation for his throwing the spear' (τεκμαίρεσθαι δὲ δεῖ ἐκ τούτων εἰκότως καὶ τὴν ἄφεσιν τῆς λόγχης).

22 In *Odysseus* 5 Odysseus says that it is likely that Ajax' bad temper will bring him harm in the future – an obvious reference to his later suicide.

23 See U. Schindel, *Der Mordfall Herodes. Nachrichten der Ak. der Wiss. in Göttingen* (*Phil.-Hist. Kl.*: 1979), pp. 203–41; *contra* M. Gagarin, *The Murder of Herodes* (Frankfurt: 1989), pp. 103–15.

24 Cf. the conclusion reached in the *Theaetetus* (171c): 'Protagoras' *Truth* (that is, his work entitled *Aletheia*) is true to nobody.' I discuss the sophists' views of truth at greater length in an unpublished paper 'The Truth of Antiphon's *Truth*'.

25 The text is uncertain here. See T. Buchheim, *Gorgias von Leontinoi, Reden, Fragmente und Testimonien* (Hamburg: 1989), *ad loc.*

26 τοὺς ἀναγκαίους διὰ λόγων ἀγῶνας. This expression probably designates speeches in law courts. There were many other occasions for debate, but only in the courts could it be said that a debate was compulsory.

27 The most recent discussion is by Buchheim, *Gorgias von Leontinoi*, pp. xviii–xix; see also D. M. MacDowell's comments, *Gorgias, Encomium of Helen* (Bristol: 1982), *ad loc.*

28 Kennedy, *Art of Persuasion*, pp. 35–9, surveys the Homeric passages that recognise oratorical qualities. More recently R. P. Martin, *The Language of Heroes: Speech and Performance in the Iliad* (Ithaca: 1989), discusses several kinds of 'speech acts' in the *Iliad*.

29 See F. Solmsen, 'The "Gift" of Speech in Homer and Hesiod', *TAPhA* 85 (1954), 1–15; M. Gagarin, 'Hesiod and the Origins of Greek Law', *Ramus* 21 (1992), pp. 61–78.

30 M. Griffith, 'Contest and Contradiction in Early Greek Poetry', in M. Griffith and D. J. Mastronarde (eds), *Cabinet of the Muses* (Atlanta: 1990), pp. 185–211.

31 J. Duchemin, *L'ΑΓΩΝ dans la tragédie grecque* (Paris: 1945); more recently M. Lloyd, *The Agon in Euripides* (Oxford: 1992).

32 S. Wilcox, 'The Scope of Early Rhetorical Instruction', *HSCPh* 53 (1942), pp. 121–55, argues that the sophists taught political, that is, deliberative, oratory; the more common view is that 'it is notorious that the earliest systems of rhetoric were occupied entirely with the business of judicial oratory': D. A. G. Hinks, 'Tisias and Corax and the Invention of Rhetoric', *CQ* 34 (1940), p. 62; cf. G. Kennedy, 'The Earliest Rhetorical Handbooks', *AJPh* 80 (1959), p. 173.

33 In addition to the speeches in Thucydides, other non-forensic speeches of the period include Gorgias' funeral oration and Thrasymachus' Assembly speech; only fragments of these survive.

34 In addition to the preliminary hearing, there were other sources of information about one's opponent's case: see A. P. Dorjahn, 'Anticipation of Arguments in Athenian Courts', *TAPhA* 66 (1935), pp. 274–95.

35 Photius, *Bibliotecha* 259.486A7–11. For Antiphon and the *Tetralogies* see above nn. 7 and 15.

36 According to the *Life* attributed to Plutarch (*X.Or.* 832f) Antiphon was born 'at the time of the Persian wars' and was slightly younger than Gorgias. This would put his birth around 480.

37 See, for example, K. J. Dover, 'The Chronology of Antiphon's Speeches', *CQ* 44 (1950), pp. 44–60.

38 G. Kennedy, *Classical Rhetoric and Its Christian and Secular Tradition* (Chapel. Hill: 1982), p. 5 and *passim*, calls this transition to written composition *letteraturizzazione*.

39 See Lavency, *Logographie*, pp. 51–9.

40 See LaRue van Hook, 'Alcidamas versus Isocrates; the Spoken versus the Written Word', *Classical Weekly* 12 (1919), pp. 89–94. Most of the specific allusions to Isocrates he sees could easily be general references to issues of the time.

41 τὸ δὲ τούτων ἐφ' ἑκάστῳ τῶν πραγμάτων ἃς δεῖ προελέσθαι καὶ μείξασθαι πρὸς ἀλλήλας καὶ τάξασθαι κατὰ τρόπον, ἔτι δὲ τῶν καιρῶν μὴ διαμαρτεῖν ἀλλὰ καὶ τοῖς ἐνθυμήμασι πρεπόντως ὅλον τὸν λόγον καταποικῖλαι καὶ τοῖς ὀνόμασιν εὐρύθμως καὶ μουσικῶς εἰπεῖν.

42 See Kennedy, *Art of Persuasion*, pp. 306–14.

43 See Cole, *Origins of Rhetoric*, pp. 97–8.

44 Solmsen, *Intellectual Experiments*, chapter 1, discusses a form of this argument, *in utramque partem disputare*.

45 For example, Kennedy, *Art of Persuasion*, pp. 168 and 170.

46 Schiappa, '*Rhetorike*: What's in a Name?', strongly disputes the traditional view of a sharp dichotomy between rhetoric and philosophy.

47 The defendant recognises that his argument will appear too subtle to many and tries to meet this objection before he begins, asking for forgiveness if he is forced to speak 'more subtly' (*akribesteron*) than usual (3.2.2).

48 In addition to Gorgias' *Helen*, one can cite the tragedians' interest in first causes of an event: see Solmsen, *Intellectual Experiments*, pp. 66–70.

49 Cole, *Origins of Rhetoric*, pp. 104–11, treats these speeches as examples of the fifth-century 'art of words' (*logon techne*), in the same genre as the speeches of Gorgias and others.

4

Classical rhetoric and modern theories of discourse

David Cohen

The past three decades have witnessed a remarkable resurgence of interest in rhetorical theory. This interest has, however, taken a number of distinct forms. Some theorists, for example, have sought to extend traditional understanding of rhetoric as a methodology for the study of argument. On the other hand, others have paid little heed to rhetoric's historical parameters as they have reconceptualised rhetoric as the analysis of fictional narrative. Still others have attempted to overcome the ancient antagonism between philosophy and rhetoric by construing rhetoric as the framework for a philosophy of discourse. Finally, in recent years post-modernist thinkers have turned to rhetoric precisely because of its repudiation of philosophical conceptions of knowledge and truth. The purpose of this chapter is to explore a variety of these perspectives on the rhetorical tradition. More specifically, the ensuing discussion will examine the ways in which diverse theorists have sought to appropriate classical rhetoric for the purposes of their own enterprise. The first part will take up seminal figures, Perelman, Booth and Richards, who regarded themselves as engaging in the construction of a 'new' rhetoric upon the foundations (or, in some cases, the ruins) of the ancient art of persuasion. The second part will turn to thinkers, such as Foucault, Derrida and Barthes, who, though they do not seek to create a 'new rhetoric', none the less find a reconnection to the classical tradition essential for their own theoretical endeavours. Though one could have included other figures as well, the sample included here represents a strikingly broad range of perspectives on the study of discourse. This breadth alone, it seems to me, testifies to the importance which classical rhetoric has assumed for contemporary theory.

1

Few would doubt that Chaim Perelman stands as perhaps the seminal figure in the revival of rhetoric as the study of argumentation. In works like *The New Rhetoric: A Treatise on Argumentation* (Notre Dame: 1969) and *The Realm of Rhetoric* (Notre Dame: 1982) Perelman goes back to the classical tradition to ground a new theory for the study of Aristotle's *Rhetoric* as the foundational text for this enterprise. Believing that the reduction of rhetoric to the 'art of the eloquent and ornate use of language' by Ramus and his followers was based upon a misapprehension of the relation of dialectic and rhetoric in the Aristotelian schema (*Realm of Rhetoric*, p. 3), Perelman sets out to restore rhetoric to its rightful place in the human sciences. Following Aristotle, Perelman distinguishes between analytical and dialectical reasoning. The latter deals with justifiable opinion and is the realm of rhetoric (ibid., pp. 2–3).

Whereas classical rhetoric traditionally focused upon persuasive public speaking the scope of Perelman's 'new' rhetoric is far broader. Oratory, according to Perelman, shares the aim of all argumentation which is to win 'the adherence of the minds addressed' (*New Rhetoric*, p. 6). Accordingly, given the changed circumstances of deliberation and communication in the modern world, there is no need to limit rhetoric to the study of public speaking: 'The theory of argumentation, conceived as a new rhetoric or dialectic, covers the whole range of discourse that aims at persuasion or conviction, whatever the audience addressed and whatever the subject matter' (ibid., p. 5). It follows from this general position that the new rhetoric may be employed to study the argumentative conventions of the various disciplines, for example law or philosophy (*Realm of Rhetoric*, p. 5). At this point, Perelman joins the perennial debate over the relationship of philosophy and rhetoric and rejects the tradition of Plato, Descartes and Kant which sharply separates these two disciplines. For Perelman, because philosophical theses cannot be founded upon self-evident intuitions they necessarily depend upon argumentation to procure adherence. Thus, he continues, 'the new rhetoric becomes the indispensable instrument for philosophy' (ibid., p. 7).

The starting point for Perelman's theory of argumentation is drawn from the new rhetoric's classical antecedents. The fundamental premise of Perelman's approach is that discourse is directed at an audience. Whereas classical rhetoric aimed at persuading a particular group of individuals through oratory, the new rhetoric casts its net far wider: 'Every speech is addressed to an audience and it is frequently forgotten that this applies to everything written as well' (*New Rhetoric*, pp. 6–7). The new rhetoric thus encompasses the entire range of 'the discursive means of obtaining the adherence of minds' (ibid., p. 8).

In investigating these means of obtaining adherence in *The New Rhetoric* Perelman addresses three main areas. First, building upon the Aristotelian tradition he further develops the notion of audience. He introduces the notion of the 'universal audience' to distinguish contingencies of persuasion in particular contexts from the ideal possibilities of persuasion according to logical proofs alone. He also uses the distinction between particular and universal audience to examine the nature of the relation of the speaker to the audience. Next, he takes up what he calls 'the starting points of argument' (p. 65). These, of course, are the premises which, following Aristotle, must be shared by the audience and speaker if persuasion is to be effective. Drawing extensively upon Aristotle's treatment of the enthymeme and common topics Perelman divides this study of premises into consideration of the nature of agreement on premises and the choice and presentation of premises. The latter section includes a lengthy discussion of the argumentative function of tropes, distinguishing between purely ornamental figures and those which contribute to producing adherence (pp. 168–9). Finally, the last and longest section of the book sets out a schema of the 'techniques of argumentation'.

The scope of Perelman's project is thus extraordinarily ambitious. He not only seeks to rehabilitate rhetoric as the study of argumentation in all its forms, but also, following Walter Jens, to establish it as the 'once and future queen of the human sciences'.[1] Since 'every discourse which does not claim an impersonal validity belongs to rhetoric', rhetoric encompasses all the academic disciplines and other discursive contexts where individuals seek to gain adherence for their views (*Realm of Rhetoric*, p. 161). Most importantly for present purposes, Perelman, to a much greater extent than other major figures in the development of the field of argumentation, explicitly grounds the new rhetoric in its classical antecedents. Indeed, one can read *The New Rhetoric* as an adaptation of Aristotle's *Rhetoric* to the contemporary world of discourse and as an affirmation of its place as the foundational text of the discipline. Those historians of rhetoric who look more to Cicero or Quintilian will of course be likely to contest this genealogy and the exclusive focus on argumentative discourse which it produces.

Like Perelman, I. A. Richards set out to revive the ancient art of rhetoric by defining a 'new rhetoric'. Like Perelman he also articulated an ambitious vision of the role this 'new rhetoric' can play as 'a philosophical enquiry into how words work in discourse'.[2] This true rhetoric, he claims, would be able to account for and remedy failures of communication. Thus, in his famous formulation, 'Rhetoric . . . should be a study of misunderstanding and its remedies' (*Philosophy of Rhetoric*, p. 3). Unlike Perelman, however, Richards sought to found this new 'philosophic discipline' of rhetoric by largely divorcing it from its ancient antecedents. He characterises the traditional rhetorical approach to discourse as 'a set of dodges that will be found to work sometimes' (p. 7), or as 'the usual postcard's-worth of crude common sense' (p. 8). More significantly he rejects the 'old' rhetoric because it concentrates on persuasion and ignores the fact that argumentation is just one mode of discourse. The new rhetoric, on the other hand, must shift focus from what Richards calls the macroscopic study of discourse to a microscopic enquiry. This enquiry must focus on the fundamental units of discourse: words. Because traditional rhetoric examines larger discursive structures it ignores the way in which the units constituting those structures acquire meaning. Thus, following from the re-orientation of rhetoric to the avoidance of misunderstanding, meaning is established as the central category for the analysis of discourse. Without a theory of the way in which words acquire meaning we are doomed to being unable to account for the failure of communication. Accordingly, three of the five principal chapters of *The Philosophy of Rhetoric* focus upon the clarification of the relation of words to their context and the way in which this relation has been misunderstood by previous theories of meaning.

After clarifying to his satisfaction the nature of meaning Richards turns to the subject of metaphor. He again distances himself from the classical tradition by dismissing its appreciation of metaphor as 'a sort of happy extra trick with words, an opportunity to exploit the accidents of their versatility . . . In brief, a grace or ornament or *added* power of language, not its constitutive form' (p. 90). What traditional rhetoricians failed to appreciate is that 'metaphor is the omnipresent principle of language' (p. 92). They 'made metaphor seem to be a verbal matter, a shifting and displacement of words, whereas fundamentally it is a borrowing between and intercourse of *thoughts*, a transaction between contexts. *Thought* is metaphoric, and proceeds by comparison, and the metaphors of language derive therefrom' (p. 94).

Richards' influential reformulation of the task of rhetoric reveals itself as fundamentally anti-rhetorical in the sense of rhetoric advanced by Perelman. Dismissing persuasion, practical reasoning and argumentation as mere epiphenomena, Richards redefines rhetoric as the study of semantics on the one hand and metaphor on the other. Perhaps because Richards' basic orientation is literary the strategic dimension of rhetoric drops out, and there is little place for Perelman's fundamental premise of rhetoric as centring on the discursive relation of a speaker to an audience. Further, following a modern trend which Barthes, Genette and other defenders of the classical conception of rhetoric will later attack, Richards' elevation of metaphor as a master trope embedded in human consciousness ignores both the manipulative possibilities of figurative language in general and the structural role which it can play in argument. Richards' work in a sense may thus be said to rehabilitate rhetoric at its own expense. The relation of classical understandings of rhetoric to Richards' 'new' philosophy of discourse consists in little more than their sharing of a common appellation.

In the United States the leading figure in establishing the legitimacy of rhetorical approaches to literature has been Wayne Booth. His major work on literature, *The Rhetoric of Fiction* (2nd edn, Chicago: 1983), focuses upon 'the technique of non-didactic fiction, viewed as the art of communicating with readers – the rhetorical resources available to the writer of epic, novel, or short story as he tries, consciously or unconsciously, to impose his fictional world upon the reader' (p. xiii). While Booth's work on the rhetoric of fictional narrative undoubtedly builds upon certain concepts from classical rhetoric, particularly audience and *ethos*, the connections are largely implicit and unacknowledged. In another influential work, however, Booth much more clearly addresses the traditional domain of rhetoric: *Modern Dogma and the Rhetoric of Assent* (Chicago: 1974) deals with what Booth regarded as the central crisis of political culture in the 1960s and 1970s: the loss of 'faith in the very possibility of finding a rational path through any thicket that includes what we call value judgements' (p. 7). This loss of faith is embodied in certain dogmas of modernism which, taken together, produce the conviction that rational discourse about values and purposes is not possible because judgements about such matters ultimately can rest only upon individual desires and ends. To find a remedy for these ills Booth proposes a return to 'rhetoric as the whole art of discovering and sharing warrantable assertion' (p. 11). In other words, Booth's aim is to revive a notion of rhetoric as the public discourse by which communities deliberate, articulate their values and reach consensus. The first part of the book is taken up with a diagnosis of the crisis of modernism and the rest develops the analysis of the rhetoric of warranted assent. The model for this rhetoric of assent draws heavily upon classical conceptions of deliberation. Booth argues that human beings are by nature creatures who manipulate symbols, communicate, exchange information, persuade and, in the process, make and remake themselves. This very Aristotelian formulation leads to a redefinition of persuasion as aiming not at imposing a preconceived view upon others, but rather at engaging in mutual enquiry and exploration (pp. 136–7). This process of enquiry and exploration, in turn, enables individuals to fulfil their natures as 'creature[s] capable of responding to symbolic offerings'. According to this again very Aristotelian argument it follows that 'the process of inquiry through discourse thus becomes more important than any possible conclusions, and whatever stultifies such fulfillment becomes demonstrably wrong' (p. 137). When individuals respect the rules and steps of enquiry the conclusions 'are as solid as the problems and circumstances allow for' (p. 138). For Booth, then, rhetoric becomes a 'supremely self-justifying activity', which can provide the basis for consensus through 'warrantable assent' as long as individuals agree on conventions by which they can reason together. This agreement offers an escape from the modernist conundrum: 'In our rhetorical terms, we can't get anywhere on any problem unless we *agree* on some knowledge for which the best proof is that we *agree* about it' (p. 139). Building upon this elevated vision of the rhetoric of assent, he then turns to an analysis of the 'proofs' by which 'warrants' are produced. Here too Booth's schema is heavily indebted to its classical antecedents, for his theory of proofs follows the Aristotelian tripartite typology of logical, ethical and emotional appeals (pp. 144 ff.).

Booth's theory of rhetoric is valuable in its reminder of the political and cultural context in which classical rhetoric operated and the social ends which it could serve. On the other hand, the foundation of Booth's argument on a teleological argument from a certain account of human nature would require a good deal more explanation before it could support the weighty claims which he rests upon it. In some sense one might regard Habermas' *Theory of Communicative Action* as attempting to provide a fuller account of the discursive preconditions for what Booth terms 'assent'. Be that as it may, in the following section it will appear that while Booth turns to classical rhetoric as a way of grounding values in the face of modernist scepticism, post-modernist theorists typically invoke the classical tradition precisely to buttress scepticism against philosophical claims of knowledge and truth.

2

Gérard Genette in 'Rhetoric Restrained' described the mis-appropriation of the classical tradition in linguistic and literary theory in the 1960s to 1970s.[3] According to Genette this period marked the culmination of a process of restriction of the field of classical rhetoric which had begun at least in the middle ages if not already in late antiquity. With the withering of the institutions which gave deliberative and epideictic oratory their social meaning, rhetoric as a whole became increasingly identified with what classical rhetoricians like Aristotle and Cicero had regarded as but one of its parts (indeed, one of its lesser parts): *elocutio*. In the contemporary period, Genette claims, this process has been carried *ad absurdum* not only to confine rhetoric to the study of figures but also to confine the study of figures to metaphor and metonymy.

Genette locates the modern origins of what he calls 'tropo-logical reduction' in the eighteenth and nineteenth century rhetorical treatises of Dumarsais and Fontanier, who, by empha-sising the primacy of the opposition between liberal and figurative meaning, 'turn rhetoric into a consideration of figuration, a turnstile of the figurative defined as the other of the literal' (*Figures*, p. 105). In essence, rhetoric is redefined: its centring in civic discourse, persuasion, argumentation and deliberation are 'forgotten', and one appendage of the 'art of rhetoric' is detached and substituted, in splendid isolation, for the whole. Genette goes on to show how the redefinition of rhetoric by Dumarsais, Fontanier and others in turn sets the stage for the further reduction of rhetoric in Russian Formalism and subsequent literary offshoots. Here, the 'figures of connection', like synecdoche, are reduced to the 'single model of spatial metonymy' (p. 110), and the array of figures of analogy are narrowed until they are all subsumed within metaphor. Genette shows how such a theory of figures of analogy, centred on metaphor alone, cannot encompass a wide variety of literary effects which a more differentiated classical appreciation would perceive. In illustration he tabulates ten separate figures of analogy to show that 'metaphor is merely one form among many others, and that its promotion to the rank of the figure of analogy *par excellence* is the result of some sort of takeover' (p. 113).[4]

As if the reduction of figurative rhetoric to the opposition of metonymy–metaphor were not enough, continental rhetorical theory, Genette claims, has taken the process of reduction even further. He criticises in particular the efforts of the Belgian school, the 'Group mu' of Liège, according to which all 'shift of meaning' is metaphor:

> If poetry is a space that opens up in language, if through it words speak again and meaning becomes significant again, it is because there is between the everyday language and rediscovered speech a shift of meaning, metaphor. Metaphor is no longer, from this point of view, *a* figure among others, but *the* figure, the trope of tropes.[5]

Exposing the inevitable distortions which this view, as promulgated by Sojcher, Deguy and others, accomplishes upon texts, Genette concludes with a call for a reassessment of the relation of metaphor to a 'new rhetoric' which would be a semiotics of all discourses. The path to such a rejuvenation of rhetoric is indicated, he says, by a line from Verdi's Falstaff: 'Torniamo all'antico, sara un progresso' (*Figures*, p. 121).

Genette's advice for a rejuvenation of rhetoric by a return to its classical antecedents was clearly a reference to work already begun by Roland Barthes.[6] In 1964–5 Barthes gave a seminar on classical rhetoric in the École pratique des hautes études. Out of this seminar came an essay on classical rhetoric originally entitled 'L'ancienne rhétorique',[7] and subsequently republished in English as 'The Old Rhetoric: An *Aide Mémoire*'.[8] The essay is interesting on two counts. First, although it takes the form of an objective presentation of the history of rhetoric from classical Greece to nineteenth-century France, it is in fact Barthes' unique interpretation of that history. As such, it is an essay which repays careful analysis to see the often subtle ways in which Barthes' own orientation to the study of discourse has influenced his appreciation of the classical tradition. This is most evident, perhaps, in his treatment of the 'merger' of rhetoric and poetics in the Roman and Mediaeval periods. Further, the essay is important because of the agenda which it indicates. Barthes devoted a seminar to the topic not because he had an antiquarian interest in the history of rhetoric, but rather because of a conviction that an account of the classical tradition was a necessary foundation for a contemporary semiotics. Thus, he introduces rhetoric as 'that metalanguage (whose language-object was discourse) prevalent in the West from the fifth century B.C. to the nineteenth century A.D.' (*Semiotic Challenge*, p. 12). The importance of that metalanguage for a semiotician like Barthes is its under-appreciated centrality for an understanding of the literature, language, instruction and institutions of the western tradition. Thus, he claims, 'a history of Rhetoric . . . is today necessary, broadened by a new way of thinking (linguistics, semiology, historical science, psychoanalysis, Marxism)' (ibid.). More specifically, Barthes believes that Aristotle offers the key for an understanding of contemporary mass-culture. Because our ideology of democracy is constructed on notions of 'the greatest number, of the majority-as-norm, or current opinion', our civilisation 'is that of the *endoxa*' (*Semiotic Challenge*, p. 92). Accordingly, the poetics, logic and rhetoric of Aristotle together furnish a 'complete analytical grid' for the 'entire language – narrative, discursive, argumentative – of mass communications . . . In a democratic system, Aristotelianism would be the best of cultural sociologies.'[9] With these grandiose visions it becomes clear why Genette looked to Barthes as indicating the way out of the 'reduction' of rhetoric to the study of one or two figures. On Barthes' view, an understanding of the classical rhetorical tradition as the metalanguage of western culture provides the means for linking language and society within a cultural sociology which encompasses the entire human activity. This linkage, in turn, provides the foundation for Barthes' own multi-faceted interpretative and critical enterprise.

Hayden White, on the other hand, in *Metahistory* (Baltimore: 1973) and *Tropics of Discourse* (Baltimore: 1978) focuses upon tropology ('tropics') as the key to historical discourse. Relying on Kenneth Burke, White identifies four master tropes (metaphor, metonymy, synecdoche and irony) which represent a 'level of consciousness on which a world of experience is constituted prior to being analysed' (*Metahistory*, p. 33). These master tropes thus permit a specification of 'styles of thought' which are embedded in any 'representation of reality' (ibid.). Applying this claim to historical discourse White argues that the four master tropes provide 'a way of characterising the dominant modes of historical thinking which took shape in Europe in the nineteenth century' (p. 38). In other words, the master tropes mark four stages in the evolution of the 'historical imagination', and each corresponds to a 'mode of employment' (romance, comedy, tragedy, satire), a 'mode of explanation' (idiographic, organistic, mechanistic, contextualist) and a 'mode of ideological implication' (anarchist, conservative, radical, liberal) (p. 29). Each of these modes, in turn, is represented by the work of one of the great nineteenth-century historians: Michelet, Ranke, de Tocqueville and Burckhardt. While the merits of White's historiographical claims are not of concern here, his methodology is illustrative of some of the problems identified by Genette and Barthes. First, although White (*Metahistory*, pp. 31–2) rejects the reductionism of the 'Metaphorical–Metonymical dyad' postulated by Jakobsen and others, as Vickers points out his account is none the less itself reductive 'in its concern with four tropes only' (*In Defence of Rhetoric*, p. 442). Further, it is also reductive in the more profound sense identified by Genette in that it wrests figurative rhetoric from its classical context and establishes it as a kind of master analytical matrix for the analysis of all discourse. Unlike Barthes' attempt to re-situate discursive and cultural analysis within 'metalanguage' of the classical rhetorical tradition, White seems to detach figural rhetoric from the schema that gave it meaning and reconstitute it as a means of uncovering the unconscious structural principles of language and thought. It is only in this way that the tropes come to signify not a persuasive authorial intention but rather the mark of an evolutionary 'Geist' silently at work beneath the textual surface of discourse.

Classical rhetoric has also provided fruitful ground for scholars motivated to question the underpinnings of the western philo-sophical tradition, particularly its epistemology and metaphysics.

Thus, Jacques Derrida has continually invoked the classical tradition as a way of articulating certain concerns about knowledge and interpretation. Although this is not the place for a systematic account of Derrida's complex and often baffling *oeuvre*, his extended essay, 'Plato's Pharmacy', does illustrate some of the uses to which a revisiting of the natal site of the philosophy–rhetoric controversy may be put.[10] The essay begins as an interrogation of Plato's criticism of writing in the *Phaedrus*, and in typical Derridean fashion soon invokes a wide variety of other texts and traditions to investigate the problem of the distinction between the 'good' and the 'bad' *logos*. The crucial term in this discourse on discourse turns out to be the *'pharmakon'*, which, as Derrida shows, plays a variety of roles in *Phaedrus* and other Platonic dialogues.

The word *pharmakon* has a variety of meanings encompassing drug, medicine, poison, remedy, charm, spell, cure and antidote. In a crucial section of the essay Derrida focuses on the way in which the Socratic *pharmakon* is prescribed as the remedy for the sophistic *pharmakon*, whose 'spell' or 'charm' Plato sees as a kind of poison requiring an antidote. Derrida here relies mainly upon Gorgias' analysis of the nature of persuasion (*peitho*) in his *Encomium of Helen* for the notion that the power of speech (*logos*) is comparable to the power of drugs in the way that it acts upon the soul. For Derrida, Plato inevitably casts Socrates as the *pharmakeus*, the 'poisoner/wizard/sorcerer', whose 'venom' penetrates the soul of those who associate with him: 'Socratic irony precipitates out one *pharmakon* by bringing it in contact with another *pharmakon*' (*Dissemination*, p. 119). What then is the Socratic *pharmakon*, the counterspell or antidote which possesses this exorcising power? It is, of course, training in dialectics, which alone can counteract the rhetorician's spell: 'The *eidos*, truth, law, the *episteme*, dialectics, philosophy – all these are other names for that *pharmakon* that must be opposed to the *pharmakon* of the Sophists and to the bewitching fear of death . . . Philosophy thus opposes to its other the transmutation of the drug into a remedy, of the poison into a counterpoison' (ibid., pp. 124–5). Yet, having established the *pharmakon* as the Platonic focal point of the opposition of rhetoric and dialectic, Derrida immediately moves to problematise the *pharmakon* and undermine the opposition concluding that in the end 'one can no more "separate" them from each other, think of either one apart from the other, "label" them, than one can in *the pharmacy* distinguish the medicine from the poison, the good from the evil, the true from the false' (p. 169). Thus, Derrida's revisitation of the classical tradition where Plato establishes the pre-eminence of philosophy over rhetoric serves to demonstrate the instability of that hierarchy and its epistemological under-pinnings. In the end, the deconstructionist reading unravels the opposition in demonstrating, at least to the satisfaction of Derrida, that the 'good' and the 'bad' *logos* of Platonic discourse are in fact indistinguishable.[11]

Like Derrida Michael Foucault turned to the classical tradition, and particularly the classical ascendancy of philosophy over rhetoric, as the origin of that western understanding of truth and discourse which he wanted to critique. Though a number of his major works are concerned with reinterpreting this heritage, perhaps nowhere did he so explicitly focus upon the theory of discourse as in his famous inaugural lecture at the Collège de France. This essay, 'The Order of the Discourse',[12] proposes to identify the procedures by which in our society discourse is 'at once controlled, selected, organised, and redistributed by a certain number of procedures whose role is to ward off its powers, to gain mastery over its chance events, to evade its ponderous, formidable materiality' (p. 109). He begins by identifying three principles of exclusion: prohibition, the division of reason and madness and the rejection of the latter and, finally, the opposition between true and false. It is that last principle of exclusion which is of greatest interest here for, according to Foucault, it finds its origin in the classical rejection of the sophist and the philosophical (that is, Platonic) production of a 'will to truth'. This 'will to truth' informs institutional structures and discursive practices in areas as diverse as education, publishing, science, economics and law. Indeed, Foucault seems to argue that this principle of exclusion has pulled the other two within its orbit as part of that framework which, since the Greeks, has operated to produce the appearance that the discourse of truth is independent of the realm of desire and power. For Foucault, on the other hand, this separation is merely an insidious mask which hides that what is really at stake in this 'will to truth' is precisely desire and power – hence his variation on the Nietzschean formulation (pp. 112–14).

Foucault goes on to identify a number of central tenets of western philosophy as corresponding to these principles of exclusion.[13] These include the notion of 'an ideal truth as the law of discourse' and 'ethic of knowledge which promises to give the truth only to the desire for truth itself and only to the power of thinking it' ('Order of the Discourse', p. 124). These philosophical tenets reinforce the principles of exclusion by denying the reality and the force of discourse itself. Whereas the sophists insisted upon discourse as an independent realm whose forces could be mastered to act upon the souls of individuals and communities, philosophy sought to banish these tricks and deceits so as to ensure 'that discourse should occupy the smallest possible space between thought and speech' (ibid.). This postulation of the transparency of discourse, where, as it were, nothing happens between thought and its physical vocalisation, of course denies the existence of rhetoric and its linkage to the production of meaning.

In this tradition discourse is reduced to signs made visible by words, and in this process of writing and reading 'discourse is annulled in its reality and put at the disposal of the signifier' (p. 125). The root of this tendency is, paradoxically, a culture which is apparently 'logophilic' but is in reality profoundly 'logophobic', fearful of the 'great incessant and discordant buzzing of discourse' (p. 126). Foucault concludes this abbreviated and schematic portrayal of this ascendancy of philosophy and repression of discourse with what is, though he does not use this label, a call for the revival of the classical understanding of rhetoric. He formulates this call in three decisions which he calls upon us to make and which, he says, will govern the work upon which he will subsequently embark: '[W]e must call into question our will to truth, restore to discourse its character as event, and finally throw off the sovereignty of the signifier' (p. 126). From the perspective of these three demands a full account of Foucault's significance for contemporary rhetorical theory would have to trace the way in which this agenda informs subsequent works such as *The Order of Things*, *Discipline and Punish* and *The History of Sexuality*, which could then be read as attempts to open our eyes to the nature and institutional settings of discursive practices and their unbreakable links to the realms of power and desire.

NOTES

1 *Realm of Rhetoric*, p. 162, quoting Jens ('alte und neue Königin der Wissenschaften').

2 I. A. Richards, *The Philosophy of Rhetoric* (Oxford: 1936), p. 8.

3 G. Genette, *Figures of Literary Discourse* (New York: 1982), pp. 103–26.

4 Cf. Paul de Man's discussion of rhetoric, metaphor and metonymy in *Allegories of Reading* (New Haven: 1979), pp. 17–19 and Brian Vickers' criticisms of de Man in *In Defence of Rhetoric* (Oxford: 1988), pp. 453–67.

5 Sojcher, 'La métaphore généralisée', quoted by Genette, *Figures*, p. 115; cf. the discussion of Richards above.

6 See Genette, *Figures*, n. 41.

7 *Communications* 16 (1970).

8 R. Barthes, *The Semiotic Challenge* (New York: 1978), pp. 11–93.

9 *Semiotic Challenge*, p. 92, and see also 'Rhetorical Analysis', in R. Barthes, *The Rustle of Language* (Berkeley: 1989), pp. 88–9.

10 J. Derrida, 'Plato's Pharmacy', appears in *Dissemination* (Chicago: 1981), pp. 61–171.

11 Cf. Lyotard's use of the opposition of Platonic and sophistic methods of argument in his enquiry into the discourse of dispute in *The Differend* (Minneapolis: 1988), pp. 14–26.

12 References are to the translation which appears as chapter 7 of *Language and Politics*, ed. M. Shapiro (Oxford: 1984), pp. 108–38. 'The Order of the Discourse' is also available in an appendix to *The Archaeology of Knowledge* (New York: 1985) and in the collection *Untying the Text*, ed. R. Young (London: 1981), pp. 51–77.

13 He also introduces the notion of 'internal limitations' on discourse which operate in conjunction with the principles of exclusion. These limitations include the traditions of 'commentary' and 'the author' but, provocative as they may be, they are not directly related to the themes addressed here.

Part II
APPLICATIONS

5

Power and oratory in democratic Athens: Demosthenes 21, against Meidias

Josiah Ober

To study politics and political life is to study power and the play of power. But what is power? A simple definition of a powerful entity might be 'one with the ability to satisfy its own desires by instrumentally affecting the behaviour of others'.[1] This simple definition leaves a lot undecided: what sorts of entities are we talking about (individuals? corporate groups?), and what are their desires? These questions can be answered (at least in a preliminary way) by applying the definition to a concrete historical situation. In the case of fourth-century Athens, it is clear enough that there were powerful individuals within society – most obviously wealthy men capable of affecting the behaviour of workers (whether slave or free) and of satisfying their desires for material goods by appropriating the surplus generated by the labour of others. On the other hand, it is equally obvious that the fourth-century Athenian demos, as a collective entity, was powerful in that it was often able to satisfy its desires for (*inter alia*) autarchy (in the Aristotelian sense) and autonomy by affecting the behaviour of both Athenian citizens and others in a variety of ways (for example, by levying taxes and paying soldiers to protect state interests and assets). In Athens, as in other societies, the spheres dominated by different powerful entities sometimes came into conflict; notable among these conflicts was the clash between public and private interests. There was a high potential for discord between powerful Athenian individuals (for example, rich men who wished to retain the use of their wealth to satisfy their private desires) and the demos (which was determined to put some part of that wealth to public use in ensuring autarchy and autonomy). A good number of 'individual vs. community' conflicts were eventually adjudicated in the lawcourts of Athens. And hence dicanic oratory was among the primary instruments whereby the power of the individual Athenian was tested against the power of the demos. The study of oratory in Athens should, therefore, be able to tell us something about how power worked in democratic Athens – and vice versa. But before we can hope to understand the instrumental role of oratory in negotiating the play of power in Athenian society, we will have to refine and expand our definition of power.

There is a large modern literature on the subject of power; here I will focus on two major paradigms. The first and more traditional approach to power, which we may call the 'coercion' paradigm, sees power as centred in the state and fundamentally based on force or the threat of force; that is, the ability to deploy violent physical coercion.[2] The state, as sovereign authority, attempts to mon-opolise the right to use force legitimately within society (for example, by police actions) and to deploy force externally (by making war). The state is the primary locus of power in that all holders of legitimate protections and privileges within society (for example, property-owners and citizens) look to the state to exert force when necessary to enforce those protections and privileges. Thus, for example, if my brother is murdered or my house is robbed, I must expect agents of the state to apprehend and punish the perpetrator, rather than taking vengeance myself. And, on the other hand, as long as I obey the laws and fulfil my various duties and responsibilities as a member of society, I can expect to remain free from the operations of power. This model sees power as essentially juridical and repressive. Both those who approve of and those who oppose the state and its ideals can agree that, according to the coercion paradigm, power is exerted in order to repress behaviour that is deemed likely to threaten the sovereign authority of the state and which contravenes its laws.

The second approach to power, which we may call the 'discourse' paradigm, is less interested in overt coercion, sov-ereignty, state apparatuses, and law as such. It focuses instead on how social and political knowledge is produced and disseminated throughout society.[3] According to this second paradigm, power is not centralised anywhere, and is neither 'legitimate' nor 'illegitimate'. Thus sovereignty is not at issue and a study of formal juridical institutions alone will not reveal the fundamental workings of power. Rather than seeing power as repressive, the discourse paradigm sees power as productive: it emerges through the production of social understandings regarding what is true and what behaviours are right, proper, even conceivable. As a consequence, the concept of freedom becomes problematic. Since power is productive and omnipresent (rather than repressive and located in the state) it is not simply a matter of my being free to do whatever is not prohibited. Rather, all of my social interactions, including my speech, are (at least potentially) bound up with a regime of power that is also a regime of truth. It is not easy to get outside power, since all forms of social communication (including speech) will depend upon generally agreed-upon truths (for example, schemes of social categorisation) as the fundamental premises of meaningful interchange. Coercive violence itself is thus part of discourse: the regime of knowledge will prescribe under what conditions one category of person may or may not perpetrate violence upon another and what constitutes violence (for example, whether a free man may strike a slave or whether it is is meaningful to speak of a husband raping his wife). The regime of knowledge/ truth/ power is thus maintained through discourse. A key question that faces the student of power working within the discourse paradigm is how, and by whom, social understandings are produced and reproduced – or challenged and overthrown.

Which of these two approaches is most useful in assessing the *dunamis* of the individual, the *kratos* of the Athenian demos and their relationship to public oratory in the fourth century? The applicability of a coercion paradigm of power to the Athenian polis, is, I believe, necessarily limited by its dependence on the notion of the sovereign state – a concept that seems to have been foreign to the demotic Athenian understanding of state and society.[4] There are, on the other hand, obvious affinities (some of which were discussed by Plato and Aristotle) between formal rhetoric and the broader realm of social and political discourse.[5] Thus, I will argue here that focusing on power as discourse will explain more about how persuasive public speech functioned in classical *demokratia* than would an exclusive focus on power as overt coercion.

If we describe the set of assumptions employed in decision-making by most Athenians as a 'regime of truth', it becomes apparent that one of the key 'truths' upon which democratic Athenian society depended was that citizens were simultaneously equals and unequals. Citizens were equals in the public realm of political (including judicial) decision-making. In the public sphere every citizen's vote had (in principle anyway) identical weight. The introduction of pay for public service and the use of the lot ensured that every citizen (at least those over thirty) had equal access to the perquisites and the risks associated with most forms of government activity (for example, magistracies).[6] In the fourth century most Athenians, including the elite, seemed willing to live with public, political equality – in any event there was no systematic effort to challenge it between 403 and 322. Yet citizens remained unequal in private life. Despite the fears of elite critics of democracy, the Athenian demos never consistently employed its collective power to equalise access to desirable material goods.[7] In so far as happiness is measured by ease of access to material goods, the rich Athenian lived a happier life than his poor neighbour. All Athenians knew that and most seemed to be quite willing to live with it. Why were elite Athenians willing to tolerate public equality and why did ordinary Athenians, for their part, willingly countenance private inequality? Opacity is not an adequate answer; the Athenian regime of truth was unable to obscure fully the contradiction or the complexity of the balancing act: Theophrastus' 'Oligarchic Man', who expresses his anti-democratic ideas in the Assembly (*Characters* 26.2) as well as to strangers (*xenoi*) and like-minded associates (26.7) and complains that it is shaming to have to sit next to his social inferiors in the Assembly (26.5), expresses in comic terms what we may guess was a fairly widespread sense of unease among the elite.[8] Aristotle (*Politics* 1301a25–39 and 1302a24–31) believed that the tendency of democrats was to generalise equality (and so to oppress superior members of society) while that of oligarchs was to generalise inequality (and so to oppress the poor); both tendencies, to Aristotle, were unjust and led to instability. In the *Politics* he unsuccessfully attempted a solution to the problem of balancing equalities by devising a system of mathematical proportions.[9] How did the Athenian regime finesse the problem?

In *Mass and Elite in Democratic Athens* I argued that powerful elite individuals and the mass of ordinary citizens who composed the demos struck and maintained a viable social contract in part through the discursive operations of public oratory. In the Assembly and especially in the lawcourts, individual speakers employed the power of speech (sharpened in some cases by formal training in the arts of rhetoric) in an attempt to explain themselves – their lives, their needs, their current circumstances, and their relationship to the demos – to mass audiences. The audience in turn assessed the form and the content of the speaker's address, sometimes responding vocally to specific comments. After the speeches had been delivered, the members of the audience exerted power through their collective judgement. In the ongoing dialectical give and take of public oratory, audience response, and demotic judgement, a set of common attitudes and social rules was hammered out. Thus Athenian ideology, the discursive basis of Athenian society, was not given from on high and was not a unique product of elite culture, but rather it was established and constantly revised in the practice of public debate. The matrix of power within which oratory was practised in democratic Athens made the *techne* of public speaking both dangerous and exciting. The Athenians were well aware of both the speaker's power – his desire and ability to sway his audience; and the power of the audience – its willingness and ability to punish the speaker for rhetorical missteps. Furthermore, the content of many speeches was overtly concerned with issues of power. In the Assembly, the question was often how Athenian military strength could be increased and how it should be deployed. In the lawcourts, the issue was frequently whether or not a display of personal power by an individual Athenian had abrogated Athenian rules regarding appropriate social behaviour.

The theme of 'personal power vs. social rules' was especially to the fore in cases involving charges of *hubris*. 'Insolent outrage' is a reasonable enough translation for the term as it was used in Attic oratory, but Athenian law never spelled out exactly what behaviours constituted acts of *hubris*.[10] Because the law did not explain to him what *hubris* was, the juryman in a *graphe hubreos* (or other action in which the law against *hubris* was invoked) had to judge the entire social context: the social and political statuses of litigant and defendant; their families, friends, and past behaviour; the location and timing of the incident; and its ramifications for the whole of the demos.[11] This lack of nomothetic specificity is a problem for the coercion paradigm with its concern for 'rule of law', but it makes perfect sense within the discursive paradigm of power. The Athenian juror did not judge litigants according to an externalised, juridicially 'given' model of appropriate behaviour. Rather, he judged within and through a regime of social knowledge and truth, a regime which his decision would participate in articulating – whether by strengthening existing assumptions about social categories and behaviour or by revising them.

For the historian, the proof of any analytic pardigm lies in its practical explanatory usefulness. In *Mass and Elite in Democratic Athens* I applied discourse analysis to the corpus of Attic oratory; here (belatedly responding to a suggestion by Daniel Tompkins) I propose to focus on a single oration. Demosthenes 21 (*Against Meidias*) is a particularly good example of the relationship between oratory and power that I have sketched out in abstract terms above. Whether or not it was formally a *graphe hubreos*, the case did centre on a charge of *hubris*. Demosthenes' speech is openly concerned with defining the limits of behaviour appropriate to the most powerful individuals in Athenian society, and with the public consequences of allowing those limits to be breached (8). Moreover, after years of neglect, a new critical edition of the speech has appeared, as have significant interpretive articles. This new scholarship has clarified (even where it has not resolved) issues of chronology, law, composition, and delivery.[12]

The specific incidents that led Demosthenes to bring charges against Meidias are laid out clearly in the speech's narrative (13–19): in the spring of 348 Demosthenes was *choregos* for his tribe Pandionis. His preparations for the presentation of his tribal chorus at the Festival of Dionysus were hampered in various ways by Meidias, a well-known wealthy politician who had an old personal quarrel with Demosthenes. Demosthenes persevered and presented the chorus, but at the Dionysia itself, in the orchestra of the theatre, Meidias punched Demosthenes in the face. At the Assembly meeting held in the theatre following the Dionysia, Demosthenes brought a *probole* against Meidias, charging him with misconduct during the festival. The vote of the Assembly went against Meidias (6). This prejudicial judgement in a *probole* did not entail punishment of the miscreant,[13] but gave Demosthenes a boost in their future dealings by demonstrating that public opinion was behind him: the demos agreed that Meidias' behaviour had been out of line. If Demosthenes wanted more than a moral victory, however, it was up to him to bring formal charges in a *dikasterion*. For whatever reason, Demosthenes did not immediately do so. Here certainty about the course of events ends.

Demosthenes 21, as we have it, purports to be a prosecutor's speech, delivered in a public lawsuit (not a *dike idia*: 25, 28) before an Athenian *dikasterion* by Demosthenes in 347/6. Yet since antiquity (Plut. *Demosthenes* 12; Dion. Hal. *First Letter to Ammaeus* 4), readers of the speech have expressed doubts about whether it was actually delivered. These doubts apparently stem from a passage in Aeschines (3.51–52) claiming that Demosthenes 'sold' (*apedoto*) for thirty minai both the '*hubris* to himself and the adverse vote of the demos given in the precinct of Dionysus against Meidias'. It has often been supposed that this passage proves that Demosthenes accepted a bribe and so did not pursue the charge in the courts after the initial *probole* in the Assembly. But then why did he write the speech? Several theories have been proposed attempting to reconcile the fact of the speech's existence with Aeschines' statement: it is claimed that certain passages show signs of incompleteness – and ergo that the speech was begun when Demosthenes still planned to prosecute Meidias but was never completed because the bribe subsequently induced him to abandon his plan. Yet the stylistic argument for incompleteness is not very convincing in and of itself; each of the supposed weaknesses, redundancies, and inconsistencies has been vigorously defended by those who suppose that the speech does represent an essentially finished product.[14]

If left unfinished and never delivered, the publication of the speech against Meidias (which concentrates on the prosecutor's bravery and steadfastness in bringing the case before the jury: 3, 40 and 120) would have been a political and stylistic embarrassment to Demosthenes. Anomalous circumstances must therefore be adduced to explain its eventual publication.[15] Furthermore, the 'no trial' hypothesis requires Demosthenes to have written a nearly complete speech *before* ever bringing a formal indictment against Meidias: Demosthenes, as prosecutor, would have suffered *atimia* if he had brought charges in a public case before a magistrate and then withdrawn them (103; and see below); Aeschines could hardly have failed to mention that juicy fact. Yet, as E. M. Harris points out, it would be very odd indeed for Demosthenes to have written the speech so early in the legal process. Harris concludes that there is no *a priori* reason for us to believe Aeschines' claim. It was made in respect to events that had occurred some sixteen years previously and few in the audience at the trial of Ctesiphon in 330 would remember the exact course of events. The fact that Meidias was not severely punished (as he clearly was not, since he was politically active in the years after 347/6) allowed Aeschines to make up the vague bribery story and leave his listeners to decide whether he meant that bribery forestalled prosecution or that the prosecutor was bribed to propose an excessively light penalty.[16] In sum, the case for supposing that *Against Meidias* was never delivered is no more compelling than one that might be made against other major public speeches in the Demosthenic corpus (for example, 20, 22 or 23). I will proceed on the assumption that we are dealing with a speech that was delivered in a *dikasterion* in more or less the form we have it, and was subsequently published by its author.

The internal evidence of the speech indicates that the trial of Meidias took place about two years after the incident in the theatre. In 347/6, stung by an (unsuccessful) attack launched by Meidias at his *dokimasia* for the office of *bouleutes* (111, 114), Demosthenes reopened the issue of the punch by lodging his complaint with one of the *thesmothetai* (presumably having summoned Meidias to appear before the magistrate as well).[17] The indictment would have been publicly announced by being posted in front of the Eponymous heroes (cf. 103). There has been considerable discussion of what procedural category Demosthenes employed in his indictment. Although Demosthenes harps on *hubris* throughout the speech, MacDowell (among others) has challenged the assumption that it was a *graphe hubreos*, arguing that the *probole* procedure covered both the initial action in the Assembly and the subsequent trial in the *dikasterion*.[18] This point of law has little bearing on my argument; in either case we are dealing with a public *agon timetos* (25: ergo a guilty verdict would be followed by a second set of speeches offering alternate penalties, any fine levied went to the state rather than to the prosecutor, and penalties would be imposed if the prosecutor withdrew the charge or failed to secure one-fifth of the votes). If the jury trial was a continuation of the *probole*, a court date was probably set at the first hearing before the *thesmothetes*; if a *graphe hubreos*, there would have been a preliminary hearing (*anakrisis*) before the magistrate at which much of the evidence would be presented.[19] As Harris points out (see above), the speech was surely written between the time that the preliminary charge was lodged and the trial itself, and surely after the *anakrisis* if there was one.

At the trial itself, Demosthenes and Meidias each used the power of oratory in attempting to persuade the jury to vote in his favour. But that power depended on a close 'fit' with audience expectations and presuppositions. This meant adapting form and content of the rhetorical performance to the ideological context determined by an audience representing a cross-section of the mature (over thirty) citizen male population of Athens – overwhelmingly men who were not members of a social elite.[20] The two litigants, on the other hand, were both celebrities, members of the same elite social category: both were very wealthy, both highly skilled speakers, both *rhetores*; that is, members of Athens' small cadre of expert politicians.[21] Thus, from the point of view of a juror whose judgement was based on established social categories, there might be little to choose between the two contestants. But social categorisation would not be the sole basis of his judgement. Both men would probably be known to him, at least by reputation – and he might well have heard them speak in Assembly or at previous trials.[22] The architectonics of each contestant's rhetorical self-presentation therefore consisted of building upon the audience's existing opinion of himself, using his rhetorical skills as his tools. The building materials included the facts of the case, the life histories of the litigants and the audience's social presuppositions.

Among Demosthenes' problems in constructing a persuasive case against Meidias was the relative slightness of the offence, a problem that was exacerbated by the passage of time. The positive vote at the initial *probole* in the Assembly was certainly in his favour, but two years later who really cared if one rich politician had bopped another in the nose? Given the existence of a strongly anti-elitist streak in Athenian popular ideology, Demosthenes must have worried that many jurors would see the incident as a silly intra-elite spat, and one that could have been solved quickly enough if Demosthenes had just been man enough to hit back. Demosthenes' central problem, then, was the tendency of the jurors to lump himself and Meidias into a single social category ('over-powerful elite politicians'). If that category were distinct from the one in which the jurors placed themselves ('regular guys'), there was a dreadful likelihood that the jurors would take on the role of spectators of a rather foolish tiff among people for whom they felt no inherent sympathy. They might simply laugh the case out of court. Thus, among Demosthenes' rhetorical goals was to draw a crystal clear set of distinctions between himself and his adversary. Meidias is to be stranded beyond an unbridgeable gulf constructed by Demosthenes' oration; on the near side stands the prosecutor, shoulder-to-shoulder with the demos. But it was more complex than that; Demosthenes must also remind the audience of his own continued possession of elite characteristics, since on these characteristics rested his claim to the privileged political position accorded the *rhetor*.[23] In sum, since the construction of social categories was a key part of Athens' truth regime (that is, the understandings the jury would use in their judgement), Demosthenes must work with a set of assumptions about the category to which both he and Meidias belonged. At the same time he must confound assumptions about the homogeneity of the category. He must explain to the audience that 'we are indeed both elite and both powerful, but we are very different sorts of men in terms of our worth to the demos'.

The actual speech negotiates these difficulties with great finesse. The unbridgeable gulf between Demosthenes/demos and Meidias is brilliantly sketched. In a number of passages Meidias is shown to be vastly wealthy and, as a direct result of that wealth, arrogant (66–67, 96, 98, 100, 194) and scornful of the demos and those he regards as his inferiors (132, 134, 185, 193–195, 198, 203–204, 211). Worse yet, his wealth gave him considerable power within the society, power which he wilfully used to destroy those ordinary citizens who stood in the way of fulfilling his desires (20, 98, 106, 109, 123–124, 137). In sum, Meidias was 'rich, bold, with a big head and a big voice, violent, [and] shameless' (201). Meidias could be depicted as *sui generis*, isolated within society in wilful self-exile (198). But elsewhere Demosthenes locates the entire class of the excessively wealthy across the gulf with Meidias. Here he suggests that Meidias' behaviour is indicative of the anti-democratic attitudes harboured by the wealthy elite: they longed to gain control of the state and if they ever did come to power, they would be merciless to the ordinary working man (208–210). In contrast to rich Meidias and his rich cronies, Demosthenes paints a picture of himself as a middling sort of man: a hoplite (not a cavalryman, like Meidias) who, along with his fellow soldiers, was shocked by lurid tales of Meidias' combined cowardice and grotesque extravagance during the Euboean campaign (133; cf. 1 and 112).

In other passages Demosthenes presents himself rather differently: not among those who are weak or friendless, but indeed as a member of the Athenian elite, able and willing to use his elite attributes – wealth, speaking ability, standing in the community – to help defend the rest of the citizens against the likes of Meidias (111, 189, 192 and 219). And thus he reveals himself as a powerful figure in his own right. Demosthenes must, of course, sidestep the appearance of arrogance. He avoids contradicting Athenian assumptions regarding the reality of popular control of affairs by pointing out that he is not alone in his heroic resistance to Meidias. Time and again, Demosthenes claims allegiance to and alliance with the laws – in one dramatic passage he literally takes the reified laws of Athens as his kin, asking the jury to contrast him, surrounded by the laws, with Meidias, surrounded by weepy relatives.[24] This striking image reveals a vital distinction Demosthenes establishes between himself and his rival. Whereas Meidias depends on his family for support, Demosthenes is a public figure, devoted to the public good. He is, at least by implication, a powerful man only through the backing of the actively expressed will of the people – just as the laws themselves are just inscribed letters unless the people are willing to act boldly in their defence (223–225; cf. 37 ff., 57, and see below). Demosthenes' wealth is meaningful to him only because it allows him to face down bullies like Meidias and to give generously to the public weal (156–157 and 189). Meidias, on the other hand, is selfish with his money: he uses it in vulgar and offensive displays calculated to humiliate ordinary citizens (133, 158–159 and 195–196). He never willingly contributes to public projects and arrogantly believes that the special tax (*proeisphora*) he is forced to pay gives him the right to harangue and berate the rest of the citizenry in the Assembly (151–169).

So far we have touched on two of the rhetorical strategies Demosthenes employed in *Against Meidias* in order to distinguish himself from his rival. First he draws a line between the elite cavalryman and the ordinary hoplite. Next, he contrasts styles of elite behaviour: the selfish, anti-democratic man interested in his private goods versus the selfless public man who takes the laws as his kin. A third, more subtle, tactic may have helped Demosthenes distinguish between the nature and function of his powers and those of his rival. At section 154 Demosthenes specifically points out the differences in their ages: he claims to be thirty-two, while his opponent is 'about fifty or a little less'. The jury might suppose that there was an eighteen-year gap in their ages, but Harris ('Demosthenes' Speech', pp. 121–5) argues convincingly that Demosthenes was lying about his own age. He suggests, no doubt rightly, that Demosthenes' primary motive here was to emphasise the disparity between the two men's liturgical records: Demosthenes' generous record looked even better if compressed into a shorter lifespan. There was, however, a pointed subtext: overstating the age difference helps Demosthenes to depict himself as a young man confronting a man considerably his senior in both years and political strength. This contrast would have considerable resonance for Athenians, raised on stories of the youthful exploits of Theseus, mythical founder of the democracy.[25]

Demosthenes had previously 'reminded' his listeners of a story, one which he claimed many of them would know well, of a youth's successful confrontation with an older, stronger, insolent man.[26] At sections 71–72, to illustrate the serious consequences that could result from acts of *hubris*, Demosthenes tells two brief tales of men who killed other men who dared offer them *hubris*. The first concerns Euthynus and Sophilus (71):

> Everyone knows – or if not everyone, many people – that on one occasion Euthynus the famous wrestler, the young man (*neaniskos*), defended himself even against Sophilus the pancratist. The latter was a strong man, dark – I'm sure certain ones of you know the man I mean. They were in Samos, just passing the time privately (*idiai*) with some friends; and because he [Euthynus] thought him insolent (*auton hubrizein*), he defended himself so vigorously that he actually killed him.

The implied parallel to young, vigorous Demosthenes and older, stronger Meidias is quite clear in the context of the oration.[27] The second tale is equally instructive (71–72):

> Many people (*polloi*) know that Euaion, the brother of Leodamas, killed Boeotus at a dinner party (ἐν δείπνῳ καὶ συνόδῳ κοινῇ) because of one blow. It was not the blow that made him angry, but the dishonour (*atimia*); nor is being hit such a serious matter (*deinon*) to free men (*eleutherois*), though it is serious, but rather being hit with *hubris*.

As in the case of the Euthynus *logos*, the story of Euaion is one of revenge for insolence offered in a specifically private context (see MacDowell, *ad loc.*). But with Euaion – to whom Demosthenes pointedly compares himself (73–76) – the speaker adds that hubristic assault brings with it the threat of *atimia*, and points to the psychological effect of insolent assault on *eleutheroi*. Demosthenes' follow-up to the double story is to point out that in his own case the context of the insult was not private but public: he was *choregos*, the assault occurred in the theatre at a public festival and was witnessed by citizens and foreigners alike (74; cf. 31 ff.). It is in the transposition of what might well have remained a private affair between rival aristocrats to the public realm dominated by the demos that the stakes involved in the play of power and ideology are most clearly exposed.

After relating the early history of his conflict with Meidias – a tale that enables Demosthenes to emphasise his extreme youth (78) – the prosecutor introduces the poignant figure of Strato the arbitrator. With the Strato *logos*, the speaker confronts his audience with the implications of private-realm aristocratic arrogance spilling over into the public realm. When we combine the salient points of the Euthynus and Euaion stories, we get a tale of justifiable revenge executed by a brave young man against an older, stronger man in order to redress the *atimia* associated with an act of *hubris*. Strato, by contrast, is far from an aristocratic youth in the first flush of his strength: an older man (as an arbitrator (*diaitetes*) he was, by definition, sixty years old), he was a worker and inexperienced in public affairs (*penes, apragmon*: 83). Moreover, says Demosthenes, Strato was no rascal (*poneros*), indeed he was a useful citizen (*chrestos*: 83; cf. 95): the exemplary ordinary Athenian who did his mandatory year's public service as arbitrator not because he was ambitious but because it was his duty.[28] Strato was assigned by lot to Demosthenes and Meidias when the former indicted the latter for slander (foul language used in the presence of Demosthenes' sister and mother, when Meidias and his brother broke into Demosthenes' home (*oikia*) demanding a property-exchange (*antidosis*): 78–80). On the day of the arbitration, Meidias did not (at first) show up and so Strato reluctantly gave a default verdict against him. After Demosthenes had gone home in triumph, Meidias arrived at the arbitrators' offices and tried to bribe Strato to reverse his judgement. Strato refused and Meidias later vindictively and manipulatively gained a judgement against Strato and so 'he expelled and disenfranchised (ἐκβάλλει καὶ ἀτιμοῖ) the arbitrator' (87). Strato, like Euaion, thus suffered *atimia* (cf. 92) at the hands of a hubristic man – and yet the meaning of *atimia* has shifted dramatically with the move from the private to the public sphere, as has the victim's power to defend himself.

The *atimia* which Euaion suffered when punched by Boeotus was personal and social dishonour: his worth was compromised in his own eyes and those of his fellows. This loss of honour (*time*) carried with it no formal political disabilities and was evidently wiped clean by Euaion's vigorous self-defence. The meaning of *atimia* for Strato was quite different: rather than being stripped of private honour, the arbitrator lost his status as a citizen. Moreover, since Meidias had secured the judgement through the legal system, there was no recourse for Strato as there had been for Euthynus and Euaion – as an *atimos*, Strato became utterly powerless (92 and 95). Having lost even the right to speak in public fora, he is put on display by Demosthenes as a mute example of the ghastly effects on an ordinary Athenian of hubristic power exercised in the public realm. Fisher (see n. 10) has emphasised the linkage of *hubris* with dishonour; indeed, what we might call the 'economy of *time*' provides the appropriate context for private acts of *hubris* and revenge for those acts. But the fate of Strato – the exemplary ordinary Athenian (*aner polites*: 88; *Athenaion hena*: 90; *ton pollon heis*: 96) who became *atimos* in the process of doing his public duty – suggests that the wilful exertion of personal power in the public realm has as its target not private or family honour, but the quality of citizenship itself. Although there is talk of *philotimia* in the speech (67, 159, 162), this attribute is associated specifically with the elite. The speech thus underlines a crucial difference between elite and demotic strata of Athenian society. The most precious possession of the elite individual was his honour. The most precious possession of the ordinary Athenian was the dignity he enjoyed because he was a citizen: the 'basket' of privileges, immunities, duties and responsibilities he enjoyed by the simple fact of his citizen status. Citizen-dignity may most readily be defined by the intersection of individual freedom (*eleutheria*: 124, 180), political equality (*isotes*: 67, 111) and security (*bebaiotes*: 222; *asphaleia*: 227).

Honour and dignity had much in common: both implied a rejection of self-abasement and an immunity from degrading violations of the body's physical integrity (179 and 180).[29] But in Greek aristocratic society, honour (as has often been pointed out) was a scarce resource in an endless zero-sum game. In the simplest two-player simulation, Player A gains in honour only at the expense of the honour of Player B.[30] Although Athenian citizenship was highly exclusivist by modern standards, dignity was not in the same sense a scarce commodity within the community of citizens. The dignity of Citizen A was not ordinarily enhanced at the expense of his fellows. In the course of the fifth and fourth centuries, the Athenian citizenry radically augmented the material and psychic value of citizenship.[31] Thus, while the total number of players did not expand much, the total 'quantity' of dignity available to the players was expansive. Dignity was a citizen's personal possession in the sense that it could be lost through individual acts (for example, engaging in prostitution) or removed by legal judgement. Yet it was simultaneously a collective possession of the demos. The downside of this collective ownership was that the total sum of dignity could be reduced (and thus each individual's immunities and so forth lessened) if the citizenry failed to act to guard its possession. It was the power of collective action that had created citizen dignity in the first place;[32] a lack of collective defence in the face of threats offered by powerful individuals could result in its loss (45, 57, 124, 140 and 142).

The chain of reasoning developed above helps to explain the argument that underlies Demosthenes' speech. It was one thing for powerful honour-driven aristocrats to attack one another and to defend themselves in private. It was quite another thing when an aristocrat began to bring his *hubris* to bear on ordinary citizens. At this point, and especially when attacks were upon citizens acting in formal public capacities (as *choregoi* or *diaitetai*: 31–34, 87), it was incumbent upon the collectivity to resist staunchly the deployment of individual power. Nothing less than the individual and collective dignity of the citizen was at stake: 'If anyone who tries to stand up for himself when quite illegally assaulted by Meidias is going to suffer this [court-mandated expulsion and disen-franchisement] and similar treatment, it will be best just to offer *proskinesis* [bow down] to hubristic men, as they do in barbarian lands, rather than try to resist them' (106). If the citizenry will not stand up to Meidias, they will cease to be dignified citizens and will devolve into salaaming subjects of the powerful few.[33]

In order to avoid this nauseating outcome, the jurors must see the situation clearly: Meidias is an exemplar (*paradeigma*: 76, 97, 227) of the powerful rich. The individual rich man, and the rich as a class, are desirous of forcing their hierarchical approach to private life and their hierarchical system of social categorisation upon the whole of Athenian political society. Intolerant of equality and freedom, they long to humiliate and subjugate all ordinary persons, whom they regard not as dignified citizens but as subhuman (185 and 208–209). Individually, ordinary Athenians were much too weak to stand up against the violence of the powerful elite. And the laws alone had no force capable of preventing their misuse by the elite. But acting collectively, in defence of the laws and customs of the democratic order, the demos was indeed powerful enough to force the elite to recognise the dignity of each citizen, and powerful enough to discipline any of those who dared to step out of line (140–142):

> All this [the tale of Meidias and his toadies], I suppose, is frightening to each one of the rest of you, living individually as best you can. That's why you should unite: individually each of you is weaker than they [the rich] are, either in friends or resources or something else; but united you'll be stronger than each of them and you will put a stop to their *hubris* . . . If a man is so powerful (*dunasthai*) that he can prevent each of us singly from getting justice from him, now, since he is in our grasp, he must be punished jointly by all for all, as a common enemy of the state.

A desirable outcome was thus possible: mass strength could trump individual strength. Yet for this desirable outcome to be realised, given the structure of Athenian legal procedure, it was necessary that a brave and resourceful individual citizen be willing to stand up to the exemplary hubristic malefactor by dragging him into court. Enter Demosthenes, the man who (as he explains in detail) has what it takes to confront the monster and bring him to justice: the necessary elite attributes of wealth and rhetorical skill and allegiance to the public good.

Yet Demosthenes makes clear that prosecuting Meidias with the support of laws and demos and in defence of the dignity of the citizenry required more than just personal strength and bravery in the face of superior strength. It also entailed a willingness to sacrifice individual honour since it meant that Demosthenes had to forgo deadly private vengeance. This 'sacrifice' meant, however, that he could have his cake and eat it too. By constructing an image of himself as a bold young elite, Demosthenes shows that he is the sort of man who *could* successfully have defended his *time*, just as Euthynus and Euaion had defended theirs. But, happily for the demos, Demosthenes is also the moderate, middling citizen who sees clearly that the interest of the state (avoiding bloodshed while simultaneously making a public example of Meidias and thus curbing the insolence of the rich as a class) must override his natural urge to dispatch his rival on the spot (74–76; cf. 219):

I think my decision [not to retaliate physically] was prudent (*sophronos*), or rather it was providential (*eutuchos*), when I acquiesced at the time and was not induced to do anything disastrous – though I fully sympathise with Euaion and anyone else who has defended himself when dishonoured (*atimazomenos*) . . . When I exercised so much care to prevent any disastrous result that I did not defend myself at all, from whom ought I to obtain atonement for what was done to me? From you and the laws, I think; and an example (*paradeigma*) ought to be set, to show everyone else that all hubristic men should not be fought off at the moment of anger, but referred to you, in the knowledge that you are the guarantors and guardians of legal protection for victims.

Later in the speech Demosthenes underlines his selflessness by pointing out that it is not he who is most in danger from Meidias (123–124; cf. 221–222):

You should all be equally angry, in view of the fact that the likeliest of you to suffer easy maltreatment are the poorest and weakest (*penestatoi, asthenestatoi*) . . . In my own case, no doubt, I repulsed lies and accusations . . . I haven't been annihilated. But what will you, *hoi polloi*, do, unless you publicly frighten everyone away from the misuse of wealth for this purpose [*hubris*]?

We can now grasp the import of the peroration and see how it relates to the proem of the speech: Demosthenes, the elite *rhetor* (cf. 189), had done his part by dragging Meidias, master of legal evasion, into court. The demos in Assembly had done its part by condemning Meidias in the initial *probole* (2–3). Now it was up to the jurors to be as true to their own interests and to the common ideals on which Athenian political life was predicated. They must use their collective power of judgement to destroy the dangerous individual and re-establish the authority of the demotic regime of truth (227):

Before the case was proved you showed your anger, you called on the victim [Demosthenes] to take revenge, you applauded when I brought a *probole* against him in the Assembly; yet now that the case has been demonstrated, and the demos sitting in a sacred precinct has given a preliminary condemnation of him . . . when it is in your power to deal with it all by a single vote, will you now fail to support me, to offer *charis* to the demos, to teach everyone a lesson (τοὺς ἄλλους σωφρονίσαι), and to secure a safe life for yourselves in future by making of him an example (*paradeigma*) to everyone?

Finally we need to consider the issue of to what degree Demosthenes' oratory was, and could have been, independent of the discursive regime that forms its deep context. In a recent article on *Against Meidias*, Peter Wilson argues that in several key passages Demosthenes loses rhetorical control of his own text: although he hoped to depict himself as a loyal democrat, his speech is hopelessly subverted by established and elitist aristocratic norms.[34] And thus (in the terminology adopted above) social power in the form of a truth regime wins out in the end – and that regime was ultimately a product of elite, not demotic, ideals and discourse. Is this actually the case? While conforming in obvious ways to demotic ideals, does Demosthenes' oratory finally and helplessly serve to subvert them? Is the democratic ideology which is so prominent in much of the speech actually twisted against itself by the irresistible power of an overarching aristocratic value system? I do not think so. Rather, it seems to me that Demosthenes' speech shows us how a central aristocratic ideal (*time*) is at once transformed by and delimited within the public democratic environment. Demosthenes tells his audience an interesting and complex story about honour and its relationship to *hubris*. By invoking the examples of Euthynus and Euaion he shows the enduring importance of honour within the 'realm of inequality' that characterised the sub-society of the elite. By exploring the two senses of *atimia* he shows how personal honour is transubstantiated into citizen dignity in the realm of equality that characterises citizen society. The example of Strato, by demonstrating the danger that 'a Meidias' represents to the individual dignity of the ordinary citizen, shows why a democracy must isolate and regulate elite behaviour patterns. And his speech itself is an example of how the democratic regime can and should use the skills and attributes of the 'good elite' speaker in reasserting order.

Demosthenes' speech participates actively in democratic ideals. Its persuasive power is overtly intended to allow the power of the people to find its target; that is, the powerful individual who embodies the continuing threat of 'non-transformed' aspects of aristocratic culture to spill over into the public realm. Oratory is thus a lens which focuses the great but diffuse power of the Athenian truth regime upon appropriate objects. The pre-trial lack of focus is symbolised by the avid but inchoate hissing and shouting against Meidias in the theatre, by the many who approached Demosthenes to urge him to follow through on the prosecution (2, 23, 198, 216, 226), and perhaps even by the overwhelming but forceless initial vote at the *probole*. Demosthenes implies that if the regime had been working smoothly, and Meidias had been a proper citizen, the latter would have listened carefully to these expressions of demotic dissatisfaction and would have conformed to the spirit of the laws without the need of a trial (61 and 63). But Meidias is a rogue-elite, who thinks he can ignore or override all signs of popular disfavour. In this situation, discourse must be translated into overt action (30). It is through the speech of the prosecutor and the subsequent vote of the people gathered as *dikastai*, that the regime is reified. At this point speech and judgement become concrete forces for action, in a way that a general regime of thought or law, that remains both everywhere and nowhere, never could. *Logos* becomes *ergon* and thus the power of the people is manifested in the life of the citizen (223–225):

> For in fact, if you cared to consider and investigate the question of what it is that gives power and control (ἰσχυροὶ καὶ κύριοι) over everything in the polis to those of you who are jurors at any given time . . . you would find that the reason is not that you alone of the citizens are armed and mobilised in ranks, nor that you are physically the best and strongest, nor that you are youngest (*neotatoi*) in age, nor anything of the sort, but rather you'd find that you are powerful (*ischuein*) through the laws. And what is the power (*ischus*) of the laws? Is it that, if any of you is attacked and gives a shout, they'll come running to your aid? No, they are just inscribed letters and have no ability to do that. What then is their motive power (*dunamis*)? You are, if you secure them and make them authoritative (*kurioi*) whenever anyone asks for aid. So the laws are powerful (*ischuroi*) through you and you through the laws. You must therefore stand up for them in just the same way as any individual would stand up for himself if attacked; you must take the view that offences against the law are common concerns (*koina*).

103

Here, several of the key themes I have attempted to elucidate are set out clearly: the power of the collectivity, the association of individual powerfulness with youthfulness, the relationship between the individual acting in defence of his own person and honour, and the need for common action in defence of common dignity.

The movement from inanimate law to political action through the medium of speech that is at the heart of the passage quoted above suggests that Athenian oratory, while deeply enmeshed in common assumptions about social categories and proper behaviour, is more than a ventriloquisation of a truth regime. The individual speaker, with his individual attributes and perspective, was indispensable as the spark that fired the system. It was in this dynamic relationship between truth regime and individual initiator/orator that Athenian democracy existed. Without the common assumptions I have dubbed the 'regime of truth', Athens would have been no more than a mob of self-interested individuals – and thus certainly would have fallen prey to the endless round of debilitating *stasis* that characterised the histories of so many Greek poleis in the fourth century.[35] Without the intervention of distinct voices and individual histories into the matrix of social assumptions, Athenian society would have been static and nightmarish, an Orwellian *1984* with the demos as Big Brother. The balance of individual and social power was always uneasy; a good part of the the enduring fascination of Attic oratory is its depiction – at the level of both form and content – of a highwire act with no net.

NOTES

1 Cf. R. Dahl, 'The Concept of Power', *Behavioral Science* 2 (1957), p. 202: 'A has power over B to the extent that he can get B to do something that B would not otherwise do.' All unattributed single number citations are from Demosthenes 21, *Against Meidias*; translations are adapted from D. M. MacDowell, *Demosthenes, Against Meidias* (Oxford: 1990), hereafter cited only as MacDowell.

2 Definition of 'paradigm': J. Ober, 'Models and Paradigms in Ancient History', *AHB* 3 (1989), pp. 134–7. What I am calling the coercion paradigm finds its philosophical underpinnings in seventeenth-century social contract theory, notably T. Hobbes' *Leviathan* of 1651 (New York: 1950), and J. Locke's *Two Treatises of Government* of 1689 (Cambridge: 1970). Contract theory explains the ultimate basis of legitimate authority by positing an exchange of complete individual freedom for the security

offered by voluntary submission to a political sovereign. Locke's definition of power (*Second Treatise*, sec. 3, p. 268) is succinct: 'Political power I take to be a right of making laws with penalties of death, and consequently all less[er] penalties for the regulating and preserving [of] property, and of employing the force of the community, in execution of such laws, and in defence of the commonwealth from foreign injury; and all this only for the public good.'

3 The discourse paradigm, developed in the 1960s and 1970s, finds its most complete expression in the work of Michel Foucault; for example, *Discipline and Punish: The Birth of the Prison*, trans. A. Sheridan (New York: 1979); *The History of Sexuality*, I, trans. R. Hurley (New York: 1980); and *Power/Knowledge: Selected Writings and Other Interviews 1972–1977*, ed. Colin Gordon, trans. C. Gordon *et al.* (New York: 1980).

4 J. Ober, 'The Nature of Athenian Democracy', *CPh* 84 (1989), pp. 322–4.

5 For Plato and Aristotle on oratory and discourse see S. Halliwell, chapter 11 below. Cf. G. Kennedy, *Aristotle, On Rhetoric: A Theory of Civic Discourse* (New York: 1991), pp. 309–12, and B. Vickers, *In Defence of Rhetoric* (Oxford: 1988), pp. 83–147.

6 The few exceptions (for example, the Treasurers of Athena, limited to the highest wealth class: [Arist.] *Athenaion Politeia* 47.1) are to be explained in terms of the demos' concern with maintaining fiscal accountability. General accounts of the opportunities and responsibilities of the Athenian citizen: R. K. Sinclair, *Democracy and Participation in Athens* (Cambridge: 1988); M. H. Hansen, *The Athenian Democracy in the Age of Demosthenes: Structure, Principles and Ideology* (Oxford: 1991).

7 Elite fears: for example, Arist. *Politics* 1318a24–26; cf. J. Ober, *Mass and Elite in Democratic Athens: Rhetoric, Ideology, and the Power of the People* (Princeton: 1989), pp. 197–8. There probably were cases in which juries convicted rich men out of greed, but no evidence that this was done consistently: see ibid., pp. 200–1.

8 For an earlier (second half of the fifth century) manifestation of anti-democratic sentiment, see [Xenophon], *Constitution of the Athenians*. Plato, *Republic* 553a–c, suggests that oligarchic attitudes were stimulated by witnessing one's distinguished father punished by death, exile or disenfranchisement in the people's court (*dikasterion*).

9 Arist. *Politics* 1280a22–24, 1282b14–84a3, 1287a13–17, 1296b15–34, 1301a25–1302a15; cf. F. D. Harvey, 'Two Kinds of Equality', *C&M* 26 (1965), pp. 101–46 and 'Corrigenda', *C&M* 27 (1966), pp. 99–100, and J. Ober, 'Aristotle's Political Sociology: Class Status and Order in the "Politics" ', in C. Lord and D. K. O'Connor (eds), *Essays on the Foundations of Aristotelian Political Science* (Berkeley and Los Angeles: 1991), pp. 120–30.

10 Definition of *hubris*: MacDowell, pp. 17–23, concluding that '[*hubris*'] essence consists of having energy or power and misusing it self-indulgently' (p. 19). See too N. R. E. Fisher, '*Hybris* and Dishonour I', *G&R*[2] 23 (1976), pp. 177–93; '*Hybris* and Dishonour II', *G&R*[2] 26 (1979), pp. 32–47; and 'The Law of *Hubris* in Athens', in P. Cartledge, P. Millett and S. Todd (eds), *Nomos: Essays in Athenian Law, Politics and Society* (Cambridge: 1990), pp. 123–38. On the 'open texture' of Athenian law and the social significance of an avoidance of strict definition:

R. Osborne, 'Law in Action in Classical Athens', *JHS* 105 (1985), pp. 40–58; S. C. Humphreys, 'Law as Discourse', *History and Anthropology* 1 (1985), pp. 241–64; S. Todd and P. Millett, 'Law, Society and Athens', in P. Cartledge, P. Millett and S. Todd (eds), *Nomos*, pp. 1–18.

11 The seriousness with which the juror would have undertaken his task is underlined by Aristotle, *Politics* 1311a1–2, who notes that the demos feared the *hubris* of the powerful just as the *oligoi* feared property confiscation.

12 Edition: MacDowell; articles: E. M. Harris, 'Demosthenes' Speech Against Meidias', *HSCPh* 92 (1989), pp. 117–36 and P. Wilson, 'Demosthenes 21 (*Against Meidias*): Democratic Abuse', *PCPhS* 37 (1991), pp. 164–95.

13 *Probole* procedure: A. R. W. Harrison, *The Law of Athens*, I (Oxford: 1968), pp. 59–64; D. M. MacDowell, *The Law in Classical Athens* (London: 1975), pp. 194–7; and MacDowell, pp. 13–17.

14 Review of history of the 'stylistic weakness' argument from Photius (*Bibl.* 491ab, citing earlier opinion), ninth century AD, to Dover in 1968: Harris, 'Demosthenes' Speech', pp. 119–20; MacDowell, pp. 24–7. Against the stylistic weakness: H. Erbse, 'Über die Midiana des Demosthenes', *Hermes* 84 (1965), pp. 135–51 (= *Ausgewählte Schriften zur klassischen Philologie* (Berlin: 1979), pp. 412–31), Harris, 'Demosthenes' Speech', pp. 121–9.

15 Thus, A. Boeckh, 'Von den Zeitverhältnissen der Demosthenischen Rede gegen Meidias', *Abhandlungen der Berliner Akademie* 5 (1818), pp. 60–100 (= *Gesammelte kleine Schriften*, V (Leipzig: 1871), pp. 153–204), suggested that the draft of the speech had been found among Demosthenes' papers after his death and published only posthumously. Wilson, 'Demosthenes 21', p. 187, suggests that Demosthenes circulated the speech himself.

16 Harris, 'Demosthenes' Speech', pp. 132–6. Wilson, 'Demosthenes 21', unaware of Harris' article, does not argue the case but speaks of the 'likelihood' that the speech 'was not risked in the public domain of the courts' (p. 165 with n. 12); by the end of his article (p. 187) likelihood has evolved to certainty. The lack of clarity and detailed argument here are consonant with Wilson's evident desire that this 'particularly edifying example of the non-transparency of classical texts' should *not* be 'what it consistently proclaims itself to be' (p. 187).

17 Chronology: MacDowell, pp. 6–11. Indictment before the *thesmothetes*: sections 3 and 32 with MacDowell's commentary *ad loc.*

18 The action was a *graphe hubreos*: Harris, 'Demosthenes' Speech', pp. 125, 130 n. 32 (with review of earlier literature); not a *graphe hubreos*: MacDowell, p. 16 and Wilson, 'Demosthenes 21', p. 165 n. 11.

19 Probably no need for *anakrisis* in cases of *probole*: MacDowell, *Law in Classical Athens*, p. 242, ergo the court date would be set immediately upon complaint being lodged.

20 Social composition of Athenian juries: M. M. Markle, 'Jury Pay and Assembly Pay at Athens', in P. A. Cartledge and F. D. Harvey (eds), *Crux. Essays Presented to G. E. M. de Ste. Croix* (London: 1985), pp. 265–97; Ober, *Mass and Elite*, pp. 142–4; and S. Todd, 'Lady Chatterley's Lover and the Attic Orators: The Social Composition of the Athenian Jury', *JHS* 110 (1990), pp. 146–73.

21 Definition of *rhetor*: Ober, *Mass and Elite*, pp. 105–12 and Hansen, *Athenian Democracy*, pp. 143–5.

22 Function of gossip in the making of a man's reputation: K. J. Dover, 'Anecdotes, Gossip and Scandal', in *The Greeks and Their Legacy: Collected Papers*, II. *Prose Literature, History, Society, Transmission, Influence* (Oxford: 1988), pp. 45–52; V. Hunter, 'Gossip and the Politics of Reputation in Classical Athens', *Phoenix* 44 (1990), pp. 299–325; and D. Cohen, *Law, Sexuality, and Society: The Enforcement of Morals in Classical Athens* (Cambridge: 1992), pp. 89–97.

23 On the balance between elite and demotic claims on the parts of *rhetores*: Ober, *Mass and Elite*, *passim*.

24 Sections 186–188. I am indebted to Danielle Allen for drawing my attention to the key importance of this passage; see also section 7.

25 The ideological underpinnings of the Theseus myth are discussed in detail in a forthcoming book by B. Strauss on fathers and sons in Athenian political ideology. On the social and political significance of acting out a culture's central myths see J. Ober and B. Strauss, 'Drama, Political Rhetoric, and the Discourse of Athenian Democracy', in J. J. Winkler and F. I. Zeitlin (eds), *Nothing to Do with Dionysos? Athenian Drama in Its Social Context* (Princeton: 1990), pp. 245–6, with literature cited. Cf. also section 69: Meidias' failure to demonstrate 'youthful enterprise' (*eneanieusato*). Demosthenes pointedly mocks Meidias' pretensions to youthful machismo at section 131: Meidias no longer thinks it *neanikos* to insult individuals, so he insults whole groups; and section 201: Meidias falsely thinks it *neanikos* to ignore 'you', the people. The root meaning of *neanikos* is 'youthful', and MacDowell's translation of *neanikos* as 'macho' is on the mark.

26 This is an example of the 'everybody knows' topos: Ober, *Mass and Elite*, pp. 149–50 and 163. This is used elsewhere in the speech (for example, 1, 16, 137, 149, 167) and helps to establish Demosthenes' solidarity with popular knowledge and wisdom.

27 At section 78 Demosthenes moves immediately to the story of his early problems with Meidias, describing himself then as a 'very young lad' (*meirakullion*) who was confronted by a violent and profane break-in by Meidias and his brother.

28 Interpretation of this passage: Ober, *Mass and Elite*, pp. 209–11. I follow Goodwin (cf. MacDowell, *ad loc.*) in translating ἄλλως δ' οὐ πονηρὸς as 'moreover not bad' rather than (per MacDowell and others) 'but in other ways not bad'. MacDowell (loc. cit.) and Wilson ('Demosthenes 21', pp. 180–1, citing Thuc. 2.40.2) seem to me to get the force of *apragmon* wrong. There is certainly an echo here of Pericles' Funeral Oration (Thuc. 2.40.1–2); both Pericles/Thucydides and Demosthenes are manipulating traditional sentiments about the link between wealth, public activity and usefulness to the community (cf., for example, the Solonian *tele*). But the point of the Strato story is that this ordinary man became Meidias' victim through no fault of his own. Strato's *apragmosyne* is his lack of overt political ambition, not an unwillingness to do his public duty. Since the Athenian laws require certain public duties, every Athenian (not just those who are ambitious) is at risk from the Meidias-type. Note too, that *chrestos*, which in elite discourse could mean 'elite',

here clearly means 'a man who is a positive asset to the state' in contrast to the *poneros* who is a public liability.

29 On bodily integrity see J. J. Winkler, *The Constraints of Desire: The Anthropology of Sex and Gender in Ancient Greece* (New York: 1990), pp. 54–64; D. M. Halperin, *One Hundred Years of Homosexuality and Other Essays on Greek Love* (New York: 1990), p. 96; and Wilson, 'Demosthenes 21', pp. 164–5.

30 Zero-sum, honour/shame-based competition and its links to a 'Mediterranean society' model: Winkler, *Constraints of Desire*, pp. 45–70 and Cohen, *Law, Sexuality, and Society*, pp. 35–69.

31 For the origins of this process see P. B. Manville, *The Origins of Citizenship in Ancient Athens* (Princeton: 1990); for its development in the fifth and fourth centuries: Ober, *Mass and Elite*, pp. 53–103.

32 J. Ober, 'The Athenian Revolution of 508/7 B.C.: Violence, Authority, and the Origins of Democracy', in L. Kurke and C. Dougherty (eds), *Cultural Poetics in Archaic Greece: Tyranny, Cult and Civic Ideology* (Cambridge: 1993), pp. 215–32.

33 Cf. section 124: anyone who stands in the way of convicting Meidias 'is simply taking away our enjoyment of free speech (*isegoria*) and freedom (*eleutheria*)'.

34 Wilson, 'Demosthenes 21', pp. 170–1, 181–2, 186–7. In arguing that aristocratic norms subverted what was ostensibly democratic discourse Wilson follows N. Loraux, *The Invention of Athens: The Funeral Oration in the Classical City*, trans. A. Sheridan (Cambridge: 1986).

35 Cf. Arist. *Politics* 1302a31–b3 (recalling much of the language of Dem. 21): men fight *staseis* in order to gain *time* and material goods (*kerdos*), and to avoid *atimia* and punishments. What stirs them up in the first place is either seeing others increasing their share of *time* and *kerdos*; or *hubris*, fear (*phobos*), pre-eminence (*hyperoche*), contempt (*kataphronesis*), or disproportionate self-aggrandisement (*auxesis*).

6

History and oratorical exploitation

Ian Worthington

Greek oratory is a vast mine of information, of which the historical must comprise the greater portion. That history holds this leading place in speeches is not surprising: history was part of an orator's training, and Isocrates for one deemed it important that an orator be able to choose the right historical example at the proper moment (4.9–10; cf. 15). Rhetorical allusion to a particular event or period inserted into a speech was calculated to have the desired effect on the audience and thus lend weight to the overall thrust of the speech. That the accuracy of the historical information contained in speeches by the Greek orators is open to doubt is no small understatement. To be fair, some of the historical narrative is valid, and from time to time can be corroborated by independent evidence; one such instance is Andocides' quoting of the law of Demophantus of 410 (1.96), which is supported by inscriptional evidence (*IG* i² 298). All too often, however, validity is not the case: the orators lie, distort, deliberately deceive, suppress the truth, and prevaricate as a matter of course. This is not surprising, given the genre in which they wrote and that they were not historians nor claimed to be: they were practitioners of rhetoric, the art of persuasion, and as such facts, persons and events were exploited, manipulated and even, if necessary, created to persuade the audience. In the Assembly the aim of symbouleutic oratory was to influence the people to vote for or against a policy; in the lawcourts, forensic oratory aimed to convict or to acquit the accused party; and at official state gatherings epideictic oratory attempted to move and to exhort the people emotionally and psychologically. To these ends the orators used their history, and historical accuracy or methodology, along the lines of the principles advocated by Thucydides (1.20 ff.), was not part of their brief.

In the first part of this chapter I wish to consider some of the problems arising from the historical examples chosen by the orators, and the implications for the audience and the speeches as we have them today. I would like to question whether a jury or a gathering at an Assembly was prepared to overlook the truth and be swayed by manipulation of past history for rhetorical (or other) reasons. In the second part of the chapter I deal with the frustration of modern scholars, faced with these important sources for the ancient Greek world who to a very large extent manufactured their history, by putting forward a potential means for evaluating the veracity of historical narrative in oratory.

1

S. Perlman has well noted and discussed that the three historical groups from which the orators were most prone to draw were mythology, the Pisistratids and the Persian Wars.[1] Perlman demonstrated how the historical example as it appears in oratory was used by the orators as a vehicle of propaganda, conditioned by the political situation of the fourth century, and he argues that it enables us to gauge contemporary attitudes and perhaps even the political leanings of the orators themselves. The use of the historical example for the purposes of propaganda grew to prominence in the fourth century, and may then have been formally included in the rhetorical handbooks as a rhetorical technique and part of the structure of a speech. That most examples are taken from these three historical groups is not overly surprising. Instead of a random selection from them, there seem to be favourite historical specifics which establish themselves as popular and patriotic topoi, fixed in the past.[2] The restoration of democracy in 403 is one (Lyc. 1.61; Aes. 3.190–192, 195, 208; Dinarchus 1.15), as is the treatment of Arthmius of Zelea by the Athenians' ancestors (Dem. 9.41–45, 19.271–272; Aes. 3.258; Dinarchus 2.24–26), or the patriotic appeal to the leadership of Pericles (Isoc. 15.111, 234, 307, 16.28; Dem. *Olynthiac* 3.21; Aes. 1.25), which was seen as a period of glory and prosperity in contrast to these orators' interpretation of their contemporary background. More often than not such topoi have little truth in them: history, as we know, does not bear out the orators' rosy-coloured view of Periclean Athens.

Not every event from past history was able to – or should – be used, as Isocrates would advise (4.74); selections had to be made and various things omitted. Indeed, we should note that the number of chosen examples occurring on any regular basis is quite few when related to the few thousands of pages of texts of the speeches we have today.[3] Since history was part of the rhetorical training, it may be said that what historical examples crop up with any sort of regularity have been carefully selected by the orators, conceivably with the audience's moods in mind. We would expect the orators to include in a speech what was popular, be it historical, abusive, racial, humorous or whatever, and thus at first sight we might well say that the orator was reflecting what periods or events the people, whose favour was curried in a speech, thought the most important. Indeed, the types of historical examples used by the orators, and in particular the changes, often minor but nevertheless evident, in the presentation of the same historical topoi by several orators, have been studied with a view to establishing the historical knowledge of the audience and its conception of certain past events.[4] When we get down to specifics, though, this does not necessarily follow: what actual historical information the orators chose and how they presented it was ultimately for their own rhetorical reasons, and had little to do with the dictates or attitudes of the audience.

Although the orators were aware of different periods of history, they did not necessarily select or relate a specific past event pertinent to a particular point of a speech. In other words, if at some stage a need arose for the inclusion of a historical anecdote in the structure of a speech say for propaganda purposes, then anything drawn from the time of the Trojan War to the Persian Wars or beyond would suffice. What mattered was not so much the actual choice but the rhetorical use of history. Yet if the audience was not particularly concerned about what example, or indeed what era, was being referred to, why, then, should a *select* stock of favourite historical topoi exist? Ought we not to expect random extractions from the past at the whim of the individual orators? Obviously some persons and events were more popular than others (indeed, oratorical practice seems seldom to invoke the great men of the past) but in a sense it was the orators on whom responsibility lies for this. Solon (or allusion to him) has a special place in the oratorical repertoire for his democratic legislation and ideals; he is someone to admire, to emulate, the ultimate people's man. Like the Areopagus, which also enjoys privileged treatment in oratory, he is an Athenian institution, and he is specifically named with great regularity.[5] But Solon's assured popularity is a result of his treatment at the hands of the orators, and it is notable how that treatment differs as time progresses, especially after the oligarchic coups of 411 and 404.[6] By comparison Cleisthenes and Ephialtes, who for propaganda and rhetorical purposes should be expected to enjoy a high profile in oratory, and whose reforms also had a significant impact on the course of Athenian democracy, are virtually disregarded. Cleisthenes crops up by name only in Isocrates, and then only three times (7.16, 15.232, 16.26), and Ephialtes – by name at least – is doomed to oblivion.[7] At least in forensic oratory, given the composition of an Athenian jury, the majority of which stemmed from the lower social stratum which his legislation had championed,[8] we should expect Ephialtes to be a popular name to conjure with as the fourth century progressed. The same goes to a large extent for Cleisthenes: the demos had willingly become his partner in his clash with Isagoras (Herodotus 5.66) and had supported him in his democratic legislation.

Solon has achieved a different status, perhaps because he was the first 'real' legislator, perhaps because of his 'pedigree', for in the historical tradition Solon was the great and paramount legislator in comparison with Cleisthenes and Ephialtes. Yet he and what he could be said to represent were used by the orators to powerful and lasting effect: Solon has a place of his own in fourth-century popular ideology; others, though they *could* fit into popular ideology, do not. Like today's publicists, the orators were responsible for taking a person, drawing on what he did (or inventing this when necessary) and what he represented (or should represent), and thus making him into what they wanted to project. A similar campaign to 'sell the product' no doubt could have been made with Ephialtes, but not so.

Thus it was the orators who decided the exact example to include in their speeches. This is not to deny that the mood or attitude of the audience was taken into account from time to time; this we should expect, but it would appear that it was the orators who attached greater worth to certain events and persons and proceeded to develop them as part of the oratorical repertoire. We should not, then, equate a specific example with the perception or inclination of the audience to that period, but merely to its expectation of a historical example as a rhetorical device. In other words, attention should not be focused so much on the audience's knowledge (or lack of) of a chosen example at a particular part of a speech, as on the actual example and the purpose it served at that part of the speech. We will return to the audience in a moment.

To a large extent mythological events may have been deemed less useful than more recent history for the conditions of the later fifth and fourth centuries (although it is to be noted that Isocrates refers to mythology a great many times), in which the Athenians themselves played a more significant and especially international role.[9] For propaganda and patriotic purposes the Athenians' role in defeating the Persians (the battle of Salamis is most frequently cited by the orators), their headship of the Delian League, and their eventual imperial hegemony in the fifth-century suited well the imperialistic position and policies of that city in the fourth. The fifth-century empire was more immediate and Athens' role in Greek affairs and international relations more influential. In the process of referring to the fifth century, there is more than merely the propaganda element at work: by choosing examples from the fifth-century *empire*, when Athenian power was at its zenith, the orators were *advocating* the Athenians' claim as hegemon of the Greeks in the fourth century.[10] By the use of such examples – information – the speeches more than pander to a common attitude but attempt to influence the Athenians at the time to imperialism, a second empire. This mood argues aginst the thesis of Cargill and Ober, for example, that the Second Athenian Confederacy was not conceived as an empire or was not seen as one.[11] The influence of the orators is evident: by their use of information and its presentation to the audience it is no surprise that in a state in which the demos was so powerful, orators such as Demosthenes and Aeschines enjoyed even greater power: testimony, from the way they used it, that information *is* power.

In exploiting history for rhetorical effect, did the orators find the people easy victims because of their ignorance of the past? As a result of Pearson's study, it is commonly accepted that the historical knowledge of the audience, to judge by the inaccuracies in speeches, was poor. Pearson noted that the orators tended not to draw their examples from the mythical past as often as they did from the later period because the audience's knowledge of events from that much earlier period was too poor, and the orator at all costs had to avoid the impression that he was lecturing his audience ('Historical Allusions', pp. 219–21). In other words, he

could never appear patronising or that he was more know-
ledgeable about any past events than the audience otherwise any
resentment would react against him. In order to overcome this we
get the recourse to the appeal to mass wisdom with phraseology
such as 'All of you will remember that' or 'You all know that',
which eventually become rhetorical topoi. [12]

This may well be true for mythological examples, but, as
Harding has well pointed out, men of the fourth century in
particular were knowledgable about current politics and recent
history given their participation in political life, either as members
of the Boule, Assemblymen, or as jurors.[13] And let us not forget the
street-talk that must have permeated Athens when the city faced
any event of significant import. True, there were cases when the
audience knowledge was minimal, perhaps exemplified by the
rhetorical appeal to mass wisdom as the orators strove to avoid the
impression they were lecturing their audience; on the other hand, it
might well be said that men, even if only on a *general* basis, *did*
know what the orators were talking about, especially if it dealt
with something from their own experience or for which the city
had won renown – hence the patriotic appeals to the fifth century
and the Persian defeats. Indeed we may even question the extent to
which the people were ignorant of mythology: after all, tragedy
was a source of knowledge about myth, and it was popular also in
the fourth century.

Plausibly the common verdict on the historical gullibility or
ignorance of the people may well be denying them some
knowledge or expertise, just as the general belief seems misplaced
that the jurors of Aristophanes' *Wasps* reflect their real-life
counterparts, greedy for their three obols a day, not concerned
with the finer (or any) points of law, prejudiced, and eager only to
find the accused guilty. Jurors in the lawcourts did have
knowledge of Athenian law and the orators paid due regard to law
and to the jurors' knowledge of it. Appeals might be rhetorical in
nature, but the actual specifics of the law did not entertain
rhetoric.[14]

What emerges from the historical narrative in speeches is that
the attendant distortion and lies appear to have been tolerated,
almost expected, by the people. When considering the people's
knowledge of events the trend has been to see the audience at
which a speech was aimed as being one and the same. Yet too little
attention has been paid to whether the audience who heard the

speeches was different from the reading one, who read the circulated speech. This would appear likely given the general lack of literacy in this period.[15] If so, then the revised speech, successful or not, circulated after a trial or meeting of the Assembly when it no longer had any influence on the outcome of that trial or Assembly debate, serves a different function, and relates to a different audience. Bound up more closely than has been argued before with the problem of revision of speeches is the extent to which the orators' lies and manipulations were accepted by the people and in what contexts, oral (that is, at a trial or Assembly) or circulated (that is, the written version of a speech for circulation). Consideration of this point calls, firstly, for a few words on revision of speeches.

There is no question that speeches were revised, as I have argued before.[16] For one thing, there is their length. If we accept for the moment that the speech we have today was about the same length as the oral, then some of our extant speeches are so long that they could not have been fitted into the allotted time for the trial. This often amounted to only one day, although it is likely that longer political or show trials could stretch to two or three days.[17] Hansen's estimate[18] that some of the longer speeches could take up to three hours to deliver cannot be proved since we have no idea how quickly the ancient Greeks read or spoke. Even if he was right, allowance has still to be made for quoting other evidence in speeches including decrees and laws (the length of which is often unknown to us), and witness testimony, and the problem is compounded by trials which involved multiple prosecutors, such as those of Cimon or of Demosthenes in 323. It is therefore likely that the oral speech was much shorter than the circulated one.

Another factor is ring composition, a stylistic device for organising subject-matter with echoes of language and themes into a symmetrical pattern within a work (be it a poem, play, history or speech). The device can operate on a series of levels: a work has a main framework or primary level, divided into a number of parts; each part may subdivide into a secondary level, and parts of this secondary level may subdivide into a tertiary level and beyond (as the structures in section 2 below will illustrate), all in corresponding ring structures, all, in effect, stories or narratives within 'the' story or 'the' narrative (which is the primary level). Thus we have ring composition within ring composition.[19]

The implications of ring composition in oratory cannot be under-rated, and I have argued that it was used widely (see n. 16). This we should expect in such a literary genre, particularly one which, like the Homeric poems, has its basis in orality, but I have further suggested that the device has implications for the two versions of a speech, the oral and the revised. Briefly, for the reading audience the composition and structure of the speech was more elaborate, while a simpler ring structuring was probably used by the orator in the oral version of the speech, where ring composition was used essentially as a mnemonic device. This would make sense in view of what orators had to cope with in the mass gatherings of the noisy lawcourts and assemblies (although revision of symbouleutic speeches was not as common as forensic speeches),[20] where it would also have been necessary to keep arguments and appeals, especially those which involved the use of past examples, as clear and concise as possible. In the revised version the emphasis seems to be on the arrangement and handling of subject-matter, for literary effect, and thus, with the outcome of an assembly debate or of a trial not hanging in the balance, it does not follow that the orator was bound to relate material as he might have done in the oral version of a speech. After oral delivery there is scope to add any amount of material omitted in the oral as a result of time constraints or which simply had not occurred to orators at the time and to arrange the material to conform to a ring structure pattern. My contention is that the historical accuracy of the evidence presented in a speech is further compromised by the probability of revisions.

The outcome of the revision process may now be applied to the extent to which the orators' lies and manipulations were accepted by the audience. Here we need to distinguish the several types of lies in speeches from the major ones to the minor ones. In the case of forensic oratory, an opponent's private life was often a good area to mine, especially if one spoke of actions in private which a jury could not check and if the opponent already was an unsavoury character. Thus in 345 Aeschines was able to exploit Timarchus' questionable reputation, and win the case. Aristogeiton emerges as a particularly sordid character in Pseudo-Demosthenes 25 and in Dinarchus 2, yet it is worth noting that some of his exploits became topoi against him, such as his treacherous activity in jail ([Dem.] 25.60–62; Dinarchus 2.10), for which episode we have only the accounts of the orators, and note Dinarchus' 'source' which is ὡς φασι ('so they say')![21]

More major lies exist. In 343 Demosthenes claimed that Aeschines spoke to the Assembly on 19 Elaphebolion 346. This could not have been the case since the decree containing the procedural rules on that day stipulated that there were to be no more speeches but only the voting. What Demosthenes said is a deliberate and manifest lie, but relying on the dim memory of the jurors, three years after the event, or that they did not know any better (explanations all too often advanced) does not explain it. Jurors were amongst the most politically active of citizens,[22] and it is odd that the same juror at a trial who at some stage before had voted on policy in the Assembly or served as a *bouleutes* would have overlooked lies or been beguiled by rhetoric when judging a case. Would not at least some of the jurors pick up on a big lie if the orator was dealing with something from their own experience? We should remember that Demosthenes' claim in 343 that Aeschines spoke to the Assembly on 19 Elaphebolion 346 took place only three years after the Peace of Philocrates, which had long-term and wide-ranging effects. Three years in a society which relied on memory, an important point to note, is not overly long. We should remember that in 343 Aeschines was not confident that the people had forgotten the details of Demosthenes' punch-up with Meidias of *five* years before, which would hardly have had the impact of the memorable Peace of Philocrates, yet by 330 he thought the outcome long forgotten, and so invented the story that Demosthenes allowed himself to be paid off (Aes. 3.52).[23]

Of course jurors must have overlooked lies and prevarications, which in any case were part of the course for the Athenian jury-system, but the question is raised why a jury did not react adversely against major lies (some of which can be proved so) in the speeches as we have them. Were jurors easily led by the orators' rhetoric or did they simply not care about the truth and thus, by extension, their duty? All of this seems contrary to their attitude to the law and their dicastic oath which they took seriously. One explanation for the apparent dilemma lies in the revision of speeches after oral delivery, for many lies can only have been the product of the revision process. The oral version of the speech, on which hung the outcome of a trial or policy debate, may well have met with a sceptical, critical audience, but not so the revised speech. This means that for the oral version the orator was on guard not to include material against which the jury might react to the detriment of his case, and ultimately of himself – after all, failure to secure one-fifth of the vote was punished by a fine of 1,000 drachmas and *atimia*. Of course, the audience of the written version was much narrower and more select than the audience at the great trials in the lawcourts or in the Assembly, and as such might be expected to recognise lies more easily. By this stage, however, the revised speech was serving a different, more literary, function as ring composition reveals, and was aimed at a very different audience.

The question is raised why the orators went to the trouble of including lies in a revised speech. Two answers are immediately obvious. First, that it was necessary to refute arguments advanced by the opposing party or further bolster proposals in the oral delivery, both of which could be accomplished by embellishment of detail and falsehoods on a grand scale in the circulated version. Second, the revised speech allowed the orator to display – and have recognised – his compositional and literary skill through the device of ring composition. I am sure that there is truth in both of these. Another, more intriguing, explanation lies in a didactic function of oratory: that in the presentation of some material there is an attempt to *influence* popular opinion rather than merely *echo* it. The question is: at whose instigation? It seems unlikely that the orator himself, at least in the forensic sphere, would have this aim, although Lysias may well have published Speech 12 (*Against Eratosthenes*) for personal reasons, to stir feeling against Eratosthenes. The answer may lie in the factional aspect of Athenian politics and the influence of groups who were influential in Athens. This may be evidenced in the handling of Conon and Timotheus, for example, as I have noted elsewhere ('Greek Oratory, Revision of Speeches', p. 69 n. 40). Their exploits together formed a historical topos ([Dem.] 13.22; Isoc. 7.12, 15.129–139; Dinarchus 1.14, 75, 3.17),[24] but they are handled very differently by Lysias (2.54 ff.) and by Dinarchus, half a century later (1.14, 75, 3.17). Isocrates links Timotheus' name with oligarchic sympathisers (15.101 ff.), but in Dinarchus he emerges as something of a popular hero (cf. Dem. 15.9–10). In the fourth century alone we know of several groups, including the Iphicrates–Callistratus–Chabrias group, into which Timotheus sometimes fitted.

The power of oratory is evident, and with it the dangers as source material for the ancient world. Thus it is more of a necessity to assess whether we can distinguish truth from lies rather than whether a certain orator has got a fact wrong or even deliberately lied about something. When historical information occurs in oratory which cannot be corroborated by independent evidence, the tendency might well be to view it with suspicion, even to deny its accuracy. To a large extent such an approach is justified, but at the same time it is a form of sitting on the fence. There will be information about which we can never determine the validity, but this should not stop us from attempting to devise and apply ways of assessing historical accuracy despite the odds. Here I suggest one method involving ring composition.

Potentially the major problem which affects the information in speeches and thus the historical veracity of oratory is the revision process, a point which cannot be stressed enough. As I have already said (see above, section 1), the circulated speeches are unlikely to be the same in form and content as were orally delivered in a lawcourt or in the Assembly. That much seems reasonably certain. Let us now consider the implications of ring composition further in the question of veracity.

Ring composition is ultimately a stylistic device and as such it should not be expected to help us to identify which particular part of a speech was original and which added, or which parts of a narrative are true or false. There are risks of placing too much emphasis on stylistic features, or at least of trying to draw too firm historical conclusions from literary techniques, as I have pointed out ('Greek Oratory, Revision of Speeches', p. 68). Yet, as is obvious in Dinarchus, Aeschines (see below) and Thucydides (see Ellis, 'Structure and Argument of Thucydides' Archaeology', pp. 344–80), parts of the structures of their works are not as sophisticated (complex) as other parts (which I shall call 'simple'), and this raises an important question: why are some parts complex and others simple? By extension, is there a correlation between sophistication and arguments which by their nature are harder to establish? In the case of the orators, a correlation is evident, for it is hard to reconcile the sophistication of complex ring structures in some parts of a speech with historical accuracy.

Now, while a complex structure does not necessarily have to indicate a bare-faced lie (thus a complex narrative may have a core of truth which has been embellished to the requirements of a structure), it does plausibly indicate that the orator was aware he had a more difficult point or argument to make, hence the need for a greater degree of sophistication. A complex structure may well then flag fabrication of a storyline. If a historical narrative, when set against independent evidence, can be shown to be both false and composed in elaborate ring structures, then perhaps we have grounds for questioning historical reliability in instances where independent evidence is lacking but the structure at that part of the speech is also elaborate. Conversely, if an argument, which by its nature was more straightforward, or which the orator deemed less important to establish, were being recounted, then the structure would be less complex.

Let us put this approach to the test with some examples, beginning with oratorical history for which we have independent evidence. Both Aeschines (3. 239–240; cf. 133 and 156–157) and Dinarchus (1.18–21; cf. 10 and 24–26) accused Demosthenes of responsibility for betraying Thebes to its destruction at the hands of Alexander the Great in 335 (although bribery is a common accusation levelled against Demosthenes, I take the episode to be a known historical event). Demosthenes allegedly had received 300 talents from the Persian king Darius III to help Thebes and to support the rebellion amongst the Greeks which had broken out on Alexander's accession in 336, but had not parted with any of it.[25] The accusation that it was Demosthenes himself who brought about the Theban downfall thanks to his venality occurs in only these two oratorical sources (Hyperides 5.17 would appear to do the same, but this passage is badly fragmented), and even then on several details there are inconsistencies between their accounts. Independent, non-oratorical, evidence on the whole Theban episode (Diodorus 17.4.8, 17.8.5–6; Plut. *Demosthenes* 20.4–5, 23.1; [Plut.] *X.Or.* 847c; Justin 11.2.7) paints a very different picture. It would seem that it was not Demosthenes himself but the Athenians in Assembly who decided against helping the Thebans, even though earlier they had supported Demosthenes' proposal of helping Thebes in its revolt and had even furnished some arms. Thus, not only do we have contradictions between Aeschines and Dinarchus but also more important inconsistencies between our independent and oratorical sources. Moreover, it is significant that Aeschines and Dinarchus can only bring *insinuations* against Demosthenes' part in the Athenian failure to support Thebes and not actual charges, let alone hard evidence. It is plausible that both the alleged money from the Persian king and the betrayal of Thebes episodes together formed a common topos to the discredit of Demosthenes, which was first used by Aeschines in 330, and reused by Dinarchus in 323, when Demosthenes was charged with complicity in the Harpalus scandal. This would hardly be surprising given that on both occasions the cases of the prosecution were weak, to say the least.[26]

Now, the structure of Aeschines and Dinarchus at these points of their speeches is very complex. I take Dinarchus first since this part of the speech is shorter than that of Aeschines and thus enables me to illustrate the different levels of the device by giving full structures. In the secondary (post-primary) level of Speech 1 the betrayal of Thebes (18–21) to its destruction forms the central element (the abbreviation D in all the following structures stands for Demosthenes):[27]

(11–13) Three of D's past actions are used to help illustrate his corruptibility.

(14) Timotheus' noble deeds, but nevertheless he was punished.

(15–16) D's actions ultimately led to the betrayal of his city.

(16–17) Timotheus did not argue the court's verdict and was prepared to die.

(18–21) Destruction of Thebes, attributed to D, is indicative of his ignoble past.

(22–23) Appeal is made to condemn D, as jury condemned others previously.

(24–26) D has betrayed Athens' allies despite his policies.

(26–27) Call made to punish men of note like D.

(28) Three of D's past exploits are used to help cast aspersions on his character.

The central element (18–21) subdivides into a tertiary level thus:

(18) D proved ineffective while Thebes was destroyed.
(18) D had 300 talents from Persia to use to help Thebes.
(18) The Arcadians welcomed the Theban embassy requesting help.
(19) The Thebans assured the Arcadians of their friendship.
(19) They could no longer endure Macedonian actions at home.
(20) The Arcadians were willing to help the Thebans.
(20) The Arcadian leader wanted 10 talents in order to help the Thebans.
(21) D did not want to spend 10 talents, despite the money from Persia.
(21) As a result the Arcadians did not help Thebes and the city was destroyed.

And some elements of this structure further subdivide into a quaternary level:

(19) Not from a desire to end friendship with the Greeks . . .
(19) Led them [the Thebans] to revolt.
(19) They would not do anything against Greece.

(20) The Arcadians were willing to support the Thebans.
(20) They explained that they had to follow Alexander in body . . .
(20) But in spirit they were pro-Theban and for Greek freedom.

(20) Astylus wanted 10 talents to help Thebes.
(20) The Theban envoys asked D [who had the Persian gold].
(20) D was begged to save Thebes by providing the money.

(21) D envisaged the salvation of Thebes . . .
(21) But he allowed other cities to provide the money.
(21) The Arcadians were bought off and no help was given to Thebes.

The structure of Aeschines 3.239–240 (part of a structure beginning at 238) is similarly complex; I give only the post secondary-levels of these chapters.

Tertiary Level:

- (238) I will show how great is D's imposture.
  - (238–239) Persian king, in danger and in need of allies, sent 300 talents of gold to Athens.
  - (239) This same thing brought about the alliance with Thebes.
  - (239–240) D betrayed the Theban allies when in danger and kept some Persian gold.
- (240) In a nutshell, the Persian gold stays with D but the danger [stays] with the citizens.

Quaternary Level (elements two and four):

- (238) Persian king, not long before Alexander crossed into Asia . . .
  - (238) Sent an insolent letter refusing gold to the Athenians.
  - (239) Persian king now overtaken by dangers upon him [Alexander's invasion] . . .
  - (239) Sent 300 talents to the Athenians.
- (239) This was owing to the crisis and need of allies [Alexander's invasion].

- (239–240) D venally kept Persian gold though he had organised Theban alliance.
  - (240) The Arcadians, though mobilised, did not help for lack of money.
- (240) D is a rich man but for his own gains serves as *choregos*.

Quinary Level (of 239–240):

- (239) D talks of Thebes and of the ill-fated alliance all the time.
  - (239) D keeps quiet about the 70 talents of Persian gold he seized and kept.
- (240) For lack of money the mercenaries did not hand over the Theban citadel.

The symmetry and echoes of subject-matter and themes as a result of ring structuring are evident; the device has been used to style a sham charge (our other source material allows us this conclusion) and so to denigrate Demosthenes very effectively. Were it not for close analysis of the other evidence, we might well accept what Aeschines and Dinarchus have to say on Demosthenes' alleged role in the destruction of Thebes – as have many scholars for several generations.[28] I would argue, then, that a sophisticated structure plausibly indicates embellishment of a storyline, at times even a lie, as the orator shaped and styled his material, whereas such a structure should not be expected if simple facts were being recounted, or an argument by nature straightforward, or which the orator deemed less important to establish, was put forward. Take, for example, the brief outline of Timotheus' exploits and demise at Dinarchus 1.14:

Secondary Level (see above for the full structure of this part of the speech):

> (14) Timotheus' noble deeds, but nevertheless he was punished.

Tertiary Level:

- (14) The patriotic exploits of Timotheus.
- (14) The jurors made no allowance for these nor betrayed their oath.
- (14) Timotheus was fined for taking money from the Chians and Rhodians.

Here, stylishly, the first element draws a contrast between Timotheus' patriotic and treacherous actions, which resulted in his condemnation. We have enough evidence dealing with Timotheus and that he was brought to trial and condemned to know that what Dinarchus says is factual (although the allegation of bribery may have been a fabricated one at Timotheus' trial),[29] but the structure here is far less elaborate and does not subdivide past the tertiary level.

Now let us consider an instance where independent evidence is lacking but for which we have a complex structure; for example, Dinarchus' insinuations at 1.41–44 that many of Demosthenes' policies and actions (which Dinarchus lists) were undertaken for purely venal reasons. These form part of a major section of the speech (which I call Past History II: chapters 29–47) as follows:

Secondary Level:

```
┌─ (29–30)  Appeal is made to punish D.
│  ┌─ (30)  D conspired with Aristarchus to murder Nicodemus.
│  │  ┌─ (31–33)  D has infected everyone with his bad luck (he is jinxed).
│  │  │  ┌─ (34–36)  D's past inactivity to the detriment of Greece (time of Agis'
│  │  │  │              war).
│  │  │  ├─(37–40)  Contrast to Athens' great ancestors, who helped the Theban
│  │  │  │              exiles.
│  │  │  └─ (41–44)  D in the past introduced bad legislation to the detriment of
│  │  │              Athens.
│  │  └─ (45–47)  D has cheated the Athenian people and is accursed.
│  └─ (47)  D advanced a cruel and unlawful course to Aristarchus.
└─ (47)  The speaker urges that D must pay the penalty for his crimes.
```

The tertiary level of chapters 41–44 is as follows:

```
┌─(41)  D is open to bribes, and is a robber and a traitor.
├─(41)  Neither he nor his luck are for the good of the city.
└─(41–44)  Ways by which D earned illegal income and served Athens
            ignobly.
```

The last element (41–44), containing the details which balance the thrust of its partner (41) further divides into a quaternary level:

```
┌─ (41–42)  D took money to introduce and to alter laws.
│  ┌─(43)  D proposed rewards and a statue for Diphilus.
│  ├─(43)  D conferred citizenship on various people.
│  └─(43)  D set up statues of the Pontic tyrants in return for a bribe.
└─ (44)  D proposed Taurosthenes for citizenship.
```

and, finally, the last element (44) further divides into a quinary level:

```
┌─(44)  D proposed Taurosthenes for Athenian citizenship.
├─(44)  Taurosthenes was forbidden by law to re-enter Attica.
└─(44)  D proposed this man to be an Athenian citizen.
```

Since we have no independent non-oratorical evidence for Dinarchus' allegations that Demosthenes did what he did only for personal gain, or, for example, that Demosthenes had the dealings with the Spartocid tyrants or with Taurosthenes that Dinarchus attributes to him,[30] and since the chapters are composed in such sophisticated fashion at multiple levels, on my method we should reject their accuracy. Such a course is not as risky, or as methodologically foolhardy, as it might seem, for the subject-matter contained in these chapters by itself raises numerous

125

problems of veracity, chronology, and even identification in the case of Conon (43) (Worthington, *Commentary*, pp. 220–1). Once again, I suggest that a complex structure, in this case lacking any corroborating independent evidence, highlights error and/or fabrication.

Naturally, we should expect denigration of an opposing party in any speech. However, it is important to distinguish between mere rhetorical invective levelled against a person, which can also be complex in structure but which appears more obviously grounded in supposition, and invective which has more significant historical repercussions (as with Demosthenes' alleged betrayal of Thebes to destruction, discussed above). The complexity of the particular narrative structure within speeches is the key to identifying problem areas; the implications from this for the veracity of oratory are obvious.

I venture to suggest, then, that complex ring structures in parts of any speech (given that the device is ubiquitous) may be connected with historical accuracy, and thus may go some way towards casting new light on doubtful narratives when independent sources are lacking. If a structural sophistication is the aim of the revised speech, then it follows that the subject-matter is adapted and worked in to fit the pattern at the expense of accuracy. This last point has been vigorously argued in the case of Thucydides by J. R. Ellis ('Structure and Argument of Thucydides' Archaeology', pp. 344–80), whose work yields significant implications for the veracity of that historian. The same is also true for the orators.

3

The shortcomings of the Greek orators are many, but it goes without saying that their speeches must not be overlooked when studying the history of the period about which they are writing. They are important indicators of the social values of the times, and valuable also for the information which they impart on various aspects of Athenian economic, judicial and political life. More bluntly, they are fun to read, of no small importance for the historian of the ancient world who all too often has to deal with less exciting or 'dramatic' source material (the Athenian Tribute Lists or the torturous naval inscriptions spring to mind). Yet the rhetorical nature of the beast makes historical information in oratory a double-edged sword. The orators knew their history from their training, hence they did not commit errors for reasons of ignorance but styled their subject-matter for their own reasons. Oratorical history may well go beyond mere persuasion at the oral delivery level of a speech and take us further into considering the function of oratory and its relationship to the audience. At the same time the people's knowledge of past events needs to be reconsidered, as the implications of a revised version of a speech suggest. Jurors, for example, may not be considered experts about past history, but in court at least, where their upholding of the rule of the law and vote mattered, they do not seem to have been as easily beguiled by rhetoric as we today tend to think they were. Historical information needs to be analysed even more carefully for inaccuracies, for the danger is clear: content has been subsumed within the literary pattern of the revised speech; history has become rhetoric, the natural preserve of the orator.

NOTES

I am very grateful to Dr J. R. Ellis and Professor S. Perlman for their comments on an earlier version of this chapter.

1 S. Perlman, 'The Historical Example, Its Use and Importance as Political Propaganda in the Attic Orators', *SH* 7 (1961), pp. 150–66, especially pp. 158–66, and see pp. 150–3 on the differences between the 'rhetorical' approach and the 'historical' approach to history. On the orators and history see also L. Pearson, 'Historical Allusions in the Attic Orators', *CPh* 36 (1941), pp. 209–29 and P. Harding, 'Rhetoric and Politics in Fourth-century Athens', *Phoenix* 41 (1987), pp. 25–39.

2 See Harding, 'Rhetoric and Politics', pp. 35–6, for what he calls 'the ancestor-theme'.

3 Over 1,200 pages of Teubner text for Demosthenes alone.

4 See especially Pearson, 'Historical Allusions' and Perlman, 'Historical Example'.

5 M. H. Hansen, 'Solonian Democracy in Fourth-century Athens', *C&M* 40 (1989), pp. 71–106 and Pearson, 'Historical Allusions', pp. 222 ff.; on the Areopagus see R. W. Wallace, *The Areopagos Council, to 307 B.C.* (Baltimore: 1991), Part II, pp. 131 ff.

6 Cf. Pearson, 'Historical Allusions', p. 222.

7 Criticisms of Ephialtes' legislation are to be found at Isocrates 8.126 ff. and 7.50 ff., for example. Allusion to Cleisthenes is also found at Isocrates 15.306; cf. 7.17 ff., especially 20.

8 On the socio-economic composition of the jury see J. Ober, *Mass and Elite in Democratic Athens. Rhetoric, Ideology and the Power of the People* (Princeton: 1989), pp. 142–4 with 127 ff., citing previous scholarship.

9 *Contra* Perlman, 'Historical Example', pp. 159–62.

10 On this see S. Perlman, 'Hegemony and *Arkhe* in Greece: Fourth-Century B.C. Views', in N. Lebow and B. Strauss (eds), *Hegemonic Rivalry from Thucydides to the Nuclear Age* (Boulder: 1991), pp. 269–86.

11 J. Cargill, *The Second Athenian League* (Berkeley: 1981), pp. 148–9 and 'Fourth-century Athenian Citizen Colonies in the Aegean: An Aspect of Naval/Military Policy', in D. M. Masterson (ed.), *Papers of the Sixth Naval History Symposium*, US Naval Academy: 1983 (Wilmington: 1987), pp. 32–8; J. Ober, 'Public Opinion and the Role of Sea Power in Athens, 404–322 B.C.', in D. M. Masterson (ed.), *Papers of the Sixth Naval History Symposium*, pp. 26–31; on an imperialistic motivation see G. T. Griffith, 'Athens in the Fourth Century', in P. D. A. Garnsey and C. R. Whittaker, (eds), *Imperialism in the Ancient World* (Cambridge: 1978), pp. 127–44.

12 The phraseology is that of Ober, *Mass and Elite*, pp. 149 ff.; cf. pp. 163–70.

13 Harding, 'Rhetoric and Politics', pp. 35–6.

14 See E. M. Harris, chapter 7 below.

15 W. V. Harris, *Ancient Literacy* (London: 1989), especially pp. 65 ff.; cf. Ian Worthington 'Once More the Client/*Logographos* Relationship', *CQ²* 43 (1993), pp. 67–72.

16 'Greek Oratory, Revision of Speeches and the Problem of Historical Reliability', *C&M* 42 (1991), pp. 55–74.

17 Ian Worthington, 'The Duration of an Athenian Political Trial', *JHS* 109 (1989), pp. 204–7.

18 M. H. Hansen, *The Athenian Democracy in the Age of Demosthenes: Structure, Principles and Ideology* (Oxford: 1991), p. 200.

19 A good discussion of the technique is given by J. R. Ellis, 'The Structure and Argument of Thucydides' Archaeology', *Class. Antiq.* 10 (1991), pp. 345–8.

20 On noise (*thorubos*) see V. Bers, 'Dikastic Thorubos', in P. A. Cartledge and F. D. Harvey (eds), *Crux. Essays . . . de Ste. Croix* (London: 1985), pp. 1–15 = *History of Political Thought* 6 (1985), pp. 1–15; on revision of symbouleutic speeches see M. H. Hansen, 'Two Notes on Demosthenes' Symbouleutic Speeches', *C&M* 35 (1984), pp. 57–70. Certainly the elaborate and high-powered content of Isocrates' orations would lend weight to the belief that his speeches were not meant to be orally delivered.

21 Cf. Ian Worthington, *A Historical Commentary on Dinarchus. Rhetoric and Conspiracy in Later Fourth-Century Athens* (Ann Arbor: 1992), *ad* Dinarchus 2.10.

22 These conform to Hansen's Group (4): the 'full' *rhetores*, who regularly attended and addressed the Assembly, moved proposals, and participated in the law courts: 'The Athenian "Politicians", 403–322 B.C.', *GRBS* 24 (1983), pp. 33–55 (= M. H. Hansen, *The Athenian Ecclesia*, II (Copenhagen: 1989), pp. 1–24).

23 See further E. M. Harris, 'Demosthenes' Speech against Meidias', *HSCPh* 92 (1989), pp. 117–36.

24 The activities of, and rewards bestowed upon, Chabrias, Iphicrates and Timotheus may also have conformed to a topos: cf. Dem. 20.75–86; Aes. 2.70, 3.243; Dinarchus 1.14, 75, and 3.17.

25 Revolts: Diodorus 17.8.2; Justin 11.2.6–10; Thebes supported by the Arcadians, Aetolians, Argives, Eleans and Athenians: Aes. 3.240–241;

Dinarchus 1.18–22; Arrian 1.7.4 and 10.1–3; Diodorus 17.8.5–6; Theban punishment: Arrian 1.7.1–10; Plut. *Alexander* 11.7–14; cf. *Demosthenes* 23.1–4; Diodorus 17.8.3–15; and Justin 11.3.6–4.10.

26 On Aeschines' weak case see E. M. Harris, below chapter 7; on that of Dinarchus see Worthington, *Commentary*, pp. 58 ff.

27 Dinarchus' entire speech is sophisticated in structure, although parts of it do not have the same depths as others. There are many other structures which could be added to lend weight to the argument put forward here: for a complete range see my *Commentary*, Appendix 2.

28 For detailed discussion and explosion of the charge, citing previous bibliography, see Worthington, *Commentary*, *ad* 1.10 and 18 ff.

29 Worthington, *Commentary*, pp. 154 ff.

30 A similar slanted view of Demosthenes and Taurosthenes is given by Aeschines at 3.85 ff.; cf. Hyperides 5.20, which is also doubtful.

7

Law and oratory

Edward M. Harris

The verdict that many Athenian writers passed on their system of justice was very harsh. Indeed, a modern student after reading their comments might easily conclude that the Athenian courts were completely under the sway of persuasive speakers and paid scant attention to the precepts of law. One of the sharpest critics was Isocrates (7.33–34), who complained that the courts in his day were far below the standard of ancient times. In the past, Isocrates claims, judges adhered to the laws and did not allow themselves to be influenced by considerations of equity. Xenophon shared Isocrates' low opinion of contemporary Athenian courts. In his work *Socrates' Defence* (4), Xenophon portrays Hermogenes warning Socrates that the men who sit in the courts are often thrown into rage and condemn innocent men to death while at other times they are moved to pity and acquit manifest criminals. In courts such as these, some claimed that it was rhetoric that counted, not the law. For instance, Gorgias in the Platonic dialogue named after him (*Gorgias* 454b–e) claims that rhetoric provides a speaker with the key to success in the Athenian courts and Assembly. Knowledge of the just and the unjust provided by the laws is not a prerequisite for winning a favourable verdict. The speaker in one of Demosthenes' orations (23.206) tells us that Athenian courts are so frivolous that they have acquitted men on the basis of a few witty remarks. Others equally guilty have been let off after their fellow tribesmen made a plea on their behalf. What is even more remarkable about this observation is that it comes from a speech composed for delivery in court!

Modern writers have been no less severe in their judgement of the Athenian legal system. B. B. Rogers, an English lawyer who translated Aristophanes in his spare time, had this to say about the Athenian courts:

> It would be difficult to devise a judicial system less adapted to the due administration of justice. A large assembly can rarely if ever form a fit tribunal for ascertaining facts or deciding questions of law. Its members lose their sense of individual responsibility to a great extent, and it is apt to degenerate into a mere mob, open to all the influences and liable to be swayed by all the passions which stir and agitate popular meetings.[1]

W. Wyse, who spent years editing the speeches of Isaeus, came to a similar conclusion:

> The speeches of the orators are a convincing proof, if proof be needed, of the vices inherent in such a system. The amount of injustice done cannot now be estimated, but it is sufficient condemnation of the courts, that appeals to passion and political prejudice, insinuating sophistry, and outrageous misrepresentations of law were judged by shrewd and experienced observers suitable means to win a verdict.[2]

M. I. Finley, though less censorious than either Rogers or Wyse, argued that the Athenian courts were staffed by men who had no professional or technical interest in law and, like the modern layman, either remained ignorant of legal terminology or tended to misuse it.[3] Since the average Athenian who sat on the court lacked legal expertise, the orators who wrote forensic speeches 'were successful advocates because of their rhetorical skill, not their juristic proficiency', and in their speeches 'stylistic demands were overriding'. One cannot help but note the similarity between the opinion expressed by Finley and that of Gorgias.

Lurking behind Finley's argument is an assumption shared by many writers both ancient and modern. This assumption is the view that the aims of rhetoric are somehow fundamentally incompatible with an interest in legal issues. Ancient rhetoric, it is believed, was concerned exclusively with matters of style and techniques of persuasion; the very nature of the subject was therefore inimical to the study of law. Since the Attic orators took obvious pains to produce speeches that displayed stylistic refinement and rhetorical power, they could not have bothered themselves with the analysis of legal questions.

My intent in this chapter is twofold. On the one hand, I would like to initiate an appeal against the rather harsh verdict that has often been passed on the Athenian courts. The Athenian system of justice was far from perfect, and the men who sat on the Athenian courts were after all only human and thus susceptible to errors and rash decisions. Yet we should not forget that the Athenians held the rule of law in deep respect and adhered to a form of government that attempted to put that ideal into practice. Nor should we underestimate the ability of the average Athenian to understand the rudimentary law-code of his native community and to distinguish sound arguments from legal sophistries. Cleon, in his speech about the Mytilenians, criticised the Athenians for their many shortcomings, but he never faulted them for being stupid (Thuc. 3.37.3–38.7; cf. Herodotus 1.60.3).

My other aim in this chapter is to question the widely held assumption about the relationship, or perhaps we should say the lack of relationship, between law and rhetoric. Some scholars appear to think that the two intellectual pursuits were hopelessly at odds with each other. Yet a careful reading of certain passages from Aristotle's *Rhetoric* reveals that no such conflict existed. In fact, Aristotle includes legal arguments among the topics to be covered in a forensic speech. The types of arguments he lists are based on sound legal principles and show no trace of sophistry.

The first part of the chapter will examine the importance of law in the Athenian courts and its consequences for our understanding of the forensic speeches of the Attic orators. The second part will look at Aristotle's view of the relationship between oratory and law and the role of legal arguments in the *Rhetoric*. The third and final part will provide a case study of the role of law in forensic oratory by analysing the legal arguments presented by Aeschines and Demosthenes at the trial of Ctesiphon. Ancient and modern scholars think that Aeschines, who lost the case by a wide margin, had the stronger legal arguments in the case. This would appear to indicate that an Athenian court might pay little attention to the law when reaching its verdict. Contrary to both ancient and modern opinion, however, it is Demosthenes who has the stronger legal arguments. When the court voted to acquit Ctesiphon, therefore, it did not ignore the law, but rather upheld the correct interpretation of the law on which Demosthenes based his case.

1

No ideal was more cherished in classical Athens than the rule of law. Pericles, in a well-known passage from Thucydides (2.37.3), praises the Athenians for their obedience to those in office and to the laws. Pericles' words are probably an echo of a similar phrase found in the ephebic oath. Every year those citizens who had reached the age of eighteen and began their duty as ephebes, swore to heed wisely (*emphronos*) the commands of the magistrates in power and the laws, both those which were in force and those which might be enacted in the future.[4] The ideal was also celebrated in Attic tragedy. Theseus in Euripides' *Supplices* (429–437) denounces tyranny because under that type of regime the law is in the hands of one man who rules by himself. Under democracy, written laws are the common possession of all citizens (*koinoi*) and enable the weak to have equal justice with the rich. Aeschines (1.4–6) asserts that what distinguishes democracy from oligarchy and tyranny is that fact that the former type of government is ruled by the established laws, and the latter two by the whim of those in power. In a democracy the bodies of all citizens are protected by the laws, while the tyrant and the oligarch rely on suspicion and armed guards to protect only themselves.

All the political institutions in Athens were subject to the rule of law. It was the law which convened the Council, summoned the Assembly, filled the lawcourts, and made the magistrates whose terms were expired yield the powers of office to their successors. In short, the entire safety and order of the community depended on the willingness of Athenian citizens to obey the law (Dem. 25.20). The main duty of the Athenian courts was not merely to settle disputes, but to uphold the laws. In his speech against Meidias Demosthenes reminds the court that the laws by themselves are lifeless and ineffective (21.224–225); it is the verdicts handed down by the courts that give the laws their vigour. Nothing could make this clearer than the oath that all those who served in the Athenian courts had to swear. This oath, known as the dicastic oath, pledged every *dikastes* to vote in accordance with the laws and decrees of the Athenian people.[5] Litigants expected the men who sat in the Athenian courts to live up to this oath and frequently reminded them of it in their speeches.[6] Speakers who addressed the court obviously placed much weight on this oath since they often mention it in the most prominent parts of their speeches, namely, at the beginning and at the end.[7]

Since the court was bound by oath to uphold the law, litigants attempted as much as possible to base their arguments on the actual text of the laws relevant to their cases. When Demosthenes prosecuted Aeschines in 343 on a charge of taking gifts while serving as Athenian envoy to Philip, he began his speech by stating that the law forbade magistrates from accepting gifts and then declared that the remainder of his speech would demonstrate that Aeschines broke this law by receiving gifts from Philip in exchange for betraying Athenian interests (Dem. 19.7–8). Aeschines rested his case against Timarchus squarely on the law which punished male prostitutes who addressed the Assembly or served as magistrates (Aes. 1.18–20). In fact, Aeschines has the law read out by the clerk and discusses its contents in some detail. When Pantaenetus brought a suit for damages against Nicobulus, the latter initiated a *paragraphe* procedure to block his opponent's suit on the grounds that Pantaenetus had granted him a full release from all claims arising from their contract. Nicobulus builds his case directly on the law which forbade cases to be brought in matters where a release had been granted (Dem. 37.18–9). Euphiletus, who was prosecuted for killing his wife's lover Eratosthenes, defended himself by citing the law that gave a husband the power to kill a man caught 'on top of' his wife without suffering punishment (Lys. 1.29–33). The speech Demosthenes composed for Euthycles to deliver in his prosecution of Aristocrates for passing an illegal decree makes copious use of the statutes about homicide to argue its case (23.22–85).[8]

It is true that in several speeches the speaker does not actually cite the law that is relevant to his case, but that tends to occur mainly in speeches given by defendants. Since it was customary for the accuser to discuss the law under which he brought his case, the defendant normally had no need to have the law read out again. The pair of speeches delivered by Demosthenes and Aeschines respectively at the latter's trial in 343 illustrates the point. Demosthenes describes the provisions of the law about magistrates accepting gifts, the interpretation of which Aeschines does not dispute. Since the case turns on a question of fact, not one of law, Aeschines devotes the better part of his speech to a careful narrative of events and does not dwell on the contents of the law. The defendant in Lysias 3 found himself in a similar position. Indicted by Simon on a charge of deliberate wounding (*trauma ek pronoias*), the defendant challenges the accuser's version of the facts by denying he started the brawl and inflicted any wounds. Though he does not cite the law, he does not ignore it for in one passage he discusses the nature of the intention required for conviction on the charge of deliberate wounding (Lys. 3.41–43). Far from passing over legal issues, the defendant is keenly aware of them and builds part of his case on an interpretation of statute.

Litigants not only referred to the laws but also expected the men sitting on the court to know them. When speaking against Pantaenetus, Nicobulus assumed that the men about to judge his case already knew the law about releases without his telling them about it (Dem. 37.18). This was not an unreasonable assumption. Unlike the modern juror, who may hear only a few cases in his or her lifetime, the *dikastes* of classical Athens would probably hear dozens of cases each year he served on the panel of those eligible for judging trials. Hansen reasonably calculates that the courts were in session between 175 and 225 days a year.[9] Out of the 6,000 men selected every year to serve as *dikastai* ([Arist.] *Athenaion Politeia* 24.3), anywhere from several hundred to 1,500 or 2,000 might be needed to judge cases on a single day.[10] Even if we set the number of men serving on a normal day as low as 600, this would mean that the average *dikastes* heard twenty cases a year. We should also bear in mind that there were only about 30,000 adult male citizens eligible for court duty in fourth-century Athens (Hansen, *Athenian Democracy*, pp. 90–4). To reach the number of 6,000 required to fill the roster each year, therefore, the average Athenian would have had to serve as *dikastes* once every five years. To put it in other terms: out of the 6,000 selected in any given year, only one-fifth had never served on the courts before.

These are of course just rough estimates and do not take into account one important factor: there may have been many men like Philocleon in Aristophanes' *Wasps*, who were addicted to judging cases, and others like his son Bdelycleon, who avoided the courts like the plague. If Philocleon and Bdelycleon are each representative of a large segment of the Athenian citizenry, we could then argue that many Athenians were willing to serve more than the average once every five years while others rarely if ever put themselves forward for court duty. This would lower the average portion of *dikastai* with no experience to much less than one in five. Although there was no professional legal education in classical Athens, there was a considerable amount of on-the-job training. Nor should we forget the amount of knowledge the average Athenian citizen might gain from his service on the Council.[11] If the young Roman was expected to memorise the Twelve Tables (Cicero, *Laws* 2.23.59), then there is no reason to doubt that the average Athenian retained a basic knowledge of the law from what he heard while listening to litigants present their cases. And despite the absence of *iuris prudentes* in Athenian society, there appears to have grown up an 'oral tradition' of jurisprudence (Dem. 54.17–19, 58.24).[12]

Although many modern scholars translate the Greek word *dikastes* as 'juryman', the men who staffed the Athenian courts acquired a considerable amount of knowledge and experience about the law and were thus unlike modern jurors.[13] The word *dikastes* means 'judge', and his duty was to decide both questions of law and disputes about facts. The role of the *dikastes* in judging legal issues is readily apparent in the case of Ctesiphon, which we will look at in the final part of this chapter. The modern juror, on the other hand, comes into court possibly (some might say preferably) without any knowledge of the laws relevant to the case he or she is about to hear. All the modern juror needs to know about the law is heard from the lawyers presenting the case and from the judge who is presiding. If an issue arises over a matter of legal procedure or about the interpretation of a statute, it is the judge who rules on the question, not the jury. In this way the modern judge can contribute to the creation of law through interpretation of statutes. Lycurgus reveals that the Athenian *dikastai* might also play this role (1.9). 'For this reason', Lycurgus argues, 'you should not be only judges of the crime, but also lawmakers (*nomothetai*)'. He explains that while many crimes are explicitly covered by the laws, some which are worse ought also to be made subject to the law and thereby punishable by the courts. By extending the scope of the laws to cover these crimes the court can set an example for subsequent cases. We might use the word 'precedent' to describe such an example. Even though this kind of precedent would not be formally binding, it could be appealed to by future litigants and thus have an influence on later cases.[14]

To be sure, Athenian literature contains many anecdotes about cases where the courts ignored the dictates of law and allowed themselves to be swayed by emotional appeals. Yet the orators also describe occasions when the courts rigorously enforced the law despite rhetorical attempts to distract them from their duty. Demosthenes (21.182) recalls how Smicrus was fined ten talents and Sciton the same amount for proposing illegal decrees. Smicrus and Sciton each had his friends, relatives and children plead for mercy, but the court remained inflexible in its resolve to punish the guilty and follow the law. And when Demosthenes (21.72–76) explains the almost evenly split votes at the trial of Euaion, he says the opinion of the court was divided because the *dikastai* could not agree about a key legal issue. Those who voted to condemn found Euaion guilty because he had retaliated against his victim in such a way as to cause his death and was thus guilty of murder. Those who voted to acquit reasoned that the victim's insult to Euaion absolved him of responsibility even though Euaion's act of retaliation was not proportional to the harm he had suffered.[15] Demosthenes' explanation of the verdict may be somewhat speculative, but it must still have seemed plausible to those who heard his speech. It would not have appeared plausible unless the audience took it for granted that the Athenian courts paid careful attention to the law when reaching their verdicts.

The forensic speeches composed by the Athenian orators amply demonstrate that litigants expected the courts to obey their oath and vote in accordance with the laws. Under ideal circumstances, the courts would make their decisions solely on the basis of the well-established facts, not on the oratorical qualities of the speeches presented by the litigants. This ideal is most conspicuous in the Areopagus, the most respected court in Athens. According to Aeschines (1.92), the Athenians held the Areopagus in such high repute because it paid no attention to how well or how poorly litigants presented their cases. Aeschines himself saw many men who had spoken well before the Areopagus lose their cases, and many who had spoken poorly win them. Litigants could also assume that most of the men who judged their cases had a good knowledge of the law and some experience in evaluating legal arguments. For these reasons, the men who pleaded in the Athenian courts could not afford to ignore the law. The Athenian courts may on occasion have yielded to emotional appeals and failed to perform their duty of upholding the law, but these few instances were regarded as aberrations from the norm, not as typical examples of the way in which the courts generally behaved.

2

If litigants knew that the courts were bound by their oaths to impose the law, what scope was there for rhetoric? If all a litigant was supposed to do was to present the facts and prove that the accused had violated the law or that the defendant was innocent of all wrongdoing, what role could rhetoric play in forensic oratory? Aristotle (*Rhetoric* 1354a) in fact criticises many rhetorical treatises for including topics such as appeals to pity and anger, which are in his opinion irrelevant to legal cases. Some communities, especially well-governed ones, do not permit the use of these tactics in their courts. Were all communities to conduct their trials in this fashion, the rhetorician would have nothing to contribute to forensic oratory. Aristotle is clearly in sympathy with such an approach and strongly disapproves of attempts to manipulate (*diastrephein*) the emotions of the dicasts. Since the primary task of the litigant is to show whether or not the deed took place, Aristotle advises legislators to draw up statutes so that judges will have little latitude and concentrate mainly on ascertaining the facts.

Aristotle knew that in reality matters were not so simple. In the *Constitution of the Athenians* (9.2), he (or one of his pupils) noted that the laws of Athens were often unclear with the result that the people had the power of decision at trials. It should come as no surprise that one of the first acts of the Thirty was to eliminate or alter the laws of Solon that contained points of dispute which might give the court broad latitude in reaching its decision (*Athenaion Politeia* 35.2). Some argued that Solon deliberately made the meaning of the laws obscure so as to unfetter the dicasts' power of decision. But Aristotle rightly dismisses this view and argues that the alleged lack of clarity in Solon's laws is caused by the difficulty of 'defining what is best in general terms'.

This passage is of central importance for it reveals that Aristotle was aware of what H. L. A. Hart has called the 'open texture' of law.[16] Hart observes that laws must be expressed in general terms (*katholou*) and as a result apply to broad categories of action and large classes of individuals (cf. Plato, *Politicus* 249a–300e). Yet because laws are framed in general terms, it is from time to time difficult to determine whether or not a given law applies to a particular action or individual. In a majority of cases, this problem does not arise. In 'hard' cases, however, the action or individual in question may meet several of the criteria for inclusion in the broad category singled out by the law, but not others. 'Open texture' is a quality found in all written law-codes. Modern legal systems often attempt to limit the amount of 'open texture' a statute may possess by formulating precise definitions of key terms, but it is impossible to eliminate it entirely. The reason for this is that no legislator can predict and enumerate all the particular cases that may in the future be tried under a given statute. The Athenians, like the Romans before the rise of the jurists, made no such attempt to provide exact definitions of wrongful actions in their law-code. In the law of *hybris*, for example, we read that a person who commits *hybris* may be prosecuted by a *graphe*, but no explanation of the term is given.[17]

This does not mean that the Athenians did not understand what the word meant. All Athenians obviously shared a common understanding of the term for otherwise communication would have been impossible. When one man called a deed an act of *hybris*, those who heard him knew what sort of action he meant. A problem only arose when there was a disagreement about how to apply the term when describing someone's actions. For instance, one Athenian might claim that an act was *hybris* by pointing out that it contained several of the characteristics normally associated with that kind of behaviour, while another Athenian might argue that the same action lacked one or two of the key elements needed to qualify as *hybris*.[18]

Aristotle (*Rhetoric* 1374a), who was fully aware of the open texture of Athenian law, rightly saw that one of the crucial tasks facing the litigant was to define clearly the nature of the wrongdoing his case involved:

> Since people often admit having done an action and yet do not admit to the specific terms of an indictment or the crime with which it deals – for example, they confess to have 'taken' something but not to have 'stolen' it or to have struck the first blow but not to have committed *hybris* or to have had sexual relations but not to have committed *moicheia* or to have stolen something but not to have committed 'sacrilege' ([claiming] what they took from a temple did not belong to the god) or to have trespassed but not on state property or to have had conversations with the enemy but not to have committed 'treason' – for this reason [in speaking, we] should give definitions of these things: what is theft? what is *hybris*? what is *moicheia*? In so doing, if we wish to show that some legal term applies or does not, we will be able to make clear what is a just verdict.
>
> (trans. adapted from Kennedy)

In fact, Aristotle begins his treatment of forensic oratory with a general definition of wrongdoing (*adikein*): willingly doing harm contrary to the law (*Rhetoric* 1368b). He next defines what he means by willingly (*hekonta*), and this leads him into an extensive analysis of the possible motives and dispositions that might lead a person to wrongdoing.[19] This is not a purely 'rhetorical' topic, one without legal significance. Aristotle's discussion reflects his awareness that wrongdoing involves more than just the objective circumstances. For the agent to be found responsible for wrong-doing, the accuser must demonstrate that he performed the wrongdoing in a certain state of mind, or, as the Romans put it, with a *mens rea*. Aristotle's exhaustive list of motives and dispositions was thus designed to help accusers deal with a central legal issue that the courts would expect them to cover in their speeches.

Aristotle's discussion of 'proofs that require no (rhetorical) skill' (*pisteis atechnoi*) combines general topoi, methods of dealing with various kinds of evidence and possible legal arguments. Some of Aristotle's arguments for laying aside the written laws were not applicable in Athenian courts where the dicasts were bound by oath to impose the law. For instance, Aristotle puts forward the possibility of appealing to unwritten law, but this was prohibited in Athenian courts (Andoc. 1.87). Nor did appeals to fairness (*epieikeia*) ever find a place in the extant speeches of the Attic orators (see Meyer-Laurin, *Gesetz und Billigkeit*). But Aristotle's other arguments for urging the court not to apply the law in a given case are juristically sound. He suggests that a litigant can point to conflicts among the laws, draw attention to ambiguous wording, or argue that a law is obsolete. The arguments he proposes for declaring contracts invalid show no trace of legal sophistry or rhetorical legerdemain either. He advises a defendant who is being accused in such a case to show that the contract was made under duress, through fraud, or in violation of the laws. These are arguments based on well-established principles of Athenian law (Dem. 37.27, 47.77, 56.2; Hyperides 3.3). What is most significant is that Aristotle did not find a discussion of legal issues out of place in a treatise on rhetoric. For Aristotle, the most important parts of rhetoric were the *pisteis*, the techniques of proof, and legal arguments figured prominently among them.[20]

3

Aristotle would never have discussed legal arguments in his analysis of forensic oratory if he had thought such a discussion would have been of little value to the litigant speaking in court. Yet the discussion of legal arguments forms only a part of Aristotle's treatment of forensic oratory. Many of the topoi he suggests for use in court speeches have in fact nothing to do with the law. Indeed, much of the second book of the *Rhetoric* is devoted to an analysis of different emotions the speaker may try to instil in his audience (1–11) and of the type of character one should assume when speaking (12–17). Book 3 treats matters of style and arrangement. One might therefore argue that legal issues, though accorded some attention by Aristotle, do not figure as prominently in the *Rhetoric* as matters of rhetoric and style, and were accordingly of far less importance for the litigant than the non-legal aspects of oratory.

In support of this argument, one might point to the trial of Ctesiphon. Ever since antiquity, scholars have believed that Aeschines, who lost the case by a wide margin (he gained less than one-fifth of the votes cast), had the stronger arguments on his side when he prosecuted Ctesiphon in 330 for proposing an illegal decree of praise for Demosthenes. According to Quintilian (7.1.2), Demosthenes and Aeschines each followed a different order of presentation in their speeches at the trial because of the respective merits of their cases. Aeschines the accuser began with a discussion of the law where he appeared to be on better ground (*a iure quo videbatur potentior coeperit*) while Demosthenes, who spoke in defence of Ctesiphon, placed almost all of his topics ahead of his discussion of the law (*patronus omnia paene ante ius posuerit*). Libanius, the author of one of the hypotheses to Demosthenes' speech, held a similar view. Libanius noted that Demosthenes both began his speech with a discussion of his policy and career and turned to those topics again at the end of his speech. This was artfully done (*technikos*), Libanius believes, for it was necessary to begin with one's strong points and to end up with them. Or, as the author of the other hypothesis phrased it, borrowing a line from Homer, Demosthenes, like a good general, 'sets his weaker troops in the centre'. If these ancient scholars are correct, then Demosthenes' victory at the trial was not just a personal triumph; it also represented the triumph of rhetoric over law.

Modern scholars have generally concurred with their ancient predecessors on this issue. The most detailed study of the legal arguments in the case still remains that of W. E. Gwatkin, who, despite some criticisms of Aeschines' arguments, concludes that 'the better reasoning is that of Aeschines'.[21] Since 'Demosthenes was *hypeuthynos* in the legal sense in 336 when the crown was proposed', Gwatkin claims that Ctesiphon's proposal was illegal and that he should have been convicted. Meyer-Laurin turns in a similar verdict (*Gesetz und Billigkeit*, p. 32): 'Aeshines hatte den Wortlaut der Gesetze auf seiner Seite ("Aeschines had the actual wording of the laws on his side")'. He believes that the outcome of the trial did not hinge on the question of the legality of Ctesiphon's decree, but on political factors. And H. Wankel, the author of an exhaustive commentary on the speech Demosthenes delivered at the trial, agrees that Aeschines had the stronger case from juristic point of view.[22] Like Quintilian and Libanius before them, these modern scholars believe that Demosthenes' oratory was so powerful that it overwhelmed the solid legal arguments put forward by his opponent Aeschines.

The fact that Aeschines devotes a much larger portion of his speech to a discussion of the laws than Demosthenes does might appear to indicate that Aeschines thought his legal arguments were far stronger than those of his opponent. But we should not make up our minds on the basis of appearances. Nor should we rule out the possibility that Aeschines knew his legal case was rather weak and consequently spun a veil of elaborate argumentation to hide its weaknesses.

Aeschines makes two main charges against the legality of Ctesiphon's decree. The first is that Ctesiphon had proposed honours for Demosthenes before he had completed his term of office as *teichopoios* and had submitted his account at his *euthynai* or audit (Aes. 3.9–31). Aeschines charges that this decree contravened the law that forbade the award of crowns to magistrates who were still subject to audit (*hypeuthynos*). His second charge against Ctesiphon's proposal is that its proposal to announce Demosthenes' honours in the theatre of Dionysus was in violation of the law which stipulated that honours granted by the Council and the Assembly could be announced only in those two places and nowhere else (Aes. 3.32–48). In his response to the second charge, Demosthenes is able to cite a law which permitted the announcement of honours in the theatre of Dionysus if the Assembly voted to allow it (Dem. 18.120–121). Scholars have generally recognised that this law provides strong support for Demosthenes' rebuttal of the second charge, but have found Aeschines' first charge unassailable.[23]

We need to look at the first charge more closely. Aeschines says that the law forbidding the award of crowns to magistrates subject to audit was passed because of the dishonesty of corrupt magistrates. These magistrates, knowing they would not pass the examination of their pilfered accounts at their *euthynai*, conspired with friendly speakers in the Assembly to have decrees of praise passed for them during their terms of office. Thus, if they were subsequently prosecuted after their accounts were examined, then the members of the court would be reluctant to convict them and thereby condemn men whose conduct in office had already received commendation from the Athenian people. Aeschines notes that Ctesiphon could have avoided breaking the law by calling for the award to be granted to Demosthenes only after he had successfully passed his *euthynai*, but failed to do so. Aeschines disapproves of the practice of inserting such a clause in decrees of praise but admits it was common at the time, and contemporary inscriptions show that his statement is correct. (We will return to these inscriptions later.) Aeschines then deals with a few hypothetical objections to his arguments. He predicts that his opponents will claim that Demosthenes was not technically speaking a magistrate when Ctesiphon passed his decree or that Demosthenes was exempt from audit at the end of his term of office since he had contributed ten minae to the project he was supervising instead of receiving public funds. He easily brushes aside these objections by proving that the office of *teichopoios* Demosthenes held was indeed a magistracy and that the contribution of money made by Demosthenes was irrelevant to the legal issue involved in the case. He sticks to what he says is the law: it is illegal to crown those in office still subject to audit and cites documents to show that Demosthenes held a magistracy when Ctesiphon proposed his decree.

That would appear to be the end of the question. We need to look, however, at the precise wording of the law. Aeschines first gives the provision of the law at 3.11 where he says it explicitly forbids the crowning of those subject to audit. At 3.26 he paraphrases the provisions of the law with similar language: 'If someone is subject to audit for one office, even a very small one, the lawgiver does not allow the crowning of that man before he undergoes his audit.' What is rather suspicious is that Aeschines does not have the actual text of the law read out by the court clerk until 3.30, where he gives a slightly different version of the law:

'The other law [of the two read out at this point] forbids the crowning of an office subject to audit' (*archen hypeuthynon*). This is a subtle variation, but it has crucial significance for the legality of Ctesiphon's decree. The version of the law given by Aeschines at 3.31 implies that it was only illegal to award a crown for a term of office; that is, for the performance of the duties attached to an office before the magistrate to receive the award passed his audit. This means that the law did not prohibit a person who held an office from receiving any crowns before undergoing his *euthynai*, but only a crown awarded for his performance in that office. In other words, a magistrate who was still *hypeuthynos* might still be able to receive a crown for some remarkable achievement, for a generous donation of money, or for earlier public service.

The next question we need to ask is, what kind of decree of praise had Ctesiphon proposed? It should come as no surprise that Aeschines never has Ctesiphon's decree read out during his discussion of the laws about crowns, but only quotes a few phrases from it after this section (3.49–50). These phrases appear to indicate that Ctesiphon's decree was a general commendation, for Demosthenes is praised for his merit and virtue and for continually saying and doing what is best for the people. The only other place where Aeschines refers to the actual contents of the decree is towards the end of his speech (3.236–237). Here he says that Demosthenes was praised for having trenches dug around the walls of Athens. Aeschines then recalls how this work resulted in tearing up the public burial grounds. A passage from Lycurgus' speech *Against Leocrates* (44) informs us that this took place right after the battle of Chaeronea when the Athenians were expecting an imminent attack by the victorious King Philip II of Macedonia. This would place Demosthenes' supervision of the work on the trenches in late 338, a year before his election to the post of *teichopoios*. This is one of several *euergesiai* ('good deeds') listed in the decree. Aeschines then repeats that in the second part of the decree Demosthenes is praised for constantly saying and doing what is best for the Athenian people. Demosthenes in his defence of Ctesiphon also quotes this phrase and adds that he was praised for donating a sum of money towards the building of fortifications (18.113–114).

These passages indicate that Ctesiphon's decree was not a decree of praise for Demosthenes' performance of his duties as *teichopoios* or as administrator of the Theoric Fund, a post he held simultaneously (Aes. 3.24). Ctesiphon's decree must have been similar to the one that Euchares moved for Callias of Sphettus in 270/69.[24] It was an award for a series of public services and contained a general commendation for his consistent devotion to the welfare of Athens.

We are now in a position to make sense of Demosthenes' reply to Aeschines' first charge against Ctesiphon. Demosthenes (18.113) rightly draws attention to the fact that he was praised not for any of the things for which he was subject to audit, but on the grounds that he had donated money. Demosthenes draws attention to the very issue Aeschines ignores, namely, the nature of the praise contained in the decree. Demosthenes stresses that he was not praised for his performance of his duties as *teichopoios* or as administrator of the *theorika*. Since Ctesiphon's decree did not praise a 'term of office' (*archen*), it is therefore not subject to the provisions of the law on which Aeschines relies. To provide evidence for his argument, Demosthenes, unlike Aeschines, has Ctesiphon's decree read out (18.118). He then sums up his argument briefly and forcefully: I made a contribution. I am praised for that reason. I am not subject to audit for what I gave. I was a magistrate. I underwent an audit for my office, not for what I contributed (18.117). Demosthenes' brevity here does not mask a rhetorical bluff. His argument is terse because it bears directly on the legal issue at stake, which is more than we can say for the convoluted arguments of the long-winded Aeschines.

To sum up so far. Aeschines adopts a broad interpretation of the statute about the awarding of crowns and construes it as forbidding any award to a magistrate currently holding office. Demosthenes takes a narrower interpretation of the statute and holds that it only applies to decrees of praise for the performance of the duties of an office, not to other types of commendation.

Several reasons favour Demosthenes' interpretation of the statute. First of all, the text of the statute is more likely to have read 'an office subject to audit' (*archen hypeuthynon*) not 'magistrates subject to audit' (*archontas hypeuthynous*) since the former is the wording that Aeschines gives right after the statute is read out to the court. Demosthenes' interpretation of this phrase is certainly the more natural one. Aeschines' interpretation, on the other hand, relies on a questionable paraphrase of these two words. Moreover, Demosthenes' interpretation is more in line with the intent of the law as explained by Aeschines (3.9–12). Aeschines says that the law was aimed at magistrates who embezzled money during their terms of office, then had friendly speakers pass decrees of praise for their performance in office to ward off prosecutions after their *euthynai*. Thus Aeschines himself says that the law was directed at decrees of praise for performance in office, not for other types of commendation.

Second, there is the argument from common sense. If the law prohibited any magistrate who was subject to audit from receiving a crown, then it would have been impossible for a general like Pericles, who was re-elected fifteen times in a row (Plut. *Pericles* 16.3), to receive a crown for a victory won in his first year of office until he either lost an election or decided not to run again for, as long as he remained in office he was *hypeuthynos* and thus ineligible to receive a crown. The law may not have been in effect during the fifth century, but it certainly was during the late fourth century, when Phocion was elected general forty-five times (Plut. *Phocion* 8.1). If we take the narrow interpretation of the statute, then a general such as Pericles or Phocion could have received a crown for a remarkable achievement immediately without having to wait for his political career to encounter a hiatus.

Third, there is the evidence that Demosthenes cites in his defence of Ctesiphon (18.114–116). Demosthenes adduces the examples of Nausicles, Diotimus, Charidemus and Neoptolemus, all of whom received the honour of a crown during their terms of office for acts of generosity. Demosthenes is not fabricating evidence for he has the decrees passed for these men read out by the clerk. These decrees do not show that the Athenians ignored the law about crowns. Rather they prove that Demosthenes' interpretation of the law was the customary one and had been followed in many previous instances.

Additional evidence comes from the speech *On the Trierarchic Crown* preserved in the Demosthenic corpus ([Demosthenes] 51). The trierarch who delivers the speech addresses the Council and informs its members that shortly before he had received a crown for being the first to launch his trireme. Yet it is also clear from the speech that the man was still serving as trierarch when he addressed the Council and was thus *hypeuthynos* at the time (Aes. 3.19). Like Nausicles and the others named by Demosthenes, this trierarch had received a crown for a remarkable achievement during his term of office.

146

Finally, we should note the decrees that call for the award of a crown and contain the clause stipulating that the award not be conferred until after the honorand submits his accounts at his audit. All of the decrees which contain this clause are motions to reward overall performance during a term of office, not for single achievements, individual acts of generosity, or long-term service to the community. There are nine in all:

IG ii² 223 (343/42): Phanodemus and Eudoxus are crowned for their service as members of the Council and for acquitting their duties as Councillors.

IG ii² 330 (336/35): Phyleus, who was elected *hieropoios*, is praised for performing his duties in that office.

IG ii² 338 (333/32): Pytheas, who was elected to supervise the fountains, is praised for excellence and justice in matters concerning the administration of the fountains.

IG ii² 354 (328/27): Androcles, selected by lot to serve as priest for the temple of Asclepius, is praised for looking after the temple 'well and piously' and for his supervision of the adjoining theatre.

IG ii² 410 (*c.* 330): A group of ten priests elected as *hieropoioi* are praised for performing their duty of conducting sacrifices.

IG ii² 415 (330/29): Callicratidas is praised for performing his duties as *anagrapheus* of documents.

Athenian Agora XV (328/27): Three members of the Council, Euthycrates, Philostratus and Chaerestratus, are praised for their *philotimia* in their performance of duties in the Council.

IG ii² 672 (279/78): Comeas is granted the award of *sitesis* and a statue in addition to the honour of a crown for his distinguished service in the office of hipparch.

IG ii² 780 (249/48 or 248/47):[25] Agathaeus is praised for performing his duties as *agonothetes*. His prize is not specified, but it is to be awarded only after he passes his audit.

None of these honorary decrees is an award for general service to the community or for individual acts of generosity.[26] This evidence lends further support to Demosthenes' narrower interpretation of the statute about crowns. Aeschines' broader interpretation of the statute was his own innovation and was apparently never followed either before or after the trial of Ctesiphon.

This conclusion profoundly alters our view of the speeches of Aeschines and Demosthenes presented at this trial. We can now see that Aeschines' legal case was in reality quite weak. Aeschines appears to have recognised that this was a serious problem, which could not be ignored, for he spent a large portion of his speech building a case for a novel interpretation of the laws about crowns. He tries to disguise this fact by postponing the actual reading of the law until he has set out his arguments using his own rather dubious paraphrase of the law rather than its true wording. It is also telling that he never has Ctesiphon's decree read out. This may well have been due to his fear that the members of the court might have recognised that the decree was not the type of decree covered under the law about crowns. Because Aeschines' legal arguments were so flimsy, Demosthenes did not need to waste his time on a lengthy refutation. All Demosthenes had to do in order to demolish his opponent's case was to deliver a few well-aimed blows. Demosthenes placed his discussion of the laws in an inconspicuous part of the speech not because he felt it was a vulnerable point in his defence of Ctesiphon, but because Aeschines' arguments about the laws did not represent as serious threat to his case as some of Aeschines' other arguments about his political career.

We have no way of knowing the precise reasons why the court voted to acquit Ctesiphon (for the verdict see Plut. *Demosthenes* 24). But one cannot argue that in finding him innocent the court flagrantly ignored the laws about crowns. Demosthenes' success was not the triumph of rhetoric over law, but instead the victory of law *and* rhetoric. Contrary to Finley's flawed assumption, Demosthenes' unmistakable devotion to rhetoric and style did not preclude a keen interest in legal issues. Demosthenes was an outstanding orator because he knew the people in his audience and how to appeal to them. When speaking in court, he knew that the dicasts had sworn to vote in accordance with the laws. His speech for Ctesiphon shows that he expected them to take their oath seriously when casting their ballots.

NOTES

1 B. B. Rogers, *Aristophanes Wasps* (London: 1906), pp. xxvi–xxvii.
2 Quoted in R. J. Bonner and G. Smith, *The Administration of Justice from Homer to Aristotle*, II (Chicago: 1938; repr. New York: 1970), pp. 288–9.
3 M. I. Finley, 'Some Problems in Greek Law: A Consideration of Pringsheim on Sale', *Seminar* 9 (1951), p. 89. Finley's claim that the orators tended to misuse legal terminology is questionable: see E. M.

Harris, '*Apotimema*: Athenian Terminology for Real Security in Leases and Dowry Agreements', *CQ²* 43 (1993), pp. 73–95.

4 M. N. Tod, *Greek Historical Inscriptions*, II (Oxford: 1948), no. 204, lines 11–15.

5 For the dicastic oath see Bonner and Smith, *Administration of Justice*, II, pp. 152–6. R. Osborne, 'Law in Action in Classical Athens', *JHS* 105 (1985), pp. 52–3, argues that the Athenian courts 'were felt to regulate conflict by effecting a redistribution' and did not 'impose any final decision' (this is simply wrong: the principle of *res iudicata* was well established in the Athenian legal system (Dem. 20.147, 38.16)). As a result, he completely ignores the implications of the dicastic oath. Nor can any mention of the oath be found in the glossary of legal terms found in P. Cartledge, P. Millett and S. Todd (eds), *Nomos: Essays in Athenian Law, Politics and Society* (Cambridge: 1990).

6 Dicastic oath quoted or alluded to: Aes. 1.170, 3.8, 198, 233; Andoc. 1.9, 105; Dem. 18.121, 19.132, 179, 239, 297, 20.118, 21.177, 212, 24.148, 175, 25.149–151; Dinarchus 3.17; Lys. 14.22, 40, 15.8–11, 18.13; Lyc. 1.79.

7 Dicastic oath mentioned at beginning or end of speech: Aes. 2.1, 3.6, 257; Andoc. 1.2; Antiph. 5.96; Dem. 18.1, 25.99, 27.68, 39.41, 45.87, 55.35; Isaeus 2.47, 4.31, 6.65, 8.46; Lys. 10.32; Hyperides 4.40; Plato, *Apology* 35c.

8 That Athenian litigants based their cases on the laws has been amply demonstrated by H. Meyer-Laurin, *Gesetz und Billigkeit im attischen Prozess* (Weimar: 1966). This important book is gratuitously dismissed by Cartledge, Millett and Todd, *Nomos*, p. 14.

9 M. H. Hansen, 'How Often did the Athenian Dicasteria Meet?', *GRBS* 20 (1979), pp. 243–6.

10 M. H. Hansen, *The Athenian Democracy in the Age of Demosthenes* (Oxford: 1991), pp. 186–8.

11 For the political education of Athenian citizens see M. I. Finley, *Politics in the Ancient World* (Cambridge: 1983), pp. 74–5.

12 On this topic see E. M. Harris, 'Response to Trevor Saunders', in M. Gagarin (ed.), *Symposion 1990, Vorträge zur griechischen und hellenistischen Rechtsgeschichte* (Cologne, Weimar and Vienna: 1992), pp. 134–6.

13 The attempt of S. Todd, 'Lady Chatterley's Lover and the Attic Orators: The Social Composition of the Athenian Jury', *JHS* 110 (1990), pp. 146–73, to compare the Athenian courts with modern jurors is very misleading. So too is the claim made by Osborne, 'Law in Action', p. 53, that the Athenian legal system was designed for dicasts 'without legal training'. The Athenian dicasts were also unlike modern jurors in so far as they did not have to remain silent during the trial. See V. Bers, 'Dikastic Thorubos', in P. A. Cartledge and F. D. Harvey (eds), *Crux. Essays . . . de Ste. Croix* (London: 1985), pp. 1–15 = *History of Political Thought* 6 (1985), pp. 1–15.

14 Cf. Lys. 14.4. Obviously this kind of decision could only act as an informal precedent since there was no statute in the Athenian law-code governing the application of precedents, nor any legal procedure for enforcing precedents. Yet one should not take the absence of such a statute as a sign of the 'primitive' nature of the Athenian legal system.

Roman law did not have such a statute either until the Law of Citations of AD 426 (*Cod. Theod.* 1.4.3).

15 For a brief analysis of the case see E. M. Harris, review of D. M. MacDowell, *Demosthenes: Against Meidias Chp* 87(1992), p. 78.

16 H. L. A. Hart, *The Concept of Law* (Oxford: 1961), pp. 124–32. Osborne, 'Law in Action', pp. 43–4, seriously misuses Hart's term 'open texture', which is relevant only to the *substantive* aspect of law, by applying it to his discussion of legal *procedure*. Osborne also misinterprets [Aristotle] *Athenaion Politeia* 9.2. Aristotle is not criticising Athenian law for its 'open texture', but simply recognising that all laws framed in general terms possess an 'open texture'. Osborne's mistake is endorsed by J. Ober, *Mass and Elite in Democratic Athens* (Princeton: 1989), pp. 144–5.

17 For the text of the law of *hybris* see Harris, review of MacDowell, *Demosthenes: Against Meidias*, pp. 77–8.

18 On the question of definitions in Athenian law see E. M. Harris, 'When is a Sale not a Sale? The Riddle of Athenian Terminology for Real Security', CQ^2 38 (1988), pp. 368–70.

19 For the meaning of this term see G. Rickert, *Hekon and Akon in Early Greek Thought* (Atlanta: 1989).

20 For a further discussion of Aristotle on proofs, see C. Carey, chapter 2 above.

21 W. E. Gwatkin, 'The Legal Arguments in Aeschines' *Against Ktesiphon* and Demosthenes' *On The Crown*', *Hesperia* 26 (1957), pp. 129–41. Cf. P. Harding, chapter 10 below.

22 H. Wankel, *Demosthenes: Rede für Ktesiphon über den Kranz* (Heidelberg: 1976), vol. 1, p. 17.

23 For example, Gwatkin, 'Legal Arguments', pp. 138–40. Aeschines (3.32) argues that the law requiring that crowns awarded by the Council only be announced in the Council and crowns awarded by the Assembly only in the Assembly and nowhere else laid down an absolute prohibition which did not allow for any exceptions. He accordingly interprets the law allowing the announcement of crowns in the theatre as applying only to crowns awarded by foreign communities (3.35–47). Demosthenes (18.120–122), on the other hand, interprets this provision as an exception to the prohibition contained in the law cited at Aeschines 3.32. Evidence from inscriptions reveals that Demosthenes' interpretation was the one generally followed: see Gwatkin, 'Legal Arguments', p. 138 n. 57.

24 T. Leslie Shear, *Kallias of Sphettos and the Revolt of Athens in 286* B.C., *Hesperia Supplement* 17 (Princeton: 1978).

25 For the date see E. M. Harris, 'When did the Athenian Assembly Meet? Some New Evidence', *AJPh* 112 (1991), p. 332 n. 28.

26 In two decrees we are told that the honorands have already passed their audit. (1) W. K. Pritchett, 'Greek Inscriptions', *Hesperia* 9 (1940), no. 20, pp. 104–11 (302/1): a group of taxiarchs are praised for performing the duties of their office. (2) *IG* ii² 488 (304/3): a group of individuals are praised for having 'justly performed their office' (*di[kaio]s arxantes*). The office they held is not named, but their number is significant: there are eleven individuals commended. If they all held the same office and comprise the total board for the office in that year, then they should be the Eleven ([Arist.] *Athenaion Politeia* 52.1).

Part III

CONTEXTS

8

Epic and rhetoric

Peter Toohey

The topic, in a sense, is a bogus one – speech-making and persuasion in Homer and Apollonius. There are speakers and speeches enough in Greek epic, but, at least in Homer and Apollonius, there is little recognisable rhetorical elaboration of the classical kind. This, of course, is understandable in the case of Homer: he was writing before rhetoric was invented. Yet, in the case of the Alexandrian writer of epic, Apollonius of Rhodes (composing after Aristotle and the major orators), the absence of speech-making, thus the absence of 'primary' rhetoric, is striking.[1] In this chapter I intend to look, selectively, at several of the speeches in Homer and in Apollonius.[2] My concern, above all, is to isolate some of the major contrasts between the speech-making habits of Homer and of Apollonius. We will see, I hope, how 'rhetorical' Homer can be. We will also see – and this is perhaps the crux of my chapter – why Apollonius may have shown so little taste for primary rhetoric.

HOMER

Homer's speeches were not shaped from any clear-cut template. How could they have been when rhetoric had not yet been invented? Even so, there seem to be sufficient traces of later rhetorical habits in Homer to justify, however tentatively, our importing aspects of this anachronistic template.[3] Such a procedure, I hope to show, can be useful in some expected, and in at least one unexpected, way. On the simplest level rhetorical analysis of Homeric speech-making may demonstrate that these speeches are not formless, but quite deliberately shaped.[4] It may also demonstrate that there is a continuity between Homer's and later rhetorical practice. More important is that such analysis shows again how vital is the *paradeigma* for Homer's speeches. This, in its turn, points to the essentially paratactic, oral nature of these utterances.[5] Thus emerges my final, most important point: these speeches, in their oral, paradigmatic, paratactic nature, betray a mind-set noted in other contexts by Ong and by Carothers.[6] Oral, or orally based cultures, they argue, externalise harmful emotions. We will, I hope, see this in the four Homeric speeches to be examined in this chapter. These addresses are not violent, but three at least are paraenetic, and the fourth may be designed to allay anger. At any rate the address of these Homeric speeches is positive, outwardly directed, and expectantly ameliorative. That, maybe, is hardly surprising. But it will, I suggest, become notable when we come to contrast the speech-making habits of the utterly literate, high-cultured Apollonius. His most prominent speeches (and there are not many of them) offer an approach markedly reflecting that interiorisation noted by Ong and Carothers as more typical of the response of literates to harmful emotion.

In the first part of this chapter I would like to tease out some of these issues in relation to Homer.[7] I will look briefly at Nestor's four major speeches in the *Iliad* (all of which might be designated as deliberative: 1.254–284; 7.124–160; 11.656–803; and 23.626–650).[8] Why Nestor? Being too old to be both a doer of deeds and a speaker of words (cf. *Iliad* 9.443: unlike Achilles or Odysseus) his appeal was based on speech. His words, Homer tells us, were like honey (*Iliad* 1.247–249).[9] Furthermore, Nestor offers us what is the longest single speech in the *Iliad* (11.656–803). His discourse thus provides a very useful indicator of the occasions and of the methods that could be used by a prominent Homeric public speaker.[10] The first of Nestor's speeches occurs at 1.254–284, where he butts into the quarrel between Agamemnon and Achilles to rebuke them, urging that they take his advice.[11] Its structure is as follows:[12]

254–258 (*exordium*):[13] The Trojans would be glad if they knew of the trouble amongst the Greeks.
259–261 (*prothesis*): Be persuaded (πίθεσθε: 259). I once associated with better men than you, and they listened to me.
261–271 (*paradeigma* = *pistis*):[14] Nestor explains how the Lapiths took his advice when he helped them fight against the Centaurs.
271–274 (*prothesis*): They were better than you and they listened to me. Be persuaded (πίθεσθε: 274).

275–284 (epilogue):[15] Advice for Achilles and Agamemnon: cease from your anger.

There are five parts to this speech, two of which (for reasons I will outline below) are repeated. What remains may approximate very loosely to the typical structure of a classical speech. Lines 254–258 attempt to gain the attention of Nestor's audience, Achilles and Agamemnon; this is the introduction or *exordium*. The *prothesis* or specific recommendation, at whose acceptance the speech aims, is repeated at lines 259–261 and 271–274. This blends, somewhat imperceptibly, with lines 275–284, an epilogue of sorts, but one which details the advice Achilles and Agamemnon ought to adopt. The 'example' (*paradeigma*), a minor narrative reminiscence (261–271), exists in place of the proofs (*pisteis*) normally adduced in support of the *prothesis* (and in place of the *diegesis* which perhaps does not suit Nestor's discursive mode of speaking; in a sense this myth 'example' is a 'narrative'). This *paradeigma* is a proof of a sort, but its logic, like most reminiscence, is wholly implicit.

We could also mention some of the rhetorical techniques used by Nestor. Amongst others there is the application of a *paradeigma*[16] (the story of the Lapiths and Centaurs) and, within that, the vivid listing of famous combatants' names (a real appeal to the past); there is the vivid frame for the example provided by the use in anaphora of forms of πείθομαι ('be persuaded': 259, 273 and 274); there are other repetitions of words and sound and, in addition, metonymy, antithesis and litotes.[17] There is also personification of a type in the *exordium*. The epilogue adapts dramatically the technique of apostrophe. That there are similarities, albeit not overwhelming ones, between this small speech and later oratory is evident. The differences are also marked. The logic of the speech is anecdotal and is deliberately tied to the character of the speaker – the latter surely a crucial point in this literary medium. The speech too is patterned in ring form – something less immediately evident in later rhetoric.[18] But the major points remain to be made. The logic of Nestor's utterance is apparent and is clearly and precisely articulated. It follows a pattern which we will observe in two of the other speeches for discussion. But it is a logic based upon the paradigm, rather than on real proof or *pistis*.

So far so good. We have seen the usefulness of rhetorical classification for this speech: it emphasises the deliberation of its structure. We have also seen that it exhibits traits shown by later oratory. We have also noted its use of the paradigm as a *pistis*. But before we can pass on to the remaining speeches we ought to look a little more at the role of the paradigm. Two points need to be made. The first, not unexpectedly, concerns parataxis[19] – something habitually invoked when discussing Homeric epic. Parataxis, of course, designates the simple linking of clauses and phrases by the use of co-ordinating conjunctions to build sentences. Parataxis functions above all by the uncomplicated use of polarity and analogy.[20] It is not, however, limited to the verbal and syntactic texture. Homer's cumulative narrative is both repetitive and stylised – doubtless the result of the constraints of the oral circumstances of its composition. This is evident not just within the narrative,[21] but within the deployment of themes and thought,[22] in characterisation, and within the shape of the poems themselves.[23] This application of parataxis accounts for a number of the characteristics of Nestor's speeches – above all for the paradigmatic nature of the Nestorean *pistis*.

Parataxis seems also to provide speeches such as this one of Nestor with their characteristic argumentative and structural mode.[24] Let us briefly reconsider *Iliad* 1.254–284. This passage exhibits two striking qualities whose origin may reside in the paratactic art of the oral poet. The first is the careful, overall structure of the speech: it is in ring form (hence the repeated *prothesis*):[25] A (254–258: *exordium*) – B (259–261: *prothesis*) – C (261–271: the *paradeigma*) – B¹ (271–274: *prothesis*) – A¹ (275–284: epilogue). This loose pattern, as I have indicated, is ultimately the product of a paratactic compositional medium. The use of the *paradeigma* is even more typical of a paratactic way of 'explaining' things. Homer likes to juxtapose. It is frequently the case that the connections between these juxtaposed elements are left unstated. That is the case with this 'example'. Why? To labour at and make obvious such connections is something that is much easier to do in a medium where revision – thanks to the provision of a pen and paper – is more possible. Homer, composing orally and with the haste that implies, could afford no such luxuries. The second point which I would like to make concerning the *paradeigma* relates back to the observations of Ong (*Orality and Literacy*, p. 69) and Carothers. The use of the *paradeigma*, at least in the context of this Nestorean speech, represents a simple means of externalising, making more manageable, and rendering more acceptable dangerous emotion. The *paradeigma* offers an indirect and oblique means for making a point. Think again of its aim in this speech. Old Nestor is attempting to dissuade two very powerful and very dangerous young men from their anger. Nestor disapproves of the actions of Agamemnon and Achilles, but he must express this without making too obvious his disapproval. The risks are manifold: he may incur their wrath himself if he is too blunt; or he may merely inflame their anger and set them all the more against one another; or he may insult one party more than the another, so causing assault or withdrawal. In such circumstances the *paradeigma* becomes an ideal means for blunting and making less offensive the potentially wrathful *paraenesis* – here appearing in the epilogue of 1.275–284. Ong's and Carothers' simple point is that potentially harmful emotion in oral societies is externalised (in the most extreme instances it may manifest itself in a character's going 'berserk' or 'running amok'). Harmful emotion must somehow be rendered acceptable – at least in the eyes of society. The means for gaining acceptance, for example, may manifest themselves as a possession-like and inexplicable outburst whose extremity and so-called divine origin renders the experience in some way *sui generis*, hence able to be tolerated.[26] In Nestor's case the 'palliative' for his blunt, almost angry, message is, I suggest, the old man's *paradeigma*. It acts as a means of palliating the simmering anger both of this aged speaker and his youthful, warrior audience. Is this application of the *paradeigma* the root of Nestor's reputation for honeyed speech?

The second of the speeches appears at 7.124–160 and represents another rebuke (or *paraenesis*). It is designed to rally the Achaeans – they have been taking a battering at the hands of Hector and the Trojans, and Menelaus has just withdrawn from a challenge to engage in personal combat with Hector. The long speech runs thus:[27]

124–131 (*exordium*): Peleus would want to die if he heard that the Achaeans were cowering before Hector.

132–135 (*prothesis*): I wish I were young again (αἲ γάρ . . . ἡβῷμ': 132–133).

136–156 (*paradeigma* = *pistis*): I once killed Ereuthalion, champion of our opponents; he had the armour of Areithous.

157–158 (*prothesis*): I wish I were young (εἴθ' ὣς ἡβώοιμι: 157). Then I would fight Hector.

159–160 (epilogue): But you all do not want to fight Hector.

The pattern of this speech is remarkable in its similarity to that at 1.254–284. (We are again witnessing a carefully constructed speech.) There is a brief but rousing introduction (124–131) balanced by a pithy apostrophe, which acts as the epilogue (159–160). Once again the prothesis is repeated (132–135 and 157–158), but this time its full purport is only apparent on the second statement. There is no *diegesis*, nor, technically, are there *pisteis*. The *paradeigma* seems to do double duty in this regard: it acts as a type of a *pistis*, but provides, at the same time, a generous, if irrelevant narrative.

Several aspects of this paraenetic speech require stress. The logic of the *paradeigma* is identical to that of the first of Nestor's speeches. It makes its claim for persuasion on that most popular of rhetorical tropes, an appeal to the past – specifically Nestor's.[28] The speech also evinces the paratactic, oral compositional mode of ring form (A–B–C–B¹–A¹), stressed also by Kirk (*Iliad*, II, pp. 24 ff.). The pattern operates here as follows: A (124–131: *exordium*), B (132–135: *prothesis*), C (136–156: *paradeigma* = *pistis*), B¹ (157–158: *prothesis*), A¹ (7.159–160: epilogue). But at the same time the technique used by this speech – the reminiscence – is totally in keeping with the ethos of old Nestor. Reminiscence is a ploy of the powerless,[29] but, and we could emphasise this, the reminiscence occurs as a paradigm. Just as we have seen with the first speech, the need here to make acceptable a dangerous rebuke is acute. Aged Nestor cannot cause Menelaus to lose face and so risk a berserk reaction. Externalisation, therefore, explains the function of the paradigm in this speech.

A *paradeigma* (11.670–761) is also at the heart of Nestor's third speech (11.656–803).[30] In this instance, however, it runs dangerously close to swamping the utterance. Indeed, its presence may be the cause for the frequent, but, as we shall see, unjust accusations made against this speech for formlessness. In this speech, while addressing Patroclus (he has come to enquire on Achilles' behalf who has returned wounded from battle), Nestor rebukes the indifference of Achilles towards the condition in which the Greeks now find themselves. He contrasts his own conduct as a young man when he fought the Epeians. Here is a breakdown of the shape and content of the address (the comments in square brackets are my paraphrastic expansions):[31]

656–665 (*exordium*): Achilles is showing no pity for the Achaeans. They are being slaughtered.

666–669 (*prothesis*): Will Achilles wait until we are all killed? I am no longer strong now [I am not, *you are*].

670–761 (*paradeigma = pistis*): How Nestor led the Pylians to a remarkable victory over the Epeians. [This is what a properly motivated warrior can achieve.]

762–764 (*prothesis*): That is what I was like. But Achilles is showing no pity for the Achaeans. He will regret this. [I would help the Achaeans if I were young, but I am not; *you are*.]

765–792 (*diegesis*):[32] Had you, Patroclus, heeded the counsel of his father Menoetius and provided Achilles with good advice, things would not have reached this pass. You might yet persuade him.

793–803 (epilogue): If Achilles will not help the Greeks, then you take his armour and help them.

The function of this most complex of speeches is sometimes said to be 'a paradigmatic exhortation, offering an example from the past to bolster its argument that Achilles should give up his anger' (Pedrick, 'Paradigmatic Nature', p. 55 and n. 2). I suggest, however, that this is to misread something which is more clearly designed to persuade Patroclus to enter the war in Achilles' stead. This point is stated outright only at the very end of the speech (793–803). On the two previous occasions when Nestor seems to be on the point of stating his purpose (the so-called *protheseis* at lines 666–669 and 762–764), he makes his point almost by misdirection. There we are tempted to interpret Nestor's utterance in light of his other speeches. It is as if he were about to say that, had he been young, there would not be this trouble (a Nestorean leitmotif). The first *paradeigma* (or *pistis*) could also be taken this way. What shifts the persuasive balance is what I have termed the *diegesis*. Its intention is to show how things have reached the state in which they are now (Greeks being slaughtered willy-nilly). The fault is all that of Patroclus and of his bad advice to Achilles. To make amends Patroclus should don Achilles' armour and fight – like Nestor did against the Epeians.

The structure and paratactic logic of this utterance require some elucidation. The speech is, at first sight, built around a very simple ring pattern: A (656–665: *exordium*), B (666–669: *prothesis*), C (670–761: *paradeigma = pistis*), B¹ (762–764: *prothesis*). But Homer breaks the mould at this point. He could have ended after lines 762–764 with, perhaps, a simple *exordium*, stating how Nestor would have fought the Trojans, and he could have finalised things with a simple lament on the low fortunes of the Achaeans. He may or may not have gone on to urge Patroclus to re-enter the war – I suspect he would not have. The structure of such a speech would have been in ring form (and the use of the *paradeigma* as a type of *pistis* is the sort of paratactic usage to which we have become habituated). But it is at this very point that the great monologue breaks from the pattern. Instead of providing us with the expected epilogue, Nestor offers us another 'digression', D (765–792: *diegesis*), then, finally, a conclusion, A^1 (793–803: epilogue), to balance the *exordium* (656–665). This *diegesis* shifts the logic of the speech away from Nestor and on to Patroclus. It makes immediately apparent that Nestor's digression was no lament, but something of a moral paradigm which ought to be applied to Patroclus. Then follows the epilogue which pulls things together. It urges Patroclus to fight. It is apparent that this complex speech has been forced to sacrifice the aesthetic niceties of simple ring structure to enable it to present a more complex form of logic. But, and I think that we cannot underline this enough, the form of logic is strictly linear and strictly paratactic. It is a form of logic that establishes itself, block-like, by accretion and by juxtaposition. Thus the connection of the *paradeigma* to its surrounds is one which remains implicit and one which we must extract. Thus too the connection of the *diegesis* to its surrounds is implicit and one which the listener must extract without assistance (especially of the anticipatory variety) from the narrator.

This address, as I hope my comments and my analysis may have indicated, is a much more sophisticated piece than those we have seen hitherto. This is fitting, for we are at a key juncture in the narrative.[33] This speech, as much as anything else, will precipitate Patroclus' re-entry into the war. That in turn will spell Patroclus' death, Achilles' re-entry into the conflict, Hector's death, and, eventually, the death (foreshadowed) of Achilles himself. It is fitting that this denouement should be marked by such a grand speech. And grand it is – long, well structured, intensely vivid, and intricate in its persuasive logic. Its logical basis does differ from Nestor's previous discourses – there he told us that had he been young, things would not have been the way they were. Here he does not say that at all. Rather the reverse: he is old now and unable to help as he might have. Therefore a new champion – Patroclus, failing Achilles – is needed. But at the same time we need to note that the persuasive strategy of this speech is as oblique as those we have already seen. Nestor builds his words about reminiscence – first concerning Pylus, then later concerning Peleus' court. The 'example', that is, is the preferred *pistis*. The *prothesis* is as indirect as ever: it could be paraphrased as 'if I were strong now – I am not, but you are. Therefore you should help.' But all that Homer allows Nestor to tell us, poignantly, is that he is too old. The understatement is striking, utterly powerful and completely persuasive.

As yet I have said nothing of the externalisation of harmful emotion to which I alluded when discussing the two previous speeches. Once again Nestor uses the *paradeigma* as a means of deflecting offence away from his potentially insulting *paraenesis*. In this instance, I suppose, though angry he is extremely anxious to avoid arousing the resentment not only of Patroclus, but also of Achilles. This, I might add, also offers a second explanation for the length of the Pylian *paradeigma*. Its extent is in part the result of the detail of this interlude. This relates to the untimely cattle raid – the cause of some of the trouble for his own folk. That fault is intended to look forward, not so much to Achilles', as to Patroclus' fault (his bad advice). In admitting his own blame, Nestor gallantly excuses, partially at least, Patroclus. (This is the type of honeyed generosity we will see Nestor making to Achilles at the funeral games.) That, I suggest, is in part designed to render Patroclus more willing to oblige, but at the same time it exculpates Nestor from the charge of presumption.

The last of Nestor's speeches occurs in Book 23. It is quite short and can be dealt with quickly. It occurs during the funeral games for Patroclus (at 23.626–650). The speech is delivered by Nestor in response to Achilles when, presumably out of respect for the age and earlier exploits of the old man, he awards him the fifth prize set aside for the chariot race. The arrangement is as follows:

626 (*exordium*): Formulaic introduction.

627–628 (*prothesis*): I am not strong now.

629–642 (*paradeigma* = *pistis*): Would that I were strong now (εἴθ' ὣς ἡβώοιμι 23.629 = 7.157) as I was at the funeral games for Amarynceus. There I won everything but the chariot race.

643–645 (*prothesis*): That is what I was like (cf. 11.762). But I am not strong now.

646–650 (epilogue): Nestor thanks Achilles for the gift of the jar.

Nestor, in his use of reminiscence, is nothing if not oblique. This short thank-you reads more as an apology. Nestor seems to be saying in his repeated *prothesis* (627–628 and 643–645) that were he strong enough now, then he would have competed and won prizes in his own right, so honouring Patroclus. Evidence of this (here we have the *pistis*) was his prowess as a young man (629–642). This oblique use of the *paradeigma*, instead of an outright *pistis* or *diegesis*, is a characteristic of the first three speeches. Note that, once again, this address is utterly in keeping with its speaker's characterisation. A very nice touch in this regard is Nestor's admission that he did not win the chariot race at the games for Amarynceus – a fine competitor, he tells Achilles with grateful modesty, but not perfect.

The paratactic structure of Nestor 's apology mirrors that of the preceding speeches: A (626: *exordium*), B (627–628: *prothesis*), C (629–642: *paradeigma* = *pistis*), B¹ (643–645: *prothesis*), A¹ (646–650: epilogue). Note that, once again, a *paradeigma*, carrying the weight of the *pistis*, is placed at the centre and has only an implicit connection made with the surrounding assertions. The use of the *paradeigma* is a prime example of a paratactic form of arguing. I wonder whether the use of the paradigm in this utterance does not suggest that there is more to it than mere apology? In the three preceding speeches the paradigm acted as a means for defusing potentially injurious situations. Perhaps Nestor's characteristic use of the *paradeigma* points to an underlying unease. Does Nestor betray fear of Achilles? Does he imply that, by not competing, despite his advanced years, he runs the risk of insulting both Achilles and his games for Patroclus? (Is this the type of fear that Priam experienced before the seemingly co-operative Achilles, in their meeting of *Iliad* 24?) Does, then, this paradigm act as a means of externalising potentially harmful emotions?

APOLLONIUS

Apollonius shows little enthusiasm for direct speech.[34] Our opportunities for viewing his modes of structuring speeches are accordingly limited. For this chapter I have selected the admittedly arbitrary figure of thirty lines or longer as constituting a speech that is sufficiently elongated to warrant consideration.[35] There are only eleven such speeches in Apollonius' poem. (This, of course, matches the generally diminished frequency of direct speech in the *Argonautica*.) It is, furthermore, striking that of these eleven speeches six do not aim to persuade. They function essentially as conveyors of factual, or, in one instance, of psychological information.[36] (I take persuasion as the *sine qua non* of the rhetorical occasion.) So there remain only five passages within the *Argonautica* of thirty or more lines which aim to persuade,[37] a remarkable feature in a poem of nearly 6,000 lines – compare Homer (50 per cent direct speech), or, even later, Roman epic poets such as Virgil, Lucan or Statius.[38] In what follows I intend to examine four of these five passages (I omit 2.209–239 primarily for reasons of space – the speech is, however, a less striking example and, perhaps, a less well structured example of what the other four attempt).

It is possible that there exists a link between Apollonius' lack of enthusiasm for direct speech, for his paucity of long persuasive speeches, and the particular nature of the five extended persuasive speeches. (We will see that these five speeches all constitute pleas or requests for favours.) The answer may perhaps be found in the observation made by Ong in *Orality and Literacy* that literates 'often manifest tendencies (loss of contact with environment) by psychic withdrawal' (p. 69). Earlier I suggested that the term 'interiorisation' captures this attitude.

'Ptolemaic bureaucracy', it seems to be true to say, 'presided over a dramatic increase in the functions of the written word'.[39] Literacy and writing in Apollonius' Alexandria, we may deduce, came to dominate the expressive culture of the elite and to displace oral traditions in a profound and hitherto unparalleled manner.[40] Perhaps the very best examples are the remarkable picture poems of Simias (collected by Powell in *Collectanea Alexandrina*) whose effect is above all reliant upon writing and upon the eye. The Alexandrian Museum offers another stark testimony.[41] Like Simias' poems, it depends wholly on writing. It is also striking that descriptions of the earliest examples of interiorised psychological states seem to date from this period. I have elsewhere argued for the 'discovery' in this period of such internalised states as melancholia, depression, boredom, and passive love-melancholy.[42] It is also most striking that such interiorised affective states play an important role in creating the emotional timbre of Apollonius' *Argonautica* and in creating the characterisation of Jason.[43] This strange congruity of a dramatic upsurge in the reliance by the elite on writing and of an 'outbreak' of passive affective conditions reinforces, if not Ong's and Carothers' rather romantic causality, at least the validity of their general observation.

I wonder whether it is being too speculative to take things a little further and to suggest a link between the lack of direct speech within the *Argonautica* and a view of the world – which I believe the *Argonautica* projects – that envisages experience as something passively registered rather than vigorously acted upon?[44] And further, I wonder whether the rhetorical prevalence of the pleas which we will look at is not but another symptom of the same outlook? Nestor attempts to control and to ameliorate his world. He disguises what seems to be a barely suppressed anger at those who baulk at this amelioration by means of his *paradeigmata*. In Apollonius' epic major speakers, even one god, seem passively to plead for assistance and for change from forces greater than themselves.

But we are moving too quickly and too far from the speeches. Let us turn now to Apollonius' extended persuasions. In their skeletal form the four speeches I have selected for discussion seem closely to resemble one another. Each possesses an introduction (an attempt to capture the attention of the addressee), a more or less detailed plea for assistance and, also attached, a promise to perform some type of a service for the addressee (this can be either good or bad, depending on the reasons for the address).[45] The order of these three elements may be varied (it depends on the self-confidence of the speaker), and, of course, the amount of detail given to each element will differ (there may also be an epilogue attached). Finally, the whole timbre and detail of presentation will be dictated and defined by the personality of the speaker.

In the first of the four speeches (3.320–366), Argus is young and seems embarrassed at what he must tell his grandfather, King Aietes. There is, thus, no clear enunciation of the plea itself (for assistance with and acquiescence in the Argonautic designs). The plea is to be understood. Here is a schema of his speech:

320–331 (*exordium*): Address to Aietes.
332–349 (plea): Request for Aietes' help.
350–354 (benefaction): An offer of help to Aietes.
355–366 (epilogue): Commendation of the Argonauts.

Argus' speech begins with an attempt to gain the goodwill of Aietes. He stresses how the magnanimous heroes of the Argo rescued Argus and his brothers after their shipwreck (320–331). Then follows the plea (332–349): the Argonauts have come for the fleece, but they do have divine sanction. Now comes the promise of the service which those, for whom the plea is being made, will render the addressee. In this instance the offer is to help Aietes in his war against the Sarmatians (350–354). And finally there is an *exordium* (but no repetition of the plea). Argus, by detailing the impressive lineage of some of the Argonauts, intends to commend this worthy throng to his uncle. It is perhaps typical of Argus' hesitance that he utilises this commendatory epilogue. Other speakers do not. We ought to compare Argus' address with those of Nestor. The logic is no longer paratactic – by which I mean that this speech is not built up by agglomeration of polar or analogous material. The seams in this speech are papered over in an unhomeric manner. There is, accordingly, no large-scale reliance on ring composition, nor does Apollonius' speaker need to rely on the paradigm. Argus' monologue is a more logical and rationally sequential performance.

These same observations could be made of the second of our four speeches (3.975–1007), delivered by Jason to Medea. It is a cool and guileful performance, but one which demonstrates the same basically tripartite structure. Once again we are reading a logically sequenced talk. Even the paradigm (of Ariadne and Theseus: 997–1004) has its superficial relevance made explicit ('thus even for you from god will there be gratitude': 1005). The utterance is structured in the following manner:

975–979 (*exordium*): Opening address to Medea.
980–989 (plea): Jason's plea.
990–1007 (benefaction): How Jason will recompense Medea.

Jason begins by emphasising his own and his crew 's worthiness – in the face of which Medea need feel no reticence (975–979). The plea itself (980–989) requests that Medea honour previous pledges and that she treat Jason as a *xeinos* (986: ironic, given the telling reference to Ariadne within lines 990–1007). The passage climaxes with Jason's plea (988–989): 'Without you I will not surmount my awful labour.' Then at once Jason offers recompense (990–1007). He will, if successful, sing of the *kleos* ('glory': 992) of Medea all over Greece. She will have a renown like that of Ariadne (997 ff.). But, it seems, this promise is a ploy – Jason understands the young girl's infatuation and he knows that what she wants is not renown but the speaker himself. Given this, given the reference to Theseus and to Ariadne (this is a *paradeigma*), and given our foreknowledge of the abandoning of Ariadne by Theseus, the promise becomes a particularly ironic one. And, I dare say, one that is completely in character with Jason.

It is Medea who makes the next long plea (4.355–390). She is reacting violently to the prospect of being abandoned by the Argonauts as part of a self-serving plan to elude Apsyrtus and the Colchians. This is a particularly powerful and blunt declamation. Yet it still follows the pattern that we have been observing. Its pattern is like this:

355–369 (*exordium*): Opening address to Jason.
370–375/6 (plea): Medea's plea.
376–390 (benefaction): Medea's threat.

It begins with a type of *exordium*, designed to rivet the attention of the addressee, Jason (355–369). Medea does not seek his goodwill, so much as she seeks to encourage his sense of obligation. Has Jason, she asks, forgotten his oaths? Has he forgotten how she has abandoned and betrayed for him her family? This proem climaxes with a devastatingly simple declaration of Medea's utter dependence on Jason: she has become his daughter, wife and sister (368–369). The plea itself is blunt (370–375/6). Medea demands Jason either save her or forthwith kill her. In the other three passages, the plea is linked with a promise of some sort of a benefaction made on behalf of the addressee. Here the reverse is the case (376–390). If betrayed, Medea threatens malefaction. Here she avers that the sort of homecoming she will face (if betrayed) will match that of Jason. As an oath-breaker Hera will not allow him happiness, and Medea herself will call down the avenging Furies.

This is the most vehement, assertive and unreferential of addresses (a leisurely paradigm would diminish its force). In that sense it might be thought to reflect the exteriorised world I have sought to demonstrate of Nestor. Recall, however, that though angry, this speech still represents an act that is built upon a sense of powerless and helplessness (that *amechanie* to which I will refer shortly). Medea is angry with perfidious Jason. But, one senses, her anger is also self-directed. As a woman and as a barbarian she cannot shape or control the course of things. That is being done for her by the treacherous Jason.

If the vehemence of Medea's plea catches much of the violence of her character (at least as it is seen in *Argonautica* 4), then Hera's long plea to Thetis for help with the Argonauts (4.783–832) admirably mirrors her scheming and guileful nature. The tripartite schema is present in this speech, but it is ordered in character with the nature of its speaker – and to stress the purport of the speech. We could represent it as follows:

783–790 (*exordium*): Hera's address to Thetis.
790–815 (benefaction): How Hera helped Thetis find a husband.
815–832 (plea): Help Jason past Scylla and Charybdis.

The introduction (783–790) emphasises to Thetis how Hera esteems Jason, how she has helped Jason in the past, but how he now faces Scylla and Charybdis. Then comes mention of the benefaction (790–815). This was something performed by Hera for Thetis at a previous time. Here she stresses that she cherished Thetis in the past – even to the point of selecting for her the best of possible husbands, Peleus, one of the Argonauts. Hera also underlines that Achilles, Thetis' son, is destined in the Underworld to marry Medea. The plea comes powerfully last (815–832). Hera requests that Thetis remember her benefactions and help Peleus – but above all Jason – to pass the dangerous Scylla and Charybdis unharmed. Hera's recounting of how she found a husband for Thetis comes close to the sort of paradigm we have become used to in Nestor's speeches. Yet the differences are marked, for in Hera's speech the reminiscence tells us of both speaker and addressee. Its connection, like that of Ariadne to Medea in the previous speech, is quite obvious. When Nestor's paradigms confuse, it is precisely because we do not know how to place the addressee within the picture. Hera's plea, despite its being uttered by a god, still reflects that interiorised world of Argus, Jason and Medea.[46]

These, then, are four of Apollonius' five longest 'persuasive' speeches – not long at all by Homeric standards. Why Apollonius has chosen to privilege these particular utterances is not easily settled. We could say of them, and of those six other essentially descriptive speeches, that they do occur at crucial junctures in the narrative.[47] Some indication as to why they should all be pleas, however, has already been suggested. But we ought to reaffirm that clear and deliberate structure is a feature of them. Each exhibits the three basic features (introduction, plea and reference to a benefaction) whose order seems to be dependent on the purpose of the address and on the speaker's character. This last point is of some importance: as was the case for Homer, speeches here do reflect the temperament of the person delivering them. But – and this point cannot be underlined enough – despite Apollonius' obvious skills at speech-making, he offers few specimens. Given his obvious competence at the task, this absence of direct speech must surely be taken as a deliberate choice.

Why? I have already suggested one answer. There may be another. This, I believe, resides in that overpowering sense of estrangement and *amechanos amplakie* ('hapless accident': 1.1053–1054) which is so much a feature of the Apollonian world-view.[48] It is as if, in this most pessimistic of creations, Apollonius is deliberately attempting to stress the gulf or fracture that exists between deeds and words, between reality or actualisation (even things themselves – the sphere of deeds) and planning or intention or even human understanding (the sphere of words).[49] Deeds, we could paraphrase, are not the result of human planning (words, that is to say, or ratiocination), but of uncontrollable chance (*amechanos amplakie*).

The theme of the gulf between reality and planning is a common one in this poem. Its simplest instance is offered by Phineus' long prediction (2.311–407: a speech which I have mentioned above). His *words* do not reveal all of the deeds or explanations of the *deeds* to be performed by the Argonauts. He does not, for example, predict that Jason and his company will meet the sons of Phrixus on the island of Ares; nor does he explain why this must be. When he narrates how the Argonauts will manage to pass the Symplegades he does not point out that this will be achieved with the help of Athena. Nor, of course, does Phineus give the Argonauts that key piece of information, how to return from Aea to Iolcus.[50] Another grim example of the disjunction between deeds and words is provided by the seer Idmon at the time of the launching of the Argo (1.440–447). He foresees, indeed predicts, his own death, but is powerless to prevent its outcome by his own actions. Compare the disastrous events in Cyzicus (1.936 ff.). The Argonauts, blown back at night to the land of king Cyzicus where they had recently enjoyed hospitality, fought the Cyzicenes and unwittingly killed the young king (1.1012–1052). 'Hapless accident' (*amechanos amplakie*: 1.1053–1054), rather than words or human understanding, seems to rule human conduct. Thus too the loss of Heracles (1.1172 ff.: he was accidentally left behind amongst the Mysians). Into the same complex should be placed the motiveless, but, for the Argonauts, utterly depressing deaths of Idmon (2.815–834) and Tiphys (2.851–863) in the land of the

Mariandyni. Or, in Book 4, the deaths in North Africa of Canthus and Mopsus (4.1485–1536), whose demise may ultimately be traced back to the loss of Heracles. This list could be continued. But it would, I suspect, serve only to reiterate the point.[51] The gulf between words (or planning) and deeds (or reality) is one of the key themes of the poem.

Is it not fitting, therefore, that at key junctures Apollonius seems to deny – sometimes his characters, sometimes his readers – insight into the planning, the words and the speeches that will reflect intention? By denying us knowledge of their intention (or by providing an incomplete account of this) Apollonius makes clear the *amechanie* to which his unheroic world is so subject. The absence of primary rhetoric, therefore, is not just another feature of the poem (a feature which undoubtedly is responsible for the unjustifiably low opinion in which the *Argonautica* used to be held),[52] but is a key aspect which allows us to establish a valid reading of the poem.

CONCLUSION

Where does all of this leave us? In a position, I hope, to be able to draw together a few tentative conclusions. From my brief survey of Nestor's speeches within Homer's *Iliad* and of some of the longer speeches in Apollonius of Rhodes' *Argonautica*, it is possible to affirm that both poets display an unexpected level of structure and of elaboration in their speeches. Whether this structure and elaboration ought be linked with later rhetoric is another question. It appears, from this cursory survey, that Homer's speeches, more elaborate and more structured than those of Apollonius, anticipate elements associated with later rhetoric. It follows, accordingly, that Homer is more fond of speech-making and of direct speech than Apollonius. Notwithstanding this Homeric 'modernity', Homer's oral products are profoundly paratactic – something that could not be said of either later rhetoricians or of Apollonius. Homer leaves the links between the portions of his speeches implicit; Apollonius tends to spell them out. This was especially notable in the case of the Homeric *paradeigma*. My final point – perhaps the most important – is that Homer's exteriorised speeches are positive, outwardly directed and expectantly ameliorative. Apollonius' prominent speeches, on the other hand, reflect an interiorisation typified by hesitance, inwardly turned anger, guile and passivity.

Why these changes? I have suggested two causes, one outside the control of Homer or Apollonius, the other likely reflecting a deliberate choice on the part of Apollonius. The involuntary mechanism may have been literacy. As Ong and Carothers suggest, literacy seems to be associated with interiorisation. Apollonius, as a result, becomes a victim of the very capacity which makes his sentimental, anachronistic enterprise possible. The voluntary mechanism may have been *amechanie*. Apollonius, by avoiding direct speech, may be attempting to point to a gulf between words and deeds, between planning and reality, a gulf that is so typified by Jason *amechaneon*.

I would like finally to return to this notion of literacy. The comparisons I have suggested highlight one notable, albeit not unvarying, difference between oral and written epic:[53] a striking avoidance of direct speech. This characteristic persists in Greek written epic. It does not in Roman epic (which, curiously enough, is probably the result of the Roman taste for rhetoric). It is of far more importance, however, that these comparisons highlight a striking aspect of a change in the Greek mind-set of the Hellenistic period. This could, as I have been attempting to demonstrate, easily be associated with the dramatic rise in literacy within this period, and the possibly related change in *mentalité* thus ushered in. I suspect, however, that while writing does indeed shape thought,[54] such an aetiology, in this case at any rate, is too reductive. We do seem to witness a change from an affective exteriorisation of strong emotion to an interiorised one. Writing must play its part in this causality. But, surely, only a part. The origins of such disorders, like those of disorders such as melancholia, are always manifold.

NOTES

My thanks for help in the composition of this chapter to Mark Golden.

1 Rhetoric may manifest itself on matters pertaining to the oratorical occasion ('primary' rhetoric) or, as 'secondary' rhetoric, it may embrace the 'generic and stylistic commonplace' (I take the phrase from W. H. Race, 'Aspects of Rhetoric and Form in Classical Greek Hymns', *GRBS* 23 (1982), pp. 5–14; the phrase at p. 5). The distinction between 'primary' and 'secondary' rhetoric is made by G. Kennedy, *Classical Rhetoric and Its Christian and Secular Tradition from Ancient to Modern Times* (Chapel Hill: 1982), pp. 4 ff. Exemplary on both forms is R. G. A. Buxton, *Persuasion in Greek Tragedy: A Study of Peitho* (Cambridge: 1982).

2 Much could be said of later Greek epic, particularly Quintus Smyrnaeus and Nonnus. Direct speech in both is not high (24 per cent and 36 per cent), but secondary rhetoric is pronounced. The introduction to F. Vian, *Quintus de Smyrne: La suite d'Homère*, I (Paris: 1963), is useful on this matter. Vian, *Nonnos de Panopolis: Les Dionysiaques*, I (Paris: 1976), pp. xlix and xxi, notes the importance of the rhetorical theory of Menander the Rhetor (see D. A. Russell and N. G. Wilson, *Menander Rhetor* (Oxford: 1981)); Menander is applied to Greek and Roman poetry (including epic) by F. Cairns, *Generic Composition in Greek and Roman Poetry* (Edinburgh: 1972). The application of the ecphrasis is a noteworthy, if well known, example of secondary rhetoric in late epic: see A. S. Becker, 'Reading Poetry through a Distant Lens: Ecphrasis, Ancient Greek Rhetoricians, and the Pseudo-Hesiodic "Shield of Heracles" ', *AJPh* 113 (1992), pp. 5–24.

3 Kennedy, *Classical Rhetoric*, pp. 9–15 and *Art of Persuasion*, pp. 35–40, stresses a number of the similarities between Homeric rhetoric and the classical form. See especially M. W. Edwards, *The Iliad: A Commentary*, V (Cambridge: 1991), pp. 55–60. There is also A. J. Karp, 'Homeric Origins of Ancient Rhetoric', *Arethusa* 10 (1977), pp. 237–58 and Cole, *Origins of Rhetoric*, pp. 33–46.

4 O. Taplin, *Homeric Soundings: The Shaping of the Iliad* (Oxford: 1992), p. 175, speaks of the 'apparent aimlessness' of this speech. He wishes to correct such a view.

5 Taplin, *Homeric Soundings*, p. 12, vehemently disputes that the *Iliad* is paratactic – in the sense used by J. Notopoulos, 'Parataxis in Homer', *TAPhA* 80 (1949), pp. 1–23. He believes – and I wholly concur – that the *Iliad* is an organic whole. That the epic is built from seemingly discrete building blocks does not render it inorganic. What matters surely is the deliberation and care with which the building blocks are arranged.

6 So W. J. Ong, *Orality and Literacy: The Technologizing of the Word* (London: 1982), p. 69, who cites in support J. C. Carothers, 'Culture, Psychiatry, and the Written Word', *Psychiatry* 22 (1959), pp. 307–20.

7 On Homer's speeches see D. Lohmann, *Die Komposition der Reden in der Ilias* (Berlin: 1970), G. S. Kirk, *The Iliad: A Commentary*, II (Cambridge: 1990), pp. 28–35; Kennedy, *Art of Persuasion*, pp. 35–40 (with bibliography); and C. J. Larrain, *Struktur der Reden in der Odyssee 1–8* (Hildesheim: 1987). Kirk also cites P. Friedrich and J. Redfield, 'Speech as a Personality Symbol: The Case of Achilles', *Language* 54 (1978), pp. 263–88, and, on the same lines, J. Griffin, 'Homeric Words and Speakers', *JHS* 106 (1986), pp. 36–57 (note the criticisms of I. J. F. de Jong, 'Homeric Words and Speeches: An Addendum', *JHS* 108 (1988), pp. 188–9).

8 Brief discussion in Kirk, *Iliad*, II, pp. 250–1.

9 Characteristics discussed, with bibliography, by K. Dickson, 'Kalkhas and Nestor: Two Narrative Strategies in *Iliad* 1', *Arethusa* 25 (1992), pp. 327–58.

10 Some important recent studies of narrative and narrators in Homer are I. J. F. de Jong, *Narrators and Focalizers: The Presentation of the Story in the Iliad* (Amsterdam: 1987); M. Lynn-George, *Epos: Word, Narrative and the*

Iliad (London: 1988); and R. P. Martin, *The Language of Heroes: Speech and Performance in the Iliad* (Ithaca: 1989).

11 Aspects of this speech are discussed in Dickson, 'Kalkhas and Nestor', pp. 339 ff.

12 My schema and wording are based upon M. M. Willcock, *A Companion to the Iliad* (Chicago: 1976), pp. 9–10. Compare Lohmann's (*Komposition der Reden*, p. 224 n. 18) rather complex analysis. He includes my *prothesis* within the same subdivision as the *paradeigma*.

13 I use these terms guardedly – in particular the notion of *prothesis*. In the Homeric context they hardly approximate real rhetorical divisions. They may offer, however, a sense of the 'rhetorical' structure of these speeches. On the divisions see Arist. *Rhetoric* 1414a ff. See also B. A. van Groningen, *La composition littéraire archaïque grecque*[2] (Amsterdam: 1960), pp. 62 ff. (using the terms *exordium* and epilogue).

14 Aristotle, *Rhetoric* 1393a, points out that the example (*paradeigma*) is a type of proof (one of the two main ones along with the enthymeme). He notes that one type of example is a narration of past events. Kennedy, *Classical Rhetoric*, pp. 9–15 and *Art of Persuasion*, pp. 35–40, notes that Homer is weak at arguing from proof (*pistis*).

15 On the specific term 'epilogue' in early Greek literature see van Groningen, *Composition littéraire*, pp. 70 ff.

16 On the following points see Kennedy, *Art of Persuasion* (index) and *Classical Rhetoric*, pp. 12–14.

17 See Edwards, *Iliad*, V, pp. 56–7.

18 I say less immediately evident with due caution. Ian Worthington has vigorously argued for the presence of detailed ring composition within the work of Dinarchus (and elsewhere). See, amongst others, 'Greek Oratory, Revision of Speeches, and the Problem of Historical Reliability', *C&M* 42 (1991), pp. 55–74 and *A Historical Commentary on Dinarchus: Rhetoric and Conspiracy in Later Fourth-Century Athens* (Ann Arbor: 1992), pp. 27 ff.

19 Which typifies oral epic. Hypotaxis (subordination) typifies the written product. The arguments on parataxis have often been rehearsed: see, for example, P. Toohey, *Reading Epic: An Introduction to the Ancient Narratives* (London: 1992), chapter 1 (with brief bibliography). Note again Taplin, *Homeric Soundings*, p. 12.

20 H. Fränkel, *Early Greek Poetry and Philosophy*, trans. M. Hadas and J. Willis (Oxford: 1975), pp. 525–7, is useful on this matter.

21 Paratactic stylisation is evident within the narrative, for example, in the case of some battle scenes. These are often highly stylised, repetitive, even formulaic events (well analysed by B. Fenik, *Typical Battle Scenes in the Iliad: Studies in the Narrative Techniques of Homeric Battle Descriptions*, (Wiesbaden: 1968)). They *seem* capable of insertion, seemingly unaltered, in a variety of contexts. When they are, they are added paratactically.

22 Parataxis often produces what some call the 'situational parallel'; for example, the simple analogy drawn in the *Odyssey* between the house of Agamemnon and that of Odysseus (1.32–43). Such parallels are added analogously, almost anecdotally to their narrative. They remain organic.

23 The *Iliad* and the *Odyssey* both exhibit a compositional style which links or juxtaposes large narrative blocks. Typical patterns of arrangement are

ring form (A–B–C–B¹–A¹) and 'spiral form' (A–B–A¹–B¹). These devices may shape the individual passage or the poem as a whole. C. Whitman, *Homer and the Heroic Tradition* (New York: 1965), pp. 249 ff., believes that the *Iliad* is arranged in ring form. W. Thalmann, *Conventions of Form and Thought in Early Greek Epic Poetry* (Baltimore: 1984), p. 52, believes the *Odyssey* is shaped in a spiral (A–B–C–A¹– B¹–C¹). See also Edwards, *Iliad*, V, pp. 45–8.

24 See, for example, S. L. Schein, *The Mortal Hero: An Introduction to Homer's Iliad* (Berkeley: 1984), p. 33, on ring composition in *Iliad* 24.599–620 (the story of Niobe); and M. N. Nagler, *Spontaneity and Tradition: A Study in the Oral Art of Homer* (Berkeley: 1974), pp. 191 ff., on ring composition between speeches within a book.

25 On ring composition in Homer see Edwards, *Iliad*, V, pp. 44–8 (with bibliography).

26 Agamemnon's apology is a fine example of this sort of thing: see E. R. Dodds, *The Greeks and the Irrational* (Berkeley and Los Angeles: 1981), chapter 1. Compare Thersites at *Iliad* 2.225–242. His blunt, paradigmless speech incurs an immediate and wrathful response from his audience.

27 My analysis is based on Willcock, *Companion to the Iliad*, pp. 77–8, and on Lohmann, *Komposition der Reden*, pp. 27–8.

28 See S. Perlman, 'The Historical Example, Its Use and Importance as Political Propaganda in the Attic Orators', *SH* 7 (1961), pp. 150–66, on one aspect of this notion of the appeal to the past.

29 Compare Phoenix (*Iliad* 9.434–605): his *paradeigmata* are remarkable in their detail. Phoenix, of course, is also old. But his social standing (he had been Achilles' tutor), did not offer him the right of being a doer of deeds and a speaker of words. Words – without the implicit sanction of social standing – were all he could offer. Were he too direct in his utterance, maybe he could have suffered the same fate as Thersites (*Iliad* 2.211–277).

30 This speech has been discussed by V. Pedrick, 'The Paradigmatic Nature of Nestor's Speech in *Iliad* 11', *TAPhA* 113 (1983), pp. 55–68 (bibliography at p. 54 nn. 1 and 2).

31 Here I depart from Willcock, *Companion to the Iliad*, pp. 132–3. The rhetorical analysis is tendentious, but the imputed logic and the persuasive technique behind it is surely not. Detailed (but confusing) analysis of this speech in Lohmann, *Komposition der Reden*, pp. 70–5 (and 263–71) whose overall breakdown is: I: 656–764: complaint against Achilles, II: 765–791: advice to Patroclus and III: 792–801: concluding view and alternative possibility. Edwards, *Iliad*, V, p. 47, has some comments on this speech.

32 Dickinson, 'Kalkhas and Nestor', pp. 341 ff., also uses the term of Nestor's speeches.

33 I note the caution of Kirk, *Iliad*, II, p. 251: 'The facile idea that length and elaboration necessarily reflect structural or emotional importance should be treated with caution'. In this instance length and elaboration do seem precisely to mirror structural and emotional importance.

34 Vian, *Quintus de Smyrne*, I, p. xxxix, has some interesting statistics (his source, which I have not yet seen, is G. W. Elderkin, *Aspects of the Speech of Later Greek Epic* (Baltimore: 1906)). He notes that direct speech accounts for 50 per cent of the text of Homer, 29 per cent of Apollonius,

24 per cent of Quintus Smyrnaeus and 36 per cent of Nonnus. Vian thinks that the statistic for Homer explains what Aristotle at *Poetics* 1448b35 meant by attributing dramatic characteristics to Homer.

35 The cut-off point at thirty is arbitrary. That it illustrates the brevity of Apollonian speech-making is, however, obvious. Nestor's speech in *Iliad* 11 is nearly 150 lines long. I note in the *Argonautica* only twelve speeches of a length between 20–29 lines: 1.675–696; 2.468–489; 2.1047–1067; 2.1123–1133; 3.56–75; 3.171–193; 3.401–421; 3.891–911; 3.1079–1101; 3.1120–1130; 4.1031–1052; and 4.1073–1095.

36 The six non-persuasive speeches are: 1.793–833: to allay Argonautic suspicions concerning the absence of the Lemnian males, Hypsipyle states her falsehood and then invites the Argonauts to stay; 2.311–407: Phineus details the route which the Argonauts must take to reach Colchis; 2.774–810: Lycus relates his relations with Heracles and his reasons for wishing to send his son, Dascylus, on board the *Argo*; 3.771–801: a 'psychological' monologue outlining Medea's conflicting emotions; 3.1026–1062: Medea explains how Jason must conduct himself during the trials; and 4.257–293: Argus predicts the route the Argonauts should take from Aea.

37 These are: 2.209–239: Phineus requests help from the Argonauts; 3.320–366: Argus attempts to convince his uncle, Aietes, to welcome the Argonauts; 3.975–1007: Jason requests Medea's help in gaining the Golden Fleece; 4.355–390: Medea requests Jason not to abandon her to Apsyrtus; and 4.783–832: Hera endeavours to persuade Thetis to assist the Argonauts past Scylla and Charybdis.

38 Virgil, *Aeneid* 1, for example, has Venus' plea to Jupiter (229–253); Jupiter's response (257–296); Venus' description of Carthage to Aeneas (335–370); Aeneas' reply (372–401); Ilioneus' address to Dido (522–558); and so on (for a full list see G. Highet, *The Speeches in Vergil's Aeneid* (Princeton: 1972)). Compare Lucan, *Civil War* 1 (Caesar's speech to his troops at 299–351), or Statius, *Thebaid* 1 (Oedipus: 56–87; Jupiter: 214–247; Juno: 250–282; Adrastus: 498–510; Adrastus: 557–672 (Linus and Coroebus); Adrastus: 682–720).

39 W. V. Harris, *Ancient Literacy* (Cambridge, Mass.: 1989), p. 128. He also notes on p. 325: 'The Hellenistic Greeks, in particular those who ruled and administered the Ptolemaic empire, developed the bureaucratic uses of writing far beyond what had been known in the classical era.' He further notes (ibid., p. 329) a lift in literacy from 10–15 per cent during the fifth and fourth centuries to an 'early modern' scale in some Hellenistic cities of 30–40 per cent. That this literacy may have been confined to the elite is suggested on pp. 116–46 passim.

40 Apollonius' eponymous city of Rhodes seems to have been an especially enthusiastic proponent of literacy. Harris, *Ancient Literacy*, pp. 130 ff., discusses its elementary education foundations.

41 Harris, *Ancient Literacy*, p. 125: 'The library was to be comprehensive, and therefore in a sense a giant retrospective of all Greek thinking – and of barbarian thinking too, which could be accepted, if not absorbed, since it could now be put into the unthreatening form of written Greek translations.'

42 'Some Ancient Notions of Boredom', *ICS* 13 (1988), pp. 151–64; 'Some Ancient Histories of Literary Melancholia', *ICS* 15 (1990), pp. 143–63; and 'Love, Lovesickness, and Melancholy', *ICS* 17 (1992), pp. 265–86.

43 See my 'Acedia and Eros in Apollonius Rhodius (*Arg.* 3.260–299)', *Glotta* 70 (1992), pp. 114–22, and 'Literary Melancholia'. The most recent defence of Jason's *amechanie* is by S. Jackson, 'Apollonius' Jason: Human Being in an Epic Scenario', *G&R*² 39 (1992), pp. 155–62.

44 So Toohey, *Reading Epic*, chapter 4 and 'Acedia and Eros'.

45 Race, 'Aspects of Rhetoric', might profitably be consulted on the 'rhetoric' of these pleas. They preserve the three key elements, as he argues, of the Greek hymn: an *arche* (the 'beginning' or *exordium*), the establishing of *charis* (in my terms the 'promise' or 'benefaction') and the request (the plea itself).

46 H. Fränkel, *Noten zu den Argonautika des Apollonios* (Munich: 1968), p. 536, stresses that Hera's agitation is reflected in this passage.

47 Even so there are many other points in the narrative when we might have expected some form of extended speech-making. Here are some random examples: when the Argonauts, before embarking, choose a leader (1.317–362); on Lemnos, Jason's leave-taking would have provided an excellent place for a very dramatic (or at the worst bathetic) address (1.609 ff.); or Cyzicus: why not have Cleite lament the death of her husband before committing suicide (1.1063–1065)? Speeches might have marked out the deaths of Idmon and Tiphys, instead Jason is *amechaneon* (2.885–893).

48 On 'estrangement' see D. C. Feeney, *The Gods in Epic: Poets and Critics of the Classical Tradition* (Oxford: 1991), chapter 2. On *amechanos amplakie* see Toohey, *Reading Epic*, chapter 4.

49 Cole, *Origins of Rhetoric*, basing himself on K. von Fritz, 'νόος and νοεῖν in the Homeric Poems', *CPh* 38 (1943), pp. 79–93, notes that 'there is no gulf between the world of thought and that of reality in the Homeric age'. The absolute reverse is the case in that of Apollonius.

50 This is Feeney's argument in *The Gods in Epic*. Ian Worthington suggests to me that Phineus' omissions may be the result of Apollonius' desire not to detract from the surprise of the later events.

51 I am profoundly indebted to Feeney, *The Gods in Epic*, chapter 2, who focuses on the role of the divine in the *Argonautica* and on human perception of the divine (humans are like words, the gods like deeds or reality). Between these spheres, argues Feeney, is a pronounced disjunction (p. 76).

52 It is significant that Book 3, the most popular section of the *Argonautica*, has the highest incidence of direct speech. The figures are *approximately* as follows: Book 1: 20 per cent; Book 2: 26 per cent (without Phineus' long speech; 33 per cent with it); Book 3: 40 per cent; and Book 4: 26 per cent.

53 W. J. Ong, *Interfaces of the Word: Studies in the Evolution of Consciousness and Culture* (Ithaca: 1977), *Orality and Literacy*, and J. Goody, *The Interface between the Written and the Oral* (Cambridge: 1987), especially pp. 263–4, are useful on this matter.

54 See Ong, *Interfaces of the Word*, *Orality and Literacy*, Goody, *Interface* and *The Domestication of the Savage Mind* (Cambridge: 1977).

9

Tragedy and rhetoric

Victor Bers

If we could witness an Attic tragedy as it was first presented in the context of the city's dramatic festivals, we would probably find it a 'preposterous entertainment', to borrow Shaw's description of grand opera. Peculiar ceremonies preceded the drama itself: an announcement of the play's subject by its author, with members of the cast, not yet concealed by the masks and costumes they would wear during the performance, standing at his side, and the purification of the theatre by the sacrifice of a piglet.[1] Each author's set of three tragedies was followed by a satyr drama, a shorter play of a genre hovering between tragedy and comedy.[2] After the full programme of tragedies was performed, jurors selected from each tribe voted first, second, and third prizes; these amateur critics announced no reasons for their choices, and since the process was in part regulated by sortition, the gods, or maybe Dionysus himself, honorand of the festival, might be thought to determine the outcome of the competition.[3] Moreover, the play itself was a medley of speaking, chanting and singing in a variety of verse forms, using a type of Greek never heard in everyday use in Athens or anywhere else. Stage movement was, almost certainly, restricted to a small repertory of gestures, and facial expression was precluded by the masks. The chorus, drawn up in a rectangle, danced (we know not how) as it sang lyrics of considerable complexity to the accompaniment of a flute.[4]

These alien strains can be understood, even prized, by regarding the dramatic festivals, in an anthropological vein, as expressions of a culture different from our own. And generations have read and enjoyed the tragedies quite unaware of these curiosities, regarding the plays as establishing the norms for western drama, in other words, as 'classical'. But obvious even from the bare texts that provide virtually all the evidence for our knowledge of tragedy[5] is the strong influence on the action by powers beyond the characters. Further, the inherited myths, the nearly exclusive source of tragic plots, were taken as historical in their fundamental outlines.[6] A tragedian's inheritance from epic and lyric poetry included an astonishing elasticity in story telling, but he could not go so far as to have *his* Penelope murder *his* Odysseus. Another principle of Greek tragedy, a tenet of Greek religious belief, assumes that the world (real or imitated) is filled with the ominous:[7] bird flight, entrails of sacrificed animals, formal announcements by oracles, dreams, the precise timing (*kairos*) of every event. By a rule of tragic plot composition, a rule to which even the most *outré* Euripidean experiment adheres, those humans endowed with mantic powers (Amphiaraus, Calchas, Tiresias, Cassandra, Theonoe), but no other, can unerringly decode those signs. Further, humans cannot always accurately distinguish their own acts from higher forces outside them.[8]

The determinism of epic and tragic plot might have produced a literature in which human characters, and even the gods when powerless to divert the course of destined actions, move through a bleak choreography devoid of human interest. Every reader knows this did not happen: puppets, to use the *cliché* for passivity, can interest us just by being made to *seem* to resist the pull on their strings. Tragic characters, even when confronted with proof of their impotence, can no more escape the sensation of freedom than the most philosophically committed determinist.[9] In the space allowed the characters of tragic drama to enjoy (or lament) their illusory freedom, the main doings are not action, for the conventions of the Attic theatre virtually excluded the performance of action on stage, but speech *about* action: action announced, contemplated and judged. The speech often does pertain to those things the modern reader relegates to the strangeness of Greek culture: oracles, divinities appearing *ex machina*, and so on. But the response to them in speech is, with very few exceptions, perfectly intelligible; and a great part of that speech is rhetorical, especially on a reasonably broad definition of the term.

A narrow view sees as rhetoric only the technically polished and highly self-conscious mode of speech-making of the *rhetorike techne* (the art of rhetoric) introduced by certain professionals, sometimes called sophists, starting sometime in the middle of the fifth century and taught by them, at least by example, to eager pupils, especially at Athens.[10] Marks of the *techne* include clear demarcations of the sections of the speech and features of the linguistic surface, such as the pervasive use of assonance at the ends of antithetical clauses. In the realm of *dianoia* ('thought') the *techne* shows frequent recourse to a largely predictable repertory of arguments of a rationalistic cast, including (under the technical term *stasis*) categorising the matter to be argued or the competence of the group judging the dispute, and advancing claims based on what is probable (*eikos*) and in accordance with nature (*phusis*). Tragedy readily accommodates these characteristic arguments, whereas the verbal tricks cannot so easily be brought over into verse, especially those tied to word order and word length.[11]

Something like this criterion seems to be in Aristotle's mind when he distinguishes the speech styles of earlier and later tragedy by opposing two adverbs which seem, at first, to have meanings more overlapping than antithetical: 'The old tragic poets made their characters speak politically; poets now make them speak rhetorically' (*Poetics* 1450b7–8). Commentators understand speaking 'rhetorically' to denote speech filled with figures of speech and thought in the manner of the *techne*. From the immediate context of Aristotle's remark and from passages elsewhere in the *Rhetoric* and *Politics*, speaking 'politically' is glossed as indicating the speaker's character, his ethics as expressed in the polis, better translated 'society' than 'city'. Like much else in the *Poetics*, a work that deplores most contemporary tragedy and sees Sophocles as the best paradigm, Aristotle's distinction of speech styles is more prescriptive than descriptive.[12] Though Aristotle devoted his *Rhetoric* to rescuing the art from attacks by Plato and others, he clearly disapproves of tragic characters speaking *rhetorikos*. In holding this attitude, he anticipates the modern distaste for undisguised rhetoric on the stage.[13]

Rhetoric under this description is easy to identify, especially in the enactment on stage of speech events that bear a strong resemblance to those that regularly took place in the city, or are even explicitly identified in the play as being that sort of event. Examples of forensic oratory include the trial of Orestes in Aeschylus' *Eumenides*, of political oratory the assembly in Euripides' *Orestes*, of display oratory the funeral oration in his *Suppliants*.[14] Every commentary points out the 'rhetorical' or 'sophistic' elements in these scenes, and it has become a commonplace to remark that the tragedies, financed and organised by the city, were performed for an audience whose most important component, Athenian male citizens, heard political speeches in the Council and Assembly, forensic speeches in the courts, and display oratory at the funerals and games. How should we interpret these connections? It is always exciting to find plausible links among different genres and, more generally, between literary works and the political and intellectual life of the society. In a field of enquiry where the evidence is sparse, one places hope in new combinations of evidence. But many readings, in my opinion, too easily assume a simple continuity between the audience's experience of persuasive speech in the courts, deliberative bodies and state funerals, and their analogues on the tragic stage. I think the connection itself between, say, a usage in the courts and in a tragedy is often uncertain; it follows *a fortiori* that the attempt to establish the priority of one over another, to identify a rhetorical strategy in a play as imitating the oratory of real life or vice versa, is often vain indeed.[15]

Consider the multiple arguments, 'lawyers'' or 'debaters'' points in our own parlance, advanced even when unrelated to the individual social and gender status of the speaker, or his circumstances in the narrative, or even his own opinion. Their prominence in discourse is often seen as a mark of rhetoric in the narrow sense. An aspiring orator paid Protagoras or another sophist for instruction not in the argument of his side in a particular case, but to develop a general ability to argue any side in any case by drawing on a repertory of arguments. Characters in tragedy, on the other hand, are not found jumping from one side of a dispute to another like adepts in the *Dissoi Logoi* ('double arguments'), spouting iambic trimeters expressing exactly contradictory propositions. This is hardly surprising, for to do so would jeopardise the minimal notions of continuity needed for a drama. A tragic character is, on the whole, expected to act from some basic motive.[16] But we meet accumulations of arguments that seem to run beyond, or even contrary to, dramatic need. Examples are easiest to find in Euripides, starting with his earliest surviving complete play, the *Alcestis*, of 438 (see n. 25), Iolaus' supplication of Demophon (*The Children of Heracles* 181–232), Andromache's extended, and one might think counter-productive, attack on Menelaus (*Andromache* 319–363), and Tiresias' and Cadmus' appeal to Pentheus to abandon his resistance to Dionysus (*Bacchae* 266–342).

But superfluity and inconsistency have also been suspected in the trial scene of Aeschylus' *Eumenides* (of 458), especially in Apollo's argument for the biological primacy of the father.[17] We might be reminded of sophistic pieces like Gorgias' *Helen*, which holds a long concatenation of arguments, not all consistent with each other, exonerating her from blame. The very accumulation suggests that the work is indeed what Gorgias calls it in the last word of the work, a *paignion* ('game').

Important for understanding the tone and focus of a dramatic scene is determining whether the author has appropriated for a heroic-age setting the polemical devices of contemporary intellectuals, and in particular the sort of detached analytical pose of a professional rhetorician or his student. Not that such anachronism would in itself be counted a flaw: no fifth- or fourth-century Greek is known to have objected to Aeschylus making the Argos of his *Suppliants* a sort of democracy with a hereditary king as leading citizen.[18] We may be sure that the *Oresteia*'s audience in 458 did not resist Aeschylus' innovation, whereby the first session of the Areopagus was convoked with mortal Athenians forming the jury panel for the purpose of judging Orestes, a mortal defendant, for killing his mother; the traditional story, which survived as the standard account (cf. Euripides, *Electra* 1258 ff. and Libanius, *Decl.* 7) despite the immense celebrity of the *Oresteia*, had the Olympian gods sitting to hear a complaint against one of their own number. The audience took the characters' situation and the issues raised by the trial seriously, and for them the play was far from an entertaining trifle. Further, the string of arguments is motivated convincingly enough within the drama. Virtually every scene that precedes the trial has shown that the chain of events leading to the matricide is no simple confrontation of pure good against pure evil. Apollo wants his 'client' acquitted; no single argument could possibly settle the issue without making the complexity that Aeschylus has taken pains to demonstrate look silly. Consequently, the arguments here almost certainly did not seem an inorganic intrusion from a later era. But what is true for one play, author, or date does not necessarily hold for another (see p. 183 below).

Scepticism is even more appropriate when it comes to the suggestion that some highly specific element in the argumentation reflects recent innovations developed outside the realm of imaginative literature. For instance, in describing Apollo's claim that the father is the 'true' parent, Kennedy remarks that Aeschylus has given Apollo a 'technical word' for proof, *tekmerion* (*Art of Persuasion*, p. 43). This might seem analogous to a lawyer in a modern play speaking of a 'writ of *certiorari*', phrasing which certainly would startle his audience. It is important to realise that Aeschylus is not after such an effect. The language spoken in the Athenian barber shops of the mid-fifth century was not nearly as distinct from forensic speech as today's colloquial speech is from any modern professional *argot*.[19] Further, any flavour of technical usage has already been blunted by its earlier appearances in the *Agamemnon* in connection with stage events already mentioned (at 352 and 1366). These are 'proofs' of a sort intelligible without reference to any contemporary intellectual developments or the evolution of Athenian lawcourts.[20] The difficulty of distinguishing organic link from mere coincidence is exacerbated by the poetic habit of deviating from the precise wording of the corresponding prosaic utterance. Frequently used words and phrases of and about political and forensic speech, like *rhetor* ('speaker'), *deinos legein* ('clever [almost always in a pejorative sense] at speaking') and *sympheron* ('advantage'), are rare or entirely missing in attested tragedy. *Pithanos* ('persuasive'), a word used by Aeschylus and Euripides (the latter with reference to a formal speech), though presumptively useful in the lexicon of real-world speakers, does not appear in any surviving oration of the fifth or early fourth century. Even as the tragedians invite their audience to draw on their knowledge of persuasive speech outside the theatre, they signal reminders that the plays are not 'really real'.

Here it is crucial to distinguish among the three major tragedians. Aeschylus is too early to hold against any Attic prose texts that are reasonably contemporary. In the *Prometheus Bound* we find the word *sophistes* with a derogatory flavour derived from its new meaning, not just an expert of some kind but a professional intellectual; but the play is not certainly by Aeschylus, nor is it datable. Sophocles seems to have made it a nearly unwavering principle to cloak words incorporating contemporary thought under a semi-transparent disguise. The *Philoctetes*, presented in 409, nearly two decades after Cleon's complaint (as Thuc. 3.38 reports) that the Athenians sat at their assemblies resembling 'men watching sophists', is much concerned with *phusis*,[21] but the word is manipulated to avoid too strong a flavour of sophistic disputation. *Phusis* is repeatedly presented as a matter of family descent, a narrower meaning than 'nature' as the term is used in general analysis. Sophocles never once has a character in the play speak of *phusis* in explicit contrast to *nomos* ('law', 'convention' or 'custom'), its expected antithesis.[22] Euripides is, notoriously, far less inhibited in employing arguments cast in contemporary formulation. His Ion, for example, links the terms *phusis* and *nomos* directly.[23] He is not above teasing the audience with explicit references to rhetorical trickery in its modern form. In the *Hippolytus* (of 428) he has the protagonist say: 'You speak of me as a clever sophist (δεινὸν σοφιστήν), who is able to force sound thinking on those who do not think' (921–924). Several years later, in the *Hecuba*, he has the Trojan queen, a formidable debater even when afflicted by appalling misfortune, remark that men do not cultivate the tyrant Peitho, though by paying tuition to learn the art they could get what they wanted (816–819). Later she seems to hint that professionals exist, men one might employ, but they are self-deluding charlatans (1193–1195). And as already mentioned, Euripides is rich in what we might suspect are portable arguments, detachable from their dramatic contexts. At the extreme of portability, we find an argument for a good thing issued from wicked lips, like the praise of peace and condemnation of war recited by the Theban herald sent by his city to deliver an uncivilised message (*Suppliants* 481–493). Rhetoric in Euripides, because it is presented dressed in almost the same clothing it wore outside the Theatre of Dionysus, takes on a flavour very different from the Sophoclean treatment, even though the two tragedians were near contemporaries.[24]

There are, then, reasons to think that apparent connections between rhetoric on and off stage may be looser and less consistent than they seem at first. This is partly a question to be addressed by objective philology, as in the assessment of putative technical vocabulary. There is also a question of aesthetic judgement, our own and antiquity's. A statement like Dale's on Alcestis' rhetorical performance promotes in the modern reader a toleration paradoxically greater than many of Euripides' contemporaries and near contemporaries had for his blatantly rhetorical passages:

> Rhetoric is a concept we tend to hold in some suspicion, as if in its nature there must be something slightly bogus; but we shall never properly understand Greek tragedy unless we realize how closely related were the rhetoric of Athenian life, in the assembly and law-courts and on other public

occasions, and the rhetoric of the speeches in drama . . . The aim of rhetoric is Persuasion, Πειθώ, and the poet is as it were a kind of λογογράφος [speechwriter] who promises to do his best for each of his clients in turn as the situations change and succeed one another. This does not by any means exclude an interest in character; the skillful λογογράφος takes that into account in its proper place. But the dominating consideration is: What *points* could be made here?[25]

Granted that the poet functions rather like a *logographos* for his characters, and granted Euripides' great popularity in his own time, still it seems that his use of rhetoric was regarded by at least part of his contemporary audience as incongruous and destructive of what they valued in tragedy. Poets of Old Comedy, many of the judges at the festival (only five first-place victories are recorded), and of course Aristotle in the *Poetics* were not so forgiving. Tragedy was rapidly changing, and to fail to discriminate among our texts in the matter of rhetoric is to miss an exceedingly important aspect of that change.

The tragedians were certainly aware that using the devices of contemporary rhetoric was an interesting gamble, similar to, or partially overlapping, the risks and opportunities in referring to current political controversy. The opportunity was obvious enough: the audience would be delighted, perhaps improved, by observing the intellectual sharpening of thought retrojected back to the heroic period.[26] The risks included chilling the play with over-intellectualised discourse: this could not only bore an unforgiving audience but appear a bizarre and tasteless anachronism. At a strictly lexical and phraseological level, the introduction of neologisms might have threatened the differentiation of tragic poetry from routine speech and the versified, but basically colloquial, language of the comic poets. It must be remembered that those writers were sitting in the Theatre of Dionysus, ears perked up for material.[27]

Another definition, one that seems to me more fruitful in the elucidation of tragedy and that relies less on the inadequate evidence for the growth of the *rhetorike techne*, regards as rhetorical anything that is said with the intent to persuade any person who shares the stage with the speaker, or even the speaker himself.[28] This approach captures at a more intimate level the dynamics of one character in his involvement with another in a theatrical idiom pervaded by a feeling of resistance and a need to make credible.[29] Here is where we meet persuasion, the abstraction or incarnate deity *Peitho*, in its (or her) protean attributes: aggression, seduction, irresistible power, weak sister of physical force and deceit. Persuasion on the tragic stage inherits all these modes and purposes from earlier literature and cult.[30]

Much that is a matter of 'fact' in tragedy is hard for the characters to accept as true, either because the event is intrinsically improbable, or because they suspect other characters of deception. An example of the first may be seen in Aeschylus' *Persians* (472), where the messenger who brings the Persian court news of the naval disaster at Salamis concludes his account with a protest: 'These things are true' (513). Some editors of the play, regarding the line as otiose, have doubted its authenticity. Broadhead defends the line with a sensible remark: 'It is natural enough after such a tale of calamity, almost passing belief.' Certainly there is a dramatic need for the characters to be seen to accept the shocking news, but this is no typical example of an 'incredible' event of legend that must escape scepticism to allow the 'story' to work: the battle of Salamis was an event whose basic historicity many members of Aeschylus' audience could personally attest. A far more normal instance occurs at Aeschylus' *Suppliant Women*, where the daughters of Danaus, in flight from Egypt and unwanted marriage with their cousins, must persuade the King of Argos that they are, despite their appearance, Argive 'nationals', descended from Io. The second variety, resistance motivated by suspicion, is exemplified in the *Agamemnon*. Clytemnestra seeks to convince the chorus of elders that the beacon signals sent (she claims) from Troy to Argos mean what she claims, that Troy has fallen: 'Having heard this much, know that you are hearing the truth' (680). For reasons intrinsic to the plot, the chorus must continue to suspect some trick and be 'vanquished by words' (583) only when the herald arrives and confirms the beacon signal.[31] But its suspicions cannot be more than vague. An irony, as befits a tragic plot, is that in this particular point she deserves its credence. Persuasion here must be attempted – and it must encounter resistance, even before Clytemnestra admits that she has 'said much to suit the moment' (1372). Cassandra is not a character under suspicion, but she can announce what is about to happen only 'from behind veils' (1178); only her declarations about the past can win the chorus' understanding (1242). She cannot persuade it that their king is to be murdered in a few moments, that is, soon enough for it to intervene.[32]

From these scenes in the *Agamemnon*, in which what has happened and is happening is available to the characters to know only through the instrument of rhetoric, the trilogy moves through several other tests of persuasion, none in a formally rhetorical cast (I can here mention only a few), before arriving at the trial scene in the *Eumenides*. As the chorus hears the shouts of their king, the twelve *choreutai* must try to persuade one another how to respond (*Agamemnon* 1348–1371). Those advocating immediate action against the killers must fail (it is especially crucial that no one pre-empt the killing of Clytemnestra). The main rhetorical business of the *Libation Bearers* is to secure, by means of an extended *kommos* ('responsive lament'), the favour of Agamemnon's ghost and for Clytemnestra to fail in dissuading Orestes from matricide. Her ultimate persuasive gesture, the display of her breast (896–897), must be overcome by Pylades' rhetorical question and sententious imperative (900–903). The action leads to the endlessly discussed victory of Peitho in the *Eumenides* (885, 970), a victory that both had to be, and still might have been allowed to fail, for Athena holds bolts of lightning in reserve (827–828).[33] Persuasion struggles with the dangers and uncertainties of the world and makes them credibly problematic to an audience that would lose interest in a drama where the 'truth' or 'the better cause' could, on its own, win all characters' immediate assent: τοῖς πράγμασιν αὐτοῖς ('by the facts themselves') as Aristotle says (*Rhetoric* 1404a5–6).

Sophocles' *Antigone* is usually read as dramatising a collision of irreconcilable wills, which is to say as something other than a conflict resolvable by rhetoric: Antigone could not persuade Creon to rescind his denial of burial to Polyneices without short-circuiting the play's action. But not only is there much room for rhetoric in the play (I can here offer only a few illustrations), much of it can be described in terms normally applied to the frankly rhetorical. The opening scene of the play is not a staple of discussion of rhetoric in tragedy.[34] The dialogue of the two sisters, Antigone and Ismene, seems to serve mainly to initiate the play's action, not resolve an issue through verbal argument, and even conjectural technical expressions of argumentation are absent. Yet the scene enacts an interchange of perception and will in which each girl voices her thoughts with the intent to influence the other.

185

I pick out a few details of the verbal texture with specific rhetorical thrust. The first line, a periphrastic vocative, both identifies a character and by its emphatic statement of close relationship (translation in only a crude sense is possible: 'O very-sister head of Ismene') functions as an appeal for a friendly hearing, in handbook terms a *captatio benevolentiae*. The speech concludes with a question ('Do you not notice that evil from our enemies marches against your own people?'), whereby Antigone pushes her sister to accept a certain view of their situation. Both facts and interpretation are at issue, though the proclamation to which she refers, Creon's prohibition of burial, has not yet been explained; and there is a trace of anticipatory reproach: perhaps Ismene is ignorant or indifferent to the fresh disaster. The tactic resembles the proem of Lysias 1, the defendant's speech in a real trial, in prompting an attitude in the listeners, even while withholding basic information.[35] When Antigone does report Creon's prohibition of burial to Polyneices, the basic datum is abundantly elaborated to make it clear why she regards it as a calamity. A challenge follows ('You will soon show whether you are noble or base': 38) that immediately turns the dialogue into a struggle over what in a symbouleutic context would be called policy (*gnome*, the word Ismene uses at 42). The notion that the decision will have enduring results, perfectly appropriate to a tragedy, recalls the orators' frequent hyperbolical claim that the impending vote in the assembly or jury will irrevocably affect the city. Ismene is seen as the literal weak sister, the *un*tragic compromiser, yet her rejection of Antigone's proposal is more than a whimper. She lays out her arguments, calling attention to their order (φρόνησον . . . ἔπειτα . . . τρίτον . . . νῦν δ' αὖ: 'think . . . next . . . third . . . now, in turn'), and makes a counter proposal. Even when the final rupture comes, Antigone now spurning Ismene's help (70–71) and bidding her sister denounce her to Creon (86), the attempt to convince does not stop right there. Antigone continues to indicate why she is resolved to act and Ismene continues both to work at dissuading her and to declare her love.

The *parodos* ends with the announcement by the chorus of a political event of sorts, a conference (*lesche*, a word not attested in this sense in prosaic Attic) convoked by Creon, who has just entered the stage (155–161). His argumentation is unmistakably rhetorical, leaning heavily to gnomic statements,[36] so I will not offer an analysis. But it is worth noting the Chorus' response to his speech (211–214): it acknowledges that he has decided what he has decided, and adds the further acknowledgment that he can do as he pleases with everyone in the city, dead or alive. By abdicating any role as judges of his words and action it defines the *lesche* to which it was called as a mere presentation of *faits accomplis*, and hence an event in which persuasion is merely an adjunct to coercion. In the meantime, Creon's coercive powers have been frustrated by Antigone's defiant act. The audience might expect that in her second appearance on the stage, now as a captive brought before Creon as the perpetrator of the forbidden burial, she would attempt to persuade him of the rightness of her deed. But the explanation she pronounces, as it is grounded on the gods' unwritten laws (454), does not constitute a defence before any human court (459). In a strict sense, her speech is not meant to persuade any mortal: she will soon say that the city agrees with her already (504–505, 509), and Creon's expected censure is dismissed as the judgement of a fool (469–470). But as in the scene with Ismene, Sophocles presents Peitho as continuing to labour, though it has been implicitly dismissed as irrelevant. Even before Creon's challenge, Antigone buttresses her argument from divine ordinance with consideration of a more pragmatic sort: as her life is unrelieved misery, death will bring a greater gain than life (461–464). At the very least, she is persuading herself or reiterating an internal argument that preceded her act, and in doing so she inevitably works to persuade the spectators to understand her defiance under a certain description.[37] Creon is not content to punish the girl. He heard her speech as making a claim: 'I hate it when someone caught in wicked acts wants to make a fair thing (καλλύνειν) of the crime' (495–496), a claim he cannot refrain from contesting. Antigone declares that nothing in his words displeases her, nor vice versa, thus there is something illogical in her attempting to refute him (502–503 would be heard as a direct answer to Creon's καλλύνειν) – illogical but dramatically right.

Somewhat as the chorus and Antigone have done, but with quite a different result in mind, Creon's son Haemon also renounces persuasion: 'Father, I am yours, and you, with counsels (*gnomas*), set out straight lines for me' (635–636). He goes on to indicate that he will not value marriage to Antigone higher than his father's guidance. Reassured, indeed delighted by his son's evidently categorical obedience (he had expected stormy resistance: 633), Creon expatiates on the dangers of rebellious children, fractious wives, such as Antigone had threatened to be, the value of discipline (*peitharchia*: 676) in general for household and city, and his resolution in the matter of Polyneices' corpse. The Chorus applauds Creon's manifesto (681–682), but this time, as if sensing the true drift of the son's words, by venturing a positive evaluation of the good sense with which the father spoke. It does allow the possibility that old age (precisely its qualification in the earlier scene for participation in the pseudo-*lesche*) has impaired its understanding, but simply by reporting how Creon *seems* to it to speak (λέγειν . . . δοκεῖς), it re-establishes the city as an arena for persuasion. Haemon renounces his own ability to criticise his father's speech, but then opens the door to criticism by attributing to 'another' the possibility of 'having something good', and offering himself as a spy on the very public opinion Creon has suppressed (683 ff.). The interchange is a masterpiece of obliquity and implication.

Creon has demanded obedience from his subjects, and met defiance. In the first sentence he utters in the play (992), Tiresias demands Creon's obedience. The seer's word is *pithou*, the imperative, in the middle voice, of the verb related to the noun *peitho*. Creon's response is not 'I will obey', but an assertion that in the past he has not 'stood apart' from Tiresias' prescriptions and has experienced their benefits. Tiresias must notice this hedging, for he concludes his report on the unmistakable tokens of the gods' displeasure with a plea to Creon to reflect on the error of his proclamation. Tiresias caps this speech by remarking that it is 'sweetest' to learn from a wise counsellor (1031–1032). The formulation anticipates the 'making sweet' suggested by the Latin word *persuadeo*, the origin of the English word. The infallible prophet has moved with great rapidity from a peremptory command to a gently worded attempt at persuasion, an exercise that his mantic authority and the extraordinarily blatant meaning of the pollution of the altars by remnants of Polyneices' corpse should have made redundant.[38] Tiresias knows his interlocutor: comparing the prophet's benign rhetoric to an assault by archers (1033–1034), Creon turns to a vituperative counter attack that, in turn, provokes Tiresias to abandon persuasion in favour of an angry proclamation of the impending disasters.[39] Only after Tiresias has left the stage and the overly deferential Chorus remarks that his prophecies have never proved false (1094) does Creon confess that he too is alarmed. Relinquishing, yet continuing to voice, his resistance (1096–1097, 1105–1106, 1113–1114), he says the word he would not say to the prophet: 'I will obey' (1099).

Few things could more quickly denature tragedy, diminishing it to an entertainment (or ritual) where only sound and spectacle mattered, than an impression that the world on stage showed less ambiguity than the everyday world of incessant debate and deliberation, public and private, presided over by Peitho.[40] And if our fragmentary evidence is a fair sample of tragedy composed in the next century,[41] rhetoric persists and also overwhelms the medium.[42] Our leading authorities, beginning with Aristotle himself, regard this as a misfortune, but Peitho argued her case before the city and won.

This chapter concentrates on rhetoric in tragedy, but I add a few observations on tragedy imitated and cited in rhetoric, specifically in forensic oratory. The comic poets watched tragedy with their own compositional requirements in mind, and there is no reason why speechwriters could not have done so too. The strong emotional responses generated by the tragedies must have impressed men faced with an urgent personal or professional need to bring jurors to anger or pity. True, the ability to induce affect in spectators was not confined to tragedy: Plato's *Ion* (535b–d) describes the intense fear suffered by audiences of Homeric rhapsodes.[43] But because tragedy was enacted by actors, not narrated, used a language that was at least *less* alien from everyday speech than epic or choral lyric, and was subject to a popular vote, it must have been seen as a more natural source of rhetorical ploys than epic.[44] Still, just as tragedy took a risk in imitating the discourse of civic institutions, so the speechwriters were in danger of losing more than they gained in borrowing from the theatre.

By a wide margin, a speech by Antiphon, the *Prosecution for Poisoning*, shows the most tragic colouring of all the preserved speeches. There is an abundance of poetic words at charged moments, and an outbreak of rhythms characteristic of tragedy (19). Further, though Antiphon's client cannot claim that his stepmother lured his father into a bath and stabbed him to death, he does call her 'a Clytemnestra' (17). The jurors who heard the speech, I conjecture, found it tasteless – moderns have been lenient, citing the speaker's youth. The merits of the case seem very weak indeed. It is easy to imagine that Antiphon was driven to compensatory stylistic extremes for his client, a young man, inexperienced in court, or so it is claimed, a bastard (we can infer) trying to make his legitimate half-brothers' defence of their own mother look monstrous.[45] The evolution of Attic forensic style, however, provides a better (or perhaps supplementary) explanation. If I am correct in thinking that many of the stylistic features of the forensic genre reflect the professional speechwriters' efforts at making their clients appear self-possessed despite the intense strain of courtroom speaking, then Antiphon's speech represents a quickly discarded experiment from the early days of the *logographoi*.[46] The intense affect which contributed to success in one civic occasion, the tragic performance, was found to be unsuccessful in litigation.[47] My guess is that other speechwriters, and even Antiphon himself, seeing that the jurors did not want to be treated to a spectacle too reminiscent of tragedy, which they demonstrated by derisive hooting and then their vote, made an adjustment in the direction of more constricted affect.

The sort of tragic colouring found in that speech is quite different from the explicit quotation of actual tragic passages in oratory. The speakers quite often quote tragedy for the same reason they quote or refer to Homer, Tyrtaeus or Solon: poetry represents a sort of unassailable wisdom. In his speech *Against Leocrates* of 330, written after the Macedonian defeat of Athens at Chaeronea, the orator Lycurgus justifies reading out passages of Euripides and Homer by attributing mere injunction to the laws but persuasion to the poets: 'Owing to their brevity, laws command what one must do, but the poets, by imitating human life and selecting the noblest of their deeds, persuade with *logos* and demonstration' (102). Just before (100), Lycurgus had quoted a long speech from Euripides' *Erechtheus* in which a mother explains her enthusiasm for allowing her husband to sacrifice their daughter, thereby saving the city from its enemies. Whatever dark shadows resided in this passage in its original dramatic home are eliminated by an indifference to context. Tragedy had itself become a source for exploitation by rhetoric in the real world of the detachable arguments first perfected outside the Theatre of Dionysus.

Lycurgus instructs the jury to attend to a verbal argument, embedded in a tragedy, that no mature Athenian could mistake as historical in its details; the exercise, he claims, will enhance the quality of their judgement of a defendant in a specific case arising out of recent events. Some fifteen years before, Euripides was invoked by Aeschines to demonstrate the insufficiency, even irrelevance, of verbal argument, here in the form of witnesses' depositions:[48] 'I have before been chosen as a judge of many arguments (λόγων κριτής), and have often heard witnesses' contradictory claims on a single incident. As any wise man does, I reckon (λογίζομαι) the truth this way: inspecting the man's nature and his life day-to-day' (1.152, quoting Euripides' *Phoenix*). By a nice twist, the words of a tragic character denouncing verbal argument of just the sort familiar from the city's courts are here put to work by a judge of many arguments, λόγων κριτής, to disregard certain verbal arguments. Peitho must have had herself a good, convincing laugh.

NOTES

My thanks to Debra Hamel, Patricia Rosenmeyer and Andrew Scholtz for their help in preparing this chapter.

1 A. W. Pickard-Cambridge, *The Dramatic Festivals of Athens*[2], rev. by J. Gould and D. M. Lewis (Oxford: 1988), pp. 67–8.

2 The technical *differentiae* of satyr drama are presented by R. Seaford in his commented edition of Euripides' *Cyclops* (Oxford: 1988), pp. 44–8. Satyr drama did not lie close enough to comedy to obviate the question whether the same man could write both tragedy and comedy (Plato, *Symposium* 223d).

3 Pickard-Cambridge, *Dramatic Festivals*[2], pp. 95–9.

4 Pickard-Cambridge, *Dramatic Festivals*[2], pp. 239–40.

5 According to Aristotle, *Poetics* 1462a11, having the text of a tragedy to read, but no performance to watch, does not preclude judging its quality.

6 Exceptions include Aeschylus' *Persians*, on which see further below, and Agathon's *Antheus* (Arist. *Poetics* 1451b21). The other pertinent *locus classicus*, a comic poet's complaint that the tragedians employ ready-made names and plots, whereas members of his guild need to invent material, is Antiphanes, fr. 191K, from his comedy *Poetry*. On the nature of the credence placed in mythological material see P. Veyne, *Did the Greeks Believe in Their Myths?* trans. P. Wissing (Chicago: 1988), and D. C. Feeney, *The Gods in Epic: Poets and Critics of the Classical Tradition* (Oxford: 1991), especially pp. 44–5.

7 W. Burkert, *Greek Religion*, trans. J. Raffan (Oxford: 1985), p. 113: 'Signs come from the gods, and through them the gods give direction and guidance to man, even if in cryptic form. Precisely because there are no revealed scriptures, the signs become the preeminent form of contact with the higher world and a mainstay of piety.'

8 The notion of joint human and divine action is captured in Sophocles' description of Ares as a 'trace-horse' (*Antigone* 140): see J. Jones, *On Aristotle and Greek Tragedy* (London: 1962), p. 172.

9 I. B. Singer summed it up: 'We must believe in free will. We have no choice.'

10 Sophistic and rhetoric cannot be separated from each other in any simple way. For the purpose of this discussion, it is sufficient to say that some, but not all, of the topics that fall under the rubric 'sophistic' touched on persuasive speech, the province of 'rhetoric'. For the sake of brevity I use the expression *rhetorike techne* though it may not have been in currency until Plato and Aristotle: see Cole, *Origins of Rhetoric*, p. 2, but against this: C. G. Thomas and E. K. Webb, chapter 1 above.

11 The tragedians did sometimes execute even the so-called Gorgianic figures of *parisosis* and *homoioteleuton*: for some examples see J. Duchemin, *L'ΑΓΩΝ dans la tragédie grecque* (Paris: 1945), p. 214.

12 See S. Halliwell, *Aristotle's Poetics* (Chapel Hill: 1986), pp. 37–9.

13 I speak only of American audiences. Brecht is perhaps the only sententious playwright of the twentieth century who enjoys enduring popularity in the United States.

14 That is, the three *gene* (genres) identified by Aristotle and others: dicanic, symbouleutic and epideictic. The last, certainly the one least well known to modern readers, is the subject of N. Loraux's study of the *epitaphios: The Invention of Athens*, trans. A. Sheridan (Cambridge, Mass.: 1986).

15 As, for instance, when L. Pearson suggests that tragic prologues may have influenced Demosthenes' construction of narrative: *The Art of Demosthenes* (Meisenheim am Glan: 1976), pp. 40–3. S. Goldhill, by contrast, attempts 'to show how the sophists do not merely constitute an intellectual background or influence on the literary world of tragedy. Rather, tragedy and sophistic writing both attest to a radical series of tensions in the language and ideology of the city of fifth-century Athens': *Reading Greek Tragedy* (Cambridge: 1986), p. 243. For some specific references in oratory to tragedy see further below.

16 'On the whole', for consistency of character and the relationship of character to action is highly problematic. Some scholars, notably Tycho von Wilamowitz in his work on Sophocles, deny that tragedy aims at consistency from one scene to another; Jones, *On Aristotle and Greek Tragedy*, claiming to be rescuing Aristotle's argument on tragedy as an imitation of an action, not of a human being, sees character in tragedy, at least until Euripides, as inchoate and unknowable, except as revealed by action. On the whole question see the collection of essays in C. Pelling (ed.), *Characterization and Individuality in Greek Literature* (Oxford: 1990).

17 A convenient précis of the scene and scholars' interpretations: D. J. Conacher, *Aeschylus' Oresteia: A Literary Commentary* (Toronto: 1987), pp. 159–69.

18 See P. E. Easterling, 'Anachronism in Greek Tragedy', *JHS* 105 (1985), pp. 1–10.

19 G. Lanata makes a similar point about medical language and poetry in 'Linguaggio scientifico e linguaggio poetico. Note al lessico del de morbe sacro', *QUCC* 5 (1968), pp. 22–36.

20 This is not to deny the possibility that Aeschylus meant the audience to notice, at some unascertainable level of consciousness, that a word used in society before the introduction of a homicide court had reappeared in that court, perhaps sharpened by the new institution. The word δικαστής ('juryman') at *Libation Bearers* 120 is a clear example. A promising candidate for a borrowing in tragedy from the symbouleutic sphere is

ἄριστα ('best') at Aeschylus, *Septem* 183 (the transmitted reading; Weil conjectured ἀρωγά ('aid')): see H. Friis Johansen, *General Reflection in Tragic Rhesis* (Copenhagen: 1959), pp. 106 ff. n. 17. The word itself is used in every sort of Greek, but the immediate contextual cues and the frequency of the word in the fifth-century political decrees that Friis Johansen adduces build a strong case. Another possible technical usage: ἀφορμή ('material') as at Euripides *Hercules Furens* 236. Vernant, who exaggerates (in my view) when he speaks of 'the almost obsessive use of a technical legal terminology in the language of the tragic writers', correctly states that the 'words, ideas, and schemata of thought are used by the poets quite differently from the way they are used in a court of justice or by the orators': J.-P. Vernant, 'Tensions and Ambiguities in Greek Tragedy', in J.-P. Vernant and P. Vidal-Naquet (eds), *Myth and Tragedy in Ancient Greece*, trans. J. Lloyd (New York: 1990), pp. 31–2. See also n. 41 below.

21 K. Alt, 'Schicksal und φύσις im Philoktet des Sophokles', *Hermes* 89 (1961), pp. 141–74 (= H. Diller, *Sophokles* (Darmstadt: 1967), pp. 412–59).

22 Admittedly, in plays not so centrally focused on *phusis*, he comes very close, as at *Ajax* 548–549 and *Oedipus Colonus* 337–338, though even there the polar expression is blunted by a variation in number and case (νόμοις/φύσιν).

23 *Ion* 643–644: δίκαιον εἶναί μ' ὁ νόμος ἡ φύσις θ' ἅμα | παρεῖχε τῷ θεῷ ('*phusis* and *nomos* together made me a just man for the god'). Euripides is apparently making mildly mischievous play with the term δισσοὶ λόγοι in the *Antiope* 21–22 Kambitsis ἐκ παντὸς ἄν τις πράγματος δισσῶν λόγων | ἀγῶνα θεῖητ' ἄν, εἰ λέγειν εἴη σοφός ('if he is skilled at speaking, a man might make from everything a contest (ἀγών) of double arguments'); the term appears in the sense 'arguments on both sides', and in grammatical dependence on ἀγών, a word often used for sophistical display. At *Hecuba* 123–124 the reference is far more subtle, for though the governing word is *rhetores* ('speakers'), we have the substitution of μύθων, a word for 'words' that shares only part of a semantic area with λόγων and has a different set of associations; further, the two arguments are reinforcing, not contradictory. In both, the audience can understand the words knowing nothing of the technical use of the term δισσοὶ λόγοι, and in both, words in the same sentence beckon the hearer to think of rhetorical exercises of his own time.

24 On specious arguments in Euripides see Duchemin, *L'ΑΓΟΝ*, pp. 207–8.

25 A. Dale, *Euripides: Alcestis* (Oxford: 1954), p. xxviii, referring to 328–368. The whole discussion (pp. xxvii–xxix) is elegant and apropos.

26 For instance, by hearing Hecuba's anachronistic appeal to the principle of *isonomia* ('equality before the law'): see J. Gregory, *Euripides and the Instruction of the Athenians* (Ann Arbor: 1991), pp. 94–102.

27 And Euripides himself satirises Aeschylus, most notoriously in the recognition scene of his *Electra*. It would be ironic if in our eagerness to allow this 'alien' element in tragedy we abandoned all efforts at discrimination.

28 For internal deliberation as a form of rhetoric see Isoc. 15.256–257. Though technical rhetoric is his main interest, the looser definition satisfies Aristotle's formulation at *Rhetoric* 1355b25–27: ἔστω δὴ ἡ ῥητορικὴ δύναμις περὶ ἕκαστον τοῦ θεωρῆσαι τὸ ἐνδεχόμενον πιθανόν. τοῦτο γὰρ οὐδεμιᾶς ἑτέρας ἐστὶ τέχνης ἔργον ('let rhetoric be defined as the ability of seeing, in regard to each thing, what persuasion is possible, for this is the role of no other art'). My definition is not so wide as to describe as rhetoric everything that induces *any* belief whatever; for example, an impression made on an audience by choral lyrics, or the totality of a work's technique, as in the title of W. Booth's *The Rhetoric of Fiction* (Chicago: 1961).

29 Though I claim that rhetoric is among the most intelligible components of tragedy, it must operate within a set of theatrical conventions that are sometimes quite different from our own. Hence the careful reader will consult studies like D. J. Mastronarde, *Contact and Discontinuity* (Berkeley and Los Angeles: 1979) and D. Bain, *Actors and Audience* (Oxford: 1977). At least some of the scenic 'grammar' these treatments delineate seems to enable the playwrights to dramatise the working of rhetoric within the technical limits of their theatre.

30 These are masterfully set out in the second chapter of R. G. A. Buxton, *Persuasion in Greek Tragedy: A Study of Peitho* (Cambridge: 1982).

31 The first part of the trilogy associates persuasion with violence and mastery: Paris, for instance, is assailed at 385 and Agamemnon at 941–942. To touch ever so lightly on an old controversy, that Peitho can be mentioned in those passages seems to me a clear sign that Aeschylus intended his audience to see his characters as feeling themselves capable of resistance to the forces that worked through her.

32 The chorus believes that Cassandra will be killed (1321), and possibly Agamemnon too ('if he will pay for the blood': 1342; note the hedging protasis), but there is a vast difference between knowing *that* something will happen and *when* something will happen; it is not the case that the chorus accepts 'Agamemnon's imminent death' (Conacher, *Aeschylus' Oresteia*, p. 48).

33 M. Gagarin is probably right in regarding Athena's persuasion as exercising greater power over the Furies than her hint that she could blast them: *Aeschylean Drama* (Berkeley and Los Angeles: 1976), p. 83.

34 It is not analysed, for instance, in Kennedy, *Art of Persuasion*, or Buxton, *Persuasion in Greek Tragedy*. Duchemin does not regard it as an ἀγών, but allows that there are 'deux tirades qui se repondent, celle d'Antigone exposants les faits . . . et celle d'Ismène essayant de justifier sa peureuse attitude': *L'ΑΓΩΝ*, p. 57.

35 C. Carey remarks that the speaker 'represents himself from the outset as the victim rather than the offender': *Lysias: Selected Speeches* (Cambridge: 1989), p. 64.

36 See Friis Johansen, *General Reflection*, pp. 114–16 on Sophocles' adroit transitions from general to specific.

37 Perhaps her reference to Polyneices as 'the unburied dead son of my mother' anticipates the argument from the irreplaceability of brothers in the 'suspect speech' (904 ff., especially 911–912).

38 See R. Parker, *Miasma: Pollution and Purification in Early Greek Religion* (Oxford: 1983), pp. 33 and 44.

39 In place of 'think of these things, my child' (1023), Tiresias now speaks an unsoftened 'consider this' (1077). In Greek, the phraseology of the two passages (they contain two of the three imperatives in -ησον found in the entire play) makes the absence of the vocative in the second more striking: ταῦτ' οὖν, τέκνον, φρόνησον as against ταῦτ' ἄθρησον.

40 See Vernant, 'Tensions and Ambiguities', p. 38.

41 It must be remembered that many of the quotations are preserved in works with a primary interest in rhetoric in general or in the gnomic, which tragic argumentation often employs. We hardly have a random sample.

42 See G. Xanthakis-Karamanos, 'The Influence of Rhetoric on Fourth-Century Tragedy', CQ^2 29 (1979), pp. 66–76.

43 According to Gorgias' most famous doctrine, *logos* in any form, that is, prose or verse, can induce strong emotions over experiences not one's own (*Helen* 11).

44 Not to mention the specific inducement of seeing trials on stage. As Thrasymachus' treatise on pity took in some aspects of delivery, there is a good chance that he drew some points from tragedy.

45 The speaker's assumption, that is, that the sons of a man putatively murdered by their mother would decline to defend her, would make Aeschylus' Orestes look perverse in hesitating, in that crucial moment in the *Libation Bearers* (see above), to kill his mother in order to avenge his father. Aristotle employs the very situation in his *Rhetoric* (1401a36–b3) to illustrate the omission of a premise, drawing the example not from actual legal argument but the *Orestes* of Theodectes, a fourth-century rhetorician who also wrote tragedies.

46 Just how quick cannot be said for our documents of fifth-century forensic speech are very few and there are almost no secure chronological pegs: see K. J. Dover, 'The Chronology of Antiphon's Speeches', *CQ* 44 (1950), pp. 44–60.

47 Not only, if I am right, was forensic speech purged of tragic flavouring, but even of many of the affective resources of routine language: I plan to present details in a book entitled *Genos Dikanikon*.

48 I count these depositions as part of rhetorical presentation despite Aristotle's assignment of witnesses to the 'inartistic' realm (*Rhetoric* 1355b37). It is rhetoric's business to put these materials before the jury for maximum persuasive effect.

10

Comedy and rhetoric

Phillip Harding

This chapter will attempt to demonstrate the influence that the genre of comic drama had on Greek rhetoric in style, vocabulary, technique and theme. To all intents and purposes this will mean the influence of so-called Old Comedy, since Middle Comedy is little more than a concept and our earliest examples of New Comedy (excluding the fragments) post-date the great rhetorical works of the late fifth and fourth centuries, upon which I shall be focusing. Just occasionally it might be possible to glimpse a stock character of New Comedy, like the braggart soldier, behind the scenes; mostly, however, I shall be taking my cue from the plays of Aristophanes. Now it is obvious that humour can be found in many places other than on the comic stage, and equally clear that not all the humour found in the speeches of the orators need have (or was likely to have) been inspired by the comic genre. The larger subject of the use of humour, in general, in ancient rhetorical theory and practice is beyond the scope of this study. It has, anyway, been treated on numerous previous occasions, especially from the theoretical point of view, from antiquity to the present. But between these works and the present enquiry stands the obtrusive figure of Aristotle, whose prim views of propriety were antipathetic to the vigour of Old Comedy, especially the more abusive elements in it, which he excluded from 'good' rhetoric. This study will overleap the bounds he set and examine the texts of the orators for echoes or applications of Old Comedy in practice.[1]

Something can, however, be salvaged from ancient theory. The examination of comedy that has come down to us in the tenth-century codex *Parisinus Coislinianus* no. 20, usually called the *Tractatus Coislinianus*, is thought by many to be an epitome of Aristotle's discussion of comedy from the lost Book Two of the

196

Poetics.[2] Whether it is or not, this text, when supplemented with material from the similarly derived prolegomena on comedy in the manuscripts of Aristophanes, provides a useful starting point for an analysis of the qualities of ancient comedy that one might look for in rhetoric. Ancient theory divided humour into humour from speech and humour from action. The first category included figures of speech like the use of homonyms, synonyms or paronyms; simile and metaphor; manner of speech; parody, puns and specific or original word formations, like the diminutive. In tone, comic language was, on the whole, of the common sort. Humour of action (which also included subject-matter) involved deception (*apate*); assimilation from better to worse or vice versa (for example, the role changes between Dionysus and Xanthias in the prologue to *Frogs*); the impossible (*to adynaton*); the inconsequential; things contrary to expectation (*para prosdokian*) and the debasement of character.[3] The comic types were the buffoon (*bomolochos*), the dissimulator (*eiron*) and the imposter (*alazon*). Straightforward abuse (*loidoria*) was different from comedy in that there was no concealment. Comic *loidoria* involved *emphasis*. This is a difficult term, for which meanings as diverse as 'innuendo' and 'fantasy' have been suggested,[4] but it is important to note here that, at least, the ancient theorists saw something different in the comic use of invective.

Modern students of Aristophanes will easily recognise what is being defined in the *Tractatus*. Aristophanic vocabulary *is* at one and the same time coarse and crude, yet rich in visual imagery and metaphor, full of neologisms, fond of diminutives, puns and parody. His action *does* depend on the unexpected, the incongruous, the fantastic, the grotesque, the inconsequential.[5] His heroes are buffoons, dissimulators and imposters.[6] Finally, Aristophanic comedy abounds in abuse, ranging from the simple form of name-calling (*aischrologia*) to out-and-out slander (*diabole*).[7] This level of agreement between the ancient and modern analyses of the essential nature of Aristophanic comedy gives us every reason to believe that what we will look for as indications of the influence of comic drama upon rhetoric is not different from what an ancient audience will have perceived as 'comic' in any speech.

But before I proceed to the analysis of passages from the orators, in which I find the influence of comic drama, it is necessary to say a few words about the comic use of *loidoria*, abuse or invective. It, too, has often been studied.[8] Scholars have found its origin in

Homeric name-calling, at which there was no one who surpassed the wrathful Achilles, a man who had no scruples about calling his commander-in-chief, amongst other things, a 'dog-eyed, deer-hearted sot' (*Iliad* 1.225). But, even in Homer, there was more to abuse than name-calling. The most abusive individual amongst the Greeks was the ever-contentious Thersites, that 'clear-voiced orator', who, however, 'spoke without judgement' (*Iliad* 2.220–224, 246). He spoke with a view to raising a laugh (*geloion*: *Iliad* 2.215), but there was substance to what he said and the opinions he voiced were popular opinions. His mistake was to overstep his bounds in the elitist social hierarchy of archaic Greece, and his mistake was made clear by the way Homer turned the laugh on him, through a thoroughly grotesque description and the laughter of his fellows at his punishment by Odysseus. So the ridiculer was ridiculed, and Pindar should have been more appreciative of Homer's affirmation of aristocratic values (cf. *Nemean* 7.22 ff., 8.20 ff.).

On the other hand, of course, it was quite appropriate for equals to abuse each other both in word and in theme. Archilochus and the other iambic poets picked up where Achilles left off. But with the advent of democracy Thersites came into his own. Now the ordinary man was expected to speak for himself and in many instances was required to initiate prosecutions on behalf of the state. In some of these – like, for example, the *dokimasia* – he would have occasion to question a candidate's qualifications and credentials. Some see here the origin of invective (*loidoria*),[9] though what is really involved is more properly defined as *diabole*.[10] This term is often used to mean 'slander' or 'false charge', but basically it denotes 'attack'. The issues that were raised in this attack were quite uniform, though, of course, they would not always be found all together in a single speech. They involved charges about a person's origin, that he was not a Greek (1), or, even worse, that he was not a freeman (2); charges about his source of income, that is, that he worked at a banausic trade (3); assertions that he was on the wrong side of the law, that is, a thief or an embezzler, especially of public funds (4); claims that his way of life was socially unacceptable, in essence, that he lacked self-control (*akolasia*) in relation to drink or sex (5); a special version of this, directed against the elite, was the charge of selling one's sexual favours in a homosexual relationship, that is, male prostitution (*hetairesis*); charges that a person was disloyal to friends (*misophilos*) or state (*misopolis, misodemos*) (6); or a coward in battle (7), either by desertion (*lipotaxia*) or flight (*ripsaspist*); finally, there were charges regarding appearance and general behaviour that were designed to suggest an undemocratic nature (8), comments about dress or hairstyle to imply elitist attitudes, or about facial expression or lack of conviviality (that is, avoidance of wine altogether) to suggest a secretive, unfriendly or exclusive character.[11]

These charges clearly reflected the sort of behind-the-scenes commentary that would constitute gossip. Underlying the whole process, however, were the social and economic prejudices that characterised Athenian society. The exploitation of these prejudicial attitudes was, of course, designed to create an immediate hostility towards the accused, but they were not only hurtful to his *psyche*. Many of them constituted real transgressions of Athenian law and involved serious penalties; at the least ineligibility for the position sought, at the worst loss of civic rights.[12] Sensibly the Athenians introduced penalties for irresponsible prosecution,[13] and rendered some of these charges liable to the law of slander (MacDowell, *Law*, pp. 126–32). If, therefore, the origin of the charges of *diabole* was, as appears credible, in a legal context, it is reasonable to assume that, at least in the early days of their use, the prosecutor had (or felt he had) some basis for his charge. On the other hand, it can hardly have escaped anyone's notice that by the time of Demosthenes these topoi had become the material for extensive sections of personal abuse, that read like virtuoso flights of pure fantasy. And, indeed, that is what they are.

A revealing passage in Cicero's *De Oratore* (2.240–241) exemplifies the rhetorical use of factual (subject-matter) as opposed to verbal humour. Cicero recounts with approval the totally fictitious (*ficta fabula*), but highly prejudicial, story created by the orator Crassus against Gaius Memmius, to the effect that in a fight over a woman he had bitten the arm of his opponent, Largus. This was the lead-up to the verbal humour of the multiple alliteration, supposedly written in acronyms on all the walls of Tarracina, *LLLMM: Lacerat Lacertum Largi Mordax Memmius* ('Mordacious Memmius lacerates Largus' limb').[14] Since Cicero states specifically that this whole story was fabricated, we can see quite clearly the attitude of the Roman rhetoricians to the use of this sort of humour, nicely combined, as it was in this case, with the verbal variety. Starting with an idea based upon prejudice (a politician fighting publicly over a woman and biting as an unmanly act), Crassus created the whole story as a backdrop to his punchline, the unforgettable (though unfounded) comic alliteration of his fictitious graffiti.

This narrative was unashamedly created to be humorous rather than hurtful. The same, I shall argue, is true of those passages of tongue-in-cheek *loidoria* in the corpus of Demosthenes, which we shall be examining later. When one asks how the transition from the hurtful to the humorous use of invective came about, the obvious place to look is the comic theatre. Whilst the first extensive application of *diabole* by an orator is to be found in the works of Lysias, it is hardly likely to have originated with him. Antiphon employed some of these charges in a work entitled *Invectives* [*loidoriai*] *Against Alcibiades*, of which we have only a fragment. They had probably been developed even earlier. At any rate, all the tricks of the trade were well known to the comic playwright Aristophanes (cf. Harding, 'Rhetoric and Politics', pp. 28 ff.). The best known victim of Aristophanic abuse, Cleon, is also the most controversial since it is notoriously difficult for scholars to believe that the poet could be so vigorously abusive if he was only in jest.[15] Other cases are easier to resolve. Euripides' mother is a good example. At *Acharnians* 478 and elsewhere Aristophanes casts the abusive charge at Euripides that his mother sold greengrocery in the agora. Free women were not expected to be seen in public, certainly not in the agora, and least of all plying a trade. This is the material of *diabole*. But the story is hardly likely to have any truth in it for Euripides' family was respectable and wealthy.[16] The humour lay, we must assume, in the incongruity.

A better example, if only because it concerns a politician, is the case of Hyperbolus. He was ridiculed by the comic poets Cratinus, Plato Comicus, Eupolis, Aristophanes, Polyzelus and Hermippus on the prejudicial grounds that his father was a slave, of foreign extraction (Lydian, Phrygian or Syrian, it did not seem to matter), his mother a bakerwoman – or maybe a moneylender (Aristoph. *Thesmophoriazusae* 845), while he himself was said to ply the banausic trade of lampmaker.[17] The tradition was so strong it was accepted by the fourth-century historian Theopompus (*FGH* 115 F 95), who claimed to know that his father's name was Chremes. An ostrakon with Hyperbolus' name, patronymic (son of Antiphanes) and demotic (Perithoidae) has proved all the statements about his father were fabricated. Consequently there is no reason to give credence to what the comedians said about his mother. The whole tradition is wrong.[18] We could (or should) have guessed as much, because his career as a politician would have been impossible, if any of the charges had been true. It is interesting that in this case we can see the influence of the comic writers upon an orator. A scholion to Aristophanes' *Wasps* 1007 reports that the orator, Andocides, at some point (probably before 416, when Hyperbolus was ostracised, but surely after the attacks by Cratinus, Eupolis and Aristophanes, at least) made the following abusive statement about Hyperbolus: I'm ashamed to talk about Hyperbolus, a man whose father still to this day works as a branded slave in the public mint, whilst he himself, a non-citizen and a non-Greek, makes lamps.[19] Not only do we know this is not true, but the Athenians showed that they did also. Whilst we cannot be sure about all the constitutional positions Hyperbolus held in his career, the fact that he was a member of the Boule in 421/20 is agreed upon. For this he had to pass a rigorous *dokimasia* that, at the least, would have scrutinised his parentage and birth as a free citizen of Athens. Thus we find Andocides, presumably in some legal context, making assertions about Hyperbolus that both he and his audience knew to be false. I can see no good reason for his doing so, nor any reasonable explanation for his being able to do so, other than that the practice of the comic stage had extended to the courts.

To conclude: name-calling (*aischrologia*) and personal attack on prejudicial grounds (*diabole*) were both components of invective (*loidoria*) and had originally been serious expressions of hostility. The full armoury available to a speaker had been constituted from a variety of sources over a long period. Ridicule had early been the purpose. When, however, the comic poets used free invention to create exaggerated, incongruous and recognisably fictitious caricature, based on the same themes, the situation changed. Now it became possible for an orator in a serious speech to make assertions of a potentially damaging and, at the same time, manifestly slanderous nature – all in the name of humour. This is the tradition of factual humour inherited by the Roman orators.

I have been at pains to put forward my understanding of the evolution of invective into the type used by Demosthenes. I hope that my subsequent examination of his *loidoria* will serve to confirm this analysis. I shall now proceed to a discussion of certain passages in the orators that reveal the influence of comedy, as it has been outlined above. It goes without saying that all orators were not equally adept in the use of comic techniques. Even amongst those who were, it was humour of fact (subject-matter) that they usually favoured. Only one orator – Demosthenes – was comfortable with the language of comedy as well. In the rest of this chapter I shall be looking briefly at Gorgias, then discussing passages or works from Lysias, Isocrates and Demosthenes, but most of all from the last, since he was the greatest master amongst the Greek orators of the use of comic humour in his rhetoric.

GORGIAS

For the prosaically minded, like J. D. Denniston, Gorgias was only a 'purveyor of puerility',[20] who exaggerated certain figures of speech, like rhyming endings and pun (*paronomasia*), and certain qualities of Greek style, especially balance (*isocolon*) and antithesis, 'to the point of absurdity' (*Greek Prose Style*, p. 10). Maybe there is more truth to this statement than he realised and absurdity was sometimes the aim. It is certainly the case that Gorgias' *Encomium on Helen*, defending her against the charge of being responsible for the sufferings of the Greeks, full as it is of exaggerated word-play and exploitation of figures of speech, concludes with one of the most notorious twists-in-the-tail (*para prosdokian*) in Greek rhetoric. In his last words he claims to have written an encomium for Helen (though he has in reality sung the praises of the logos), and 'a bit of fun' (*paignion*) for himself. Thus Gorgias himself invites us to read his speech as a tongue-in-cheek exercise. As such, it makes more entertaining reading. It is all too easy to misinterpret humour, if one does not know the context. [21]

LYSIAS

Lysias' fame in antiquity rested upon the simplicity of his language (Dion. Hal. *Lysias* 2–3), and his ability to delineate character (*ethopoiia*: Dion. Hal. *Lysias* 8). The first quality was the very antithesis of comic style, but the latter left scope for comic characterisation. Perhaps Lysias' most memorable creation in this medium was the *physically handicapped person* of Speech 24, an *alazon*, if ever there was one, and one who, through the perverse incongruity of his arguments, personified the comic representation of rhetoric as the skill in 'making the worse into the better argument'.[22]

There is also another element of the comic stage in the speech, revealed in the ambiguity of the title, *Peri tou adynatou*. The preposition *peri* is used for a speech that is 'about' or 'concerning' a subject, not 'on behalf of' or 'in defence of' a person, for which the preposition *hyper* is regularly used. Furthermore, whilst the word *adynatos* in the masculine signifies a physically handicapped person, in the neuter *to adynaton* denotes the comic theme of the 'impossible', which is often created by the perverse turning upside-down of the accepted world through the paradoxical or absurd.[23] In the genitive, the form of the masculine and the neuter is identical. So the title of the speech warns us that it is simultaneously *about* a physically handicapped person and *about* an upside-down world (*mundus perversus*). Indeed, it is by turning arguments on their head that the defendant proceeds to vindicate his right to continue to receive the small dole (two obols in Aristotle's day, one at the time of this speech, if we are to believe the speaker) given by the Athenian state to people who possessed less than three minas (300 drachmas) and were so physically handicapped that they could not ply a trade (Arist. *Athenaion Politeia* 49.2). His prosecutor had charged that he was neither as poor nor as handicapped as he claimed; in short, that he was an imposter (*alazon*). He was probably correct. In writing a speech for this individual Lysias decided to take the bull by the horns and use the technique of comic imposture (*alazoneia*) as his form of attack. Thereby, he reduced the whole issue to the level of the ridiculous (the case was, after all, about only one obol), and probably hoped in that way to gain some sympathy for his client. We do not know the outcome.

Imposture and incongruity are everywhere. It is incongruous to have an individual of this sort speaking in his own defence so sophisticated a speech on such a pitiful issue. The whole speech is, thus, a parody of the *dikanikos logos*, or rather it stands in the same relationship to serious rhetoric as the comic perversion of tragedy (paratragedy) does to its original – language of the high style put into the mouth of a comic character in an inappropriate situation. Any doubt about this is removed by the opening gambit of his proem.

Amongst the great variety of introductions in the armoury of the Greek speechwriter was the claim – usually kept for a politically and legally inactive person (*apragmon*), whose lifestyle had been misinterpreted or misrepresented – that the speaker was actually grateful to his opponent for bringing him to court, because it gave him the opportunity to explain his way of life and clear himself of calumny. But it is a perversion of this topos for an utter rogue, as the defendant clearly is, to open his speech in the same way, especially since he scrupulously avoids, throughout the speech, giving any specific information about his income or his health or his trade. The imposture is compounded when he goes on to allege that his prosecutor was not motivated to prosecute by any of the usual stimuli, such as profit or personal hostility, but by envy. That his opponent could make any profit out of prosecuting such a poor person as himself is such a ridiculous idea that he breaks off in mid-sentence with a dramatic *aposiopesis*; that he was prosecuting out of personal enmity is inconceivable, because the defendant has not had any relationship, friendly or hostile, with the prosecutor. Why not? Because the prosecutor is such a base person that he would not touch him with a barge-pole. In this way he arrives at the outrageous and incongruous conclusion that his prosecutor envies him, because he is a better citizen, and has brought him to court for this reason. Thus we enter the *mundus perversus*, the topsy-turvy world.

Here is not the place for a detailed analysis of this superb speech, but I cannot resist a brief paraphrase of some of the key passages that reveal the defendant as a rogue, who could have played the lead role in any Aristophanic comedy. In sections 4–9 he offers to explain his circumstances. This is his chance to disclose the source and size of his income and the nature of his disability. Of course, he does neither. Rather he exploits pity, but in a comically exaggerated form – his father left him with nothing when he died; his mother had been an invalid until her death two years previously and he had dutifully shouldered the burden of looking after her in her sickness; he has no children to do the same for him; his business (whatever it is) hardly sustains him; only the dole keeps the wolf from the door. But this exaggeration is only the lead-up to the incongruous and impossible perversion of his conclusion: the prosecutor is the best witness to his poverty, for if he (the defendant) should be chosen to perform the choregic liturgy (a public service imposed only on the very rich) and were to challenge his opponent to an exchange of property (*antidosis*),[24] then that person would choose to be *choregos* for ten dramas rather than exchange property once. This is a manifest *adynaton*.

Sections 10–12 argue a paradox. The defendant has obviously been seen riding on horseback. His prosecutor has charged that this proves he is physically fit. Carefully confusing this with the separate allegation that his income was larger than allowed, the defendant proceeds to the obtuse argument that his riding on horseback proves that he is disabled, because, if he were rich, he would ride on a mule with a soft saddle! But, if he rode a mule, his opponent could not argue that he was not disabled. If that is not enough, he throws out the enigmatic irrelevance that he walks with two canes, not one like most people (ironically implying that makes him a rich man), but his opponent has not used that fact to prove that he is able-bodied. Of course, he says, he uses two canes for the same reason that he rides on horseback. The argument against the charge that he is physically fit then concludes with another *adynaton*. If the Council decides that he is physically fit, there is nothing to prevent him from being selected for the archonship,[25] and his prosecutor, on the other hand, from applying for the dole.

Passing on to the charge that he is a violent and unrestrained character (anti-social behaviour of a type, we might note, that typifies the comic hero), he defends himself not by fact, but by resorting to an argument from popular prejudice.[26] Everyone knows, he says, that an old, disabled and impoverished man cannot behave this way; his circumstances keep him on the straight and narrow (*sophron*); only the rich, young and strong can push people around. This, of course, reflects a popular prejudice about the rich that their wealth leads to lack of self-control (*akolasia*), a prejudice that is in stark contrast to the claim of the elite to be 'reasonable men' (*sophrones*).[27] The idea that only poverty keeps a man honest (*sophron*) and hardworking is a comic reversal of this elitist image; it is found most explicitly in Aristophanes, *Plutus* 563. It also appears in Isocrates, *Areopagiticus* 4, to which I shall refer later. This section concludes with the revealingly ironic charge that his opponent is trying to make him into a character in a comedy. The prosecutor had also made allegations about the nature of the business the defendant was engaged in, deducing its unsavoury nature from the equally unsavoury clientele. The response to this is a reduction to absurdity. All Athenians frequent one business establishment or another, therefore all Athenians are unsavoury. But this outrageous argument involves a reversal of the basic premise of the prosecutor's charge.

The conclusion of the speech is full of pitiful appeals, but two final points should be noted. He deflects the imaginary charge that he was not a good democrat by the standard defence that he had not collaborated with the Thirty Tyrants. Instead he had gone into exile in Chalcis, 'even though he could have enjoyed full citizen-rights without fear under them' (25). From what we know of the Thirty's policy to exclude the poor from the franchise,[28] this would have been absolutely impossible – unless, that is, he was indeed wealthy. Finally, he descends to the ludicrous banality of denying the implication that he was, in essence, embezzling public funds (the sort of *diabole* that was frequently thrown at a politician or magistrate), by reminding the jury that he was only receiving 'a mere obol'. In this brilliant speech Lysias has used many of the techniques of the comic dramatist – exaggeration, incongruity, parody, absurdity, the impossible and, furthermore, as he makes his own character admit, he has masterfully taken the comic hero off the stage and put him in court.

ISOCRATES

Humour can be found in strange places, but none so strange as Isocrates' *Areopagiticus*. On the face of it this is a very serious speech, criticising the faults of fourth-century democracy and praising the way of life of past generations, especially those who had lived under the supervision of the Areopagus. Isocrates is usually taken as a *laudator temporis acti*, as a conservative who either lived in the past or, at least, projected his ideal virtues back into the past.[29] In this speech, it appears, the ideal virtue is *sophrosyne* (controlled behaviour), the opposite of *akolasia* (lack of self-control). Yet there are reasons to doubt this interpretation. In the first place we know that the Athenians had the habit of retrojecting all civic virtues upon an imaginary ancestry,[30] and, secondly, we recognise in Plato's *Menexenus* (published about thirty years earlier than the *Areopagiticus*) a tendency amongst intellectuals to parody this national propaganda. Furthermore there are internal indications that the work may not be as serious as it seems.[31]

The first of these can be found close to the beginning of the speech (4), where Isocrates introduces his central subject, namely, *sophrosyne*, in a very surprising manner for one who ran an educational establishment for the very rich. 'Wealth and power', he says, 'are attended by stupidity (*anoia*) and lack of self-control (*akolasia*), while *sophrosyne* and *metriotes* (moderation) belong to those in need and the lowly'. This is the same negative popular view of wealth that was adopted by that scoundrel, the handicapped person, and that is put into the mouth of Poverty (*Penia*) in Aristophanes' *Plutus*: 'I shall proceed next to speak to you about *sophrosyne* and I shall demonstrate that propriety lives with me, whilst it is characteristic of Wealth to be insolently arrogant' (563–564). The scornful reaction of Chremylus, the character whom Poverty is trying to persuade, shows how ridiculous an idea this is. It is not only ridiculous, but also incongruous for Isocrates to adopt this definition of *sophrosyne*, the virtue he specifically associates with the noble ancestors of Athens' timeless past, instead of using the elitist view of it as the 'aristocratic ideal of quietude, restraint and eukosmia' (North, *Sophrosyne*, p. 144).

The idea that something is amiss is strengthened by the presence of some clear echoes of Aristophanic themes in the speech and, in addition, some probable examples of comic technique. First, the echoes. In sections 25–26 Isocrates contrasts the politicians of the present, who enter politics to feather their own nests, 'looking around from the day they entered office to see if the previous magistrate had left anything behind for the taking', with those of the good old days, who believed that magistrates should behave like household slaves (*oiketai*) to a Demus, which is ironically designated as a tyrant. Of course, it was a popular prejudice about politicians that they were on the make, and this prejudice was the basis of the charge of embezzlement that was a frequent element in the *diabole* against a magistrate. But it was not new in Isocrates' day. It was rife in the fifth century, not least in comedy. Aristophanes most frequently levelled this charge against Cleon, most vigorously in *Knights*. By contrast, those pitiful characters who speak the prologue of that play, usually given the names Nicias and Demosthenes, are specifically identified as *oiketai* (Demus' household slaves). Were these the sort of politicians Isocrates had in mind? Again in section 34 the statement that in Isocrates' day many people drew lots in front of the lawcourts (that is, for jury duty) to find out whether they would have the bare necessities of life or not, is really a situation out of Aristophanes' *Wasps*, where a child asks his father what they will buy their meal with, if the magistrate does not empanel a court that day (303–306). It is, however, the situation described in sections 48–49 that both embodies a crucial theme of the *Areopagiticus*, namely education of the young, and at the same time provides the clearest indication of humorous intent. It is, in fact, a parody of a parody.

One of the primary concerns of the Areopagus in the 'good old days', or so we are told, was the education of the young (43). Close surveillance and strict punishment was their way of preventing wrongdoing (47). As a result the young of those days, unlike the young of Isocrates' generation, did not frequent the gambling dens or consort with flute girls, but stuck to their appointed tasks. They stayed away from the agora if they possibly could and, if forced to go there, behaved with utmost respect and modesty (*sophrosyne*). They never talked back to their elders or made fun of them (the verb is *loidoreo*) – that was a worse crime in their eyes than parent abuse was for his generation.[32] As for eating or drinking in a tavern, not even a respectable slave would think of that. Dignified behaviour was their aim, not horsing around (*bomolocheuesthai*). In those days witty men were considered mistakes of fortune rather than naturally talented (*euphyeis*), as would be the case now, he said.

If all this sounds familiar, it is. Even those who treat the speech seriously recognise that this passage is remarkably similar to the words put into the mouth of that old pederast Dikaios Logos in Aristophanes' *Clouds*.[33] That character, of course, was aiming his criticism at the new learning of the sophists, especially rhetoric ('the art of making the inferior argument win'), which was, of course, the very art that Isocrates was teaching. Furthermore, the credibility of the educational system of the 'good old days' was destroyed by the way it had been represented by Dikaios Logos in *Clouds*. It was, consequently, utterly incongruous for Isocrates to claim to be teaching that sort of old-fashioned stuff, that was more to the liking of a Strepsiades than a rich young Athenian. It was equally out of character for Isocrates to reject natural ability.[34] These echoes of Aristophanic themes are reinforced by vocabulary and technique. In the above passage, for example, there is a humorous incongruity in criticising *loidoria* at the same time as exploiting its themes, and in associating the *bomolochos* (the comic buffoon) with the man of intelligent wit (*eutrapelos*). In the latter case the humour is double, because Isocrates dismisses the *bomolochos* just as he is praising ideas made popular by a *bomolochos*, Strepsiades. In fact, this speech is full of incongruity. The examples given must suffice.

Isocrates also employs the comic device of exaggeration, especially in preparation for a reduction to absurdity. The idea that even good slaves behaved with sophrosyne in the 'good old days' is an example of this technique, with the added incongruity that slaves were, of course, not part of the educational system, and the unexpected (*para prosdokian*) that slaves should be capable of an aristocratic virtue at all. Another example of this same technique of combining incongruity, the unexpected and exaggeration to produce an absurd result can be found in section 35, where Isocrates maintains that, despite the decline in standards, so much virtue (*arete*) and self-control (*sophrosyne*) remain still on the Areopagus in his day that even unendurably bad men quit their evil ways when they become members of the Council! Similarly, in sections 29–30, the exaggerated presentation of the religiosity of the ancestors (*progonoi*) leads to the banal absurdity that in the 'good old days' the sun always shone at harvest time.

Let me give one last example of Isocrates' use of the comic device of the unexpected (*para prosdokian*). In section 57 he enlivens his speech with some drama in the form of an imaginary interruption by a nameless student (*tis*), who warns him that, if he goes on talking the way he is, people will think he is an enemy of democracy (*misodemos* – one of the prejudicial themes of *diabole*). This sets him up for a response that is both surprising and incongruous: it would be a real disaster for him, he says, if he should seem to be proposing an oligarchic revolution by praising the *politeia* as it was in those golden years (59); in the first place, that was real democracy (a kind that could be found at Sparta also at that time), and in praising it he was only praising the democratic constitution, as he always does (60–61). In fact, it is his belief that any form of democracy is better than the alternatives. Why, if a person compared contemporary democracy with the rule of the Thirty Tyrants, he would think it divine (62). Neatly, Isocrates caps a passage that is full of incongruity by the unexpected and perverse selection of the most notorious example of oligarchic abuse in Athenian history as his point of comparison. The whole argument is topsy-turvy.

Not to belabour the point, it should be clear that the *Areopagiticus* is not a narrow-minded piece of bourgeois bigotry, as is usually thought,[35] nor is it in praise of the 'good old days'; rather, it is a work of elegant humour parodying a whole range of popular prejudices, not least the idea that the past (especially the education of the past) is always better than the present.

DEMOSTHENES

We come, finally, to Demosthenes, master of the spoken word in all its moods. Demosthenes employed the techniques, themes and vocabulary of Old Comedy in his rhetoric to a greater extent than any of his predecessors. That said, there is no doubt that his forte was in harnessing the topoi of *diabole* to the vocabulary of comedy to create humorous but negative characterisations (or caricatures) of his opponents. His excellence in this field left a lasting impression upon subsequent rhetoric. I shall begin, however, not with this usage, but with an example of his skill at a gentler, more subtle, form of humour.

Studies of the *First Philippic*[36] have revealed the way Demosthenes effectively supported his seemingly innocent proposals by humorously or satirically showing that the reality was exactly opposite. In essence he created the sort of topsy-turvy world (*mundus perversus*) that we saw in Lysias' speech through the use of irony, incongruity and paradox, and the reduction to absurdity of which Isocrates was so fond. His seemingly innocent proposals are not put forward until section 19, but before that the ground has been well laid for his comic or satiric treatment of the topic. Right at the outset he presents the Athenians with a paradox: the worst aspect of our present situation resulting from the past is the best feature with respect to the future (2). The reason he gives for this is a *para prosdokian*: our hope that things will get better is based on the fact that our present problems are the result of our own failure to do our duty. In section 7 he explicitly calls Athens' past behaviour an *eironeia*, and compounds that in section 9 by the use of the hunting metaphor, in which Philip is the hunter and Athens the obliging quarry that sits still and waits to be caught. Finally, in section 11 he jokingly rams home the point by stating that, if Philip should get sick and die, it would make no difference, Athens would soon create a new one. As in a comedy, it seems, Philip is only a fantasy figure created by Athens' fear and lack of concern.

After this introduction the recipe for success of section 19 seems all too obvious: the Athenians should prepare a force to make war on Philip, a real force, not of mercenaries but one that belongs to the state, led by a general, whom it should follow and obey. It should also be provided with operating funds. This ingenuously simple solution encapsulates, of course, all the things Athens has failed to do in the past. The rest of the speech makes this point by repetition of key themes that exemplify the way in which Athens' past performance has failed to meet the main demands of the proposal. In each case the incongruity between what Athens has been doing and what she should be doing is made increasingly apparent as the ironic representation of actuality approaches the absurd.

So, the suggestion that the force be a real one is antithetical to the reality that the Athenians keep voting or threatening huge forces that never actually materialise. The charge is developed by repetition (20, 30, 44), until it is reduced to the absurd picture (45) of Athens sending out a general armed with high hopes and an empty decree (itself an ironic exaggeration of the 'empty triremes' of 44). This creates the incongruous result that their enemies laugh (here vocabulary cleverly reinforces the absurdity), whilst their allies are scared stiff. Again, that the force should belong to the state is contrasted with Athens' use of mercenary forces, who in section 24 are described as 'winning victories over friends and allies', not over the enemy, and then, after a sidelong glance (παρακύπτω is comic vocabulary) at Athens' war, turn tail and run off to serve the Persian satrap Artabazus with their general in tow. This last is, of course, an incongruous reversal, since generals are meant to lead. Thus Demosthenes recalls his next suggestion that whatever force Athens sends out should be led by a general, 'whom it should follow and obey'.

It is not only the soldiers, however, who are of the wrong sort, the generals are not playing their part either. In a manner rather reminiscent of a stock character in New Comedy, the braggart soldier (*miles gloriosus*), they prefer to conduct processions and festivals at home, rather than campaign abroad: 'Just like people who create clay figurines, you elect taxiarchs and phylarchs for the agora, not the war' (26). Any fighting they do is against each other in the lawcourts, not against the enemy in battle (47). This leads to the absurd incongruity that Athens' generals are like footpads and cloak-snatchers, for they prefer a death imposed upon them by a jury as punishment for crime to a fitting end fighting the enemy. This theme is cleverly extended into a comment on the quality of the leadership in Athens as a whole – in politics as well as in war (46). Conversely, the Athenians themselves must shoulder their responsibilities as soldiers and taxpayers. They are repeatedly reminded that no one can fight a campaign if he cannot hire a crew for the triremes or pay the soldiers. And fighting, or making war on, Philip is the purpose of the whole exercise. Success in that arena goes to those who are ahead of events, not those who follow. But the Athenians make war on Philip the way barbarians box, covering the place where they were last hit. So, Philip leads and the Athenians follow and, incongruously, he has become their general, whilst they have been reduced to the status of barbarians (39–41).

The *First Philippic* was a speech with a serious purpose, but Demosthenes cleverly used satiric humour in his description of Athens' past performance in order to make manifest the paradox that the solution to her present difficulties was as ridiculously simple as he outlined in section 19, while at the same time as difficult as getting the state and its generals and all the citizens to change their ways. This is an excellent example of the more subtle way in which Demosthenes could employ comic technique to advantage, rather similar in many respects to the use Isocrates made of them, but it was not his favourite. As I mentioned above, Demosthenes' preference was for the more vigorous methods of comic invective. He tried his hand at this first in one of his earliest political speeches, the *Against Androtion*, that he composed for a client, Diodorus, in 355/4.

Androtion was a respected politician whose public career had spanned thirty years already by the time of this case, and was to continue for at least ten more. He was a wealthy member of the elite class. He had only recently been governor of the city of Arcesine on the island of Amorgos, by whose citizens he had been greatly honoured for his integrity and goodwill.[37] Since then he had been on the Council of 500, for whom he had proposed the standard honour of a golden crown at the end of their year in office. Whereupon two personal enemies, Euctemon and Diodorus, indicted him under the catch-all political charge of unconstitutional proposal (*graphe paranomon*). They maintained that the crown was illegal, because the Council had not performed all its tasks, especially of making sure that the required number of ten triremes was built during their year in office. Their case was clearly very weak, so Demosthenes devoted the large part of the speech he wrote for Diodorus to extraneous matters, that is, to personal abuse (*loidoria*), as frankly admitted in section 21.

The charges levelled against Androtion were: (1) that his father had been a state-debtor, but had escaped rather than pay his debt

(33–34); (2) that he himself had been a male prostitute (21–32); and (3) that his behaviour towards people who owed arrears of taxation had been high-handed and contemptuous (47–58). These charges were manifestly fabricated, since, if either of the first two had been true, Androtion would have lost his citizen rights.[38] Diodorus is aware of this possibility, but excuses his not prosecuting on these grounds by hinting that he will bring two separate cases in the future. He never did and the fact that he offers no substantiation for his *diabolai* shows why. The real purpose of these allegations only becomes clear in the discussion (42–59) of Androtion's collection of arrears of *eisphora*.[39] This was one of the issues that had created the hostility between Euctemon and Androtion. Euctemon had been a member of a commission for the collection of arrears, but had been removed (probably at his *euthyna*) on the instigation of Androtion. Somehow Androtion had become responsible for the collection (42–47). There is no reason to believe there was anything illegal about this. Euctemon was almost certainly corrupt. It was clearly a matter of some importance to the prosecutors to get their own back on Androtion for this.

The description of Androtion's performance in this function begins at section 47 and extends over twelve paragraphs. It is the highlight of the speech. Its purpose is specifically to demonstrate that he was 'shameless, brash, thieving, overbearing and fit to be a citizen in any other constitution than democracy'. In other words, that his performance had been worse than Euctemon's. We are told that Androtion took the Eleven, the superintendents of the state prison, with him, when he went knocking on people's doors. Thus men found themselves imprisoned in their own houses (a nice incongruity). This, it is maintained, was worse than the time of the Thirty Tyrants when people were arrested in the agora but at least safe in their own homes (a paradoxical exaggeration with which Lysias could not have agreed). One could even see a man – poor or rich – who was short of the ready cash at that moment, either climbing over the roof to his neighbour's or hiding under the bed to avoid being dragged off to jail, like slaves not freemen. And all this under the eyes of the wife, whom he had married as a free citizen (53).

This fantastic description has the air of a scene from New Comedy about it. But more is to come. Androtion supposedly seized the persons of two prostitutes, Sinope and Phanostrate, even though they did not owe any *eisphora*. This, the greatest indignity, is, of course, an incongruous absurdity. Prostitutes were not liable to the tax for two reasons: they were women and they were not citizens. But throughout this vivid description we are reminded of the irony of it all: Androtion, whose father was imprisoned by the Eleven but escaped, now takes the Eleven with him to people's houses, turning them into prisons and making the people go to ridiculous extremes to escape; Androtion, the male prostitute, is depicted behaving outrageously towards members of his own profession (ὁμοτέχνους πόρνας: 58); Androtion, who on two counts deserves to be deprived of his citizen rights, is seen treating citizens as slaves. So, this scene provides the context for understanding the factors that influenced Demosthenes' choice of prejudicial themes from the stockpile of *diabolai*, and gives an instructive lesson in the way these passages of *loidoria* are concocted.

This surprisingly artful first attempt at the technique of negative characterisation through humour was, nevertheless, rather blatant in its fabrication and failed to shake the reputation of Androtion. I very much doubt that Demosthenes expected otherwise. Comic abuse can help a litigant win a good case, but is hardly a sufficient basis for success by itself. In writing the speech for Diodorus, who clearly had only a grudge to stand on, he 'made the best of a bad argument'. By contrast, late in his career (330), when his skill in this area was fully developed, he unleashed all his talents against his great opponent, Aeschines, in a case he was almost certain to win: the speech *On the Crown*. Indeed, this was no contest either in fact, because the sympathies of the Athenian people were surely with Demosthenes, or in rhetorical skill. Aeschines might have been an actor earlier in life, but, when Demosthenes referred to him as a third-class performer (*tritagonistes*), he was not thinking only of the past. Demosthenes was the unsurpassed master of the use of theatre in rhetoric, especially comic theatre. He literally buried Aeschines under a storm of comic vocabulary, comic techniques and comically abusive topoi.

A recent study has shown the carefully worked out counterpoint between tragedy and comedy in Demosthenes' speech.[40] In brief, in order that I may not obtrude on another writer's turf, the defeat at Chaeronea is depicted as a tragedy inflicted by Fate upon Athens. In this way her noble stand, true to her past history, can be seen as a heroic death. 'Better to die with honour, than live in shame'. The agent of Fate was Philip. As such, he is described as a natural phenomenon: a thunderstorm (194) or a winter torrent (153). But Fate and Philip needed help from within in the form of a whole crop of traitors (61). They were seduced by bribes. The worst of these was Aeschines, because it was a greater crime to betray Athens than any other city. He acted as Philip's collaborator (*synergos*), colleague-in-the-contest (*synagonistes*: 41), in short, as his hired hand (*misthotos*: 52), who assisted in reaping the crop (51). The comic counterpoint that is developed throughout the speech by repetition, only to burst forth in two magnificent passages of virtuoso abuse (126 ff. and 256 ff.),[41] underscores the fact that Aeschines has played a supporting role all his life.

From the very beginning of the speech Demosthenes takes up the theme of *loidoria* (10). He insinuates that Aeschines' speech is solely abuse by stating in vigorous, picturesque and clearly humorous language that he will not play that game. He will stick to the facts and only respond to abuse reluctantly, when he is compelled to or when the people want him to (11). The passage begins with an elaborate double pun that is impossible to translate into English: 'Sharp-natured (*kakoethes*) as you are, Aeschines, you were dim-witted (*euethes*) to think (*oethes*) that I would drop discussion of the facts of my political career and turn my attention to your *loidoria*.' The comedy of the pun is heightened by the dramatic device of direct address. It is compounded a few words later by the vivid metaphor: 'I am not so fever-struck.' Demosthenes states that he will deal first with the slanderous lies with which Aeschines has attacked his political career and only then make reference to 'that parade of verbal diarrhoea' if the people want him to. All this comic business is nicely used in the comic irony of pretending reluctance to do something everyone knows full well he wants to do.[42] And of course it is Demosthenes who descends to the lowest forms of *loidoria*, not Aeschines.[43]

Space does not allow a detailed analysis of the comic characterisation of Aeschines in *On the Crown*. It would be difficult, in any case, to improve upon the excellent presentation of the evidence by Galen Rowe (see n. 40). Demosthenes reveals his debt to the comic stage in his rich use of comic vocabulary (for example, 'this gossip-gathering-agora-dandy, the very devil of a bureaucrat': 127); crude comic expletives (for example, 'go to Hell', literally 'split in two': 21); parody (for example, 'using such pompous words, shouting out as though in a tragedy "O earth and sun and virtue" and that sort of stuff': 127); diminutives ('the pretty mannikin': 129; 'midget': 242, who was in service to 'minor magistrates': 261; and 'little old hags': 260); oxymoron ('the very best of the third-part players': 129); puns (most obviously between the name Aeschines and the Greek word for 'shame': *aischyne* – this is used surprisingly rarely but with telling effect, as, for example, in 136 where 'Philip sent Python of Byzantium with a view to putting the city in disgrace/in the hands of Aeschines'); and an abundance of metaphors.[44] Through these and other verbal tricks of the comic playwright's trade Demosthenes created his caricature of Aeschines as a figure out of comedy.

Other indications reveal that this figure was that of an *alazon*, an impostor. He was a fake politician, because he pretended to be working for Athens when he was in the service of Philip; he was a fake doctor, who knew no cures but turned up at the wake (243) and was, in fact, symptomatic of the sickness in the cities (45); incongruously, however, his greatest fault was to be a fake actor.[45] But the most devastating thrust of the two main passages of *loidoria* in *On the Crown* is to show that from his birth onwards Aeschines has been a servant and a collector of scraps from other people's tables. Exploiting many of the prejudicial topoi of *diabole*, especially those regarding origin, status and profession, but exaggerating them into comic fantasy, Demosthenes depicts a man whose father was a slave to a schoolteacher, and whose mother, given the name of the comic bogey-woman Empousa, ministered to others as a priestess and a prostitute. Born to servants, he was reared in service – grinding the ink and sponging off the benches at school, assisting his mother at her Dionysiac revels (where, of course, he got carried away and lost his wits like the others), and receiving as his pay (*misthos*) sops and rolls and cakes. The description in both cases is pure theatre. When he came of age he became a secretary to minor officials or 'hired out' his voice (trained in Dionysiac revels) to a troupe of actors, where he played a supporting role (*tritagonistes*). In another theatrical scene Demosthenes describes the way Aeschines waged war on his audience from the stage, a very different sort of war from the one Demosthenes fought, just as Aeschines was a very different sort of politician from Demosthenes. The comedy is brilliant fabrication but not gratuitous. It serves as counterpoint to the serious accusation that Aeschines was Philip's hireling. What else could one expect from a person raised like that? So comedy crosses over into reality.

No discussion of Demosthenes' rhetoric would be complete without reference to his other great opponent, Philip of Macedonia, whose existence as a personality is almost totally the creation of the orator. Were it not for one of Aeschines' more successful attempts at drama, the unforgettable scene when Demosthenes lost his voice (2.34 ff.), we would only know Philip as Demosthenes portrayed him: a hard-drinking, bisexual, perfidious pirate.[46] But Philip has to play another role in *On the Crown* as the thunder or torrent that represents the hand of Fate. Despite that, Demosthenes cannot avoid literally cutting him down to size in one masterly passage of bathetic incongruity (66–69). Here, Demosthenes returns to a theme he has raised twice already in the preceding paragraphs and demands of Aeschines what policy it befitted the city to adopt when it saw Philip aiming for tyrannical rule over Greece. He follows this rhetorical question with an extended period, which hinges on the clause, 'Philip, against whom we have our contest (*agon*)'. Pivoting chiastically around this statement are, on the one side, Athens and her adviser (*symboulos*), Demosthenes,[47] and their memory of the city's perpetual struggle (*agon*) for primacy, honour and repute; on the other, Philip (and, of course, his colleague-in-the-contest, Aeschines), who is aiming to gain mastery, honour and repute in the future. So, the present contest is over the same prize and pits Athens' past against Philip's future. But, while it is a serious, if not tragic, issue, that the national image that the Athenians had so carefully cultivated for themselves,[48] referred to by Demosthenes at the beginning and end of this passage, was in a very real sense the compulsion that left them little choice but to fight at Chaeronea, the comic counterpoint is seen in Philip's stop-at-nothing passion for power.

The city of Athens has *always* striven for glory and repute, but Philip is a Johnny-come-lately, as is emphasised by his origin in 'Pella, a puny place, at that time without any repute'. Athens strives for the benefit of Greece, Philip for tyranny and empire over Greece. But the real difference lies in the way they go about achieving their respective ends. Athens expends men and money, but Philip is extravagant with parts of his body. An eye, a collar bone, a hand, a leg, he is willing to throw away any part of his body Fate should demand of him 'so that he could live in honour and repute with what was left'. The concept of Philip, a truncated tyrant, trying to live with honour and repute (an impossibility for a tyrant) is grotesquely bathetic and perversely incongruous. It serves to emphasise how impossible it was for him ever to acquire those virtues that had been handed down to the Athenians from the timeless past by their ancestors. At the same time we may well surmise that, eight years after Chaeronea and six years after the death of Philip, the humour of this last passage was bitter sweet.

In this chapter I have indicated some of the ways in which the practices of the comic stage influenced the Greek orators in style and method. I have only been able to discuss the more obvious instances and my study does not pretend to be exhaustive. I do hope, however, that what I have demonstrated here will be a stimulus to closer and more sensitive reading of the orators.

NOTES

1 Aristotle's view of humour in rhetoric is only revealed in passing in Book 3 of the *Rhetoric*; for example, 1419b7, where he refers to a fuller discussion of 'jokes' in his *Poetics*. This section is, however, lost and we have to infer his views from later works, such as the *Tractatus Coislinianus*, which is often thought to be an epitome of Book 2 of the *Poetics*: see for example R. Janko, *Aristotle on Comedy* (London: 1984). More useful is the excellent discussion of the topic by Cicero in *De Oratore* 2.216–290, though this also is infused with Aristotelian attitudes to wit and humour, probably derived via Theophrastus. On the subject of ancient views of humour in rhetoric see, in general, E. Arndt, *De Ridiculi Doctrina Rhetorica* (dissertation, Bonn: 1904); L. Cooper, *An Aristotelian Theory of Comedy* (New York: 1922); M. Grant, *The Ancient Rhetorical Theories of the Laughable* (Madison: 1924); and the work of Janko cited above. It is rather neglected by Kennedy, *Art of Persuasion*.

2 For text, translation and discussion of this work see Janko, *Aristotle on Comedy*.

3 Other elements, such as 'dirty dancing', are not relevant to the present study.

4 See the discussion of these terms in Janko, *Aristotle on Comedy*, pp. 201 ff.

5 For these terms see the relevant sections of K. J. Dover, *Aristophanic Comedy* (Berkeley and Los Angeles: 1972).

6 On these types see C. Whitman, *Aristophanes and the Comic Hero* (Cambridge, Mass.: 1964).

7 The only thing we have difficulty with is agreeing on the nature of the humour in the *loidoria* of Old Comedy, that is, whether it was meant to hurt or not. See, most recently, J. Henderson, 'The *Demos* and Comic Competition', in J. J. Winkler and F. I. Zeitlin (eds), *Nothing to Do with Dionysos? Athenian Drama in Its Social Context* (Princeton: 1990), pp. 271–313, especially 293 ff.

8 See, most recently, S. Koster, *Die Invektive in der griechischen und römischen Literatur* (Meisenheim am Glan: 1980).

9 I. Bruns, *Die literarische Porträt der Griechen* (Berlin: 1896), pp. 469 ff.

10 W. Voegel, *Die Diabole bei Lysias* (Basel: 1943).

11 These topoi were first systematically analysed by W. Suss, *Ethos: Studien zu alteren griechischen Rhetorik* (Leipzig: 1910), pp. 247 ff.

12 See P. Harding, 'Rhetoric and Politics in Fourth-century Athens', *Phoenix* 41 (1987), pp. 28 ff.

13 See for example D. M. MacDowell, *The Law in Classical Athens* (London: 1978), pp. 62–6.

14 This is the felicitous translation of E. W. Sutton in the Loeb edition of the *De Oratore*.

15 The most recent scholar to feel this difficulty is Henderson, 'Comic Competition'. His case is not very strong. His view that Aristophanes seriously expected to hurt Cleon politically, but failed, goes beyond the available evidence, especially if one looks at other cases like Euripides and Hyperbolus. His assertions about Aristophanes' political leanings are even harder to credit. The idea that Aristophanes' views are to be identified with the views expressed by the chorus in the parabasis of *Knights* because it voiced the opinions of the aristocrats 'to whose world the comic poets belonged' ('Comic Competition', p. 298) is illogical (what about the views of other choruses?), and the very notion that one can extract Aristophanes' opinions from the words of characters in his plays – even the chorus – was discredited long ago: see for example A. W. Gomme, 'Aristophanes and Politics', in *More Essays in Greek History and Literature* (Oxford: 1962), pp. 70–91. On the other hand, the treatment of Aristophanic invective by Koster, *Invektive*, pp. 72–6, is disappointingly brief and bases its incredible conclusion, that the comedians stayed closer to the facts than the orators, almost exclusively upon his attacks on Cleon, as though he and his fellow comedians did not abuse all politicians and thinkers and artists, and ordinary citizens as well.

16 See Harding, 'Rhetoric and Politics', p. 30.

17 The evidence is laid out in J. Kirchner, *Prosopographia Attica* (Berlin: 1901–1903), no. 13910 and J. K. Davies, *Athenian Propertied Families* (Oxford: 1971), no. 13910.

18 See now the discussion of the whole tradition in my commentary on Androtion F 32 in *Androtion and the Atthis* (Oxford: 1994). The ostraka have also vindicated the citizen birth of Cleophon against the comic tradition: see E. Vanderpool, *Ostracism at Athens* (Cincinnati: 1969), p. 27.

19 See A. E. Raubitschek, 'Theopompos on Hyperbolos', *Phoenix* 9 (1955), pp. 122–6 and my forthcoming discussion cited in the note above.

20 J. D. Denniston, *Greek Prose Style* (Oxford: 1952), p. 11.

21 Context would include, amongst other things: the nature of the audience, their expectation of the work, previous literature on the subject and reaction to that literature in educated circles.

22 See for example Aristoph. *Clouds* 112 ff. Cf. C. D. Adams, *Lysias: Selected Speeches* (Norman, Ok, and London: 1970), p. 237.

23 See G. O. Rowe, 'The "Adynaton" as a Stylistic Device', *AJPh* 86 (1965), pp. 387–96 and 'Demosthenes' First Philippic. The Satiric Mode', *TAPhA* 99 (1968), p. 363 and n. 8.

24 See the definition of this procedure in MacDowell, *Law*, pp. 162–4.

25 The implication is that people with physical disabilities were debarred from holding public office. We have no evidence to support or reject this notion, though it is consistent with the prejudices of Athenian society.

26 On the subject of popular attitudes at this time see K. J. Dover, *Greek Popular Morality in the Time of Plato and Aristotle* (Oxford: 1974).

27 On the elitist connotation of *sophrosyne* see H. North, *Sophrosyne* (New York: 1966), pp. 143–4; cf. P. Harding, 'In Search of a Polypragmatist', in G. Shrimpton and D. J. McCargar (eds), *Classical Contributions. Studies in Honor of M. F. McGregor* (New York: 1981), pp. 42–3.

28 Xenophon, *Hellenica* 2.4.1; Lys. 25.22; Diodorus 14.32.2; cf. P. Krentz, *The Thirty at Athens* (Ithaca and London: 1982), pp. 65–6.

29 See for example K. Bringmann, *Studien zu den politischen Ideen des Isokrates* (Göttingen: 1965), pp. 75–95; North, *Sophrosyne*, pp. 142–4; R. W. Wallace, *The Areopagos Council, to 307 B.C.* (Baltimore: 1991), pp. 145–73.

30 See N. Loraux, *The Invention of Athens*, trans. A. Sheridan (Cambridge, Mass.: 1986).

31 See P. Harding, 'Laughing at Isokrates: Humour in the Areopagitikos?', *LCM* 13 (1988), pp. 18–23, though I disown the typographical errors.

32 To judge from Aristophanes, 'father-beating' was a favourite pastime of the young in fifth-century Athens! Cf. *Birds* 1347 ff.

33 For example, North, *Sophrosyne*, pp. 143–4. On the pederastic proclivity of the *dikaios logos* see Dover, *Aristophanic Comedy*, pp. 113–16.

34 Cf. his own specific statement in *Against the Sophists* 14 that 'abilities with words and in all other activities are engendered in those who have natural ability (*euphyeis*) and have been trained by experience'.

35 As, for example, by Bringmann, *Studien*.

36 See, recently, Rowe, 'Demosthenes' First Philippic', pp. 361–74. It does not matter for my purposes whether we call the speech comic or satiric, though I prefer the latter. The point is that the author of the speech employed techniques that were used by the writers of comedy.

37 Cf. *IG* xii, 7, no. 5 = M. N. Tod, *Greek Historical Inscriptions* (Oxford: 1948), no. 152 = P. Harding, *From the End of the Peloponnesian War to the Battle of Ipsus* (Cambridge: 1985), no. 68. On Androtion's political career see the introduction to Harding, *Androtion and the Atthis*.

38 See Harding, 'Rhetoric and Politics', pp. 33–4.

39 A capital levy imposed on property-owning citizens; on the question how many were eligible to pay (as few as 1,200 or as many as 6,000) see P. J. Rhodes, 'Problems in Athenian *Eisphora* and Liturgies', *AJAH* 7 (1982), pp. 1–19.

40 G. O. Rowe, 'The Portrait of Aeschines in the Oration *On the Crown*', *TAPhA* 97 (1966), pp. 397–406. On Demosthenes' and Aeschines' speeches, and especially that Demosthenes ultimately had the law on his side, see E. M. Harris, chapter 7 above.

41 For a detailed analysis of these passages see H. Wankel, *Demosthenes: Rede für Ktesiphon über den Kranz*, II (Heidelberg: 1976), pp. 670–785, 1117–73.

42 See, for example, Aristoph. *Clouds* 535 ff., *Frogs* 1 ff. It is a hallmark of Demosthenes' extended sections of *loidoria*, which he works up with such relish, that they are introduced by a statement of his distaste for such things: see for example 18.126, 256.

43 Bruns, *Die literarische Porträt*, p. 572, missed the point entirely when he criticised Demosthenes for departing too far from the facts in his attacks on Aeschines in this speech. By contrast he found Aeschines' pedestrian attempts preferable, because they were closer to the evidence (p. 579). It is hard to credit an opinion of this sort, given that the evidence we have comes mainly from the orators themselves.

44 For the themes of Demosthenes' metaphors see G. Ronnet, *Étude sur le style de Démosthène* (Paris: 1971), pp. 147–76.

45 See the discussion in Rowe, 'Portrait of Aeschines', pp. 400–2.

46 See especially *Olynthiac* 2.5, 17–20. Theopompus (*FGH* 115 FF 224, 225a–b, 236) held much the same opinion of Philip. For a discussion of Theopompus' attitude to both Philip and Demosthenes, and the suggestion that he might have been Demosthenes' informant about life in the Macedonian court, see G. Shrimpton, *Theopompos the Historian* (Montreal: 1991), pp. 157–80.

47 This was the 'image' Demosthenes cultivated for himself in Athenian politics: see Harding, 'Rhetoric and Politics', p. 36 and n. 41.

48 Most clearly set out in Loraux, *Invention*.

11

Philosophy and rhetoric

Stephen Halliwell

> Hence came about that split – absurd, harmful and deplorable as it is –
> between the tongue and the mind, whereby one group of people
> teaches us to be wise, another to be eloquent.
>
> (Cicero, *De Oratore* 3.61)

For much of the history of European culture, philosophy and
rhetoric have been regarded as indispensable categories in the
analysis of intellectual activity and in the organisation of academic
or scholastic institutions. Yet during many periods of this history
there has been uncertainty and debate about the scope of
philosophy and rhetoric as individual pursuits or disciplines, and
therefore about the relationship that does or should obtain
between them. One of the most notable exemplifications of this
statement is the very period in which articulate concepts of
philosophy and rhetoric first began to emerge – the classical period
of fifth- and fourth-century Greece, above all in the cosmopolitan
culture of Athens which either produced or attracted most of the
protagonists in a controversy which was to have lasting repercussions for the history of ideas. It is easy, with hindsight, to
characterise this controversy as a confrontation between
philosophy and rhetoric. But it is safe to do so only if, from the
outset, we appreciate two essential qualifications called for by this
description.

The first is that to regard the phenomenon in these terms is
almost inescapably to observe it, in some measure at least, from the
point of view adopted by two of its participants, Plato and
Aristotle. Not only are their ideas most fully known to us, but also
they have been profoundly influential in establishing the very
categories which we now use to understand the cultural setting in
which those ideas were created and shaped. For it was these two

thinkers, more than any others, who formulated explicit concepts of both philosophy and rhetoric, and who offered extensive interpretations of what they saw as the divergences between the two. But the notion of a confrontation between philosophy and rhetoric also needs modifying by a general recognition that we are not here dealing with the rivalry of fixed or autonomous practices, but with a complex interplay between modes of thought and educational programmes whose identity and character were involved in processes of development and (self-)definition. It is vital, therefore, to try to grasp the dynamic and contentious context within which Greek concepts of philosophy and rhetoric were in active formation.

At stake in the emergence and elaboration of these concepts was, in part, the status of intellectual authority and cultural influence – an authority that would give the practitioners and teachers of certain activities a pre-eminent claim to wisdom and expertise (*sophia*), and a corresponding right to present themselves as possessors of politically, socially and educationally valuable knowledge. Claims to the title of such *sophia* were made by or on behalf of a large range of figures, many of whom we have become accustomed, principally in the wake of Platonic usage, to calling 'sophists'. We know, however, that the term *sophistes* was flexible and unstable for much of the classical period, and that it could be used in both laudatory and pejorative senses;[1] and whatever special conclusions might be argued for this specific noun, there can be no doubt about the wider desirability, for all intellectuals active in the classical context, of the entitlement to be described as *sophos*. It is this background which explains the development of a further set of terms, *philosophos* and its cognates, whose earliest usage was unsettled and which was to remain open to variable interpretation until well into the fourth century.[2] But *philosophia* became at any rate gradually associated with individuals and schools of thought that aspired to comprehensive understanding of the world, whether the material and natural world, the principles of human nature and society, or, most ambitiously of all, the world conceived as the totality of all reality. It was in the particular domains of human wisdom – the domains of psychology, ethics and politics – that the evolution of 'philosophy' became entangled with the potentially competing claims of a 'rhetoric' which asserted its own general competence in the sphere of public discourse.

That formulation, as I have already suggested, is one which owes much to the perspective so influentially constructed by philosophy's own proponents, and above all by Plato. But to suppose, as Thomas Cole has recently urged, that the very conception of 'rhetoric' should be regarded as an invention of philosophy, is an excessively radical way of analysing what was in fact a tangled (and not wholly recoverable) development of terminology, ideas and practice.[3] The term *rhetorike* itself probably came into use around the turn of the fifth and fourth centuries, as a way of denoting increasingly explicit attempts to define, formalise and offer instruction in the (putative) 'art' of the public speaker (*rhetor*). The term was not a Platonic invention: at its first occurrence in the *Gorgias* (448d9), Socrates refers to 'so-called *rhetorike*', thereby indicating unambiguously that the word already had some currency.[4] It is possible, if uncertain, that the earliest surviving use of *rhetorike* is in the short essay *On the Sophists* by Alcidamas, where the word shows no signs of being novel.[5] Alcidamas' work, whatever its precise date and connections, allows us a glimpse of the milieu of intellectual and educational polemic in which the relationship between philosophy and rhetoric was enmeshed at this time. Attacking certain 'so-called *sophistai*', Alcidamas stands up for his own interpretation of the art of public speaking. When he says that those who confine themselves to written discourses possess 'only the smallest portion of *rhetorike*' (1), he might be taken to be merely stressing the difference (which is his main theme) between 'live' oratory and its written simulation. But evidently more than this is at issue, since Alcidamas also criticises his opponents' neglect of 'history' and literary culture (*paideia*), and he wishes his own conception of rhetoric to be associated with the term 'philosophy' (2, 15). Although these details are tantalisingly allusive, it is clear that Alcidamas was writing from familiarity with an active debate about the sources, methods and contents of intellectual *sophia* in contemporary society, and that ideas of both rhetoric and philosophy lay close to the heart of this debate.

1

To derive a much fuller, though polemically slanted, picture of some of the questions which were generated in this context, we need to turn to Plato himself. Whether, in the end, we wish to accept, reject or modify Plato's perspective on the controversy, his exploration of it represented a powerful challenge for contemporary and later thinkers, beginning with Isocrates and Aristotle. For Plato, the ramifications of what was at issue, in terms of politics, ethics and psychology, made the contest between philosophy and rhetoric into nothing less than a choice of 'lives' (see further below). A complete examination of Plato's position would have to encompass practically the entirety of his written work, from the *Apology* (with its paradoxically simultaneous use and rejection of rhetoric) to the *Laws* (with its self-conscious application of 'persuasion' in the presentation of a legal code to the inhabitants of a city).[6] Contrary to a common stereotype, there is no simple or invariable Platonic attitude to rhetoric, and no static understanding of philosophy's dealings with it. While the *Gorgias* and *Phaedrus* can, as here, be treated as central expressions of some of Plato's most abiding anxieties, many other works contain material that supplements or even qualifies these dialogues.

Moreover, while it is one of Plato's purposes to elaborate distinct concepts of philosophy and rhetoric, this enterprise can in turn be used to question the status of his own aims and procedures as a writer. As Plato's critics have often been quick to notice, his dialogues contain elements which could themselves be judged rhetorical; and it is likely that, though the judgement is often a delicate one, Plato himself would have been prepared to concede the description in certain cases.[7] Contrary to the impression which he sometimes creates, Plato should not be counted as a mere opponent of rhetoric. Behind his often hostile stance, he raises questions whose scope ought, I shall contend, to make them of positive concern to proponents or defenders of rhetoric, and indeed to others besides.

An initial impression of Plato's perception of the competitive interplay of philosophy and rhetoric can be gained from the end of the *Euthydemus* (304c–307c). The main part of the dialogue has dramatised an encounter between Socrates and two brothers, Euthydemus and Dionysodorus, who in Plato's terms count as 'eristic sophists'; that is, exponents of a technique of casuistic refutation which exploits purely verbal ambiguities, and which elevates the show of clever debating skills above the substance of serious knowledge. Against the specious virtuosity of these figures, practised partly at the expense of the young Cleinias, Socrates has given illustrations of his own contrasting interest in exploring the relationship between knowledge and happiness, and in doing so by engaging Cleinias in co-operative, step-by-step enquiry (Socratic dialectic). In the last part of the work, Crito tells Socrates of the views of an unidentified teacher of rhetoric who had observed his conversation with the two brothers, and had expressed criticism of both the sophists and Socrates, scorning a certain conception of 'philosophy' in the process (304e7). Socrates in turn rebuts this criticism by commenting on this person's intermediate status between the philosopher and the politician; and the work ends with Socrates urging Crito, who is concerned about a choice of education for his sons, not to be put off 'philosophy' by its inferior practitioners.

The last part of the *Euthydemus* evokes, and projects back on to a fifth-century scenario, an atmosphere of rivalry similar to that suggested by Alcidamas' *On the Sophists* (see above). The two brothers, Socrates, and the unnamed critic (who has often been identified with Isocrates)[8] are all dramatised by Plato as candidates for the description of *sophos*, which would mark them as possessors of, and educators in, a knowledge of cardinal value to their society. Euthydemus and Dionysodorus are said to profess a wide range of expertise, including both the ability to communicate virtue or excellence (*arete*), and the skills of forensic oratory (272a, 273c). The anonymous critic is also a teacher of orators (305c), seemingly with a view to the rhetoric of political life in general. Set against both of these is Socrates himself, who does not make any overt claims to proficiency of his own, but shows an attachment to something that he calls 'philosophy', and hints at its inter-connections with *arete* on the one hand, knowledge on the other (275a1–6, 288d8). In fact, the dialogue suggests that the term *philosophia* is broadly available as a near-synonym of *sophia*, and its flexibility is only too evident. Socrates uses it in addressing the two brothers, ostensibly to mean the desire for knowledge or wisdom (whatever such wisdom might turn out to be); and it is later used also by Crito, a less than formidably cerebral character, apparently to denote intellectual argument and discussion (304e7).

The overall effect of these and related details of the dialogue is to depict a situation in which contrasting modes of thought and discourse are seen as contenders for the title of *sophia*, and perhaps *philosophia* too, and as challengers for the cultural authority to determine the advanced education of Athenians of the wealthier classes (such as Cleinias, cousin of Alcibiades, and Crito's sons).

The importance of rhetoric, as the ability to engage effectively in public discourse (whether forensic or political), is evident from its place in the practices of the two brothers and the unnamed critic, though their exact views on the subject are not aired in the work. Nothing in the *Euthydemus* entails the strict separation or the mutual incompatibility of rhetoric and *philosophia*, but Plato's deployment of the divergence between Socrates and the others serves to convey the possibility of a particular identity for philosophy. In the second of the sections in which Socrates controls the discussion (288d–292e), it is intimated that philosophy is a search for the knowledge and the *sophia* which would constitute the supreme 'art' of human living – the statesmanship or political wisdom (*politike*) which could control, for the best, the practice and use of other, subordinate arts, and thus bring about human happiness. Among the subordinate arts in question is that of speech-making (*logopoiïke*, 289c–290a), since Socrates and Cleinias agree that it is one thing to be able to make or compose a speech, another to know how to use one. In this same context Plato makes Socrates indulge in some typical (and perhaps 'rhetorical') imagery, by comparing public rhetoric to activities such as snake-charming. But beyond this tendentious and sarcastic characterisation, the passage broaches a question which is crucial to Plato's larger interest in rhetoric and in its relationship to (Platonic) philosophy.

The *Euthydemus* acknowledges an art of rhetoric – an art of skilled and effective public discourse – and acknowledges too that when practised by its best exponents it is a fine and worthwhile activity (307a6). But it sets these acknowledgements against an insistence (foundational for Plato's thought) that all human activities must be subject to the jurisdiction of ethical knowledge and judgement. This insistence is itself, of course, a far-reaching 'philosophical' thesis, and acceptance of it depends on an extensive series of premises and arguments. But whether or not it is finally acceptable, it introduces an issue of penetrating importance for the status of any art or theory of public discourse, especially within a culture such as that of classical Athens where public speaking was integral to the conduct of political and social life. If rhetoric is understood as a purely formal art – an expertise in the organisation and manipulation of linguistic structures, independently of subject-matter – then its ethical standing and influence will have to be determined, both in particular cases and in general, from a vantage-point which lies outside rhetoric itself. But if that is so, then experts in rhetoric cannot maintain, as many Greek rhetoricians apparently wished to do, that they were possessors and teachers of insight into the nature of human excellence (*arete*), the principles of political life, or the conditions of happiness. To sustain this larger position, the rhetorician needs to vindicate rhetoric as a more-than-formal art, whose ideas and techniques are supported by both intellectual and moral authority.

This is the fundamental challenge to rhetoric which is adumbrated by the *Euthydemus*, and it is one whose validity can be secured separately from its particular setting within Platonic doctrine. But to see how Plato develops his version of the challenge, we must turn to the conceptual arguments which are explored in the *Gorgias* and *Phaedrus*. In the *Gorgias*, the challenge to rhetoric is expressed directly in Socrates' conversation with Gorgias (448d–461b). Gorgias, *qua* rhetorician, describes himself as possessing 'knowledge about speeches/discourses' (*logoi*, 449e1, etc.); but when interrogated by Socrates, he finds himself torn between two possible positions: one, that the rhetorician knows how to deploy language persuasively on any and every subject; the other, that his art somehow contains ethical and political principles *within* itself. Gorgias' difficulties partly stem from the fact that while he needs to present himself as the holder and communicator of socially valuable skills, he also wishes to avoid responsibility for the abuse of rhetoric by his pupils. This conjunction of attitudes creates its own tension, quite independently of the particular and problematic view of moral knowledge (knowing the good entails *being* good) which Socrates advances at 460b–c. The idea that rhetoric has superior persuasive power even to specialised arts in their own fields of knowledge (456a7 ff.) requires the model of a subject-neutral technique or facility, and this corresponds to the notion, which already had wide currency, that the effective orator can in principle speak to, or on either side of, any issue. But for a teacher like Gorgias to commit himself wholly to this model would leave him vulnerable to Socrates' suggestion (459a–b) that the effectiveness of such persuasion cannot appeal to the rationality of its audiences. It would also undercut the rhetorician's pretensions to a larger *sophia*, an overarching sagacity about what Gorgias calls 'the greatest and best of human affairs' (451d7–8). In short, Gorgias is suspended between claiming for himself a formal, subject-neutral command of *logoi*, or professing a general wisdom about the nature and workings of political societies. Whatever Gorgias' personal entitlement to affirm either of these attributes, the first part of the dialogue leaves an unanswered question about the problematic relationship between them.

It is sometimes said that the thematic structure of the *Gorgias* moves away from rhetoric as such towards broader issues of morality. But this is to beg the very question posed by Plato's perspective. The shape of the dialogue embodies the view that the full examination of any theory of public discourse requires, and should embrace, a scrutiny of its bearing upon ethical and political principles. In that sense the *Gorgias* never leaves, though it enlarges the considerations bearing upon, the central issue of rhetoric's character and use. After Gorgias' own equivocal stance, his associates Polus and Callicles both present new defences of the power of rhetoric, a motif introduced by Gorgias himself at 455d ff. If rhetoric is truly powerful, there is a strong *prima facie* case for deeming it to be worth having, and for regarding its teachers as the masters of a social asset. But in expounding the power of rhetoric, Polus and Callicles are shown as inescapably adopting and advertising a morality of their own: one which assumes material criteria of human success or happiness; treats survival, pleasure and self-interest as the goals of life; and downgrades the values of much common morality (such as principles of social justice) to the status of a fiction designed to protect the weak against the strong. These two figures represent a severe but serious response to the exposure of Gorgias' dilemma. For if morality can be shown to be a cultural concealment of a necessary (because 'natural') competition for self-gratification and power, and if rhetoric can be seen to be a productive instrument of power, then Socrates' challenge has been rebutted. On this view, Gorgias' equivocation is discarded, and rhetoric emerges as a decidedly more-than-formal art: an art which contains the secret to success for any individual or group capable of using it in their own interests.

Against the tough extremism of Polus and Callicles, Socrates cannot complain that there is anything wrong with the connection made between their view of morality and their praise of rhetoric; indeed, Plato clearly wishes the connection to be seen as a true *description* of one way in which rhetoric actually does function in the hands of some people. But Socrates sets himself to show that there is something wrong with this view of morality itself, and to maintain the position crystallised in the maxim that it is better to suffer than to perpetrate injustice. The cumulative force of Socrates' arguments, whose detailed implications and difficulties cannot be examined here, asserts the irreducibility of ethical standards which override the individual's pursuit of his own gratification: power divorced from goodness, Socrates insists, cannot be a formula for human happiness. In the case of Polus, the rebuttal turns out to be relatively straightforward, since he is shown as finding it hard to rid himself of a given language of ethical evaluation, within which the notion of 'shame' attaching to injustice seems unavoidably to imply an evil that exists within the doer himself. Even Callicles, who argues much more vehemently than Polus for the principle of the superiority of the naturally 'stronger', is brought to agree that a pure hedonism is hard to uphold, and that pleasures can be judged, by apparently independent criteria, as 'better' or 'worse'. But it is important that Plato dramatises a breakdown in the conversation between Socrates and Callicles; there is no real agreement between them, and their exchange ceases to be co-operative from 505c. The significance of this breach in the discussion is that it marks a gross divide between the principal premises, as well as the underlying commitments, adopted by the two men. And it thereby enacts the idea, which Socrates spells out at 500c, that what is at stake between them is nothing less than a fundamental 'choice of lives'.

Viewed as a whole, therefore, the *Gorgias* constitutes an investigation into the relationship between rhetoric and human values. But for all the dark colours and polemical accents of the drama, both in the depiction of the antagonists and in Socrates' pejorative account of rhetoric as a branch of 'flattery', the work does not purport to offer a definitive account of rhetoric. Rather, by means of the strong contrasts which run through the dialogue, there emerges a basic configuration of three possible conceptions of rhetoric: one, as an essentially formal art of discourse, open to use for many different purposes, and necessarily subject to guiding standards which lie outside the art itself; two, as an instrument of practical self-interest, the pursuit of power, and the manipulation of others; three (though this is the most briefly glimpsed of all, at 480–481b), as a possible ally and medium of social justice.

Within a dramatic framework of a very different kind, the *Phaedrus* too circles around the question of rhetoric and morality. Here the formal capacity of rhetoric to argue any case is implicit in the paradoxical thesis of Lysias' speech, that a boy should yield himself not to a lover but to a non-lover. Socrates draws attention at an early stage to the distinction between formal and substantive criteria of rhetorical excellence, by asking whether hearers are expected not only to admire Lysias' vocabulary and phrasing, but also to praise him for saying 'what is appropriate' (*ta deonta*, 234e–235a). Such distinctions were already familiar within the analysis of oratory, and Plato is developing his critique from inside, so to speak, the framework of rhetorical categories.[9] As in the first part of the *Gorgias*, the challenge to rhetoric can here be seen as carrying a point that is potentially independent of Plato's own commitments (his espousal of philosophy as the agency of supreme knowledge and values), for it is a challenge to provide an account of how a single art can both present itself as a formal facility with words, and yet encompass an understanding of the human goals and subject-matter with which public discourse is inescapably concerned. The later parts of the *Phaedrus* make much of the fact that existing programmes of rhetorical teaching are heavily slanted towards adeptness at 'controversy', *antilogike* (261d10); that is, an ability to speak on either side of any given issue. The more such (apparently) formal skills are emphasised, the greater the need to question the sources of putative authority and influence which underlie such practices. In short, if rhetoric presents itself as a technical adroitness with *logoi*, its status can only be instrumental, not self-sufficient, and it will remain subject to the principle which we earlier met in the *Euthydemus*, and which is conveyed in the *Phaedrus* by the words of the Egyptian god Theuth: 'One man is able to create the products of art, and another to judge the degree of harm or benefit which they hold for those who intend to use them' (274e7–9).

This quotation belongs to the discussion of writing which forms the last part of the *Phaedrus*, and the context alerts us to a special feature of this work. While the *Gorgias* and *Phaedrus* both accentuate the problematic relationship between formal and substantive conceptions of rhetoric in its familiar public applications, and press the question whether the persuasive power of such speech is purely manipulative or can be grounded in a deeper understanding (ethical, political, psychological), the *Phaedrus* develops the point into a much broader examination of what might be called the uses of *logos*. From the beginning of the dialogue, we are made aware of what is educationally at stake in the contrast, experienced by the young soul of Phaedrus, between the rhetorician Lysias and the figure of Socrates, who describes himself (ambiguously) as 'a lover of *logoi*' (228c1–2). This contrast dramatises the issue of what kind of discourse, what kind of interest in language, Phaedrus should devote himself to; and it gives us another glimpse of the status of cultural authority for which Plato regards rhetoric and philosophy as being rivals. The critique of rhetoric which Socrates gradually elaborates, first by ironically competing with the speech-making of Lysias and later by explicit analysis, depends upon a framework of general categories: truth and falsehood; justice and injustice; knowledge, belief and ignorance; and the form and content of any discourse, whether written or spoken. The framework is used in part to construct a condemnation of much existing rhetoric, on three main grounds: first, as excessively concerned with persuasion through an audience's beliefs and prejudices, regardless of the truth;[10] second, as amorally neutral or fickle with respect to the values to which it makes nominal appeal; third, as inordinately given to a repertoire of formal techniques and devices, at the expense of a knowledge of how (to what purpose) any kind of discourse should be used.

It need not immediately concern us whether Plato is here being entirely fair to the practice or principles of rhetoric in his own time, for his ultimate aim is in any case much more than polemical. The direction of the argument is towards a normative redefinition of the concept of rhetoric – a statement of its ideal form. And the kernel of this statement is that rhetoric needs to be underpinned by a rigorous and co-ordinated study of 'nature', of psychology, and of varieties of discourse or argument (269e–272b). All successful discourse, Socrates maintains, requires knowledge of the truth of those aspects of reality upon which it pronounces; and such knowledge must be based on the intellectually systematic procedures of 'dialectic' which are described at 265b–266c.[11] This means that the rhetorician, as someone who purports to deal with subjects as important yet disputable as justice and love, must, if his discourse is to have a respectable claim to attention, possess an analytical and critical understanding of many major features of the world. Among these features is the psychology of the human mind itself, since it is upon this that every piece of rhetoric aims to work a persuasive effect. Because audiences are variable, the orator must have a grasp of the multifarious nature of human emotions, beliefs and mentalities. But it is not sufficient for this grasp to be coherent in the abstract; it has to be capable of application in direct practice, and this will involve a correlation between psychological insight and a knowledge of the communicative possibilities of language itself. By the latter Plato denotes something much more than technicalities of speech-structure or specific adversarial strategies of the kind which available rhetorical manuals supplied. These are, at best, antecedents to, or functional components of, a true art of discourse (266d–269c). Such an art, in order to merit that description, can be constituted only by a unified comprehension of man, society and reasoning. And that, for Plato, necessarily means that a properly constituted rhetoric must be dependent upon, must be informed by, the 'master-art' of philosophy (see especially *Politicus* 303d–311c).

Even this severely selective and compressed account of some key ideas in the *Phaedrus* and *Gorgias* makes it clear that the Platonic critique of rhetoric is counterbalanced, at every point, by the Platonic espousal of philosophy: the attempt to delimit the capacity of the former is simultaneously an assertion of the supremacy of the latter. The motif of a 'choice of lives', which we saw in *Gorgias*, is no hyperbole, but a symbol of the momentousness of the issues which Plato takes to be involved. It is a choice, Plato is committed to arguing, between the pursuit of truth (philosophy), and the acceptance of merely plausible beliefs (rhetoric); between objectivity of knowledge and values, and a pervasive relativism of ideas and judgement; between a mode of thought that seeks to grasp the general structure of reality, and one which is tethered to the prejudices of particular audiences; between a rational method of enquiry which strives to enter and change the soul of the individual from within, and a repertoire of techniques which manipulate the minds of mass audiences from outside. Expressed in this summary, though not inaccurate, form, the contrast throws equally into relief the ambitiousness of Plato's claims for his own enterprise, and the extent to which he demotes the possibility of a human wisdom which arises from the ordinary, non-philosophical beliefs and practices of men.

It is for these twin reasons that Plato's critique of rhetoric has itself sometimes been rebutted by those who allege that philosophy, at least in its Platonic version, avows absolute standards that are otherworldly and therefore irrelevant to the common conditions of human lives. Indeed, Plato allows some such point of view to be expressed in the *Gorgias*, where the robust Callicles is allowed to sneer at the uselessness, the practical ineffectualness, of 'philosophy'.[12] This criticism touches on a sensitive Platonic nerve. It becomes a central anxiety of Plato, revealed above all in the ideal city of the *Republic*, to defend the concept of a philosophy (an access to ultimate truth and absolute goodness) which can still put itself into practice, and make sense of itself, within the actualities of what, for the purposes of most rhetoric at least, counts as the 'real world' of human society. But it is important to realise that even a radical rejection of the tenets of Platonic philosophy will not make irrelevant, or constitute an adequate response to, the central concern in Plato's critique of rhetoric. For that concern – a concern, at heart, about the sources of rhetoric's authority over human minds – remains of pressing importance for anything which professes to be a coherent art of persuasive discourse. Any such art can hardly, in the end, afford to limit itself to a purely formal scope, since the goal of persuasion entails a necessary contact with the convictions of an audience. Rhetoric, if it is to make reasonable claims for itself, must explain how and why there can be a reliable connection between its methods and its results. The explanation need not satisfy the demands of Platonic philosophy, but it must be one which can maintain rhetoric's teachable rationale, and justify its role in the shaping of belief and action. With that urgent (though ambitious) requirement in mind, it is time to consider Aristotle's thoughts on the relationship between philosophy and rhetoric.

2

Aristotle's *Rhetoric* has been interpreted by some scholars as an attempt to fulfil Plato's requirements, especially those of the *Phaedrus*, for a philosophically respectable rhetoric, and by others as setting out a position which is substantially independent of, and perhaps in conflict with, Plato's. As this divergence suggests, it is not easy to be confident about the historical relationship between the two thinkers' views on the subject. Aristotle is said to have 'taught' rhetoric during his first period in Athens (367–347), when he was a member of Plato's Academy (Cicero, *De Oratore* 3.141; Diog. Laert. 5.3). Does this mean that he did so with Plato's support or even encouragement? Many have assumed so, but it is impossible to say. To this period, at any rate, belong two lost Aristotelian works on rhetoric: a dialogue, *Gryllus* (of whose contents we can say virtually nothing), and a conspectus of earlier handbooks of rhetoric, the *Synagoge Technon*. It also seems probable that parts of the extant *Rhetoric*, especially the treatment of style in Book 3, are datable to these years; yet it is certain that the work was subsequently revised or added to, since it contains references to events of the 330s, at a time when Aristotle had returned to Athens to found his own school, the Lyceum (335–322). These sparse facts are insufficient to allow us to discern how Aristotle's conception of rhetoric developed, at various stages of his career, in relation to works such as the *Gorgias* and *Phaedrus*. But while the *Rhetoric* itself does not explicitly address Platonic texts,[13] there can be no doubt that Aristotle became familiar with these, and that his arguments effectively embody a response to the issues explored by Plato. This is not, however, to concede that we can reach a clear-cut verdict on the work's attitude to Platonic concerns. For all its lucidity and method, the *Rhetoric* represents an intellectual stance of real subtlety.

Aristotle's perspective shares one key assumption with Plato's: both observe rhetoric from the vantage-point of philosophy. The Platonic concept of philosophy as the 'master-art', the authoritative source of political wisdom (*politike*), to which rhetoric and other practices must be subordinated, is restated precisely by Aristotle in the *Nicomachean Ethics* (1094b2–3). In the *Rhetoric* itself, as well as in another passage of the *Ethics*, this assumption is revealed by the quasi-Platonic criticism of 'sophists' and others who confuse rhetoric with *politike*, and thereby implicitly deny the special status of 'philosophy' to which Plato and Aristotle are equally committed.[14] This does not mean that Plato and Aristotle possess an identical concept of either the values or the methods of enquiry which constitute *politike*. But they do share a basic allegiance to philosophy as the intellectual and educational enterprise which can provide the fullest grasp of *politike*, the fullest insight into the ethical and political principles of human societies. And they agree in defining philosophy partly by contradistinction to what they regard as the closely neighbouring practices of 'sophistic' and rhetoric, practices which themselves lay claim to expertise in the affairs of the city, and which locate this expertise predominantly in possession of an 'art of discourse'.

But if Aristotle is on Plato's side in his estimation of the rivalry between philosophy and rhetoric, and of the necessary sub-ordination of the latter to the former in the sphere of *politike*, his approach to rhetoric is none the less distinct in several immediately striking respects. To begin with, Aristotle does not doubt, as Plato had pointedly done, that rhetoric is entitled to the description of an 'art', a *techne*: he treats it as such from the outset of the *Rhetoric*, and refers to it consistently in these terms on many occasions throughout his writings. To accept the status of rhetoric as a *techne* is to acknowledge that it has a rational foundation, that the connections between its methods and its results can be coherently described and taught, and that it possesses a legitimate and proper function within human affairs. It is this cardinal fact which explains the very existence and character of the *Rhetoric*, for this is not a detached critique of either the theory or the practice of rhetoric, but an attempt to contribute, albeit from an avowedly philosophical angle, to the clarification of the art's structure and to furtherance of its study. Moreover, Aristotle perceives and stresses the respectability of rhetoric in terms which are specifically designed to satisfy, or at any rate to assuage, the concerns of philosophers. He builds his account of rhetoric around the central contention that it is, or can be, an art of reasoning. Where Plato had emphasised dichotomies between knowledge and belief, rational certainty and irrational conviction, to the benefit of philosophy and the disadvantage of rhetoric, Aristotle adopts a point of view allowing him to see a continuity between rhetoric and other modes of rational thought, as remarked at the very opening of the *Rhetoric*, where Aristotle programmatically connects rhetoric with 'dialectic', by which he (unlike Plato) denotes the general ability to argue critically on the basis of common beliefs and probable considerations. And the continuity is confirmed by a passage such as *Posterior Analytics* 71a9–11, which explicitly asserts that the basic forms of argument (induction and deduction) are shared by rhetorical persuasion with all rational enquiry and instruction.

Aristotle's account of rhetoric rests, then, on the premise of an affinity with dialectic which is asserted at the outset of the treatise. This means that the rhetorician's rational ability to devise effective persuasion involves a secure grasp of forms or patterns of argument, grouped by Aristotle into the two basic categories of 'enthymemes' (quasi-deductive considerations from probable or likely premises) and *paradeigmata* (quasi-inductive 'examples' of what are posited as relevant generalisations): see especially 1356a35 ff. The capacity to use these types of reasoning incorporates a familiarity with various topoi – argumentative themes or headings – which Aristotle catalogues most fully in the later chapters (18–26) of Book 2. This aspect of the work can be read as acknowledging and incorporating what I have called the 'formal' conception of rhetoric, which makes the art independent of any special subject-matter or body of knowledge.[15] Aristotle's recognition of this point is, in fact, evident. Included in his initial statement of the rhetoric–dialectic affinity is the principle that neither art belongs to any system of knowledge, *episteme* (1354a3), and this is reiterated several times subsequently (1355b7–8, 1355b34–35, 1358a21–22). What is most remarkable about Aristotle's openness to the formal conception of rhetoric is that he is led by it to grant, without disquiet, two correlative principles that had already been articulated by rhetoricians of the sophistic age, and had accordingly aroused Plato's deepest suspicions: one, that rhetoric can be employed to make a case, to find persuasive considerations, on *any* subject (1355b26–27); the other, that for any given issue it lies within the capacity of rhetoric to discover and marshall arguments on *either* side (1355a29–36).

Aristotle's position on the rational character of rhetoric as an art places him in a potentially equivocal attitude towards the Platonic critique. On the one hand, rationality is certainly a *sine qua non* if Plato's anxieties are to be addressed at all; and in this sense Aristotle's detailed exposition of the types of argument which a rhetorician must comprehend can be taken as a possible or partial fulfilment of the requirement which Plato himself lays down at *Phaedrus* 271b, where an ordered understanding of 'the varieties of speeches/arguments (*logoi*)' is prescribed as an essential component of a true art of rhetoric. But if the formal conception is stressed in isolation, there is a real risk of presenting rhetoric in the very terms which Plato had polemically scrutinised in both the *Gorgias* and *Phaedrus*. Thus, Aristotle's definition of rhetoric, mentioned a moment ago, as 'the capacity to discern the available means of persuasion about each [sc. and any] subject' (1355b26–27),[16] is not immediately easy to distinguish from the first description of the art of persuasion which Gorgias offers in Plato's dialogue (*Gorgias* 456a–c), where he claims that the proficient rhetorician can out-perform even the arguments of specialists in their own domains. But we saw earlier that Gorgias has severe difficulty maintaining a formal account of rhetoric in conjunction with the more general profession of ethico-political knowledge, *politike*, which he also wishes to make. Even if the formal view did not occasion

237

troubling paradoxes (as it does when Gorgias asserts that a rhetorician could out-argue a doctor on a medical issue, 456b–c),[17] it would generate an apparently insoluble puzzle. A purely formal grasp of, say, patterns of argument, or structures of discourse, ought not to be able to make sufficient contact with people's *beliefs*, particularly those which underlie and determine their civic lives, to open them fully to the rhetorician's persuasion: in this sense, the rhetorician whose art is entirely formal ought to be no better a persuader than the logician. For this precise reason Plato shows Gorgias coupling his formal account of his art with substantive claims of sagacity and knowledge. And it is for the same reason that Aristotle does not, after all, allow the formal model to hang unsupported by a larger framework of considerations about the content of rhetoric.

The combination of these further considerations with the idea of a formal facility in types of argument (dialectic) is encapsulated in the two parts of Aristotle's famous remark that 'rhetoric is, so to speak, an offshoot of dialectic and of the study of ethical principles,[18] which it is appropriate to call *politike*' (1356a25–27). This proposition follows on from the statement that the rhetorician needs not only to have a grasp of procedures of reasoning, but also to understand something about 'ethical principles, virtues . . . and emotions' (1356a22–23). Here, then, Aristotle appears to be satisfying the second element in Plato's stipulation at *Phaedrus* 271b that a true rhetoric must involve ordered knowledge of 'the varieties of speeches/arguments (*logoi*) and of the soul'; that is, a conjoint comprehension of reasoning and psychology. In broader terms, it looks as though Aristotle has taken Plato's point, or at any rate is in agreement with him, that rhetoric cannot justify its standing as a general agency of judgement and decision-making in the life of the city, unless its theorists and practitioners can assert, and offer to communicate, at least some of the principles of ethical and political wisdom, *politike*. Aristotle evidently reckons with the fundamental significance of rhetoric's immersion in the affairs of the polis, the affairs of social life, particularly in the case of the two most practical of the three branches into which he divides the art, forensic/legal and symbouleutic/deliberative.[19] As a result, the *Rhetoric* gives formulations of forensic and symbouleutic oratory which revolve entirely around the kinds of subject-matter, with their attendant *protaseis* or thematic 'propositions', which the practitioners in these branches must aim to master. And these *protaseis* not only include substantive details of, for instance, taxation, military defence, or commerce (in the case of deliberative rhetoric), or the motives for crime and the relationship of criminal acts to written and unwritten laws (in that of forensic), but also supply reflections on the central concepts and values – happiness, expediency, justice – guiding the vital decisions of political assemblies and judicial courts.

The rhetorician who embodied in himself the tenets of Aristotle's presentation of the art, therefore, would have a stock of 'facts and figures', of legal parallels, and the like, at his disposal. But he would have something more than that. He would also display an adeptness at discerning and analysing the ethical and political implications of the issues with which he dealt. If, in his formal facility at reasoning, he approximated to the ratiocinative powers of the dialectician, he would equally have an important affinity, in the broader sweep of his skills of forensic or deliberative argument, with the moral philosopher or the student of *politike*: that, inescapably, is the entailment of Aristotle's formulation of rhetoric as 'an offshoot of dialectic and of . . . *politike*'. But it is at just this stage in the interpretation of the *Rhetoric* that we are confronted by the complexity, and perhaps the inevitable ambiguity, of its relationship to Plato's critique. For the combination of dialectical and ethical accomplishments which Aristotle posits, within this definition of the art, can be read up to a point as a way of meeting the Platonic requirement that a philosophically respectable rhetoric must integrate political wisdom with its formal resources. But it is only 'up to a point' that the *Rhetoric* can be read this way, because of one decisive difference between the assumptions of the two thinkers: the *politike* which Plato demands of an ideal rhetoric can be supplied *only* by philosophy itself; but the *politike* presupposed and partially expounded by Aristotle's treatise is not directly philosophical at all, but belongs rather to the domain of popular, widely held beliefs and values. What this difference amounts to is that whereas Plato wishes rhetoric to be wholly dependent on philosophically derived knowledge, Aristotle believes that rhetoric can reputably work with and, so to speak, inside the realm of what we might call 'common discourse'.[20]

3

The realm of 'common discourse' – the general *logos* of speech, argument and reasoning – is the territory over which the emergent self-consciousness of both philosophy and rhetoric asserted their rival claims in classical Greece. Greek rhetoric presented itself as a persuasive 'art of *logos/ logoi*', and as such set itself to formalise, to translate into method, some of the modes of speech and the techniques of argument by which the minds of audiences could be engaged and moved, above all in those public and institutional contexts which exert a structural influence on the social, ethical and political life of a community. But it is because of rhetoric's involvement in, and application to, the common discourse of its society, that it faces a problem about its self-definition. If rhetoric professes to be a formal or subject-neutral art, an art capable of speaking about *everything* (*Gorgias* 457a5–6), then the categories of language or *logos* with which it operates (whether linguistic,[21] stylistic, structural or argumentational) cannot themselves provide substantive principles or evaluative criteria capable of informing beliefs or motivating actions. On this model, rhetoric will be a purely instrumental vehicle of whatever ideas it may serve on any particular occasion, and its use will be subject to appraisal and control by reference to values that are not encompassed by rhetoric itself. If, by contrast, rhetoric arrogates the status of an art that can both interpret and shape human commitments, then its contents will call directly for ethical and political scrutiny.[22] Plato and Aristotle, as advocates of a philosophy which they held to have the authority to assess rhetoric, both undertook such scrutiny. Plato's driving concern, I have argued, was that rhetoric should be subordinated to the 'master-art' of philosophy itself, which alone could supply the knowledge and the goodness that will guarantee rhetoric's beneficial exercise within a community. Aristotle, while he sympathised with the priorities expressed in this view, was much readier to see a role for a well-informed rhetoric as an agency of the common currency of beliefs and values that circulate within a society's public discourse.

These attitudes were, and should be, the beginnings not the end of a vitally important debate. Rhetoric, after all, need not remain silent in the face of philosophy, nor desist from challenging philosophy's credentials in turn. If the rhetorician's putative capacity to 'speak about everything' poses difficulties for the definition of his art, analogous consequences surely follow from the idea that it is within the philosopher's competence to comprehend all things (Arist. *Metaphysics* 1004a34 ff.). If rhetoric's relationship to the common *logos* is problematic, so too, in multiple ways, is that of philosophy, not least in its Platonic version.[23] Some such considerations seem to have been part of the basis for the intellectual stance of Isocrates, who distanced himself both from theoretical or abstract philosophising (for example, 10.1–5) and from a wholly formalised art of rhetoric (13.9–13), while still claiming the term *philosophia*, as well as 'political discourses' (*politikoi logoi*), for his own enterprise.[24] Isocrates bases his 'philosophy of discourse'[25] upon a conception of *logos* (both rational and ethical) as the defining feature of all human society and culture (especially 3.5–9), and he offers an educational programme whose purpose is a practical intelligence and effectiveness in the prevailing realities of political life. From the perspective of my earlier argument, it seems apt to say that Isocrates largely collapses the distinction between philosophy and rhetoric, and aims to produce a new compound – a principled political insight, expressed in the forms (whether spoken or written) of public oratory – that operates entirely within the realm of 'common discourse'.

But Isocrates goes so far in allying his own *philosophia* to common discourse, and in preferring the flexibility of approximate beliefs to the elusive certainty of final knowledge (10.5, 13.8, 15.184), that it is possible to discern a kind of vacant space at the heart of his pronouncements – an absence of compelling grounds for accepting any one set of beliefs rather than any other. For all its later influence on humanistic ideals, the Isocratean programme can hardly answer all the questions about the relationship of philosophy and rhetoric which had been raised by the intellectual controversies of the fifth and early fourth centuries. Those questions, as I have tried to suggest in this chapter, ultimately revolve around the multiple concept of *logos* – *logos* as speech, reason, argument, explanation, deliberation and theory. It is part of the unexhausted legacy of Greek thought that such questions remain as a permanent challenge to the proponents of both philosophy and rhetoric, and perhaps not to them alone: to work for answers to them is to advance, if not towards the grand (re-) marriage of the two arts which Cicero wished to announce, then at least towards a realisation of the ways in which wisdom and eloquence are badly in need of one another.

NOTES

1 W. K. C. Guthrie, *A History of Greek Philosophy*, III (Cambridge: 1969), pp. 27–34.
2 Cf. further below. The question of Pythagorean connections is controversial: see, for example, W. K. C. Guthrie, *A History of Greek Philosophy*, I (Cambridge: 1962), pp. 164–6, 204–5.
3 Cole, *Origins of Rhetoric*, chapter 1, especially p. 2; on the term *rhetorike*, p. 98 is more cautious.
4 The term also occurs without any sense of novelty at *Euthydemus* 307a6, though this may be later than the *Gorgias*. Isocrates 3.8 (dated *c.* 368) suggests that the adjective *rhetorikos* was established usage; cf. Plato, *Republic* 8.548e5. See too M. Gagarin, chapter 3 above.
5 Despite Cole, *Origins of Rhetoric*, pp. 118 and 173 n. 4, Alcidamas' work may well be earlier than Plato's *Phaedrus*: for one view, see F. Blass, *Die attische Beredsamkeit*[2], II (Leipzig: 1892), pp. 345–6.
6 On *Laws* see C. Bobonich, 'Persuasion, Compulsion and Freedom in Plato's *Laws*', CQ^2 41 (1991), pp. 365–88. A recent, harsh account of Plato's views of rhetoric is given by B. Vickers, *In Defence of Rhetoric* (Oxford: 1988), chapter 2.
7 Plato allows Callicles to accuse Socrates of his own rhetoric at *Gorgias* 482c–e. The perception of Plato's own writing as rhetorical is at least as old as Cicero, *De Oratore* 1.47. One recent treatment is provided by H. North, 'Combing & Curling: *Orator Summus Plato*', *ICS* 16 (1991), pp. 201–19.
8 See R. S. W. Hawtrey, *Commentary on Plato's Euthydemus* (Philadelphia: 1981), pp. 189–96.
9 Cf., for example, Thuc. 1.22.1 (?); Lys. 10.7; Isoc. 9.10–11 and 13.16–17. Cole, *Origins of Rhetoric*, chapter 1, is wrong to argue that Plato and Aristotle 'invented' the form–substance dichotomy in the conception of rhetoric.
10 When Plato accuses rhetoricians of preferring 'probability' (*eikos*) to truth (*Phaedrus* 267a, 272d–e), he may exaggerate their avowed position, but he makes a conceptually urgent point: if persuasion is treated as an overriding goal, then truth cannot be guaranteed to be the persuader's best strategy in every case.
11 This is an instance of philosophy's attempt to distinguish and distance itself from rhetoric by means of intellectual or argumentative *method*: see G. E. R. Lloyd, *Magic, Reason and Experience* (Cambridge: 1979), chapter 2, especially pp. 79–102.
12 *Gorgias* 484c–486c. Cf. the contrast between philosopher and rhetorician at *Theaetetus* 172a–177b.
13 There is an incidental mention of *Phaedrus* at 1408b20; cf. n. 14 below.
14 *EN* 1181a12–15, *Rhetoric* 1356a27–8 (with an allusion to Plato, *Gorgias* 464c); cf. *Metaphysics* 4.2, 1004b17–26, especially the motif of the 'choice of life' at 24–25 (with p. 230 above).
15 A further part of the formal conception is usually taken to be the category of 'style'; but I have qualified this view in 'Style and Sense in Aristotle *Rhetoric* Book 3', *Revue Internationale de Philosophie* 47 (1993), pp. 50–69.
16 Likewise with dialectic: *Rhetoric* 1355a33 ff., *Topics* 163a36 ff.

17 The claim need not be authentically Gorgianic, but it dramatises a possible extension of the formal conception. It also acquires piquancy if we reckon with the use of rhetorical argument in medicine itself: see Lloyd, *Magic, Reason and Experience*, pp. 88–98.

18 'Ethical principles' translates *ethe*, which here embraces both individual 'characters' and *ethe politeion*, features of political constitutions.

19 The third – epideictic – impinges less upon practical decision-making, though that does not mean that it lacks implications for moral and political values.

20 I have discussed some ethical dimensions of this relationship in 'Popular Morality, Philosophical Ethics, and the *Rhetoric*', in D. Furley and A. Nehamas (eds), *Aristotle on Rhetoric and Philosophy* (Princeton: 1993).

21 'Linguistics', in the classical Greek context, could be regarded as a branch of rhetoric: see Plato, *Cratylus* 425a4; Arist. *De Interp.* 17a5–6.

22 In terms of rhetoric's own later tripartite scheme of *inventio, dispositio, elocutio*, such scrutiny concerns the source and authority of the first of these divisions.

23 Plato himself perhaps recognises this, to the extent of formulating questions in the *Phaedrus* that apply to all *logoi*: see especially 258d, 277b–278e.

24 *philosophia*: for example, 4.6, 47–50, 12.9, 13.21, 15.181 ff.; *politikoi logoi*: 13.21, 15.46, 260.

25 4.10; a similar phrase occurs at [Arist.] *Rhetorica ad Alexandrum* 1421a16.

12

The Canon of the Ten Attic Orators

Ian Worthington

The so-called 'Canon of the Ten Attic Orators', which was established at some date between the third century BC and the second century AD, has had a dominating effect on the survival of the orators whose works we have today.[1] The canon as we have it names ten orators: Antiphon, Andocides, Lysias, Isocrates, Isaeus, Demosthenes, Aeschines, Hyperides, Lycurgus, and Dinarchus. As is immediately evident, the list is in neither alphabetical nor chronological order (for Lysias was born before Andocides, and Aeschines, Hyperides and Lycurgus were born before Demosthenes). Moreover, while Antiphon is said by Quintilian to have been the first to write speeches (3.1.11), Dinarchus is not the last orator to have lived and worked, but was followed by others – Demetrius of Phalerum to name but one. We do have some speeches by other orators; about half a dozen by Apollodorus, for example, which have survived in the orations of Demosthenes;[2] or there is the speech *On The Twelve Years* (which today exists only in fragments), attributed to Demades, but this is a later composition which could even be the product of imperial times.[3] Thus most of what is extant comes from the orators of the canon.

The canon is fundamental to any study of Greek oratory and rhetoric, and accordingly it has received a fair share of attention in numerous books in these areas over the years. All too often, however, discussion of the canon and the chosen ten orators is subsumed under more detailed treatment of particular orators or of oratory and rhetoric in general – examples of this range from Blass' magisterial work, the two volumes by George Kennedy on Greek and Roman rhetoric, to Konrad Heldmann's recent study of rhetoric.[4] Studies specifically on the canon are few, especially in recent times.[5] Such a neglect is perhaps to be expected, given the

244

paucity and nature of the evidence, which does not allow us to determine why the ten we have were chosen or to identify the compiler or even the date of compilation with any degree of accuracy. The date of compilation may be put at any time between the third century BC and the second century AD, and often scholars are content to leave it that.

Since no new evidence has come to light the question may be raised why this chapter has made an appearance. There are several answers as justification. Thirty years since A. E. Douglas' article (see n. 5), the last full and formal study of something so significant and yet so controversial as the canon, is a long time, and this in itself is a good reason for a fresh treatment. Most importantly, however, a major aim of the present chapter is to reconsider the nature of the canon and the rationale which led to what must be viewed ultimately as a destructive compilation. This may be achieved by tracking the related areas of dating, authorship and the intellectual background of the canon. The more condemnatory view which I propose is not one which appears when we consider the common attitude to the canon, and indeed it is not one which has been sufficiently stressed before. Given the importance of the related areas for the questions to be addressed, they must again come under scrutiny. The fact that new evidence is lacking, and thus many of the arguments are by necessity speculative, should not stop us from posing new questions about the canon and its less praiseworthy effects, rather than merely sitting on the fence.

Over a period spanning a large part of the fifth century and most of the fourth, a considerable number of orators must have lived and worked in Athens. Many orators must have been at work in other Greek cities too. But it is really Athens which was the main centre for oratory and thus the place to be for establishing a reputation, and this is shown by foreigners who moved to live there (Dinarchus from Corinth is one example). Schools which taught oratory and rhetoric flourished in Athens in both the fifth and the fourth centuries, and these subjects were an integral part of education. Also flourishing were litigation in the law-courts and political activity in the Assembly, conditions which called for a greater need for oratorical ability and led to advances in rhetoric, the intellectual pursuit of oratory. An offshoot of the increased litigation was the rise of the professional group known as the *logographoi* (speechwriters), who for payment wrote forensic speeches for others, and, like Antiphon, may also have given legal advice (Thuc. 8.61.1). Logography was a lucrative profession, and there were those who were content to remain *logographoi* rather than enter the political realm, or those who were constrained to do so because of their non-Athenian status, which debarred them from full participation in political and judicial life.[6]

The many orators at work must, by implication, have led to the composition of a large number of speeches. This supposition is reinforced by some ancient authorities who ascribe a number of speeches to a particular orator: thus Antiphon was credited with over 60 ([Plut.] *X.Or.* 833c); Lysias with 425 ([Plut.] *X.Or.* 836a); Isocrates 60 ([Plut.] *X.Or.* 838d); and Dinarchus with anything from 60 to 160.[7] We might expect to possess a representative selection of the various orators of the fifth and fourth centuries, together with a veritable army of speeches, thereby allowing us to assess the styles of a whole *corps* of Greek orators, as well as providing us with a large body of directly contemporary evidence for that period. Unfortunately, as is so often the case with most exponents of literary genres from the classical period, we have information on no more than a handful of the orators who lived and worked. Indeed, some are known to us by name only, such as the enigmatic Coccus (Quintilian 12.10.21; cf. *Suda*, s.v.) or Hippias ([Plut.] *X.Or.* 838a). Furthermore, only a portion of these orators' works has survived. We have only thirty-four speeches by Lysias, for example, and Dinarchus has fared even worse: only three of his speeches survive today, of which the second and third are incomplete.

The existence of the canon, though, has given the group of ten something of an exclusive reputation, and its influence is immediately obvious in that it is the origin of references to a collection of orators which occur in a variety of other sources from the second century AD onwards. The list was used with variation by Hermogenes at περὶ ἰδεῶν (*On Types of Style*) B 10–11, where he names Demosthenes, Lysias, Isaeus, Hyperides, Isocrates, Dinarchus, Aeschines, Antiphon, Critias, Lycurgus and Andocides as the best writers of political speeches (but it is emphasised that Critias is not one of the ten), and by the second century AD lexicographers Harpocration (*Lexicon of the Ten Orators*) and Pollux (*Onomastikon*).[8] It also provided the basis for Pseudo-Plutarch's *Lives* of these orators, which, in turn, was a major source for Photius' *Bibliotheca* and *Lexicon* of the ninth century AD, and no doubt of the *Suda* of the tenth century AD. Six anonymous manuscripts from the tenth to the fifteenth centuries, which give the ten orators of the canon (one in a different order from the other five), together with the number of their speeches, are perhaps the latest recordings of the original model.[9] Not all of the later authorities cite ten orators: a codex of the *Bibliotheca Coisiliana* (codex 387, fol. 153), for example, is notorious in giving the names of only nine. Dinarchus is excluded, for reasons unknown, unless by the post-classical period the criticism of his style and oratorical ability from Dionysius onwards had taken effect. Yet on the same codex is a work (fol. 113) in which the ten orators are given and Dinarchus is included. Moreover, a Bodleian codex also includes Dinarchus,[10] and there is no apparent reason, given that his name occurs almost consistently with the other orators in a variety of sources, to reject him from the original ten.

These inconsistencies have led A. E. Douglas ('Canon of Ten Attic Orators', p. 31) to question the validity of the term canon (or authoritative list) in the first place. Douglas points out that a canon designates a permanent and influental list, whereas we see fluctuations in the number and particularly the order of those included in the Canon of the Ten Attic Orators as we have it today. These are valid points, but in my view allusion to a canon regardless of fluctuating order brings to mind a deliberate selection of orators regarded as worth preserving and listed together as such. Rather than use the inconsistencies to which Douglas draws attention as grounds for disputing the accuracy of the term canon, I suggest we should see them as the result of simple copying error. The number of orators in the canon has a bearing on the date of composition, to which we will return.

The selection of the ten orators has proved a disaster for the survival of works by those who missed out. A disaster not only for the orators affected but also for posterity in that we have no real knowledge of other orators and their talents. In this respect the genre of oratory does not stand alone: we have extant plays by only one Old Comedy writer, and by only three tragedians, which is equally unfortunate since fragments of plays by other playwrights show great literary merit. Various reasons explain the deficit here, stemming from simple loss of texts to the 'canonisation' of Aeschylus, Sophocles and Euripides in Lycurgan times – a canon again influential in the transmission of texts, or, more correctly, the lack of transmission. And the same unfortunate influence applies to the Canon of the Ten Attic Orators. It is more than plausible that the scholars and copyists of later antiquity may have disregarded the works of other orators, if indeed they had managed to survive into later times, in favour of the chosen ten. In doing so they condemned many orators to unwarranted extinction. Worse still, while we can only presume that whoever drew up the list regarded the ten as special, it does not necessarily follow that they were the most outstanding of the Attic orators of their times, and therefore the right choice for survival. Admittedly, this is something of a circular argument since the non-chosen are lost, but it would be defeatist merely to leave it at that, for the problem of inclusion has a direct bearing on the compilation of the canon.

The canon of the ten, then, presents us with something of a *fait accompli*: out of the numerous orators who were living and working in Athens someone decided to draw up a list of ten, and that is what we are left with today. It is of course impossible for us to guess the criteria which led to inclusion, a dilemma compounded by the fact that since some of those included in the canon have been thought unworthy. Into this category, Dinarchus is probably the one who springs most readily to mind. His style has been criticised by ancient and modern critics from Dionysius of Halicarnassus onwards, although much of this criticism, particularly of his compositional abilities, is refuted by the identification of complex ring composition in his speeches.[11] Then there were other orators who were excluded from the list when we might think their inclusion should have been automatic – Demetrius of Phalerum, for example, who was one of the more influential teachers of rhetoric in Athens, and who wrote on a wide variety of subjects.[12]

In his series of essays on Lysias, Isocrates, Isaeus and Demosthenes[13] and in the introduction to those essays (περὶ τῶν ἀρχαίων ῥητόρων, *On The Ancient Orators*), the Augustan critic Dionysius of Halicarnassus gives us some insight into his literary tastes, and presumably those of the day.[14] In the preface to that work he criticises the declining standards of oratory as a result of the so-called 'Asianist' influence, and presses the need for a return to oratory of classical Greek standards (on this see further below). While this seems a common theme of rhetoricians of the Augustan age, we cannot say that Dionysius' particular tastes and feelings as regards the Greek orators were universal. Nor can we say that all aspects of rhetorical theory and technique in the orators were adequately covered by one critic, and that there were not other critics dissatisfied with a recent treatment. And dissent need not just apply to the orators of the canon: another, equally influential, Augustan critic, Caecilius of Calacte, was criticised by the author of *On The Sublime* – Pseudo-Longinus – for favouring Lysias over Plato (32.8).[15]

Since we have no means to become acquainted with any of the other orators, the destructive nature of the canon is clear. This should make us more cautious when we come to assess the styles of the various orators we do have: all too often assessments tend to be made in absolute terms. While the characteristics of an individual orator certainly should be described, it is important to avoid value judgements on the quality of his style and use of language, for example, when our judgement is based on only an extant portion of Greek oratory, which may have survived for reasons unconnected with contemporary evaluations of the quality of the Greek. Demosthenes, then, becomes the greatest orator to have survived, but, heresy here, not necessarily the greatest of all the ancient Greek orators. The canon has a lot to answer for – all the more so if it happens to be the product of a personal, arbitrary decision.

Given the effect of the canon on the study of Greek rhetoric and our evaluation of Greek oratory, the importance of the related areas of its dating and authorship cannot be stressed enough, and they deserve closer attention than has normally been paid. The type of evidence is a major handicap, and by necessity we must enter the realm of speculation. But this is justified speculation, for if we can determine either one or both of these related areas, with some degree of plausibility, we may be clearer as to why the handful of orators we have today were included, and whether or not their inclusion was an arbitrary decision.

The dating of the canon is problematical, and leads on to the question of authorship.[16] We know that the canon was compiled between the third century BC and the second century AD, and indeed this is the only statement on that matter that cannot be disputed. One period in which the canon could have been compiled, and which has received some consent,[17] is the third to the second centuries BC, and thus several scholars of either Alexandria or Pergamum come to mind: Aristophanes of Byzantium, librarian at Alexandria, or his successor, Aristarchus, or Apollodorus of Pergamum.[18] Indeed, support is lent to this period since the type of exercise involved in the cataloguing of texts of various authors for the great libraries may well have led on to the compilation of canons in various genres, as Kennedy has suggested.[19] A selective list or 'canon' of nine lyric poets seems to have been produced by Aristophanes of Byzantium,[20] and Pfeiffer (*History of Classical Scholarship*, I, p. 206) would argue that similar lists of orators, historians and philosophers followed before too long.

There are arguments, nevertheless, against the formation of a select list or canon of the orators in this period. After the death of Demosthenes, and particularly during the hellenistic age, Attic oratory declined before the so-called 'Asianic' trend, and was not to be effectively challenged until the Augustan age. Alexandrian tradition would almost certainly have included some of the orators of the new-wave trend, yet Dinarchus, expounding an Attic style, is the last of the ten. For the Alexandrians or Pergamenes to finish with him in any survey of oratory up to and including their own time is odd.

Furthermore, Cicero does not refer to the existence of any specific canon before his time. Douglas has put forward persuasive arguments to this effect ('Canon of Ten Attic Orators', pp. 31–4), but one or two more may be added. Firstly, on *De Oratore* 2.22.92:

Quod non tam facile in nostris oratoribus possumus iudicare, quia scripta, ex quibus iudicium fieri posset, non multa sane reliquerunt, quam in Graecis; ex quorum scriptis, cuiusque aetatis quae dicendi ratio voluntasque fuerit, intellegi potest.

Of this truth we can judge less easily in the case of our own orators, since they have left but very few writings on which a judgement could be based, than as regards the Greeks, from whose works the method and tendency of the oratory of every generation may be understood.

The implication is that numerous works by different orators were still in circulation in Rome, an implication reinforced by *Brutus* 9.36, where, in a list of many orators, Cicero is explicit that no speeches of Demades were extant in his time, and, further, it is possible that Critias' works, or at least some of them, were also extant in Cicero's time. Thus the other orators' speeches were readily available, which one would not expect if the canon of ten already existed.

Secondly, at *De Oratore* 2.22.93 ff. and *Brutus* 7.26 ff. and 82.285 ff., Cicero refers to a wide range of Attic orators, including several from the fifth century – Pericles, Alcibiades, Thucydides, Critias, for example. Several named do not appear in any canon, but nowhere does Cicero express surprise at the exclusion. He is simply citing various orators to illustrate points put forward at those parts of his works. This is evident, to take an example, in his presentation of the list of orators in *Brutus* 82.285 ff. It is his reaction to the movement at this time in Rome towards a return to the Attic style (see especially 289–291), and again nowhere does Cicero criticise his predecessors or contemporaries for drawing up a canon which excluded orators he thought highly of – nor does he pretend that his is any definitive list. Cicero's silence shows that the idea of canonising selected Attic orators had not yet occurred to literary minds, much less that one was in existence.

Dionysius of Halicarnassus, who was working in Rome between 30 and 8 BC (*Rom. Ant.* 1.7.2, 1.3.4), also does not refer to a canon. His silence is, in my opinion, even more significant than that of Cicero, and more under-rated than has previously been made out, for on it hinges the dating problem. It is difficult to believe that Dionysius would have ignored an existing work, as Dobson suggests in his entry on that critic in the *Oxford Classical Dictionary*, given that he is so methodologically careful and thorough when dealing with material and criteria. The latter point is evidenced by the pains he took to establish an accurate chronology of Dinarchus' life and the rigorous criteria that he applied to distinguish genuine speeches from the spurious in his essay on that orator (see especially *Dinarchus* 10–14). Dionysius would have felt bound to refer to any canon on what we may class as academic grounds.

Jebb (*Attic Orators*, I, pp. lxvi–lxvii) has suggested that Dionysius disregarded the canon because of its arbitrary nature and that it was more of a hindrance than a help to the type of approach he intended to adopt towards the orators. The suggestion does not hold weight. Dionysius pulls no punches in criticising those whose methodological approaches lack foundation and led to inaccuracy. A case in point is the first chapter of his essay on Dinarchus, where the mediocre biographical investigations of Callimachus, the Pergamene grammarians and Demetrius of Magnesia, which adversely affected their literary opinion of Dinarchus, are castigated. Indeed, his attempt to identify Dinarchus' genuine speeches, the focus of his essay, was prompted by what he saw as his predecessors' shortcomings.

Accordingly, we should expect him to discuss the canon, all the more so if it was an arbitrary compilation or conflicted with his findings, if only to question its validity and the methodology of the compiler. The approach he took to the orators, in particular linking historical study with the rhetorical, demanded due consideration of all existing works. We are led to the plausible conclusion that Dionysius did not refer to the canon, let alone discuss it, because at the time he was writing it did not exist. Thus the canon cannot be a product of Alexandrian or Pergamene times.

This points to a later dating, and the silence of Cicero and Dionysius takes us to a late first century or even second century AD date. Douglas would prefer the latter, but on the basis of two passages in Quintilian (10.1.76, 10.1.80) and the brief biographies of the orators by Pseudo-Plutarch (which may well have stemmed from the list), we should look to the first century. Here a stumbling-block, for the value of the Quintilian passages has been doubted, and thus examination of them must be made first, even though at some length.

At 10.1.76 Quintilian states: *sequitur oratorum ingens manus, ut cum decem simul Athenis aetas una tulerit*. The Loeb translation is: 'There follows a vast army of orators, Athens alone having produced ten remarkable orators in the same generation'. 'Ten remarkable orators' is misleading: there is nothing in the Latin to allow anything but 'ten' (*decem*). Thus although Quintilian does not actually state the existence of a canon, the reference to *decem* is strikingly coincidental, and has been accepted as referring to such an authoritative list. Yet arguments against this have been advanced, most strongly by Douglas ('Canon of Ten Attic Orators', pp. 34–6), who believes that the canon came into existence only in the second century AD. Douglas points out that *aetas* in both Cicero, *Brutus* 9.36 (discussed above), and the Quintilian passage means 'generation'. Therefore, instead of *decem* ('ten') meaning anything akin to a 'canon' covering a period of 120 years, these ten orators are simply ten who were working in Athens in the same generation (*simul aetas una* implying exact contemporaneity) – all the more so in view of the reference to Demosthenes, Aeschines and Hyperides at 77–78 which is followed in 78 by *his aetate Lysias maior* ('Lysias comes from a previous generation'). For Douglas, Quintilian is here saying: 'There now follows a vast host of orators; their large numbers can be illustrated by the fact that in a single generation Athens produced no fewer than ten'.

This is a strong argument, but not a conclusive one: *aetas* can mean 'age' in a wider context (here the age of the orators); *ut cum* has to be explanatory (as Douglas noted); while *simul* must denote concurrence in time. Thus another interpretation of Quintilian 10.1.76 is: 'There follows a vast host of orators, since in the time of the age of the orators Athens produced the ten'. I add the definite article (indicating a canon) for the following reasons. Having briefly cited Demosthenes, Aeschines and Hyperides, who were contemporaries, Quintilian then turned to Lysias, and in doing so necessarily makes the chronological change to an earlier generation (*his aetate maior*). Yet what makes 10.1.76 so different and what needs to be borne in mind above considerations of the temporal aspect of the passage is the specific number. This is unusual in Quintilian, who does not specify any numbers in this way when referring to literary and historical writers elsewhere (for example, 10.1.66 ff.). Even more to the point is that *decem* stands by itself in this passage; when Quintilian uses the word elsewhere in his works it is linked to another word or performs a function so that the specific context is clear, not ambiguous.[21] Thus at 3.6.22 we have *elementa decem* ('ten elements'); at 8.3.54 *decem mensibus* ('ten months'); at 8.5.5 *decem genera* ('ten types'); and at 10.4.4 *decem annis* ('ten years'). At 10.1.76 the numeral *decem* stands alone, and this indicates not a general reference to ten orators at any one time, but *the* ten.

Furthermore, the implicit criticism of Quintilian 10.1.80, despite Douglas' arguments, can be interpreted to refer to a recognised group with which Quintilian does not agree, and still be linked with the reference to Demetrius of Phalerum in 80: *ultimus est fere ex Atticis, qui dici possit orator* ('he is almost the last from Attica who can be called an orator'). This is geographical: Demetrius was virtually the last from Attica before the rise of the great centres elsewhere in the hellenistic world, not that he was virtually the last of the Attic orators in terms of style. Quintilian is merely voicing his opinion of Demetrius, and we should agree with Cicero that he was an example of the intermediate school (*De Oratore* 2.95, *Orator* 92).

There are also grounds for doubting Douglas' explanation ('Canon of Ten Attic Orators', pp. 37–8) for Quintilian giving the figure ten at 10.1.76: that Quintilian may have confused the story of Alexander demanding the surrender of ten Athenian statesman in 335 after the razing of Thebes with a canon of ten Attic orators.[22] Quintilian's apparent confusion on this issue verges on the incredible. Moreover, not all of the ten whose surrender was demanded in 335 were orators – the mercenary Charidemus, for example (who was the only Athenian actually handed over to Alexander)[23] – and if Quintilian were aware of the episode he must have known the identities of those involved.

At 12.10.20-24 Quintilian names twelve Greek orators, an incompatible figure with a canon of ten, and a context, one would expect, for citing an already existing canon (cf. Douglas, 'Canon of Ten Attic Orators', pp. 36–7). Douglas also draws attention to the similarity with Cicero, *Brutus* 82.285 ff., and thus parallels his argument there that since neither Cicero or Quintilian explicitly refer to a canon, one cannot exist before the time of Quintilian. But from 12.10.10 ff. Quintilian is merely repeating the Ciceronian position in the anti-Asianist controversy, and, as with Cicero's works discussed above, the number of orators cited is not significant: Quintilian chooses those he wishes to refer to in order to fit his discussion. That is why at 10.1.76-80, having talked about the *decem*, he then goes on to give select details involving only six orators (one of whom, Demetrius of Phalerum, is not included in the canon), and similarly at 12.10.21 ff., where, we should note, he sandwiches Plato between Demosthenes and Pericles.

Furthermore, ought we to expect that Quintilian specifically refers to this canon? In effect, he has already done so, at 10.1.76, and the educated audience who would have read his works would know to what he referred there, and likewise recognise the context of his criticisms in Book 12. Nor does Quintilian actually refer to canons of other genres. Although Douglas argues ('Canon of Ten Attic Orators', p. 36), that *grammaticorum consensus* of 10.1.53 refers to canons of epic, iambic and lyric poets going back to Alexandrian times,[24] this is by no means certain.

Regardless of the ambiguity caused by *simul aetas una* at 10.1.76, what stands out in that passage is the reference to *decem*. This points to an already existing canon in the time of Quintilian. We may thus reject the arguments of Douglas and thereby disregard the second century AD for the canon's compilation.

As a result, we go back to a period before Quintilian but after Dionysius of Halicarnassus, in which case, as Brzoska suggested a century ago, the Augustan critic of the first century BC, Caecilius of

Calacte, becomes prime suspect. The case for Caecilius' authorship of the canon receives further weight from the fact that the *Suda* tells us he wrote a treatise on the ten orators (περὶ τοῦ χαρακτῆρος τῶν δέκα ῥητόρων, *On the Character of the Ten Orators*), which discussed questions of authenticity. The veracity of the *Suda*'s testimony (since so little of Caecilius' own output exists) has been doubted, but that Caecilius did compose such a work is supported by references to Caecilius (and presumably to this treatise) in the *Vitae* of the ten orators by Pseudo-Plutarch. Thus, for example, we find that Caecilius thought 25 of Antiphon's alleged 60 plus speeches were spurious ([Plut.] *X.Or.* 833c); that he agrees with Dionysius that only 233 of Lysias' 425 speeches are genuine ([Plut.] *X.Or.* 836a); and that he considers 28 of Isocrates' 60 orations genuine, thereby disagreeing with Dionysius' figure of 25 ([Plut.] *X.Or.* 838d).

Despite the questions raised about the *Suda*'s reliability with the title, even, of Caecilius' work, not to mention its attribution to that critic,[25] the *Suda* provides the first actual instance we have of the number ten specifically connected with the Attic orators. If we accept that the canon did not already exist before Caecilius' time, then it seems likely from the title of his treatise that in the process of his study on the Attic orators who were known in his day, Caecilius drew up a list of the ten to whom he attached the most importance. Yet against this is Dionysius' silence, for Caecilius and Dionysius were contemporaries in Rome and had the same range of scholarly interests, writing both historical and rhetorical works. That the two knew each other and, it would seem, enjoyed a friendship,[26] almost certainly means they must have discussed their interests together, however informally. Again, Dionysius' silence would seem to sound out the death-knell, this time for a Caecilian authorship of the canon.

I would argue that the death-knell on the issue need not peal out just yet. To begin with, it is stretching credibility too much to posit a later date than Caecilius for the invention of the canon. To do this would take us too close to the time of Quintilian, and his tone at *Institutio Oratoria* 10.1.76 does not imply that the *decem* were so recently chosen. We can rule out Dionysius as a possible compiler since his critical essays would not call for another treatment of the orators which would inevitably overlap. Besides, he would presumably have alluded to it in the essays since he includes cross-references to his other writings in his other critical works.[27] I have suggested that Dionysius' silence indicates that no canon was actually in circulation at that time since he is quick to criticise those whose works have a bearing on his own, and that were either still in circulation or preserved in the works of others. Caecilius' ten would thus have excited comment. A plausible explanation for the dilemma is also the simplest one: Caecilius published his treatise after Dionysius' works.[28] Kennedy has already suggested (*Art of Rhetoric in the Roman World*, p. 364 with n. 86) that Caecilius' writings may post-date those of Dionysius, and he has drawn attention to the introduction of Dionysius' *On The Attic Orators*, which could not have been written before Caecilius' work was in circulation. I am extending this view more than Kennedy has done by connecting the implications of the timing of both treatises more closely with the date and 'authorship' of the canon. We can then see why Dionysius would not refer to any canon. Here the relationship between the two men has a relevance. If they were rivals, as some would argue, we wonder why Dionysius would have neglected the chance to poke criticism in advance of his rival's work.[29] More than likely, I suggest, is that Dionysius' silence stems from a reluctance to pre-empt the other's treatise, simply out of friendship.

If we accept that Caecilius was the author of the canon, then we must ask why he selected the ten orators we have today and ended his list with Dinarchus. Such questions take us into a consideration of the literary background against which the Augustan critics lived and worked.

Dionysius and Caecilius had much in common in their approach to the orators. Both were interested in matters of authenticity as well as style, and both are apparent exponents of a return to Attic standards in rhetoric after the Asianist rhetoric which followed the death of Demosthenes. Oratory in Athens after the fourth century had suffered a dramatic decline, partly because of the rise of new intellectual centres in the hellenistic world and partly because of radically changed political conditions in the city of Athens itself.[30] True, men such as Demetrius of Phalerum and Demochares, nephew of Demosthenes, were at work, there were also some advances in rhetorical theory,[31] and even Theophrastus had written a rhetorical work (now lost).[32] Nevertheless, the intellectual output was vastly inferior to what had preceded it. In the third century a style of rhetoric known as the Asian, responsibility for which, with due criticism, has been attributed to Hegesias of Magnesia,[33] came to dominance.

The term 'Asianist' was coined by critics of the first century AD and has literary as well as politico-geographical connotations, the latter arising from the conquests of Alexander III of Macedonia. The Asianist style was far removed from the classical, and included elements of form and language from the various geographical regions of the hellenistic world which, even in republican times, were felt to debase the Attic style – note the derogatory remarks of Cicero, *Brutus* 13.51 and *Orator* 24–27 (cf. Quintilian 12.10.16 ff.). Discontent with the Asianist rhetoric probably began in the mid-first century BC, as is evident in the works of Cicero,[34] and by the Augustan age an anti-Asianist push, or movement, had come more to the fore.[35] Perhaps the reason for the movement was because Rome by then had replaced Greece as the centre of rhetoric, although Kennedy (*Art of Rhetoric in the Roman World*, pp. 352–3) has suggested that such a return to a classical and less hybrid form had connotations connected with purity, and was thus in keeping with the Augustan moral policy. The suggestion cannot be proved, but it is an intriguing one. If Dionysius and Caecilius were influenced by the political background and carried this over into the literary, then their works may be seen in a new light.

The alternative view has been put forward by G. P. Goold that Dionysius and the other Greek rhetoricians at Rome were more concerned with preserving classical Greek models for teaching and aesthetic purposes, and thus for ensuring the preservation of a 'Greek heritage', than with trying to influence Roman writers and oratorical ideals to ways Greek.[36] Dionysius and his associates thus become a 'professorial circle', and not a literary one. This I find less credible, given the didactic tone to their works, but even if the 'professorial circle' theory were true, the present argument is not affected. These rhetoricians had a distinct view of Attic oratory, and it comes as no real surprise that for posterity a selection of the Attic orators would be made as examples of the classical style prior to what was seen as its eclipse in the hellenistic period. Indeed, given the importance Dionysius attaches to the Attic style, and that he does not seem to refer to an anti-Asianist movement proper in his writings, it is quite possible that he was responsible for spearheading such a movement in the Augustan age.[37]

Now, Dionysius was held in high repute in Rome, and it is plausible that he exerted some influence on the literary circle of which he was part, and which included Caecilius.[38] That Caecilius' work was prompted by Dionysius' own essays is not impossible – given the contacts between the two men it is only to be expected; also it is interesting that Dionysius wrote essays on seven of the orators usually included in the canon. Critical literary works for the most part follow on from what has preceded. Thus we find that Theophrastus' treatise *On Style* heavily influenced Cicero's *De Oratore* (*Orator* 79), and Cicero's rhetorical writings had a direct influence on Dionysius.[39] The author of *On the Sublime* was prompted by Caecilius' περὶ ὕψους (*On Sublimity*) to write his treatise because he did not think Caecilius had gone far enough, especially with his discussion of *pathos*, the emotional element (cf. 1.1 and 8.1).[40] Quintilian's views on certain orators in *Institutio Oratoria* 10.1.76 ff. echo those of Dionysius in the fragmentary περὶ μιμήσεως (*On Imitation*), but Quintilian does not refer to Dionysius. Clearly Quintilian's *decem* had an ultimate source, and it is plausible that this was Caecilius' work.

Caecilius' study of the orators, like that of Dionysius, was anti-Asianist in outlook, and was in keeping with the intellectual trends of Augustan Rome. This gives us a clue as to why Dinarchus, and not one of the orators who followed him, such as Theophrastus or Demetrius of Phalerum, is deliberately fixed last in the list. For Dinarchus is the last of the true Attic orators in terms of his literary style; Antiphon is at one end of this literary spectrum and Dinarchus at the other. Despite Quintilian's view that Demetrius was virtually the last of these orators (a view that seems confused, as was mentioned above), Demetrius has moved away from the pure Attic style, and we should agree with Cicero (*De Oratore* 2.95, *Orator* 92), that he was an example of the intermediate school. Caecilius selected his ten orators as representatives of the Attic style, and necessarily had to conclude with Dinarchus. To judge by the number of times Caecilius' name appears in Pseudo-Plutarch's *Lives of the Ten Orators*, his work is one of the main sources of information (along with Dionysius' essays) for the author of those lives.[41] Thus the Canon of the Ten Attic Orators comes into being.

To conclude. The Canon of the Ten Attic Orators justly deserves attention in view of its paramount importance and the controversies attached to it. Having tracked dating and author-ship, plausible inferences and judgements (for the paucity of evidence does not allow us too many absolutes) may be made on the nature and effects of the canon. The Asianist style which remained dominant for no small period of time may be used in the argument against an Alexandrian or Pergamene date for the canon, which we should expect to have included orators from the Asianist trend. On this basis, together with Cicero's silence on the matter, the compilation of the canon may be placed in the period between Cicero and Quintilian, and given Dionysius' silence Caecilius seems the ultimate source of the canon as we have it today. Caecilius' assessment of the Greek orators was prompted by the intellectual trend of the first century, and later critics and rhetoricians were to accept his selection and ranking of the orators as a canon.

Caecilius' critical expertise is some comfort for us since it follows that the ten were not arbitrarily selected but were well chosen as examples of the 'pure' or classical Greek oratory of the classical period. Thus Dinarchus is the last of the ten because he is the last exponent of a pure Attic style; the same is not true for those who followed him. Unfortunately we have no means to determine why Caecilius chose the orators he did. At some stage he must have been guided by some personal concerns, and this raises the question of the universal favour of his list. More importantly, while the exercise ensured the survival of works by the chosen ten, and for this it should be stressed that we have every right to be grateful, the destructive aspect of the canon, in part stemming from the nature of the beast, sentenced the speeches of other orators to probable extinction. As a result, we need to adopt a more condemnatory approach to the canon, rather than be swayed by at least one modern scholar's somewhat sweeping view that the labour of Dionysius and other critics resulted in the 'preservation of the living voice of Hellas'.[42]

NOTES

Professors Mark Golden, Carol Thomas, Michael Winterbottom and Cecil Wooten read earlier versions of this chapter, and I am very grateful for their comments. Translations of Cicero are taken from the Loeb Classical Library.

1 For the sake of convenience I use the modern term 'canon' to denote an authoritative list or selection: it should be said that the Greeks did not use the term in this sense (in the ancient rhetorical sense *kanon* was a stylistic model, provided by and represented by an individual author), and indeed it was not coined as such until 1768: see R. Pfeiffer, *History of Classical Scholarship*, I (Oxford: 1968), p. 207, and II (Oxford: 1976), p. 163 n. 2. Pfeiffer's criticism of the term 'canon' at I, p. 207, is worth bearing in mind.

2 See Kennedy, *Art of Persuasion*, pp. 246–9; cf. G. H. Macurdy, 'Apollodorus and the Speech Against Neaera', *AJPh* 63 (1942), pp. 257–71.

3 See F. Blass, *Die attische Beredsamkeit²*, III.2 (Leipzig: 1898), p. 272 and Ian Worthington, 'The Context of [Demades] *On The Twelve Years*', *CQ²* 41 (1991), pp. 90–5. Other orators are discussed by Blass, *Die attische Beredsamkeit²*, III.2: for example, Hegesippus (pp. 135–46); the author of [Demosthenes] 17 (pp. 146–51); Polyeuctus of Sphettus (pp. 151–3); Demades (pp. 266–78); Aristogeiton (pp. 278–83); Pytheas (pp. 283–8); Stratocles (pp. 333–5); Demochares (pp. 336–41); and Demetrius of Phalerum (pp. 342–50).

4 K. Heldmann, *Antike Theorien über Entwicklung und Verfall der Redekunst* (Munich: 1982), pp. 133 ff. for example.

5 For example, I. Brzoska, *De Canone Decem Oratorum Atticorum Quaestiones* (Breslau: 1883); P. Hartmann, *De Canone Decem Oratorum* (Göttingen: 1891); L. Radermacher, 'Kanon', *RE²*, X (1919), cols. 1873–8; A. E. Douglas, 'Cicero, Quintilian, and the Canon of Ten Attic Orators', *Mnemosyne* 9 (1956), pp. 30–40.

6 These included the metics Isaeus, Lysias and Dinarchus. Metics were allowed to appear on their own behalf in the polemarch's court: [Arist.] *Athenaion Politeia* 58.2 and 3 with P. J. Rhodes, *A Commentary on the Aristotelian Athenaion Politeia* (Oxford: 1981), *ad loc.*; A. R. W. Harrison, *The Law of Athens*, I (Oxford: 1968), p. 192 n. 1, and especially pp. 193–6, and II (Oxford: 1971), pp. 10–1. The metic orators known to us seem not to have brought cases regularly: Lysias Speech 12 (extant) and Dinarchus' speech against Proxenus (indictment quoted at Dion. Hal. *Dinarchus* 3; cf. [Plut.] *X.Or.* 850e) were delivered by the two orators themselves.

7 Demetrius of Magnesia (apud Dion. Hal. *Dinarchus* 1) gives him over 160, Pseudo-Plutarch and Photius 64 (*X.Or.* 850e), and the *Suda*'s figure is 160 or 60: see Blass, *Die attische Beredsamkeit²*, III.2, pp. 298–306 for a list, with Ian Worthington, *A Historical Commentary on Dinarchus. Rhetoric and Conspiracy in Later Fourth-Century Athens* (Ann Arbor: 1992), pp. 10–2.

8 Cicero also refers to Critias (*Brutus* 7.29, *De Oratore* 2.22.93); probably at least some of Critias' works were extant in the time of Harpocration and Pollux, in which case at some point after the second century AD they became lost – the influence of the canon and Harpocration's emphasis that Critias was not part of it?

9 See G. Shoemaker, 'Dinarchus. Traditions of his Life and Speeches with a Commentary on the Fragments of the Speeches', unpub. Ph.D. thesis (Columbia University: 1968), pp. 22–6 with further bibliography.

10 On this see Hartmann, *De Canone Decem Oratorum*, p. 12.

11 Dion. Hal. *Dinarchus* 1, 5–6, 8; cf. [Plut.] *X.Or.* 850e, and, for example, R. C. Jebb, *The Attic Orators²*, II (London: 1893), p. 374; Blass, *Die attische Beredsamkeit²*, III.2, pp. 307 ff.; J. F. Dobson, *The Greek Orators* (London: 1919), pp. 302–7 and his entry in the *Oxford Classical Dictionary*; and Kennedy, *Art of Persuasion*, pp. 256–7. On a re-evaluation of Dinarchus' style see Worthington, *Commentary on Dinarchus*, pp. 27–36.

12 Diog. Laert. 5.80-82. Quintilian (10.1.80) and Cicero (*Brutus* 9.37 ff., *Orator* 92, *De Oratore* 2.95) held Demetrius in high repute; further on Demetrius, see Blass, *Die attische Beredsamkeit²*, III.2, pp. 342–50; Dobson,

Greek Orators, pp. 312–13; Kennedy, *Art of Persuasion*, pp. 284–90; Heldmann, *Antike Theorien*, pp. 98 ff.

13 Cf. his essay on Dinarchus, composed for different reasons (to distinguish Dinarchus' genuine speeches from the spurious) and thus not included with the other four. See below.

14 Cf. the introduction to Dionysius' *On The Ancient Orators*, and on the work see G. Kennedy, *The Art of Rhetoric in the Roman World* (Princeton: 1972), pp. 350 ff.; on Augustan tastes, Kennedy, ibid., pp. 301 ff., and see also further below. On Dionysius as a critic see especially W. Rhys Roberts, *Dionysius of Halicarnassus on Literary Composition* (Cambridge: 1910); Kennedy, *Art of Rhetoric in the Roman World*, pp. 342–63; Heldmann, *Antike Theorien*, pp. 122 ff.; and (in a discussion of Dionysius' historiographical principles) C. Schultze, 'Dionysius of Halicarnassus and his Audience', in I. S. Moxon, J. D. Smart and A. J. Woodman (eds), *Past Perspectives* (Cambridge: 1986), p. 122.

15 On Caecilius see most conveniently Kennedy, *Art of Rhetoric in the Roman World*, pp. 364–9 with bibliography. In defence of Caecilius is W. Rhys Roberts, 'Caecilius of Calacte', *AJPh* 18 (1897), pp. 306–7.

16 On the dating of the canon see, for example, Jebb, *Attic Orators*, I, pp. lxv ff.; cf. Kennedy, *Art of Persuasion*, p. 125 and *Art of Rhetoric in the Roman World*, pp. 366–7; Douglas, 'Canon of Ten Attic Orators', pp. 30–40; Shoemaker, 'Dinarchus', pp. 11–28 (discussed from the viewpoint of Dinarchus' inclusion); Heldmann, *Antike Theorien*, pp. 99 and 133 ff.; and the works cited in n. 5 above.

17 The second century BC is accepted without question by Fowler in the Loeb edition of Pseudo-Plutarch's *Lives of the Ten Orators* (on p. 342); cf. Jebb, *Attic Orators*, I, p. lxvi.

18 Pfeiffer, *History of Classical Scholarship*, I, pp. 172 ff. on Aristophanes; pp. 210 ff. on Aristarchus; and pp. 253 ff. on Apollodorus.

19 *Art of Persuasion*, p. 331 – he points out there is no proof of this. On the Alexandrian library and its librarians see especially Pfeiffer, *History of Classical Scholarship*, I, pp. 87 ff.; cf. G. M. A. Grube, *The Greek and Roman Critics* (Toronto: 1965), pp. 123–32.

20 Pfeiffer, *History of Classical Scholarship*, I, pp. 181–8 and 205–7.

21 I exclude instances where *decem* is part of a compound number (3.1.10, 4.2.69, 4.2.71, 7.4.42, 7.6.2) or proper name (5.13.35); the context of 5.11.34, in which *decem* stands alone, is quite clear. The same argument applies to occurrences of the word at *Decl.* 252, 265, 278, 318, 370 (numerals); 248, 265, 338, 364 (specifics), and *Decl. Maior* 8 (specific). Instances of *decem* in Quintilian were collected for me from the PHI compact disk collection of Latin literature by Dr Peter Toohey, to whom I express my thanks.

22 On Thebes see Diodorus 17.15; Arrian 1.10.4–6; Plut. *Demosthenes* 23.4, *Phocion* 17.2; [Plut.] *X.Or.* 841e, 847c, 848e; and Justin 11.4.10–11; cf. Aes. 3.161. Although the sources name different statesmen who were to be surrendered, the list in Plutarch, *Demosthenes* 23.4 is to be preferred: A. B. Bosworth, *A Historical Commentary on Arrian's History of Alexander*, I (Oxford: 1980), pp. 92–6.

23 Arrian 1.10.6 with Bosworth, *Commentary on Arrian, ad loc.*

24 Cf. Radermacher, 'Kanon', cols. 1873–8. On a canon of nine lyric poets see above with n. 20.

25 For example, see Douglas, 'Canon of Ten Attic Orators', pp. 39–40 – criticisms which he admits are open to dispute.

26 See Dion. Hal. *Ep. to Pomp.* 3. That they were friends is normally accepted: Jebb, *Attic Orators*, I, p. lxiv, and II, p. 450; Kennedy, *Art of Rhetoric in the Roman World*, p. 364; cf. Schultze, 'Dionysius of Halicarnassus and his Audience', p. 122.

27 Cf. Kennedy, *Art of Rhetoric in the Roman World*, p. 344, and the reference to Bonner in n. 62.

28 Kennedy, *Art of Rhetoric in the Roman World*, pp. 366–7, suggests that Caecilius' *On The Character of the Ten Orators* was 'perhaps responsible for the formation of the canon'. Cf. Shoemaker, 'Dinarchus', p. 17, that Caecilius' work followed Dionysius' essay on Dinarchus, and also J. Tolkiehn, 'Dionysios von Halikarnass und Caecilius von Kalakte', *Wochenschrift für klassische Philologie* 3 (1908), cols 84–6.

29 On rivalry between the two see E. Ofenloch, *Caecilii Calactini Fragmenta*, Teubner text (Leipzig: 1907), p. xiii.

30 See Kennedy, *Art of Persuasion*, pp. 301–3, with 264 ff. and *Art of Rhetoric in the Roman World*, pp. 350 ff. on the decline of oratory and hellenistic rhetoric; see too Blass, *Die attische Beredsamkeit*², III.2, pp. 350 ff.; Jebb, *Attic Orators*, II, pp. 438 ff.; and Dobson, *Greek Orators*, pp. 308–14. Note Pfeiffer's criticisms of the intellectual capabilities and output of some other centres, especially Pergamum: *History of Classical Scholarship*, I, pp. 234 ff.

31 See Kennedy, *Art of Rhetoric in the Roman World*, pp. 114 ff. and 351 ff.

32 Diog. Laert. 5.42 ff., especially 47–49; cf. Athenaeus 1.21a–b; Cicero, *De Oratore* 2.217 ff., 3.37 ff.; Quintilian 8.1–11.1. At *Orator* 79 Cicero refers to Theophrastus' treatise *On Style*, which heavily influenced that orator's *De Oratore*; on Theophrastus see Kennedy, *Art of Persuasion*, pp. 273–84 and Grube, *Greek and Roman Critics*, pp. 103–9.

33 Cicero, *Brutus* 82.286, *Orator* 226, 230, for example, with Jebb, *Attic Orators*, II, pp. 441–2 and Grube, *Greek and Roman Critics*, pp. 122–3. Dobson, *Greek Orators*, pp. 313–14, is justly critical, for example: 'Hegesias is important only on account of the debasing influence which he exercised over his Greek and Roman followers'. On Asianism see the works cited in n. 30 above.

34 Cicero, *Brutus* 13.51 and *Orator* 24 ff.; Jebb, *Attic Orators*, II, pp. 437 ff. and Grube, *Greek and Roman Critics*, pp. 181 ff.

35 Kennedy, *Art of Persuasion*, pp. 330–5 and especially *Art of Rhetoric in the Roman World*, pp. 352 ff., and Jebb, *Attic Orators*, II, pp. 437 ff.

36 'A Greek Professorial Circle at Rome', *TAPhA* 92 (1961), pp. 168–92, especially pp. 190–2.

37 On this cf. Kennedy, *Art of Rhetoric in the Roman World*, p. 352; I believe Grube, *Greek and Roman Critics*, pp. 81 ff., overstates his case for the first century BC.

38 Cf. W. Rhys Roberts, 'The Literary Circle of Dionysius of Halicarnassus', *CR* 14 (1900), pp. 439–42 and Grube, *Greek and Roman Critics*, p. 207.

39 See Kennedy, *Art of Rhetoric in the Roman World*, p. 353 with n. 77.

40 Note, however, the remarks of Rhys Roberts, 'Caecilius of Calacte',
pp. 307 ff. The date of *On the Sublime* is suspect, but I follow the common
belief, based on Chapter 44 dealing with the decline of oratory, that it is
first century AD: for some discussion with bibliography see Kennedy, *Art
of Rhetoric in the Roman World*, pp. 370–2, and on Pseudo-Longinus see,
for example, Grube, *Greek and Roman Critics*, pp. 340–53 and Kennedy,
Art of Rhetoric in the Roman World, pp. 369–77.

41 Cf. Ofenloch in the Teubner Caecilius at pp. xxi ff. and L. Radermacher,
'Dinarchus', *Philologus* 58 (1899), pp. 161–9.

42 Goold, 'Greek Professorial Circle at Rome', pp. 191–2.

Bibliography

Adams, C. D., *Lysias: Selected Speeches* (Norman, Ok, and London: 1970).
Alt, K., 'Schicksal und φύσις im Philoktet des Sophokles', *Hermes* 89 (1961), 141–74.
Arndt, E., *De Ridiculi Doctrina Rhetorica* (dissertation, Bonn: 1904).
Bain, D., *Actors and Audience* (Oxford: 1977).
Barthes, R., *The Semiotic Challenge* (New York: 1978).
—— *The Rustle of Language* (Berkeley: 1989).
Becker, A. S., 'Reading Poetry through a Distant Lens: Ecphrasis, Ancient Greek Rhetoricians, and the Pseudo-Hesiodic "Shield of Heracles" ', *AJPh* 113 (1992), 5–24.
Bers, V., 'Dikastic Thorubos', in P. A. Cartledge and F. D. Harvey (eds), *Crux. Essays in Greek History Presented to G. E. M. de Ste. Croix on his 75th Birthday* (London: 1985), 1–15 = *History of Political Thought* 6 (1985), 1–15.
Blass, F., *Die attische Beredsamkeit*[2], 3 vols (Leipzig: 1887–98).
Bobonich, C., 'Persuasion, Compulsion and Freedom in Plato's *Laws*', *CQ*[2] 41 (1991), 365–88.
Boeckh, A., 'Von den Zeitverhältnissen der Demosthenischen Rede gegen Meidias', *Abhandlungen der Berliner Akademie* 5 (1818), 60–100 (= *Gesammelte kleine Schriften*, V (Leipzig: 1871), 153–204).
Bonner, R. J. and G. Smith, *The Administration of Justice from Homer to Aristotle*, 2 vols (Chicago: 1938; repr. New York: 1970).
Booth, W., *The Rhetoric of Fiction* (Chicago: 1961; 2nd edn, 1983).
—— *Modern Dogma and the Rhetoric of Assent* (Chicago: 1974).
Bosworth, A. B., *A Historical Commentary on Arrian's History of Alexander*, I (Oxford: 1980).
Bowra, C. M., *Pindar* (Oxford: 1964).
Bringmann, K., *Studien zu den politischen Ideen des Isokrates* (Göttingen: 1965).
Bruns, I., *Die literarische Porträt der Griechen* (Berlin: 1896).
Brzoska, I., *De Canone Decem Oratorum Atticorum Quaestiones* (Breslau: 1883).
Buchheim, T., *Gorgias von Leontinoi, Reden, Fragmente und Testimonien* (Hamburg: 1989).
Burkert, W., *Greek Religion*, trans. J. Raffan (Oxford: 1985).
Buxton, R. G. A., *Persuasion in Greek Tragedy: A Study of Peitho* (Cambridge: 1982).
Cairns, F., *Generic Composition in Greek and Roman Poetry* (Edinburgh: 1972).

Carey, C., *Lysias: Selected Speeches* (Cambridge: 1989).

—— 'Structure and Strategy in Lysias XXIV', *G&R*² 37 (1990), 44–51.

—— *Apollodoros Against Neaira: [Demosthenes] 59* (Warminster: 1992).

—— and R. A. Reid, *Demosthenes: Selected Private Speeches* (Cambridge: 1985).

Cargill, J., *The Second Athenian League* (Berkeley: 1981).

—— 'Fourth-century Athenian Citizen Colonies in the Aegean: An Aspect of Naval/Military Policy', in D. M. Masterson (ed.), *Papers of the Sixth Naval History Symposium*, US Naval Academy, 1983 (Wilmington: 1987), 32–8.

Carothers, J. C., 'Culture, Psychiatry, and the Written Word', *Psychiatry* 22 (1959), 307–20.

Cartledge, P., P. Millett and S. Todd (eds), *Nomos: Essays in Athenian Law, Politics and Society* (Cambridge: 1990).

Cohen, D., *Law, Sexuality, and Society: The Enforcement of Morals in Classical Athens* (Cambridge: 1992), 89–97.

Cole, T., *The Origins of Rhetoric in Ancient Greece* (Baltimore: 1991).

Conacher, D. J., *Aeschylus' Oresteia: A Literary Commentary* (Toronto: 1987).

Cooper, L., *An Aristotelian Theory of Comedy* (New York: 1922).

Dahl, R., 'The Concept of Power', *Behavioral Science* 2 (1957), 201–15.

Dale, A., *Euripides: Alcestis* (Oxford: 1954).

Davies, J. K., *Athenian Propertied Families* (Oxford: 1971).

Davison, J. A., *Companion to Homer* (London: 1962).

de Jong, I. J. F., *Narrators and Focalizers: The Presentation of the Story in the Iliad* (Amsterdam: 1987).

—— 'Homeric Words and Speeches: An Addendum', *JHS* 108 (1988), 188–9.

de Man, P., *Allegories of Reading* (New Haven: 1979).

de Romilly, J., *Magic and Rhetoric in Ancient Greece* (Cambridge, Mass.: 1975).

—— *The Great Sophists in Periclean Athens* (Oxford: 1992).

Denniston, J. D., *Greek Prose Style* (Oxford: 1952).

Derrida, J., 'Plato's Pharmacy', in *Dissemination* (Chicago: 1981), 61–171.

Dickson, K., 'Kalkhas and Nestor: Two Narrative Strategies in *Iliad* 1', *Arethusa* 25 (1992), 327–58.

Diller, H., *Sophokles* (Darmstadt: 1967).

Dobson, J. F., *The Greek Orators* (London: 1919).

Dodds, E. R., *The Greeks and the Irrational* (Berkeley and Los Angeles: 1981).

Dorjahn, A. P., 'Anticipation of Arguments in Athenian Courts', *TAPhA* 66 (1935), 274–95.

Douglas, A. E., 'Cicero, Quintilian, and the Canon of Ten Attic Orators', *Mnemosyne* 9 (1956), 30–40.

Dover, K. J., 'The Chronology of Antiphon's Speeches', *CQ* 44 (1950), 44–60.

—— *Aristophanic Comedy* (Berkeley and Los Angeles: 1972).

—— *Greek Popular Morality in the Time of Plato and Aristotle* (Oxford: 1974).

—— 'Anecdotes, Gossip and Scandal', in *The Greeks and Their Legacy: Collected Papers*, II, *Prose Literature, History, Society, Transmission, Influence* (Oxford: 1988), 45–52.

Duchemin, J., *L' ΑΓΩΝ dans la tragédie grecque* (Paris: 1945).

Easterling, P. E., 'Anachronism in Greek Tragedy', *JHS* 105 (1985), 1–10.

Edwards, M. W., *The Iliad: A Commentary*, V (Cambridge: 1991).

Elderkin, G. W., *Aspects of the Speech of Later Greek Epic* (Baltimore: 1906).

Ellis, J. R., 'The Structure and Argument of Thucydides' Archaeology', *Class. Antiq.* 10 (1991), 344–80.

Erbse, H., 'Über die Midiana des Demosthenes', *Hermes* 84 (1965), 135–51 (= *Ausgewählte Schriften zur klassischen Philologie* (Berlin: 1979), 412–31).

Feeney, D. C., *The Gods in Epic: Poets and Critics of the Classical Tradition* (Oxford: 1991).

Fenik, B., *Typical Battle Scenes in the Iliad: Studies in the Narrative Techniques of Homeric Battle Descriptions* (Wiesbaden: 1968).

Finley, M. I., 'Some Problems in Greek Law: A Consideration of Pringsheim on Sale', *Seminar* 9 (1951), 72–91.

——— *Politics in the Ancient World* (Cambridge: 1983).

Fisher, N. R. E., '*Hybris* and Dishonour I', *G&R*² 23 (1976), 177–93.

——— '*Hybris* and Dishonour II', *G&R*² 26 (1979), 32–47.

——— The Law of *Hubris* in Athens', in P. Cartledge, P. Millett and S. Todd (eds), *Nomos: Essays in Athenian Law, Politics and Society* (Cambridge: 1990), 123–38.

Foley, J. M., *The Theory of Oral Composition: History and Methodology* (Bloomington: 1988).

Foucault, M., *Discipline and Punish: The Birth of the Prison*, trans. A. Sheridan (New York: 1979).

——— *The History of Sexuality*, I, trans. R. Hurley (New York: 1980).

——— *Power/ Knowledge: Selected Writings and Other Interviews 1972–1977*, ed. Colin Gordon, trans. C. Gordon *et al.* (New York: 1980).

——— 'The Order of Discourse', in M. Shapiro (ed.), *Language and Politics* (Oxford: 1984), 108–38.

Fränkel, H., *Noten zu den Argonautika des Apollonios* (Munich: 1968).

——— *Early Greek Poetry and Philosophy*, trans. M. Hadas and J. Willis (Oxford: 1975).

Friedrich, P. and J. Redfield, 'Speech as a Personality Symbol: The Case of Achilles', *Language* 54 (1978), 263–88.

Friis Johansen, H., *General Reflection in Tragic Rhesis* (Copenhagen: 1959).

Fritz, K. von, 'νόος and νοεῖν in the Homeric Poems', *CPh* 38 (1943), 79–93.

Gagarin, M., *Aeschylean Drama* (Berkeley and Los Angeles: 1976).

——— *Early Greek Law* (Berkeley and Los Angeles: 1986).

——— *The Murder of Herodes* (Frankfurt: 1989).

——— 'The Ancient Tradition on the Identity of Antiphon', *GRBS* 31 (1990), 27–44.

——— 'Hesiod and the Origins of Greek Law', *Ramus* 21 (1992), 61–78.

Genette, G., *Figures of Literary Discourse* (New York: 1982).

Gentili, B., *Poetry and Its Public in Ancient Greece*, trans.T. Cole (Baltimore: 1988).

Goebel, G., *Early Greek Rhetorical Theory and Practice: Proof and Arrangement in the Speeches of Antiphon and Euripides* (Ph.D. dissertation, Madison: 1983).

Goldhill, S., *Reading Greek Tragedy* (Cambridge: 1986).

Gomme, A. W., 'Aristophanes and Politics', in *More Essays in Greek History and Literature* (Oxford: 1962), 70–91.

Goody, J., *The Domestication of the Savage Mind* (Cambridge: 1977).

——— *The Interface between the Written and the Oral* (Cambridge: 1987).

Goold, G. P., 'A Greek Professorial Circle at Rome', *TAPhA* 92 (1961), 168–92.

Grant, M., *The Ancient Rhetorical Theories of the Laughable* (Madison: 1924).

Gregory, J., *Euripides and the Instruction of the Athenians* (Ann Arbor: 1991).

Griffin, J., 'Homeric Words and Speakers', *JHS* 106 (1986), 36–57.

Griffith, G. T., 'Athens in the Fourth Century', in P. D. A. Garnsey and C. R. Whittaker (eds), *Imperialism in the Ancient World* (Cambridge: 1978), 127–44.

Griffith, M., 'Contest and Contradiction in Early Greek Poetry', in M. Griffith and D. J. Mastronarde (eds), *Cabinet of the Muses* (Atlanta: 1990), 185–211.

Grube, G. M. A., *The Greek and Roman Critics* (Toronto: 1965).

Guthrie, W. K. C., *A History of Greek Philosophy*, I and III (Cambridge: 1962, 1969).

—— *The Sophists* (Cambridge: 1971).

Gwatkin, W. E. Jnr, 'The Legal Arguments in Aeschines' *Against Ktesiphon* and Demosthenes' *On the Crown*', *Hesperia* 26 (1957), 129–41.

Halliwell, S., *Aristotle's Poetics* (Chapel Hill: 1986).

—— 'Style and Sense in Aristotle *Rhetoric* Book 3', *Revue Internationale de Philosophie* 47 (1993), 50–69.

—— 'Popular Morality, Philosophical Ethics, and the *Rhetoric*', in D. Furley and A. Nehamas (eds), *Aristotle on Rhetoric and Philosophy* (Princeton: 1993).

Halperin, D. M., *One Hundred Years of Homosexuality and Other Essays on Greek Love* (New York: 1990).

Halverson, J., 'Havelock on Greek Orality and Literacy', *Journal of the History of Ideas* 53 (1992), 148–63.

Hansen, M. H., 'How Often did the Athenian Dicasteria Meet?', *GRBS* 20 (1979), 243–6.

—— 'The Athenian "Politicians", 403–322 BC', *GRBS* 24 (1983), 33–55.

—— 'Two Notes on Demosthenes' Symbouleutic Speeches', *C&M* 35 (1984), 57–70.

—— 'Solonian Democracy in Fourth-century Athens', *C&M* 40 (1989), 71–106.

—— *The Athenian Ecclesia*, II (Copenhagen: 1989).

—— *The Athenian Democracy in the Age of Demosthenes: Structure, Principles and Ideology* (Oxford: 1991).

Harding, P., 'In Search of a Polypragmatist', in G. Shrimpton and D. J. McCargar (eds), *Classical Contributions. Studies in Honor of M. F. McGregor* (New York: 1981), 41–50.

—— *From the End of the Peloponnesian War to the Battle of Ipsus* (Cambridge: 1985).

—— 'Rhetoric and Politics in Fourth-century Athens', *Phoenix* 41 (1987), 25–39.

—— 'Laughing at Isokrates: Humour in the Areopagitikos?', *LCM* 13 (1988), 18–23.

—— *Androtion and the Atthis* (Oxford: 1994).

Harris, E. M., 'When is a Sale not a Sale? The Riddle of Athenian Terminology for Real Security', *CQ²* 38 (1988), 351–81.

—— 'Demosthenes' Speech against Meidias', *HSCPh* 92 (1989), 117–36.

—— 'When did the Athenian Assembly Meet? Some New Evidence', *AJPh* 112 (1991), 325–41.

—— 'Response to Trevor Saunders', in M. Gagarin (ed.), *Symposion 1990, Vorträge zur griechischen und hellenistischen Rechtsgeschichte* (Cologne, Weimar and Vienna: 1992), 133–8.

—— review of D. M. MacDowell, *Demosthenes: Against Meidias*, *CPh* 87 (1992), 71–80.

—— '*Apotimema*: Athenian Terminology for Real Security in Leases and Dowry Agreements', *CQ*² 43 (1993), 73–95.

Harris, W. V., *Ancient Literacy* (Cambridge, Mass.: 1989).

Harrison, A. R. W., *The Law of Athens*, I and II (Oxford: 1968, 1971).

Hart, H. L. A., *The Concept of Law* (Oxford: 1961).

Hartmann, P., *De Canone Decem Oratorum* (Göttingen: 1891).

Harvey, F. D., 'Two Kinds of Equality', *C&M* 26 (1965), 101–46.

—— 'Corrigenda', *C&M* 27 (1966), 99–100.

Havelock, E., *Preface to Plato* (Oxford: 1963).

—— *The Literate Revolution and Its Cultural Consequences* (Princeton: 1982).

—— *The Muse Learns to Write* (New Haven: 1986).

Hawtrey, R. S. W., *Commentary on Plato's Euthydemus* (Philadelphia: 1981).

Heldmann, K., *Antike Theorien über Entwicklung und Verfall der Redekunst* (Munich: 1982).

Henderson, J., 'The *Demos* and Comic Competition', in J. J. Winkler and F. I. Zeitlin (eds), *Nothing to Do with Dionysos? Athenian Drama in Its Social Context* (Princeton: 1990), 271–313.

Heubeck, A., 'L'origine della lineare B', *SMEA* 23 (1982), 195–207.

Highet, G., *The Speeches in Vergil's Aeneid* (Princeton: 1972).

Hinks, D. A. G., 'Tisias and Corax and the Invention of Rhetoric', *CQ* 34 (1940), 61–9.

Hobbes, T., *Leviathan* (New York: 1950).

Humphreys, S. C., 'Law as Discourse', *History and Anthropology* 1 (1985), 241–64.

Hunter, V., 'Gossip and the Politics of Reputation in Classical Athens', *Phoenix* 44 (1990), 299–325.

Jackson, S., 'Apollonius' Jason: Human Being in an Epic Scenario', *G&R*² 39 (1992), 155–62.

Janko, R., *Homer, Hesiod and the Hymns* (Cambridge: 1982).

—— *Aristotle on Comedy* (London: 1984).

Jebb, R. C., *The Attic Orators*², 2 vols (London: 1893).

Jeffery, L., *Archaic Greece: the City States c. 700–500 B.C.* (London: 1976).

Jones, J., *On Aristotle and Greek Tragedy* (London: 1962).

Karp, A. J., 'Homeric Origins of Ancient Rhetoric', *Arethusa* 10 (1977), 237–58.

Kennedy, G., 'The Earliest Rhetorical Handbooks', *AJPh* 80 (1959), 169–78.

—— *The Art of Persuasion in Greece* (Princeton: 1963).

—— *The Art of Rhetoric in the Roman World* (Princeton: 1972).

—— *Classical Rhetoric and Its Christian and Secular Tradition from Ancient to Modern Times* (Chapel Hill: 1982).

—— *Aristotle, On Rhetoric: A Theory of Civic Discourse* (New York: 1991).

Kirchner, J., *Prosopographia Attica*, 2 vols (Berlin: 1901–1903).

Kirk, G. S., *The Iliad: A Commentary*, II (Cambridge: 1990).

Koster, S., *Die Invektive in der griechischen und römische Literatur* (Meisenheim am Glan: 1980).

Krentz, P., *The Thirty at Athens* (Ithaca and London: 1982).

Lanata, G., 'Linguaggio scientifico e linguaggio poetico. Note al lessico del de morbe sacro', *QUCC* 5 (1968), 22–36.

Larrain, C. J., *Struktur der Reden in der Odyssee* 1–8 (Hildesheim: 1987).

Latte, K., 'Hesiods Dichterweihe', *Antike und Abendland* 2 (1946), 152–63.

Lavency, M., *Aspects de la logographie juridique attique* (Louvain: 1964).

Lloyd, G. E. R., *Magic, Reason and Experience* (Cambridge: 1979).

Lloyd, M., *The Agon in Euripides* (Oxford: 1992).

Locke, J., *Two Treatises of Government* (Cambridge: 1970).

Lohmann, D., *Die Komposition der Reden in der Ilias* (Berlin: 1970).

Loraux, N., *The Invention of Athens: The Funeral Oration in the Classical City*, trans. A. Sheridan (Cambridge, Mass.: 1986).

Lynn-George, M., *Epos: Word, Narrative and the Iliad* (London: 1988).

Lyotard, A., *The Differend* (Minneapolis: 1988).

MacDowell, D. M., *The Law in Classical Athens* (London: 1975).

——— *Gorgias, Encomium of Helen* (Bristol: 1982).

——— *Demosthenes, Against Meidias* (Oxford: 1990).

Macurdy, G. H., 'Apollodorus and the Speech Against Neaera', *AJPh* 63 (1942), 257–71.

Manville, P. B., *The Origins of Citizenship in Ancient Athens* (Princeton: 1990).

Markle, M. M., 'Jury Pay and Assembly Pay at Athens', in P. A. Cartledge and F. D. Harvey (eds), *Crux. Essays Presented to G. E. M. de Ste. Croix on his 75th Birthday* (London: 1985), 265–97 = History of Political Thought 6 (1985), 265–97.

Martin, R. P., *The Language of Heroes: Speech and Performance in the Iliad* (Ithaca: 1989).

Massenzio, M., 'Il Poeta che Vola', in B. Gentili and G. Paioni (eds), *Oralita: Cultura, Letterature, Discorso*, Atti del Convegno Internazionale, Urbino, 1980 (Rome: 1985), 161–77.

Mastronarde, D. J., *Contact and Discontinuity* (Berkeley and Los Angeles: 1979).

Meyer-Laurin, H., *Gesetz und Billigkeit im attischen Prozess* (Weimar: 1966).

Nagler, M. N., *Spontaneity and Tradition: A Study in the Oral Art of Homer* (Berkeley: 1974).

North, H., *Sophrosyne* (New York: 1966).

——— 'Combing & Curling: Orator Summus Plato', *ICS* 16 (1991), 201–19.

Notopoulos, J., 'Parataxis in Homer', *TAPhA* 80 (1949), 1–23.

Ober, J., 'Public Opinion and the Role of Sea Power in Athens, 404–322 B.C.', in D. M. Masterson (ed.), *Papers of the Sixth Naval History Symposium*, US Naval Academy, 1983 (Wilmington: 1987), 26–31.

——— 'The Nature of Athenian Democracy', *CPh* 84 (1989), 322–4.

——— 'Models and Paradigms in Ancient History', *AHB* 3 (1989), 134–7.

——— *Mass and Elite in Democratic Athens: Rhetoric, Ideology, and the Power of the People* (Princeton: 1989).

——— 'Aristotle's Political Sociology: Class Status, and Order in the "Politics" ', in C. Lord and D. K. O'Connor (eds), *Essays on the Foundations of Aristotelian Political Science* (Berkeley and Los Angeles: 1991), 120–30.

——— 'The Athenian Revolution of 508/7 B.C.: Violence, Authority, and the Origins of Democracy', in L. Kurke and C. Dougherty (eds), *Cultural*

Poetics in Archaic Greece: Tyranny, Cult and Civic Ideology (Cambridge: 1993), 215–32.

—— and B. Strauss, 'Drama, Political Rhetoric, and the Discourse of Athenian Democracy', in J. J. Winkler and F. I. Zeitlin (eds), *Nothing to Do with Dionysos? Athenian Drama in Its Social Context* (Princeton: 1990), 237–70.

Ofenloch, E., *Caecilii Calactini Fragmenta* (Leipzig: 1907).

Ong, W. J., *Interfaces of the Word: Studies in the Evolution of Consciousness and Culture* (Ithaca: 1977).

—— *Orality and Literacy: The Technologizing of the Word* (London: 1982).

Osborne, R., 'Law in Action in Classical Athens', *JHS* 105 (1985), 40–58.

Parker, R., *Miasma: Pollution and Purification in Early Greek Religion* (Oxford: 1983).

Pearson, L., 'Historical Allusions in the Attic Orators', *CPh* 36 (1941), 209–29.

—— *The Art of Demosthenes* (Meisenheim am Glan: 1976).

Pedrick, V., 'The Paradigmatic Nature of Nestor's Speech in *Iliad* 11', *TAPhA* 113 (1983), 55–68.

Pelling, C. (ed.), *Characterization and Individuality in Greek Literature* (Oxford: 1990).

Perelman, C., *The New Rhetoric: A Treatise on Argumentation* (Notre Dame: 1969).

—— *The Realm of Rhetoric* (Notre Dame: 1982).

Perlman, S., 'The Historical Example, Its Use and Importance as Political Propaganda in the Attic Orators', *SH* 7 (1961), 150–66.

—— 'Hegemony and *Arkhe* in Greece: Fourth-century B.C. Views', in N. Lebow and B. Strauss (eds), *Hegemonic Rivalry from Thucydides to the Nuclear Age* (Boulder: 1991), 269–86.

Pfeiffer, R., *History of Classical Scholarship*, I and II (Oxford: 1968, 1976).

Pickard-Cambridge, A. W., *The Dramatic Festivals of Athens*[2], rev. J. Gould and D. M. Lewis (Oxford: 1988).

Powell, B., *Homer and the Origin of the Greek Alphabet* (Cambridge: 1991).

Pritchett, W. K., 'Greek Inscriptions', *Hesperia* 9 (1940), 97–133.

Race, W. H., 'Aspects of Rhetoric and Form in Classical Greek Hymns', *GRBS* 23 (1982), 5–14.

Radermacher, L., 'Dinarchus', *Philologus* 58 (1899), 161–9.

—— 'Kanon', RE^2, X (1919), cols 1873–8.

—— *Artium Scriptores* (Vienna: 1951).

Raubitschek, A. E., 'Theopompos on Hyperbolos', *Phoenix* 9 (1955), 122–6.

Rhodes, P. J., *A Commentary on the Aristotelian Athenaion Politeia* (Oxford: 1981).

—— 'Problems in Athenian *Eisphora* and Liturgies', *AJAH* 7 (1982), 1–19.

Rhys Roberts, W., 'Caecilius of Calacte', *AJPh* 18 (1897), 302–12.

—— 'The Literary Circle of Dionysius of Halicarnassus', *CR* 14 (1900), 439–42.

—— *Dionysius of Halicarnassus on Literary Composition* (Cambridge: 1910).

Richards, I. A., *The Philosophy of Rhetoric* (Oxford: 1936).

Rickert, G., *Hekon and Akon in Early Greek Thought* (Atlanta: 1989).

Rogers, B. B., *Aristophanes Wasps* (London: 1906).

Ronnet, G., *Étude sur le style de Démosthène* (Paris: 1971).

Rowe, G. O., 'The "Adynaton" as a Stylistic Device', *AJPh* 86 (1965), 387–96.

—— 'The Portrait of Aeschines in the Oration *On the Crown*', *TAPhA* 97 (1966), 397–406.

—— 'Demosthenes' First Philippic. The Satiric Mode', *TAPhA* 99 (1968), 361–74.

Russell, D. A., 'Ethos in Oratory and Rhetoric', in C. Pelling (ed.) *Characterization and Individuality in Greek Literature* (Oxford: 1990), 197–212.

—— and N. G. Wilson, *Menander Rhetor* (Oxford: 1981).

Schein, S. L., *The Mortal Hero: An Introduction to Homer's Iliad* (Berkeley: 1984).

Schiappa, E., 'Did Plato Coin *Rhetorike*?', *AJPh* 111 (1990), 457–70.

—— *Protagoras and Logos: A Study in Greek Philosophy and Rhetoric* (Columbia, SC: 1991).

—— '*Rhetorike*: What's in a Name? Toward a Revised History of Early Greek Rhetorical Theory', *QJS* 78 (1992), 1–15.

Schindel, U., *Der Mordfall Herodes. Nachrichten der Ak. der Wiss. in Göttingen (Phil.-Hist. Kl.*: 1979).

Schultze, C., 'Dionysius of Halicarnassus and his Audience', in I. S. Moxon, J. D. Smart and A. J. Woodman (eds), *Past Perspectives. Studies in Greek and Roman Historical Writing* (Cambridge: 1986), 121–41.

Scodel, R., *The Trojan Trilogy of Euripides, Hypomnemata* 60 (Göttingen: 1980).

Seaford, R., *Euripides' Cyclops* (Oxford: 1988).

Sealey, R., 'From Phemios to Ion', *REG* 57 (1970), 312–55.

—— 'The *Tetralogies* Ascribed to Antiphon', *TAPhA* 114 (1984), 71–85.

Shear, T. L., *Kallias of Sphettos and the Revolt of Athens in 286 B.C.*, *Hesperia Supplement* 17 (Princeton: 1978).

Shoemaker, G., 'Dinarchus. Traditions of his Life and Speeches with a Commentary on the Fragments of the Speeches', unpub. Ph.D. thesis (Columbia University: 1968).

Shrimpton, G., *Theopompos the Historian* (Montreal: 1991).

Sinclair, R. K., *Democracy and Participation in Athens* (Cambridge: 1988).

Solmsen, F., 'The "Gift" of Speech in Homer and Hesiod', *TAPhA* 85 (1954), 1–15.

—— *Intellectual Experiments of the Greek Enlightenment* (Princeton: 1975).

Sperduti, A., 'The Divine Nature of Poetry in Antiquity', *TAPhA* 81 (1950), 209–40.

Suss, W., *Ethos: Studien zu älteren griechischen Rhetorik* (Leipzig: 1910).

Swearingen, C. J., 'Literate Rhetors and their Illiterate Audiences; the Orality of Early Literacy', *Pre/Text* 7 (1986), 145–62.

Taplin, O., *Homeric Soundings: The Shaping of the Iliad* (Oxford: 1992).

Thalmann, W., *Conventions of Form and Thought in Early Greek Epic Poetry* (Baltimore: 1984).

Tod, M. N., *Greek Historical Inscriptions*, 2 vols (Oxford: 1948).

Todd, S., '*Lady Chatterley's* Lover and the Attic Orators: The Social Composition of the Athenian Jury', *JHS* 110 (1990), 146–73.

—— and P. Millett, 'Law, Society and Athens', in P. Cartledge, P. Millett and S. Todd (eds), *Nomos: Essays in Athenian Law, Politics and Society* (Cambridge: 1990), 1–18.

Tolkiehn, J., 'Dionysios von Halikarnass und Caecilius von Kalakte', *Wochenschrift für klassische Philologie* 3 (1908), cols 84–6.

Toohey, P., 'Some Ancient Notions of Boredom', *ICS* 13 (1988), 151–64.

—— 'Some Ancient Histories of Literary Melancholia', *ICS* 15 (1990), 143–63.

—— 'Acedia and Eros in Apollonius Rhodius (Arg. 3.260–299)', *Glotta* 70 (1992), 114–22.

—— *Reading Epic: An Introduction to the Ancient Narratives* (London: 1992).

—— 'Love, Lovesickness, and Melancholy', *ICS* 17 (1992), 265–86.

Untersteiner, M., *The Sophists*, trans. K. Freeman (Oxford: 1954).

Usher, S., 'Individual Characterization in Lysias', *Eranos* 63 (1965), 99–119.

van Groningen, B. A., *La composition littéraire archaïque grecque*[2] (Amsterdam: 1960).

van Hook, LaRue, 'Alcidamas versus Isocrates; the Spoken versus the Written Word', *Classical Weekly* 12 (1919), 89–94.

Vanderpool, E., *Ostracism at Athens* (Cincinnati: 1969).

Vernant, J.-P., 'Tensions and Ambiguities in Greek Tragedy', in J.-P. Vernant and P. Vidal-Naquet (eds), *Myth and Tragedy in Ancient Greece*, trans. J. Lloyd (New York: 1990), 29–48.

Veyne, P., *Did the Greeks Believe in their Myths?* trans. P. Wissing (Chicago: 1988).

Vian, F., *Quintus de Smyrne: La suite d'Homère*, I (Paris: 1963).

—— *Nonnos de Panopolis: Les Dionysiaques*, I (Paris: 1976).

Vickers, B. F., *In Defence of Rhetoric* (Oxford: 1988).

Vlastos, G., *Socrates* (Ithaca: 1990).

Voegel, W., *Die Diabole bei Lysias* (Basel: 1943).

Volkmann, R., *Die Rhetorik der Griechen und Römer in systematischer Übersicht*[2] (repr. Hildesheim: 1963).

Wallace, R. W., *The Areopagos Council, to 307 B.C.* (Baltimore: 1991).

Wankel, H., *Demosthenes: Rede für Ktesiphon über den Kranz*, 2 vols (Heidelberg: 1976).

White, H., *Metahistory* (Baltimore: 1973).

—— *Tropics of Discourse* (Baltimore: 1978).

Whitman, C., *Aristophanes and the Comic Hero* (Cambridge, Mass.: 1964).

—— *Homer and the Heroic Tradition* (New York: 1965).

Wilcox, S., 'The Scope of Early Rhetorical Instruction', *HSCPh* 53 (1942), 121–55.

Willcock, M. M., *A Companion to the Iliad* (Chicago: 1976).

Wilson, P., 'Demosthenes 21 (*Against Meidias*): Democratic Abuse', *PCPhS* 37 (1991), 164–95.

Winifrith, T. J., Review of E. Havelock, *The Muse Learns to Write*, *CR*[2] 38 (1988), 158.

Winkler, J. J., *The Constraints of Desire: The Anthropology of Sex and Gender in Ancient Greece* (New York: 1990).

Worthington, Ian, 'The Duration of an Athenian Political Trial', *JHS* 109 (1989), 204–7.

—— 'The Context of [Demades] *On The Twelve Years*', *CQ*[2] 41 (1991), 90–5.

—— 'Greek Oratory, Revision of Speeches and the Problem of Historical Reliability', *C&M* 42 (1991), 55–74.

——— *A Historical Commentary on Dinarchus. Rhetoric and Conspiracy in Later Fourth-century Athens* (Ann Arbor: 1992).

——— 'Once More the Client/*Logographos* Relationship', *CQ*[2] 43 (1993), 67–72.

Xanthakis-Karamanos, G., 'The Influence of Rhetoric on Fourth-century Tragedy', *CQ*[2] 29 (1979), 66–76.

Young, R. (ed.), *Untying the Text* (London: 1981).

Index

The index refers to the text only.